Corporatism

The Secret Government
of the "NewWorld Order"

Jeffrey Grupp

Purdue University

CORPORATISM

The Secret Government of the "New World Order"

Copyright © 2007 by Jeffrey Grupp
All Rights Reserved

Published by Progressive Press under the Banned Books USA imprint
www.progressivepress.com

ISBN 0-930852-71-0
EAN 978-0-930852-71-9
Length: 153,000 words including Bibliography and Index, on 412 pages.

Reprinted March 2010. Printed in USA.

Topics:
Autism, brainwashing, chemtrails, communism, concentration camps, corporatocracy, denatured modern existence, economics, false flag terrorism, fascism, fluoridated water, genocide, globalization, GMO food, Morgellons disease, New World Order, Orwell, population reduction schemes, secret government, vaccines, 2012, 9/11.

BISAC Subject Area Codes

POL042030 Political Science : Political Ideologies - Fascism & Totalitarianism

PSY021000 Psychology : Industrial & Organizational Psychology

SOC038000 Social Science : Freemasonry

3   Corporate Communism   111

4   Secrecy, Terror, Theft, and Destruction: Corporatist Strategies, Tactics, and Economics   197

5   The Global Contamination of Humanity: The Primary New World Order Tactic   293

6   The Corporatist Dream-State: A World of Death Camps   373

WORKS CITED   393

INDEX   403

QUOTATIONS

"Whoever tries to seek happiness through hurting others, cannot find happiness."

—Buddha, *Dhammapada* v. 131

"Multi-national corporations have no ethics. They will deal with the Devil himself if they can make a profit."

—Robert Steele, former CIA covert operations[1]

"An entire generation pumping gas, waiting tables: the slaves of the slaves of white collars. Advertising has us chasing cars and clothes, working jobs we hate, so we can buy shit we don't need. We're the mental children of history… No purpose or place. We have no great war. No Great Depression. Our great war is a spiritual war. Our great depression, *is our lives*. We've all been raised on television to believe that one day we'd all be millionaires and movies stars and rock stars… but we *won't*…"

—From the film, *Fight Club*

Some even believe we are part of a secret cabal working against the best interests of the United States, characterizing my family and me as "internationalists" and of conspiring with others around the world to build a more integrated global political and economic structure—one world, if you will. If that's the charge, I stand guilty, and I am proud of it.

—David Rockefeller, *Memoirs*, p. 405

Hitler's motive for the invasion was entirely economic—the Third Reich was growing desperately short of oil, and he needed to capture the Soviet oilfields in and around Azerbaijan as quickly as possible.

—Greg Felton, *Enemies By Design: Inventing the War on Terrorism*, p. 292

---

[1] Quoted in Karel 2004.

"The polls… that don't really mean anything. The polls aren't important…"

—Laura Bush, July 6, 2006[2]

To study corporatism in fine detail… you find out that what corporatism is most specifically is a study of *psychology*—not the sort of phony psychology that you learn about in colleges and universities, which is just about behavior modification and trying to get people to fit into corporatized culture… [and] about labeling any sort of behavior that does not fit into the corporatist state as 'abnormal'… But when you study corporatism, what you really find out is that it's a genuine study of one's self, and you find out why and how one has become the way they are, and why a person has the pains and sadnesses and frustrations one does in a corporatized culture, due to the fact that people have been despiritualized, and they are being forced to fit into a communist system which is a despiritualized system… which can only give rise to utter misery.

—Jeffrey Grupp, on the Nutrimedical Report,[3] June 4, 2007

---

[2] This is a word-for-word quote: there is no typo in this quotation. This is from CNN's "Larry King Live," where Laura was commenting in response to Larry King's question: "How do you handle it emotionally when people say 'polls are down?'" George W. Bush was also present at this interview, and he expressed the same sentiments: opinion polls are irrelevant, and not what successful leaders take into consideration.
[3] This is Dr. Bill Deagle's radio show, www.nutrimedical.com.

1 Corporatism: The New World Order

"Have you ever considered that we may be on the wrong side?... What if the democracy we thought we were serving no longer exists? And the Republic has become the very evil we have been fighting to destroy?"

—Padme, from *Star Wars, Episode III: Revenge of the Sith*

[W]e need to accept responsibility for America's unique role in preserving and extending an *international order* friendly to our security, our prosperity, and our principles. (emphasis added)

—From "statement of principles" web page of the Project for a New American Century think tank's web site[4]

This book is about the imprisonment and destruction of human consciousness and the human spirit of the citizens of the world by the massive monopolistic corporations of the world that control resources, land, war, medicine, information, food, transportation, water, mail, education, and thought. Examples of these corporations include General Electric, Wal-Mart, Duke Energy, Corrections Corporation of America, 7-Eleven, General Motors, Diebold, The US Postal Service, AOL, Phillip Morris, Dell, Starbucks, Microsoft, The Federal Reserve, Budweiser, Lockheed Martin, News Corp., Gap, Blackwater, KinderCare Learning Centers, United Water, Nike, CACI, McDonalds, Boeing, Monsanto, Ignite!, National City Bank, Borders, Exxon, Titan, Thomson Learning, Merck, AT&T, The University of Texas, Viacom, and Halliburton, to name a few. Some of these may appear to you to be government organizations (e.g., US Postal Service, Corrections Corporation of America, University of Texas, CACI, etc.) and you may be surprised to see them described here as for-profit corporations. This is because not many people know that the largest corporations in America and worldwide are *identical to government*: in the contemporary world, the average citizen of the world has no idea that the education, water, food, resources, energy, information, medicine, and any of the other industries that the citizens of the world depend on for their survival, are all indistinguishable from government.

According to Jim Fetzer, philosophy professor at the University of Minnesota, Duluth:

> ...th[e] merger of big business with big government, which Mussolini described as *corporatism*, ... is defined by rampant militarism..., where the leader tends to be identified with the state, and criticism of the leader is treated as unpatriotic or even treasonous, is *exactly* what we have emerging here [in the United States]: an American-style fascist

---

[4] As of November 18, 2006, this web page was located at this URL: http://www.newamericancentury.org/statementofprinciples.htm.

government... [For example,] the President has imposed his own interpretation upon the law,... He now figures out what the law is, whether or not to enforce [the laws], and what they mean.[5]

This is a horror-state in the making, for reasons I will point out in this book. Even though the effects of corporatism pervade America, and even though corporatism literally constructs the behavior and thought of all Americans, as I will point out, Americans are largely oblivious to the existence of corporatism, and instead, they are blinded with distracting and vacuous notions of "democracy," given to them by educators and the mass media. Similar to the way air is all around us, inside and outside of us, but unseen by us, Americans do not notice the corporatism that is everywhere, pervading their world and sustaining their existence, and they do not notice the Orwellian-corporatist influence on them (on their minds, behaviors, beliefs and volitions) throughout the moments of their lives. Americans are imprisoned, but have been taught to erroneously believe they are free.

The apparently extreme nature of these claims might surprise some readers, but you will see that they are astonishingly easy to prove (as I do at length in later chapters). For example, consider the succinct way this corporate influence is described in a remark from Lindsey Williams, author of *The Energy Non-Crisis*,[6] from the Rense Radio Show on December 14, 2005, where he was describing the power of the corporations and the people that control it.

It literally reaches into every portion of a human being's life. Every issue in the world is related to crude oil... [For] the person that lives in a cardboard shack ... in a third-world country, or the elite of America, everything is related to and influenced by crude oil.

What Williams was talking about is how food production, transportation, printing, and nearly any industry in contemporary civilization, has been made to be dependent on one resource: *oil*. Civilization exists the way it does because of oil and the oil corporatists, and since civilization shapes human thought and behavior (as I will show in later chapters), then, ultimately, oil and the oil corporatists shape human thought and behavior. But it is not just oil that is monopolized in order to dominate, control, and crush humanity; the industries that depend on oil are also monopolized by small numbers of corporatists in a similar fashion. "The top [largest] five corporations now control more than 50% of the world's market in the automotive, airline, aerospace, electrical, electronics, and steel industries."[7]

---

[5] Professor Fetzer uttered this on the Rense Radio Show (which can be heard in the archives at www.rense.com), September 9, 2006.

[6] 1980, Master Books.

[7] Geyman 2006, 26.

It is critical to know that this control and engineering of human behavior and thought is *deliberately* carried out by the corporatists. Consider what Lamb and Mikel write about the way that corporations secretly plan ways to advertise to the young girls of America in order to make them shallow, superficial, media- and consumerist-crazed shoppers and television junkies:

> By the time your child is four years old, she has probably watched tens of thousands of advertisements,[8] most of them designed to appeal to her little heart and mind. Marketers know how to reach young children

---

[8] This is apparently not any sort of a guess being made by Lamb and Mikel, but rather a scientific finding. Consider what the following article says about this issue (the article cites data that matches what Lamb and Mikel give in their book):

Parents who put their babies in front of the TV to watch videos that are supposed to make them smarter are being duped, say some University of Washington researchers who published a study Monday on TV watching by children 2 and under. "We're in the midst of a large, national, uncontrolled experiment on the next generation," said Dr. Dimitri Christakis, a pediatrician at Children's Hospital and Regional Medical Center in Seattle and a researcher at the University of Washington. "What the effects of that will be—good or bad—we don't know yet." Parents who in the past would read and sing and play with their children are choosing TV, videos and DVDs for their kids in the belief that this screen time is good for them, Christakis said. They believe the marketers of baby videos and TV programs and are ignoring warnings from the American Academy of Pediatrics that very young children should not watch any TV, said Frederick Zimmerman, lead author of the study who is an economist who works for the university as a researcher in health sciences. "The best available evidence suggests that there's harm (in babies watching TV) but it's by no means conclusive," Christakis said. Other studies have found a connection between early TV viewing and attention deficit disorder, aggressive behavior and poor cognitive development, Zimmerman said... Unlike the common perception that parents use TV as an electronic baby sitter, the study found instead that the No. 1 reason babies watch TV and videos is because their parents think it is good for them, Christakis said... But the study published Monday in the Archives of Pediatrics and Adolescent Medicine shows babies are watching a lot more TV than necessity demands... By 3 months of age, 40 percent of infants are regular viewers. That number increases to 90 percent of 2-year-olds, the study found... Parents told the researchers they allowed their children to spend this time in front of the TV because they thought it was good for the child's brain (29 percent), because the kids found it enjoyable or relaxing (23 percent) or because they use it as a baby sitter (21 percent)... Zimmerman said he was especially concerned that parents are being convinced by video marketers who say certain videos are beneficial, when there is no evidence to support those claims. Christakis said parents are being preyed upon by marketers who make "outrageous claims" that are unsubstantiated. He said the baby videos overstimulate children and that is what keeps them so engaged... (From "Babies Watch Too Much TV, Study Finds: 90 Percent of 2-Year-Olds Are Regular Viewers," Associated Press, Donna Gordon Blankinship, May 9, 2007.)

because they employ developmental psychologists to conduct research on what kids desire and respond to. These psychologists don't care about your child's healthy development; their job is to help companies acquire cradle-to-grave brand loyalty so they can "own" your children.[9]

We will see that civilization did not have to evolve this way, and this single-resource-dependency might not be accidental. For example, the hemp plant is even *more* versatile and productive than crude oil, and it could be used in even *more* productive and diverse ways than crude oil is in order to fuel a civilization,[10] but hemp has been made *illegal* by American politicians and lawmakers (who are largely either part of, or are lobbied by, Big Oil). Corporatists have taken steps in the past to deliberately steer civilization into being dependent on one selectively chosen resource, while banishing others, in order to have total domination over the world citizenry, since the semi-covert troupe of corporatists will monopolize the one resource that the citizens of nations depend on. The same sort of domination will be shown below to currently exist for the production of food, medicine, education, water, and any other basic life necessity (but where each of these industries is currently dependent on Big Oil, due to the way that the corporatists have set-up and structured the global monopolies in the contemporary world).

Even though they don't know what *corporatism* is, Americans have largely been fooled into believing that the current corporate-monopoly culture (or a perfumed picture of it that they have been taught about through media and education) is natural, good, and inevitable. But we will see that it is not, and rather, we will see that it is unnatural, fabricated, demented, and genocidal.

Like the Nazi citizenry of the 1930s, Americans have been tricked into financing and working for their nation's demise, which, it can be shown, is continually being planned by their corporatist government in secret. For example, Americans are kept in the dark about what their tax dollars are being spend on, and this book shows how the US government uses those tax dollars

---

[9] Lamb and Mikel 2007, 4. Rampton and Stauber (2002) present examples throughout their book about how corporations secretly plan ways to change people by changing their perceptions, thoughts, priorities, opinions, and behaviors, where corporations regularly hire third-party "experts" (such as paid-off scientists—I will document an instance of this with vaccines in chapter 5) to advocate their products and control consciousness. On the second page of their book, they write:

> In order to understand the manipulations that are practiced today in the name of science, it is necessary also to understand the particular habits and practices of a particular class of experts who specialize in the management of perception itself—namely, the public relations industry. "Perceptions are real," proclaims the website of Burson-Marsteller, the world's largest PR firm. "They color what we see... what we believe... how we behave. They can be managed... (ellipses in the original)

[10] See Clarke 1995.

for the imprisonment and destruction of humanity—not just for the people of Iraq, El Salvador, Thailand, Mexico, and Cambodia, for example, but also for *all* ordinary Americans. Carroll Quigley, former Chair of Political Science at Georgetown, and Bill Clinton's former top advisor at Georgetown, is famous for writing a book called *Tragedy and Hope*, that gives inside information on what the most powerful secret government forces in the world are planning for the citizens of the world,[11] and Quigley revealed that it is to be an *end* to civilization and a start to a new type of feudalism (i.e., a medieval type of slavery), called *neofeudalism*, that will encompass the globe.[12]

For the reader of this book who does not understand the severity of what I am getting at by making these remarks, and for anybody who believes that the atrocities and "mistakes" of the US government since 2000 are merely coincidences (these "mistakes" include invading oil-rich Iraq on the false assertions that Iraq was a threat and had WMDs, failure to warn or help citizens in New Orleans when Katrina approached and then later hit and destroyed the city, complete failure to secure America's protective borders while Americans are preached to daily through the media about the dangers of Al-Qaeda and Hezbollah getting WMDs into the United States, "coincidentally" causing the recession of 2000 and 2001 by raising interest rates and failing to warn Americans about the onset of the recession, the odd events surrounding the 2000 Presidential election and other elections after that, the "coincidence" that the media did not tell Americans about the long pre-planning by certain members of the US government to set up the North American Union, the odd ambiguities and savagery of "The Patriot Act" and the follow up bills such as HR 6166 that passed in the fall of 2006 (it was passed as S3930 in September 2006, the Military Commissions Act) and Public Law 109-364 that was signed October 17th 2006,[13] RFID chips being planted everywhere and the drive to get all humans "chipped" with the 'Verichip,"[14] the strange failure of NORAD to

---

[11] Quigley could develop this picture because he had special inside access to their files, documents, plans, and so on, and the groups that comprise the secret world government are the Federal Reserve, CFR, the CIA, the World Bank, the World Health Organization, the IMF, the WTO, among others that I will discuss later in this chapter

[12] Quigley 1966, 324. Thanks goes to Professor Michael Coffman for informing me of this quote.

[13] This law allows the President to declare a national emergency for any reason whatsoever, without the approval of Congress, and it authorizes the use of the US military *against US citizens*—something that has not been "legal" for hundreds of years.

[14] I actually suspect that the Verichip is a planned distraction set up by the highest powers of government. Those powers tell us that they want humanity "chipped"—to have a Verichip implanted into them, much in the way as portrayed in an X-Files episode. At the time that I write this book, the Verichip program is largely a failure, and virtually nobody is signing up to "get chipped." I hold the opinion that humans are going to be, and are currently being, chipped via Morgellons disease (See Nutrimedical Report Radio Show, www.nutrimedical.com, April 3, 2007, for interesting commentary

stop the planes on 9/11, and there are other odd things that occurred before 2000, such as the speech given by George Bush Sr. on September 11, 1990—exactly eleven years to the day before 9/11—for war in Iraq to initiate a "New World Order,"[15] which was an old Hitlerian phrase), such persons must understand that such a large number of "coincidences" show that they are *not coincidences at all*, and rather they are predictable signs that what is *really* going on right under the noses of Americans and all other world citizens, which is a repeat of what has happened so often in "recorded history:" a gradual takeover and *crushing* of the people.

American Education and Media:
Fiat Education

The 'old man' that came across in dangerous sailing ships,... that traversed the length of the continent,... that was based in freedom and liberty and strength and honor,... is a dying breed. And the 'new man' is an individual who can't even put 2 and 2 together, who can't think, and who accepts whatever he is told.
—Alex Jones, on the Infowars Radio Show, February 15, 2007

Before introducing corporatism in more detail, I will discuss some reasons why corporatism is virtually unnoticed by Americans, even though it is *the* primary element influencing and constructing their lives, thought, and behavior.

In general, it seems that Americans still actually believe that they are free, and that they control the United States, since they have been taught that the United States is a democratic nation (controlled by the people). But there is no actual evidence that Americans have this sort of control, as I will point out in this book, since, to give just one example, the laws and rules of America are not voted on by ordinary Americans; they are created in Congress and the Supreme Court, and ordinary Americans are forbidden to participate in the lawmaking processes of Congress and the Supreme Court. Americans do not vote on the laws that govern business and commerce, or their food, medicine, drinking water, education, and so on. Rather, the ultra-rich people who are in charge of Congress, the Presidential Branch, and the Supreme Court do that, and it is standard to see that they do not implement policies that are what the people would appear to want—for example, lawmakers create things like "the Patriot Act," or the "National Uniformity in Food Act," both of which clearly are

---

on this issue), and Verichip is perhaps merely a distraction of some sort, to create fearmongering and to get the American citizenry to feel they are watched and controlled, so as not to rebel. (Jeff Rense is the first person I know to have made the aforementioned suggestion about Morgellons.)

[15] I cite this part of that speech later in this book.

terrorizing ordinary Americans nationwide.[16] For that reason, the behaviors and thoughts of the people—which are created by the laws and rules of the nation— are dictated by those in power, even though ordinary Americans commonly believe their daily lives are created by the *free will* of their own daily lives. For these and other reasons I will discuss, ordinary Americans are merely slaves that believe they are free—"freedom is slavery," as the old Orwellian party slogan goes.

Under such a spell, the citizenry will be tricked into allowing the nation's wealth and laws to be devoted to the interests of the ultra-rich controllers, rather than on the interests of the general citizenry. The citizenry will be fooled into allowing the nation's wealth and laws to be devoted to war rather quality health care or education, they will accept "minimum wage" (and most other wages for most other professions) to remain stagnant for over a decade while inflation runs wild, they will allow the dissipation of unionization in America, and so on. As you will see in this book, America is a massive experiment in social engineering, where the citizenry can be taught to defend, or even *fight for*, policies, social customs, laws, and ways of life that only induce ignorance, powerlessness, and sadness everywhere (e.g., the 8-5 workday, the existing reserve banking system that exists in America, mass militarization of the world, de-unionization, the corporatization of and destruction of the family, etc.). Americans are taught to guard and protect that which imprisons them.

The spirit of science, which involves the radical skeptic and the hard-nosed empirical perspective, is largely gone from contemporary American education. Also, the spirit of philosophy, which involves the hard-nosed, no-nonsense logician, and which often involves the person who becomes an expert in all subjects (an expert in *the study of reality*), is often castigated in contemporary American education. In contemporary America, college and university administrators, and technology, science, or other professors, are typically financial profit-seekers rather than educators,[17] and American education is now often merely about *believing what one has been told*, rather than a quest to question, and to be skeptical of, all that one has been taught and told (which is the true spirit of science). For example, so much of what college science students are taught in school is *merely told* to them, in a sort of "fiat education," and the students uniformly believe it, faithfully following their professors and educators, even though real data is hardly ever presented to them to prove what

---

[16] Examples of this terrorization from these and other "acts" can be seen everywhere, such as is described in this story: "New Airport Scanner Gets Personal: It Peers Through Clothing, Alarms Privacy Advocates," Associated Press, February 23, 2007.

[17] See "College Officers Profited by Sale of Lender Stock," New York Times, April 5, 2007, by Jonathan D. Glater, for an interesting and rare media disclosure of the fact that college and university administrators are secretly corporatists. Also see Angell 2005 (pages 1-10) for in-depth discussion of this regarding biomedical technology professors and university programs.

is presented to them in the education system, and even though they nearly never do the experimentation for themselves in order to *understand* and *verify* what they have been told. Medical students, for instance, will be *just told* that

    i. vaccines are safe, and that they have miraculously eliminated diseases at various times in the past (the general public is also told this disinformation)[18]

    ii. the pharmaceutical industry creates a lot of new drugs each year that are safe and effective[19]

    iii. "natural medicine" is inferior to "orthodox medicine" (orthodox medicine = Big Pharma, drug-prescribing "medicine")

    iv. nutrition is *not* an important issue in understanding disease and treating patients[20]

There is not one piece of real data anywhere that supports i - iv. Medical students will only be *merely told* this information, *without seeing actual and/or correct data,*[21] and without doing the experimentation and/or research for themselves to see that this information is correct. Medical students will be told that any information conflicting with what they are told in medical school is *erroneous*, and is to be ridiculed.

In the climate of degenerate fiat education, a genuine, passionate, and scientific inquiry of reality—as exemplified in the following bold and fearless passage from Descartes—is nearly extinct:

> Several years have now passed since I first realized how numerous were the false opinions that in my youth I had taken to be true, and thus how

---

[18] To see why this is blatant non-information (to see why there is no data to support this "good vaccine theory"), see chapter 5, and see Miller 1999, Tenpenny 2005, Kirby 2005, Golden 1998, Ayoub 2005 and 2006, and Horowitz 1996 and 1999. I will give an example later in this book that shows how top medical school textbooks actually hide data about vaccines that reveals the vaccines to be extremely harmful and fatal.

[19] To see why this is not true (to see why there is no data to support this theory), see Angell 2005.

[20] The total avoidance of studying nutrition in medical school is discussed by many nutritionists, such as Mary Ann Block, in the Forward to Richards 2006. I have heard Dr. Russell Blaylock of the University of Mississippi discuss this on the Rense Radio Show (www.rense.com) on July 24, 2006, and I have heard Dr. Lorraine Day, and Dr. Carolyn Dean (author of *The Magnesium Miracle*, Ballantine Books, 2007 [2003]) discuss this issue on the Rense Radio Show a few different times. Dr. Lorraine Day discusses these issues in famous DVD lecture, "You Can't Improve Upon God" (available at www.drday.com), Rockford Press, Thousand Palms, CA. Day's lectures were given and recorded in early 2000s.

[21] There are, in fact, too many instances of medical students using textbooks in medical school that have misinformation, bad data, missing data, and so on. I give specific examples elsewhere in this book (such as when I discuss the book, *The Immune System*, by Stanford professor, Peter Parham (New York: Garland Publishing) in chapter 3).

doubtful were all those that I had subsequently built upon them. And thus I realized that once in my life I had to raze everything to the ground and begin again from the original foundations, if I wanted to establish anything firm and lasting in the sciences.[22]

The American educational system and the mainstream media (especially the so-called "cable news channels"), which are the two sources that nearly all Americans get their information from, present a very narrow, surprisingly unscientific, and mostly unverifiable account of reality. Also, both the American educational system and the mainstream media are in extraordinary agreement. Both, for example, will unquestioningly and thoughtlessly assume and agree that Europeans were not in North America before Columbus (1492), that water automatically freezes at 32 degrees Fahrenheit,[23] that economic recessions are spontaneous and unplanned, that atomic weaponry is the most destructive weaponry that humans have yet developed, that the space shuttle is high-tech, that mercury-, cancer-, virus-, aspartame-, MSG- and aluminum-filled vaccines are safe and effective for infants, that the Vietnam War was about the so-called "threat of communism," that vitamin E or vitamin C are something to be leery of lest one overdose,[24] that there are checks and balances in the US government, that there is no known cure yet for cancer, that the American medical system is the best in the world, that Americans have the best standard of living of any nation in the world, and so on—even though no evidence whatsoever exists for these and nearly countless other ideas that could be listed, and which fill both the American educational system and the mainstream media. (In fact, abundances of simple empirical evidence exists that could *disprove* each of these claims just stated.)

The American educational system and the mainstream media will both agree that, for example, World War II was a spontaneous event, without any unseen pre-planning by any secret or unseen groups that had the power to do so. The

---

[22] This is from Meditation One of the famous Cartesian *Meditations*.

[23] If this were so, then we could not have entire oceans full of water that is significantly below 32 degrees farenheit, but unfrozen.

[24] Medical schools do not cover nutrition in any detail for their medical students, as just stated in a footnote above, and instead they focus all attention on drugs and surgery. There have been recent front-page blockbuster news story reports in the mainstream mass media about how vitamins, such as vitamin E and C, are claimed to be deadly and dangerous. (For example, see "Antioxidant Supplements Tied to Death Risk," Reuters, February 27, 2007, by Michael Conlon.) In these mass media accounts of the "dangers" of vitamins, it is usually claimed that "teams" of scientists arrived at the conclusions in these reports, making it appear that the information is credible. In discussing the famous Johns Hopkins University research findings on vitamin E, that came to the conclusion that vitamin E is dangerous, but which was really a statistical nightmare, Dr. Ray Strand[24] said: "I am not a conspiracy theor[ist], but it makes you very suspicious when you see how poorly these studies have been put together." (This is a quote from an interview from the Rense Radio Show, www.rense.com, November 30, 2004.)

war supposedly "just happened," and the extraordinary wealth and power gained from the war by specific politicians and corporations was "just a coincidence." Both the American educational system and the mainstream media will assume and adhere to this "spontaneous history" theory about World War II (or perhaps about almost any event in history: *it just happens, nobody plans it*), but both will not mention how IBM secretly and illegally sold the Nazis hoards of computers and census machines in the years leading up to and throughout World War II[25]—as documented in the Holocaust documents—

---

[25] See Black (2001) for a complete account. If I happen to bring this up to the average person I meet in my daily life, their first response is to aggressively deny this, saying, for example, "Why should I believe that? Just because somebody writes a book and says something does not make it true!" This is, of course, an excellent objection. The standard account of history is one where Germany went from being a broken nation to the world's supreme superpower with an army and organizational ability that truly baffled the rest of the world, in just a few years. The mysterious thing is that Germany did this in just five years at most. Teachers, historians, and the news media, typically will merely tell us that this turnaround occurred because under Hitler's rule, "Germany underwent an amazing recovery," but they will typically not tell us specifically *how* or *why* this rather miraculous and unprecedented recovery took place in any way that makes sense or hashes out any of the facts. They will typically tell us, for example, that "industry in Germany under Hitler was productive," and that accounted for the unheard of and strange recovery. But this supposed explanation is mysterious, due to the quick pace of the turnaround, when no clear and reasonable cause is typically given. For this reason, finding a *specific cause* would appear to be a much more reasonable way to analyze these events of history. And when one finds that bargain-rate computers and census machines were sold to the Nazis by IBM under special terms that the rest of the world did not have (as Black shows, this is documented in the Holocaust documents, and even at the Holocaust museum in Washington D.C.), which was driven by a miraculous new invention (the computer), there appears to be a *specific cause* found, but one which educators and media in the United States have mysteriously left out of their account of history. (There were many other ways, in addition to IBM's interactions with the Nazis, that the Nazi empire was financed and built-up by their supposed enemies during World War II (see Horowitz 2001, chapter 1).)

What is most interesting about this issue of IBM selling or "donating" computers away to "enemy nations" is how the IBM in the 1990s and early 2000s did the same thing, but this time gave them to China. (This issue is widely known among researchers, and it was discussed on the Rense Radio Show in a discussion between Charles R. Smith and Jeff Rense, November 17, 2004.) IBM supplied China with so many supercomputers that they literally raised the computer sophistication of the Chinese by several decades. This, when combined with other things that I discuss about China in this book, give an eerie forewarning about what the future holds regarding World War III, especially when we consider that the US national debt—which is so large that it will never be paid back (and that means that the US is insolvent)—has a collateral on it, which is US land (national parks, etc.), and the Chinese might want to collect their collateral some time in the near future. (For More information on this, see Thorn [2003], chapter 26, especially pages 189-190.) This issue is even more threatening when one considers that American big business is, and has been, moving off of the US soil, and largely into literally building-up and giving super-strength to the Nazis, wherein they gained overwhelming superpower status. In gaining such strength, the Nazi empire baffled and astonished the rest of the world, but this was only because the world did not know all the facts: the world did not know that the Nazis were getting their efficiency and strength because, unlike the rest of the world, the Nazis were the first automated empire, which is the real reason for the Nazi Empire coming to power as it did. Amazingly, American media and education are largely in complete agreement in *not* informing the world about this "secret" about World War II, which radically changes the history of that war. If media and education are in agreement on presenting a false account of history, then Americans will be oblivious to the real, verifiable story of World War II, and the rest of history—and perhaps even the real story of the history and origin of the human race.

Media and education also have ubiquitously agreed that the Democrats and Republicans are in control of the United States, and that that there is, for example, no secret, "invisible" government behind them, controlling them. Media and education have agreed that there was a jetliner that hit the Pentagon on September 11, 2001, that democracy is the best or the only legitimate form of government, that America is a democracy, that comets come from the Oort cloud, that the FDA is a regulative agency, that AIDS came from monkeys (or that HIV is the cause of AIDS), that there are shortages of usable crude oil which have caused the price increases in oil since 1999, that chemotherapy is an effective treatment for cancer, and so on—but in each of the cases just listed, *not a single bit of evidence exists for any of these ideas*. People are *merely told* that these things are true over and over throughout their lives, and hence they start to appear to them as obvious facts, even though no evidence or proof is ever presented.

The American education system and the mainstream American media involve a plethora of unverifiable and unproven ideas, thus helping to construct a fake picture of reality in the minds of nearly all Americans. If the average American was asked to prove any of the things just listed, or nearly all of the things she has been taught in school or through television, she would be unable to do anything more than say, "well, um, that's just what everybody knows, and what everybody has been taught." It is mass agreement that creates mass delusion, just like, for example, how everybody has been taught to believe and accept (without evidence) that Diet Coke (which contains aspartame) is safe merely because everybody drinks it: soda and soda machines are everywhere— in high schools and colleges, cities and hospitals, child-oriented TV-commercials and churches—and, well, how could Diet Coke be so dangerous if

---

China (and other countries), where slave labor can be readily utilized. These controlling corporatists may have interest in decimating the US economy (signs of this occurring are evident, as I discuss in chapter 3) in order to transfer that wealth to the Chinese economy.

everyone is drinking it? (Of course, the quantity of people drinking a soda does not causally determine if it is safe or not!)

The Unverifiability of the Account of Reality Given in American Education and Media

As I am implying here, quite literally, *very* few ideas involved in American media and education are verifiable. Verifiability, which is the ability to confirm the existence of something by seeing it with one's own eyes and directly perceiving it with their senses, is the key to the scientific attitude and the scientific mode of discovery: that which is perceivable by the senses is scientific information, that which is not, is either philosophy or math, or history or art (or propaganda, in the case of American education and media). But Americans are not taught to think like scientists and critical thinkers, nor like poets and artists. Rather, in schools, they are taught to follow directions and to believe what teachers tell them, lest they fail a test or even fail out of school. Thus, Americans are taught from an early age to follow what they are told rather than what they see. Loosely speaking, America is a culture replete with people who will reject the idea that they can *see* that the sky is blue, if they are merely *told* that it is green. Consequently, America is a culture that believes that mercury-filled vaccines for 12-hour old babies are safe (I am referring to the HepB vaccine[26]), that fluoridated water is healthy, and that milk and meat are healthy, just because they have been told so, and even though the catastrophic holocaust-level effects of these are seen everywhere. As Alex Jones satirically said on February 15, 2007, "if you don't believe everything you hear, you are a conspiracy theorist. Don't even question [anything], or you're a nut!"[27]

Then Jones went on to discuss how psychologists (such as Dr. Patrick Leman, of the Royal Holloway University of London), have devised a test that checks for mental illness in a person by checking how much one doubts things, and by checking how much of a skeptic one is—as if the more skeptical one is, the more mentally ill one is.[28] *But being a skeptic is the key to the scientific*

---

[26] See chapter 5 for more information.

[27] Jones said this on his radio show, www.infowars.com.

[28] Information about this test can be found in the following article, "The Psychology of Conspiracy," BBC, February 14, 2007, http://news.bbc.co.uk/2/hi/programmes/ conspiracy_files/6354139.stm. The doctor's test consisted of 15 questions, and the subject tested is asked to tell their level of agreement or disagreement to them. The questions were as follows:

1) There was no organised conspiracy involved in the assassination of John F Kennedy. 2) For the most part, government serves the interests of a few organised groups, such as business, and isn't very concerned about the needs of people like myself. 3) I can normally do what I want to do in the world today. 4) Princess Diana's death was an accident. 5) It is difficult for people like myself to have much influence in public affairs. 6) We seem to live in a pretty

attitude, and for that reason, these psychologists contrived a "test" that shows that one's ability to question and be a scientific thinker is now considered by some to be a mental illness. As Jones joked: "if you think the government is corrupt, that's mental illness."

What if one wanted to do something as harmless as question whether or not milk is needed as part of a person's diet? Does that make one "conspiratorial" or "mentally ill?" The problem is this: most information people have is erroneous, as I am showing here, and thus a rational thinker (a skeptic) can only be castigated in American culture: they will be seen as a troublemaker, as somebody who is needlessly challenging "what everyone knows," even though the skeptic almost surely will have the right information. For example, in America, it is *widely* believed that consumption of milk and/or various dairy products is utterly *essential* for building strong bones, and that without them, a person may experience a "calcium deficiency," which we are told can lead to osteoporosis, and death. But in fact, it is astonishingly easy to verify that this is patently absurd. For example, there is not a single case of calcium deficiency caused by diet ever recorded *in human history* for any culture not experiencing starvation conditions.[29] And there are no known cases of weak bones due to a failure to consume meat and dairy foods in vegan cultures.[30] In other words, if calcium deficiency occurs, it is not found in a situation where a person has adequate food available, and the cause must be something *not* to do with food. There are no instances where a vegan culture (such as some hunter-gatherer cultures) with adequate vegetables available undergoes instances of calcium deficiency, and it is widely known that "primitive peoples" were mind-bogglingly healthy (e.g., cancer free, etc.) at the times of their contact with civilization.[31] Cancer, for example, has been called a *disease of civilization*. Calcium deficiency occurs when a person is either starving, or when a person does not take part in eating adequate food (for example, if a person lives on

---

rational and well-ordered world. 7) My closest friends are very unpredictable. I never know how they are going to act from one day to the next. 8) When I am with my closest friends, I feel secure in facing unknown new situations. 9) Most politicians are sympathetic people and do a good job. 10) I feel very uncomfortable when my closest friends have to make decisions which will affect me personally. 11) The attack on the Twin Towers was not a terrorist action but a conspiracy involving certain Western governments. 12) The American Moon landings were faked. 13) I am certain that my closest friends would not lie to me, even if the opportunity arose and there was no chance that they would get caught. 14) I can rely on my closest friends to keep the promises they make to me. 15) Governments are suppressing evidence of the existence of aliens.

This test can be viewed in the following news article: "Conspiracy Test," BBC, December 8, 2006, http://news.bbc.co.uk/2/hi/programmes/6161425.stm.

[29] See Anderson 2004-2006

[30] See Anderson 2004-2006

[31] See Proctor 1999 24; Rubin 2003, 116.

Hostess cakes alone). (Osteoporosis, which is nowadays typically blamed on "calcium deficiency," is caused by lack of use of bones, such as when a person's bones weaken during bed rest, or with the sloth of old age. Osteoporosis is caused by sloth.[32]) This can be verified in almost any medical anthropology book,[33] to name just one source, or by merely visiting milk-free cultures (such as some gatherer cultures) to verify what I have just written with your own eyes. See how easy it is to show that there are myths that virtually all Americans believe, and which nearly all Americans consider to be *facts*, but which do not have a shred of evidence to support them, and which one can disprove in seconds!

It seems that few Americans suspect that there is an ocean of unverifiable non-facts that they have been spoon-fed throughout their life, and which form the basic constituents of their thoughts, their picture of the world, and the overall veneer of American culture. As I am showing in another book I am currently writing on the subject of brainwashing in American culture, a mixture of information from television and from education literally *creates consciousness* for contemporary Americans, but nearly all of this consciousness is based on, and built up out of, *non-reality*—which is the textbook definition of *brainwashing*: to be tricked into believing that an unreal reality is the actual one.

Media and education in America form an Orwellian-scale nationwide deception, where nearly all sources and accounts of information are false, but at the same time are in agreement with one another. When Americans go to church, they are told the same falsehoods they hear in school, on television, and from politicians, and so on. For example, I may hear about the threat of al-Qaeda on television, in movies, at church, in conversation with friends, in the news paper, and so on, but all along, there is no evidence presented that al-Qaeda even exists (and, in a chapter below, I prove it does not—or, rather, I prove that it is merely a CIA PMF[34]). Sadly, this sort of pervasive "agreed-upon

---

[32] See Anderson 2004-2006 for more information on this and similar "food myths."

[33] For example, in a famous medical anthropology textbook, McElroy and Townsend (1989), pages 168-169, we are told that deficiencies in calcium occur if there is consumption of food grown in areas where there are problems with the soil (such as if it is depleted of nutrients), not by avoiding milk and/or dairy products. Thus, it is not diet, in this case that causes calcium deficiency, but rather culture (specifically, cultural practices, such as over-farming [or other practices, such as producing GMO food], which produces "empty food", where a potato, for example, has little more value than a Hostess cake [see Pawlick 2006]) that causes it.

[34] PMF stands for "privatized military force," which is a secretive, for-hire military force—a corporate army.

disinformation" among people often also exists in the scientific community also, as the milk example just given shows.[35]

Confusion on this mysterious issue of "calcium deficiency" is widespread, and academic work is often surprisingly sloppy and riddled with unscientific assumptions. For example, on page 198 of their book, *Medical Anthropology*,[36] McElroy and Townsend inform us that

> [c]alcium is another nutrient that is deficient in the modern U.S. diet. The classic picture is that of an elderly woman with a broken hip, due to the demineralization of her bones cause by the combined effects of the aging process and low stores of the mineral."

This is all McElroy and Townsend say about this issue, and they do not cite references—as if the issue is *so obvious* and widely known that no proof of the claim that aging causes osteoporosis is needed. Implicit in this passage is the idea that aging causes "demineralization of ... bones", but, again no data is presented by them. But isn't the old lady they refer to also the same person who, in American culture, becomes more slothful and couch-ridden as she ages (this is not the case among aging women in many other cultures)? Muscles weaken with lack of use, so why wouldn't this also be the case with bones (as I have heard many doctors and nutritionists claim it is)? And why don't the vegan hunter-gatherers with active elderly women involve any cases of osteoporosis at all?[37] In fact, American elderly women have osteoporosis rates higher than any other country, and, osteoporosis is a relatively new ailment since the 1970s (and thus it came about *after* human life-spans reached their purported current 70+ average in America, showing that women did live to old ages before osteoporosis became widespread), which further adds serious problems to the assumption McElroy and Townsend are making that aging causes osteoporosis.[38] And lastly, Americans are told that the fluoridated water

---

[35] Examples are many. I have more than once talked with prominent anthropologists who have acted as if Elaine Morgan's aquatic ape theory is merely a "conspiracy theory," and where Morgan is just a troublemaker, as if she does not present any data, and as if the public has taken to her theory just because they are merely unscientific, and perhaps foolish and delusional. Also, as another example, I can't tell you how many times I have had physicists that I have conversed with tell me that instantaneous communication between bodies is *impossible*, even though in the early 1980s Alain Aspect proved it occurs between quantum entangled particles. I could list nearly countless other examples, which I will however not, in the interests of keeping this discussion brief.

[36] 1989, Boulder: Westview.

[37] See Phillip Goscienski, *Health Secrets of the Stone Age*, Second Edition, Better Life Publishers, 2005.

[38] For interesting information on the osteoporosis facts and non-facts, see the excellent, scholarly article, "A New Disease, A New Marketing Opportunity," by Susan Sellman (*Nexus Magazine*, Volume 5, #6, October-November 1998, http://www.nexusmagazine. com/articles/osteoporosis.html).

they drink builds strong teeth and bones due to the fluoride in the water, so if that's the case, then why is there so much osteoporosis in the United States? Does that prove that fluoride *does not* strengthen teeth and bones?

Sellman also discusses[39] how a diet dominated by meat, or heavy use of pharmaceuticals, can also lead to artificially manufactured osteoporosis, but where the ailment will be mysteriously blamed (by medical schools and their lobbied researchers) *not* on the meat and drugs, but rather on *aging* (which is exactly what McElroy and Townsend also assert), even though the elderly of some other cultures (especially primitive cultures) who do not even consume dairy, or the elderly of America before 1970, exhibited no osteoporosis. McElroy and Townsend seem to be merely making a completely unverified assumption that aging causes "demineralization of ... bones", but it is an assumption that must be rejected, until scientifically proven, since there appears to be counter-evidence in Sellman, and which I presented in the previous paragraph. Now the critical issue is the following:

> This example shows how the assumptions that the general public make are often the same ones that academics make, and vice versa. *It would therefore seem that this implies that American media is influencing the thought of academics*, and this example shows that academics are not free of the mass brainwashing that pervades American culture.

Believe the Unverifiable Account of Reality that You are Taught in School and on TV, or You are a "Conspiracy Theorist"

Nearly any of the ideas and concepts that do not fit into and agree with the unverifiable picture of reality conveyed by the American educational system and the mainstream media typically will be quickly, aggressively, and angrily called a "conspiracy theory!" "quackery!" and so on, by educators and media celebrities. For example, consider the following New York Times article about Laetrile—a natural substance, and a mere vitamin (vitamin B17)—which is argued by many nutritionists to prevent cancer and even cure early-stage cancer, but which has been *banned* by the FDA, even though the FDA has not shown why Laetrile should be banned, why it is dangerous,[40] and if it really is ineffective as a treatment:

> The Senate Health and Science Research Subcommittee... seemed to generate an unusual air of excitement when it gathered last summer... The subject under discussion was the ... anticancer chemical Laetrile...,

---

[39] Ibid.

[40] Often it is claimed that Laetrile (vitamin B17) is dangerous because it has cyanide. But the cyanide it has is locked up in a molecule, and is not free-floating cyanide, and thus is not dangerous at all. Also, vitamin B12 has copious locked-up cyanide, and it has never been found to be dangerous for the cyanide it contains. So this "cyanide danger" of Laetrile is merely fabrication.

an extract of the lowly apricot pit… The unprecedented meeting had been called because 12 states had voted to legalize Laetrile, even though it is banned by the Federal Government from importation and from interstate commerce. The states had done it—and had given doctors the right to prescribe Laetrile for their patients—against the advice of such powerful and determined agencies as the Food and Drug Administration (FDA), the National Cancer Institute and the American Cancer Society—*all of whom had branded Laetrile as a worthless nostrum, the ultimate in quackery.*[41] (Emphasis added)

This sort of name-calling pervades the mass media, and, in turn, serves as a teaching tool, instructing the citizenry on how to respond to virtually any sort of dissenting voice that falls outside of the mostly *unverifiable*, metaphysical picture of reality that is spoon-fed to the citizenry in the classroom and in the hypnotic trance of televisual stimulus. If one merely questions the picture of reality found in media and education, and/or if one merely presents simple empirical counter-evidence (as I did with the milk example above) about the narrow and unverifiable ideas about reality that Americans have been spoon-fed through education and media, one will typically be ridiculed or even terrorized by the masses: "conspiracy theorist!" "kook!" "traitor!" "communist!" "terrorist!" "you're ignorant!" "you're paranoid!" Yes, one may even be considered a "terrorist" (which, according to H.R. 6166, the Military Commissions Act), a bill passed by the 109th Congress in the fall of 2006, means any American can be secretly arrested, tortured, and killed by the US government), as if merely presenting simple scientific data means that you are identical to Osama bin Laden, and, *ipso facto*, you are a person who wants to kill millions of American children.

In America, Empirical Research is Now Often Called "Conspiracy Theory" or "Terrorism"

For example, David Horowitz accused Professor Mark Levine[42] on August 1, 2006, on the Hannity and Colmes show on the Fox News Channel of being "with the terrorists," as George W. Bush often puts it[43]: "Mark Levine is an

---

[41] "Why Laetrlie Won't Go Away," New York Times, Lee Edison, Nov. 27, 1977.

[42] Professor Levine is the author of *Why They Don't Hate Us* (2005, Oxford: Oneworld Publications), which is an empirical study about Levine's own travels through the Middle East that shows that citizens of Arab countries, of course, do not hate Americans, and, of course, are not "terrorists," and rather, like Americans, they are merely people (and what could be simpler than that thesis!) trying to survive from day-to-day, raising children, trying to stay safe, and being victimized and terrorized by governments and corporatists.

[43] Bush is known for saying: "you are either with us, or you are with the terrorists." Bush started saying this shortly after September 11, 2001, such as on the evening of

apologist for the terrorists... Anybody who writes a book about why they *don't* hate us, referring to the Arab Middle East, has no credibility whatsoever." The public has been very well trained to carry out this juvenile name-calling and non-analytic quick-conclusion-making whenever somebody questions the unscientific and mostly unverifiable view of reality that the American mass media and the government-mandated, UN-created,[44] American education system have constructed.

If I give my students the clearest, simplest evidence of something that is in disagreement with the narrow view of reality they have been conditioned to believe in, even by presenting simple, straightforward empirical data that they can verify with their own eyes, that evidence will nevertheless typically *not* jar them from their brainwashed dream-state, and often a student will raise their hand and say something like, "but isn't that just a conspiracy theory?" They have been taught that the sky is green, and to believe that it is blue is something that only fools ("conspiracy theorists") would do.

Other students of mine will often become irritated with me for merely having the nerve to challenge them in a classroom setting. They will be surprised that I have interest in presenting simple empirical data that challenges their preestablished, spoon-fed, absurdist picture of reality, as if I am *out of place* for presenting simple, straightforward evidence to them in an academic setting. As if I am supposed to hide that evidence from them so that I can instead teach them a false account of reality.

This example with my students shows how easily control of a citizenry can be grasped in a nation that tends to have belief-systems that are anti-scientific, and which cherishes belief rather than hard evidence. The system *governs itself.* Icke writes:

> When few people wish to control and direct a mass of humanity, there are certain key structures that have to be in placed... First you have to set the "norms", what is considered right and wrong, possible or impossible, sane or insane, good and bad... This pressurizes [citizens] to conform and serves as a warning for those others in the herd who are... thinking of breaking away... This creates a situation fundamental to the few controlling the many in which the masses police themselves and keep each other in line... It is like a prisoner trying to escape while the rest of his cellmates rush to stop him. If that happened we would say the prisoners were crazy, how could they do that? But humans are doing precisely this to each other every day by demanding that everyone

---

September 20, 2001 in a famous speech from Washington, D. C., which can be read at this web page: http://www.whitehouse. gov/news/releases/2001/09/20010920-8.html.
[44] See Tabor for a detailed discussion of how the American education system in the United States has been deliberately and secretly hijacked and shaped by the United Nations from the end of World War II to the present.

conform to the norms to which *they* blindly conform. This is nothing less than psychological fascism—the thought police with agents in every home, everywhere. Agents so deeply conditioned that most have no idea they are unpaid mind controllers... This is part of the divide and rule strategy so vital to ensuring that the herd will police itself. Everyone plays a part in everyone else's mental, emotional, and physical imprisonment... Once you set the norms in a society, there is no need to control every journalist or reporter or government official. The media and the institutions take their "truth" from those same norms and therefore ridicule and condemn by reflex action anyone who offers another vision of reality. Once you control what is considered "normal" and possible, the whole system virtually runs itself.[45]

Brainwashing: Being Tricked into Believing that Non-Reality is Reality

The masses of people in the modern world are taught to believe in a reality that does not exist; they are taught to believe in *non-reality*. This is the textbook definition of *brainwashing*,[46] and I will show in detail below that it is currently being carried out against the citizenry of the world. Reality is there for anybody to witness, if they merely use their senses and observe. But, unfortunately, so often people will not do this, and thus they will consequently only see *unreality*. When they do, reality for them can be described as being *hidden in plain view*: it is there all around and they can know it immediately if they merely use their *senses* to do so (this is what a scientist does in her attempt to understand reality); but they do not, and instead they trust their *ideas*—that is, their *inaccurate* ideas—about reality. For example, no matter how many times I remind my next-door neighbor that Americans were never presented with empirical evidence (sense information), such as video footage, that a plane hit the Pentagon on 9/11, she will nevertheless demand that there *was* a plane that hit the Pentagon on 9/11, she will not believe there are reasons to conclude that there was no plane there on that day.

This book is about what I consider to be the most important "hidden" issue in the world today: the philosophy of *corporatism*, which is the governing system of the contemporary world. Corporatism is the political and economic system where *corporations are government*, and where they specifically use their control of resources and information in order to shape and control the citizens of the world in a way analogous to how tightly shaped and controlled the brainwashed Nazi citizens were in the 1930s, and in a way analogous to how a strict dog owner controls and shapes her dog: the world the owner lets the dog see is the only world the dog will know (and the only world the dog will believe

---

[45] Icke 2001, 1-2.
[46] See Taylor 2004 for more information on the highly developed definition of brainwashing.

is real), and the behaviors (and thoughts) that the dog exhibits that are permissible in the eyes of the owner are the only ones that, through time, the dog learns to perform. I will prove that America (and the rest of the world) is a purely corporatist system in the next chapter. But before that, in this first chapter, I will discuss a few issues that need to be clarified in order to productively discuss corporatism throughout the rest of this book. There will be those who assert that I am merely a "conspiracy theorist" for showing that America is a corporatist nation (and that the world is moving toward a state where it is a global-Orwellian corporatist plantation), but the evidence I present in this book is simple and empirical.

Corporatists vs. Workers

In the contemporary America, few of us grow the majority of our own food, nearly none of us make our own clothes, build our own homes, make our own cars, and so on. In fact, we depend on other persons for nearly *all* the goods we use for daily existence. Therefore, all of us, to some degree, are living in, and dependent on, the *corporatist* system, where gigantic monopolistic and undemocratic businesses sell us (for profit) the goods we need for our basic daily survival. All of American society (including politicians, the military, law-enforcement workers, and judicial workers) are in servitude to these corporate assemblages, and most of us cannot help but be employed by them also. Even though few in the corporation and in the corporatist society seem to become concerned with this power the corporations have, we will see that corporatism of the corporatist society controls every facet of life, down to the minutest detail, and unfortunately for the purpose of creating a world of mass-misery.

Corporatism—which is a form of government where corporations dictate and rule the lives of people—can assume many forms. On one extreme, corporatism can be politically *anarchistic*: the corporation, where goods and services are produced, governs and controls people, but there is no centralized group of people in power; rather, all workers are of equal status, distributing wealth quite evenly, productively working together to produce the needed goods to be sold for profit.[47] On the other extreme, corporatism can be *fascistic* and *communistic*: in the corporation, one person or one small board or group of people dictate over the mass of workers at the corporation, distributing wealth very unevenly, ultimately leading to mass poverty, and to situations where the corporation merely becomes a forced-labor camp and/or death camp. The second variety, fascistic-communist corporatism (which I will merely refer to as *corporatism* hereafter) is the one I am primarily concerned with in this book (and I will only discuss anarchist corporatism in a few places below), and is the governmental system that describes the United States and most of the contemporary world. This type of corporatism, as we will see, inevitably leads

---

[47] Examples of these sorts of corporations are the Argentine factories documented in Lewis, 2004.

to global depression, poverty, slavery, mind-control, and all-encompassing *1984*-like circumstances, most of which are currently fully developed, or well on their way to being implemented in the United States (and in the rest of the world).

More specifically, the fascistic-communist sort of corporatism I am concerned with is a political and economic system where

a) The *corporatists* (the corporation controllers), and/or

b) The *corporations* (where the corporation is merely a group of people working together in order to accumulate monetary income),

control the economy and the social and psychological structure of a nation. a) and/or b) *are the government* in a corporatist system, regardless which of a) or b) is manifested, or if some mixture of them is manifested. a) is a governing system that involves rule by a tyrant or by very few tyrants, and b) is a governing system that involves rule by an abstraction, an *idea*.

a) can only be manifested in a society when the citizenry is fooled into believing that power and control of the society derives from the corporatists, rather than the workers. In reality, all power in a corporatist state resides with the labor force—*the workers*—who are the engine of society, but in a fascistic corporatist nation, workers are tricked into believing they are powerless and that oppression of them is to be tolerated.

Without workers, civilization does not exist. Without corporatists, however, workers can merely keep producing. There is a big secret being disclosed here: as illustrated in the cases of anarchistic corporatism in South America[48] and elsewhere, corporatists (the tyrants described in a)) are not needed, and corporation controllers must take measures to ensure that workers do not figure that out. The existence, power, and labor of workers determines all; but in a system where a) is in place, workers are typically fooled (brainwashed) into believing that power does not reside with the laborer and with the raw "force" of labor. Rather, workers are fooled into believing power comes from a) and/or b), not from them.

In reality, a) and b) exhibit no power whatsoever: the corporation and the corporatists are dependent on the real power, which is the "force" of labor. In a fascistic corporatist setting, if a workforce decided, as a group, that they desired their situation to involve some quality, call it x (x may be higher wages, more profit sharing, shorter hours, etc.), usually all they have to do is merely decide, as a group, that x is to be implemented, and to take measures to ensure that it is (e.g., strike), and rarely will the "all-powerful" corporatist be able to do anything about it (they will likely only be able to stop x from being implemented if it is truly impossible that the corporation can give rise x).

---

[48] See Lewis 2004.

Workers, not knowing the power they hold, may go a lifetime without ever realizing their power, and they may falsely imagine throughout their lives that a) and b) are sources of control and authority in their lives. If they do believe this, then they will indeed go along with a) and b), and they will give up the power they have.

The "Corporatists" can be defined as follows:

Corporatists = $_{def}$ Those members of the ultramassive, monopolistic, global corporations at the highest ranks, and who control others but are not controlled by other members of that same corporation in return.

As we will see, the corporatists are a separate social class in America, and in the next section I will show that they include the majority of politicians in Washington D.C., since US politicians tend to be either corporatists or working for corporatists in some way.

In this book I will define the rest of the population (RP)—all those who are not corporatists—as follows:

RP = $_{def}$ The members of a population who are not corporatists, and who are not working *immediately* under the corporatists as convert agents for the corporatists.

Corporatism is an economic system that has shown up at many points in history. It is the economic and political system that best describes the United States (even though most Americans are told and believe otherwise), and it may be the governing system most frequently used by humans who are not members of hunter-gatherer and/or inchoate farming communities. Even though few Americans realize it, it is not a secret that the United States is a corporatist nation. For example, in Title 28 of the US Code of Law, it is stated that the United States is a *Federal Corporation*. The system of corporatism varies in levels of quality (where "quality" can be defined as the level of prosperity for each strata of society, and how/if each level has all its basic life needs met: safety, genuine education, etc.), depending on the objectives of the fascistic corporatists and what the nature of the labor is. A productive corporatist nation (the aforementioned *anarchistic* corporatist system), where maximum financial, technological, and educational wealth is sought for all citizens in all strata of society, eliminates and/or does not involve wasteful "government leaders," corporatist bankers, and any other sort of shady groups working for the corporatists (the CIA, CFR, IMF, WTO, NATO, WHO, FDA, UN, EPA, FBI, MI-6, USDA, the Vatican, and so on) that work against the people, taking on criminalistic and/or genocidal qualities.

In the world today, the system of corporatism in place is the aforementioned fascistic-communistic corporatist system, and since this system involves an oppressed and unknowingly terrorized citizenry, this system requires the existence of a plethora of "institutions" (police, public education, a reserve banking system, "regulating agencies," doctors, etc.) that stand between the corporatists and the people, and which have the sole function of dominating, controlling, molding, shaping, and socially engineering the people in the way that the corporatists desire, and in a way that hides the mass torment of the citizenry (i.e., making them believe they are free even though they're slaves). Therefore, contemporary corporatism in America and all over the world is found to involve all sorts of secretive control-groups that have little function other than to overshadow and terrorize the world citizenry. These are the masses of militaries, politicians and "lawmakers," think tanks, secret militaristic and intelligence agencies, lobbyists, trade organizations, philanthropic organizations (e.g., Bill and Melinda Gates Foundation[49]), education administrators, "regulating agencies" (FDA, EPA, etc.), and torture armies (such as the UN,[50] or the CIA), just to name a few. These pollute the corporatist system to such a degree that they turn it into a feudalist system. They corrupt the system of corporatism in a way where they literally rob the populace and even some of the lower-level (non-monopolistic) corporatists of the mass of their wealth.

As you will see over the course of the first few chapters of this book, America is, and has been since the 1870s, a corporatist nation. We will also see that the United States is a communist nation, in the truest sense of the world "communism." And as you will see later in this book that America is also an Orwellian state, with all the standard characteristics: invisible and fabricated terror networks that are advertised by the big media as being continually ready to strike, mass brainwashing, staged war, mass poverty, and, eventually, the migration of virtually all the citizens into compact, dirty, disease-ridden cities—or what are more appropriately called labor camps, or concentration camps. Politicians and mainstream media personalities repeatedly tell Americans that the United States is a democracy, and they trust that the mob-like majority will, in general, not look into or question any of the issues I discuss in this book—wherein, in the meantime, corporatism more firmly is set in place while Americans are not looking. The worldwide corporatist empire that is approaching full power will dramatically transform the world in the coming years, so much so that things like family, rights, anonymity from

---

[49] This is an agency that is non-profit and therefore can avoid taxes. It is an agency that is primarily involved in delivering vaccines to the children of the world (with the help of the WHO). In chapter 5, I will show that vaccines are perhaps the stealthiest of the secret government torture-tools. Microsoft, which is Bill Gates's foundation, has also been involved in the seediest of corporate corruption. See Ramptom and Stauber 2002, pages 8-13.

[50] To see why I refer to the UN as little more than a "torture army," see the Introduction chapter of Tabor (2006), and also see "UN Child Sex Slave Scandals Continue: Wave after wave of child abuse reports pour forward from all over the globe," Infowars.net, Steve Watson, Wednesday, January 3, 2007.

government, unbrainwashed minds, and even the human body or human consciousness as we have known it, will all be obsolete.

A Coup of the US Government in the Late 1800s

Many researchers and political thinkers seem to think that a governmental coup d'état took place with the theft of the 2000 Presidential election by the PNAC-supported, corporatist-funded neoconservative Bush Administration,[51] wherein afterward the United States has been incrementally and deliberately dismantled in order to set up the North American Union, and, ultimately, the corporatist New World Order. This is, however, incorrect. As we will see, the coup d'état of the US government occurred in the late 1800s *by the corporatists*, and the Bush Administration is merely a recent unelected, deliberately appointed,[52] emanation of that coup d'état that has secretly been in place for over a century. The most successful fascist rule is the one that is disguised as freedom, and which fools the citizenry into believing they are free.

Corporations are not accountable to any higher authority. Americans are told (via the mass media, the education system, and perhaps the churches) that there are all sorts of rules and limitations that limit and govern the activities of the ultramassive monopolistic corporations. But we will see that if one looks closer, they will find that there are literally no regulations *at all* that corporatists and their corporations must abide by. To give just one of a plethora of examples that could be given, consider the Tribune Company,[53] a giant autonomous media company, which owns news media (11 news papers, including the Chicago Tribune and the LA Times, etc.) that reaches 80 percent of US homes,[54] and controls a lot of television, including the popular television show, *South Park*. If one were to investigate the Tribune Company, and the corporatists that control it, such as its CEO, Steven Fitzsimmons, one would find that *government* personnel (Senators, etc.) dominate the board of the Tribune Company, and thus it is a government run corporation—which is what is found in a corporatist state: corporatism involves a unification between big government and big business (in this case, big media business). In fact, this is true for all of the big media corporations: CEOs and board members are members of the FCC, are senators, and so on.[55] PNAC, for example, is indistinguishable from The Weekly Standard (which is published by News

---

[51] To give just one example, Charlotte Iserbyt, former Reagan Administration Dept. of Education official, on the Rense Radio Show, November 29, 2006, uttered this conviction.

[52] See Miller 2005.

[53] The Tribune Company was being bid-on for buyout by various other larger corporations, such as the Carlyle Group, just before this book went to press. It was not clear if a buyout was going to take place.

[54] This is according to the Tribune website, http://www.tribune.com/about/index.html.

[55] See Bagdikian 2004, Pappas 2003.

Corp.). PNAC and the Weekly Standard each have the same street address, many of the same members, and so on.

There are literally too many examples to list of how politicians are involved at the top of big media corporations, and there are no clear boundaries or distinctions between the US government and big media—which is precisely what *corporatist* media would be. How can there be government regulation of the media when media is owned by the government? The same question could be asked about any of the other industries or institutions that the US government owns: medicine, public education (including universities), weapons and war, food, and so on. Corporations own and control nearly all of the world's resource wealth, and we will see in chapter 2 that this means that corporations control all people, and their behavior and thought. Without corporations, most people would die.[56]

Corporations did not originally exist in this way. Corporations began in the 1700s under a heavy cloak of *actual* regulation. It was in the first half of the 1800s that corporations began battling against this regulation. Between 1870 and 1890, corporations attained full control of the United States, and a corporate tyranny (a corporatist nation) emerged.[57] Consider the following passage from Professor Korten about this evolution into corporatism:

> Gradually... corporations gained sufficient control over key state legislative bodies to virtually rewrite the laws governing their own creation. Legislators in New Jersey and Delaware took the lead in watering down citizens' rights to intervene in corporate affairs... A conservative court system that was consistently responsive to the appeals and arguments of corporate lawyers steadily chipped away at the restraints a wary citizenry had carefully placed on corporate powers. Step by step, the court system set new precedents that made the protection of corporations and corporate property a centerpiece of constitutional law.[58]

Corporatists infiltrated government positions in the United States, and shaped government to their interests. This removed and eliminated the power of the Constitutional government in the United States, and it put governance in the hands of those corporatists that had the most money and thus who had enough money to gain government offices.

Few issues are more central to American corporatism than the invasion and thorough takeover of the US government by the corporatists (and by those who have been specifically appointed by the corporatists) since the late 1800s.

---

[56] This is because Americans do not have basic life skills (farming, making clothes, etc.) since they spend most of their daily work-time at a corporation, rather than sustaining themselves and taking care of basic survival activities, taking care of their children, and so on.

[57] See Korten 2001, 63-66 for lucid discussion of this evolution.

[58] Korten 2001, 65.

This is the aforementioned coup d'état of the US government that occurred in the late 1800s: those who had enough money to buy their way into Washington in order to destroy Constitutional activity did not hesitate in doing so.

This was a covert implementation of a secret government, which still exists today, and which has been for a century dressed in the garb of US government politicians, thus forming a government designed not to serve We the People, but rather one for corporations alone. From the late 1800s onward, although the members of government may have looked like politicians, and although they may look like they are debating issues on the floor of Congress, they are not: *they are acting*. When one watches the film, *Forrest Gump*, one may be so taken by the dramatic story and the convincing acting that they forget that Forrest is an actor, and that they are really watching a person named Tom Hanks, who in "real life" does not act at all like Forrest Gump. This is precisely what most of Washington D.C. is *really* all about, and many Americans have no idea (and would be completely shocked if they knew) that this is the case, since they do not know what politicians really do in-and-out of each day, such as consult lobbyists, covertly work as corporatists and in imperialistic think tanks, avoid reading legislation before it is voted on, collaborating with Big Pharma and with the military-industrial complex in various ways, and so on. This is analogous to how, in the classic 1950s film, *Invasion of the Body Snatchers*, there were people who were "not what they appeared to be." When you looked at their faces, they appeared to be one person, but deep down, behind the skin-veil, they were secretly a whole different person altogether. This is a core theme of American corporatism that will be discussed in this book.

9/11: Initiation into the New World Order

Above I said that it can be verified that the American education system is full of disinformation. But one thing it seems to have at least *partially* correct is the level of violence that has existed throughout human history. This violence is a horror far worse than the most horrifying Hollywood horror film. This horror, of course, has not been absent in parts of Europe and the USA over the past 60 years, but the typical pervasive horror-qualities of many eras of history (pervasive slavery and concentration camps, seemingly endless martial law and Gestapo-like practices, the pervasive jailing and torture of citizens for speaking against the controlling powers of the land, and so forth) have been somewhat absent since 1945 in some parts of the Western world. But that mode of human existence is in the first stages of being implemented back into the places it has been somewhat absent, as you will see in this book.

There is a secret plan to turn the entire world into an Orwellian horror-state, and the plan has been firmly in motion since the late 1800s, intensifying from 1970 to 9/11/2001, and it reached what appears to be its penultimate phase with 9/11, as you will see later in this book. Most Americans are still not conscious of this, but it is a plan that has been put in place by the controlling powers of

America (the corporatists) and signs of its horror can be seen all around: Guantanamo Bay, "preemptive warfare," secret CIA prisons, the fabrication of Orwellian-style enemies that live in caves and exist in "networks" or "cells" all around, which are never seen but which Americans are told "could be in your neighborhood," media controlled by the corporatists (including the military-industrial complex corporatists: e.g., GE owns NBC, CNBC, MSNBC, etc.; The Carlyle Group owns Qwest Communications, Insight Cable, etc.), Halliburton currently building *massive* "detention camps," complacent citizens, Rex84, destruction of the power of the Constitution, mass child vaccinations with poisoned vaccines, foiled elections with decisions made before recount and where the lesser votes reveal the winner, false flag terrorism (when a government attacks its own country under a disguise of being an enemy), voting machines, draft legislation, "soma" (e.g., Prozac, Ritalin, Zyprexa, etc.), nationwide social engineering, chemtrails, DU, mass extinction, transhumanist and posthumanist philosophy—and that is just the beginning.

In general, Americans do not understand the transformation taking place, nor do they see that America, as it was during the 60 years prior to 9/11, no longer exists. If they were to merely read the publicly available corporatists' plans and documents (such as NSSM 200, and a few other corporatist-government documents I will cite later) that discuss their plans for global control, global slavery, global genocide programs, and global poisoning of the citizens who remain, they would see the future of their kismet. I can confidently assert that, unfortunately, soon they will understand even if they do not look into the issues.

I am of course not the only researcher to argue that the aforementioned changes are being currently implemented, and that their full implementation is nearly upon us. Many of the researchers and professors I cite in this book also argue for the same position. For example, Berman (2006) has written a book-length account for why America is plummeting into a dark age, which, according to him, is similar to how Rome plummeted. This may be true, but "dark age" is, I will argue, not quite the right term that properly describes current metamorphosis going on with the United States. Rather, I will show that the United States is right in the midst of a transformation into a *corporatist* state, rather than into a dark age: America is moving into a *full* corporatist-Orwellian world government and into what the corporatists have called a *New World Order*, as George Bush Sr. said exactly 11 years to the day before 9/11, when he was discussing the first Iraq War: "[The war in Iraq is] a rare opportunity to move toward an historic period of cooperation. Out of these troubled times...a new world order can emerge."[59]

---

[59] George Bush Sr., September 11, 1990.

The Corporatists

Since a significant percentage of Americans have lived the past 60 years in America partly outside of the standard horrific nature of history, it is hard for some of them to fathom and countenance the reality of something like Rwanda, the slaughter of Jericho, the American holocaust of the Native Americans, or present-day war- and DU-devastated Iraq. Many Americans are fooled into believing that prosperity, peace, plentitude (of resource wealth), and democracy are normal, rather than anomalous.

Currently America is in a nightmare scenario, since it is controlled by a fascistic, communistic group of psychopaths who are well-organized, oppressive, ultra-secretive, determined, ultra-violent, and, according to some researchers, secretly occultist and/or satanic,[60] which would not be entirely surprising given their Nazi ancestry (discussed in chapters below). These American communists and fascists have control of the greatest military force in the world—no other country even compares—and the two Iraq Wars prove they are ready and eager to use it excessively for murderous activities without logical reason, without being provoked, to merely usurp energy reserves in order to give more power to their global corporations, and, apparently, for the thrill of spreading mass misery (via false flag terror, for example).[61]

---

[60] See Maxwell 2000; Jones 2006, 2005; Pinto 2006; Howard 1989. One of the most convincing accounts I have seen that shows that the secret corporatist government is satanistic found in the first 30 minutes of a lecture given by Dr. Michael Coffman in his DVD, "World Events and Prophecy," which can be acquired at Coffman's website, www.discerningtoday. org. I do not want to take a position on whether or not Coffman is correct in maintaining that current world events correspond to the Bible's account of the so-called "end-times" (many people were also saying the same thing about Hitler's run for "World Order"). What is interesting is how in the first 30 minutes of his lecture, Coffman goes through all sorts of texts written by people in or associated with the New World Order that exhibit outright claims of satanistic worship. Also, Coffman discusses how these people attempt to align themselves, to some degree, with Buddhism, as if Buddhism has something to do with worship of any sort, or with magic and belief in Satan. This is flatly incorrect, however, since Buddhists reject all sorts of belief, and only endorse meditation in order to reach nirvana. Consider the Buddha's own words: "For hate is not conquered by hate: hate is conquered by love. This is a law eternal. Many do not know that we are here in this world to live in harmony. Those who know this do not fight against each other." (*Dhammapada* v. 5-6) Also, Buddhism is widely recognized for being a philosophy of poverty, compassion, and love—all of which are not existent in Satanism. Therefore, there is no credibility in the idea that Satanism has anything to do with Buddhism. Also, Buddhism is entirely aligned with science (see Grupp 2005 [conclusion], 2006), and thus cannot have anything to do with unscientific belief, such as the unscientific nature of something like Satanism.

[61] See Jones 2006 for an account of why the miscellaneous terror attacks in Iraq over the past half decade have been false flag attacks, conducted by, for example, the CIA, British Intell, and so on. I also discuss why this is the case later in this chapter. Also,

The controllers of America that I am discussing here are not necessarily Congress or George W. Bush (who are merely actors and dummy ventriloquists used by the "invisible" corporatist-government that secretly rules America [and the world], as will be discussed in this introductory chapter). The group I am referring to who controls the United States from behind-the-scenes, *the corporatists*, are the controllers and owners of the world's ultra-massive, monopolistic corporations. As mentioned, they have infiltrated politics (e.g., Dick Cheney, James Woolsey, Steve Forbes, Al Gore, etc.) and thus the American public in general may know something about *some* of them; but most corporatists are, in essence, not visible to the populace, and those that are will not reveal their genuine intentions to the citizenry.

Some researchers assert that the secret government is satanic since certain symbols, such as the "all-seeing" eye of Horus (Horus is the Egyptian sky god), pervade the corporatist's symbology, but do not show up elsewhere in culture.

---

consider how the following news reports of miscallaneous terror attacks are given through news reports that have occult masonic numerology involved (e.g., 117➔711, 93, 9x3=27, etc.): "Suicide Bombers Kill 93 in Iraq Nine U.S. Soldiers Die in Separate Blasts," Associated Press, by Lauren Frayer, March 6, 2007; "Suicide Car Bomb Kills 17 in Baghdad," Associated Press, by Sameer N. Yacoub, January 17, 2007; "Suicide Bombings Around Iraq Kill 27," Associated Press, April 23, 2007; "Bombs Kill at Least 183 People in Baghdad Latest Spasms of Violence Leave a Total of 233 Dead," by Steven R. Hurst and Lauren Frayer, April 19, 2007. Most stories of miscallaneous terror events in Iraq are given through numerological language.

The faces that the corporatists display on television show them as kind, cheery, philanthropic people who are interested in selflessly helping others (think of Bono and the vaccine-pushing Gates Foundation, for example). But we will see in this book that this is a false image—an act fit for a Marquis de Sade novel—and in fact they are a fascist group that currently is subjecting most people of the world to a harsh existence, to ubiquitous torture (even though the people often do not know they are being tortured, since they are tricked into believing that they are free), and in the near future this will escalate into an overt global tyranny of horror (in the places it is not such already, like Iraq and Africa) far worse than any the world has yet seen and literally beyond the imagination of most people.

The fascist leaders and fascist groups that have full tyrannical control of the United States are not in the media limelight, and certainly most Americans do not even know their names: Louis V. Gerstner, Jr., Rex Tillerson, Ben Bernanke, William H. Swanson, Paul Wolfowitz, Edward E. Whitacre, Jr., Ivan G. Seidenberg, Richard Perle, Stanley O'Neal, David Rockefeller, Walter James McNerney, Jr., Robert Iger, William Kristol, Rupert Murdoch, H Lee Scott and Sam Walton, Jack Welch, Steve Forbes, Lynne Cheney, Joseph Coors, to name of a few of the thousand or so that could be listed. These are controllers of supermassive corporations (for example, Boeing, The Carlyle Group, Walt Disney, Coors, GE, etc.), of supermassive media corporations (for example, News Corp), they are corporatists that *also* work in the US government (for example, Rumsfeld, Cheney, Bush, Giuliani, etc.), and they are lobbyists or those who work in the most powerful think tanks (Rumsfeld, Perle, Forbes, Fukuyama, Kurzweil, etc.).

As we will see, ultra-powerful corporatists and their think tanks, lobbyists, and militaries govern and create policy in the United States (and the world), and their policies are for fascism (corporatism), militarism (such as the so-called preemptive warfare philosophy), secret spying on American citizens,[62]

---

[62] This is not a new issue, and it predates the Bush Administration. And this issue is now widely known to be going on, but a short time ago it was not, and it shocked many Americans when they found out about this secret spying. This policy was announced to the world with the Patriot Act, and its implementation announced in the *widely* discussed story broken by the USA Today, and which was later admitted to be correct by the Bush Administration. Consider this passage from NPR about the USA Today story:

All Things Considered, May 18, 2006 · *USA Today* disclosed last week that the National Security Agency had been secretly collecting the phone records of tens of millions of Americans with the help of major phone companies. It was a big scoop. Other newspapers -- including *The New York Times* and *The Washington Post* -- soon confirmed that the NSA had created the database... In its article, *USA Today* reported that AT&T, BellSouth and Verizon had provided data to the government -- and had even been offered money by the NSA to do so. But after its publication, Verizon issued a statement saying it had

impoverishing the vast majority of the population of the United States and the world, slave labor, death camps, torture, fake (staged) wars and terrorism, controlling all information and media, genocide (more formally called "population control"), posthumanism, among other basic Orwellian features. If the reader believes what is being written here is outlandish and the stuff of "conspiracy theory," it would very likely be the case that such a reader believes that due to his lack of knowledge of history,[63] and due to the reader's lack of knowledge of the real state of technology that the corporatists have at their hands (but which is kept secret from the RP).[64]

Corporatist Governance Means a Fascist World

In this book (especially in chapters 2 and 3), I will show that America is secretly controlled by monopolistic corporations and by the people appointed by the monopolistic corporatists to create policy that is desirable to the corporatists. America is not controlled by the RP, or by the politician-actors. Since corporations have a fascist structure, if corporatists control America, then America is consequently a fascist nation. Thomas J. DiLorenzo, economics professor at Loyola College, tells us that

> [w]hen most people hear the word "fascism" they naturally think of its ugly racism and anti-Semitism as practiced by the totalitarian regimes of Mussolini and Hitler. But there was also an economic policy component of fascism, known in Europe during the 1920s and '30s as "corporatism," that was an essential ingredient of economic totalitarianism as practiced by Mussolini and Hitler. So-called corporatism was adopted in Italy and Germany during the 1930s and was held up as a "model" by quite a few intellectuals and policy makers in the United States and Europe. A version of economic fascism was in fact adopted in the United States in the 1930s and survives to this day. In the United States these policies were not called "fascism" but

---

never provided any information about the domestic phone calls of its customers. (*NPR.org*)

[63] For a good refresher, I recommend the reader read *American Holocaust*, by David Stannard, Oxford University Press, 1992. The typical American appears to have a strange idea that the horrors of history are far away from us now. But that merely is a product of not focusing on the recent derangements all around, such as the child-sex scandals involving so many priests that were revealed in the last five years, the derangement of American controlled Iraqi prisons, the 2000 American Presidential election, just to name a few things.

[64] To get ideas of what this technology is all about, see the section on Morgellons disease in chapter 5, and see Fukuyama 2002, Kurweil 1999, and see the DVD lecture, *Weapons of Mass Control*, by Bob Fletcher, 1997, available from World News Insight, P.O. Box 216, Bayview Idaho, 83803.

"planned capitalism." The word fascism may no longer be politically acceptable, but its synonym "industrial policy" is as popular as ever.[65]

This innate nature of corporations is true of both small corporations, and for the giant monopolizing mega-corporations, but in this book I am only concerned with the latter.[66]

Americans do not understand that *corporations are government* and politicians are not government (but rather, politicians are the policymakers for the governing corporatists). Rather, Americans have been fooled into believing that politicians are working for the people, that politicians control and regulate the United States, and that the United States is a democracy. Undoing this "education" of non-facts is one of the goals of this book, and it will take me many pages, given the life-long, convincing, relentless, non-education Americans receive from birth to death.

Simple study of the daily activities of politicians will reveal, to anyone who looks, that the mass media portrays politicians inaccurately, and that politicians are not politely working for "the people." Rather, they are implementing policy that has not been created by voters, but which has been created by a few unelected policy-creating groups (called think tank and New World Order organizations, and I will describe them at length in a later chapter), who write the policy and shape the military and the world in a way suitable to the interests of those in control of corporations. Corporatism is the all-pervading dominant engine of the United States, controlling and creating government and policy, war and business, media and education, and even the structure of moment-to-moment consciousness of American citizens.

---

[65] DiLorenzo 1993.

[66] Some readers might assume that only the ultra-massive corporations are corporatistic (governmental) in nature, since it is in those companies that we find situations where it is clear that business = government, and where, for example, a CEO will be a senator, a board member a member of the Executive Branch of the US government, or a top stock holder a member of the FDA, FCC, EPA, or some other aspect of the US government. But it is not true that only the ultra-massive corporatists are the real corporatists, and the smaller corporatists are not. This is the case for many reasons. First, the smaller corporatists contribute to enforcing the corporatist way of life for Americans, and the same thought control and oppression that the ultra-massive corporatists set forth will be present in the smaller corporations, since the smaller corporatists learn from the ultra-massive corporatists and use the law-system of the ultra-massive corporatists. Also, the smaller corporatists share some (but not all) of the traits, on a smaller-scale, as the ultra-massive corporatists do (these characteristics are outlined in chapters 2 -5). For example, smaller corporatists often possess capital (unlike nearly all non-corporatists in the United States), control resources, create mass-misery, tyrannize human consciousness, and contribute to corporate terrorism and misery.

Corporatist Methods

Much of this book involves an empirical study of the *tools and techniques* that corporatists use to implement and carry out their Orwellian corporatism. There are thirteen primary tools that corporatists use to assure their fascistic domination:

1. Communist labor structure,
2. The fabricated "business cycle,"
3. Contamination of the people (via fluoride, vaccines, pollution, Morgellons, food [pesticides, GMO food[67]], etc.).
4. False flag terrorism,
5. Fabricated and staged wars,
6. The fabrication of Orwellian sorts of unseen/invisible "terrorist" networks and enemies,[68]
7. Using media (including the corporatist-created "education system") to create pervasive mass brainwashing and to implant constant fear about unseen/invisible enemies,
8. Monopolization and covert poisoning of basic resources needed by the citizenry for survival (food, air, water, medicine, land/soil, etc.),

---

[67] The specific reason GMO food is so devastating and harmful to humans is for the following reasons. Human bodies need building blocks in order to replace cell material during the process of cell reproduction (among other reasons). One of the things that is reproduced in this process is the DNA double helix. Humans get their DNA material from food (in food are other pieces of DNA from other living things). The DNA in your body is the DNA that was in other living creatures. When we eat food, we take in the DNA matter from the food, and some of that DNA in the food will be used to create our DNA. For these reasons, the DNA of creatures in nature is being shared repeatedly and endlessly: all creatures are sharing from the same pool of DNA material. *GMO food consists of DNA that exists nowhere in the animal kingdom or the plant kingdom; it is literally extraterrestrial DNA.* For that reason, the pre-established pool of DNA that plants and animals are sharing in nature will be contaminated with entirely new DNA matter. Since DNA is responsible for giving plants and animals the structure of their bodies, that means that the consumption of GMO food will alter DNA and the altered DNA will result in altered structure reproducing cells, and thus of human bodies, and of all the bodies of all plants and animals on earth. Thus, the massive worldwide use of GMO food that is currently going on worldwide by the global corporatist farming system will make humanity dependent on, and replete with, *extraterrestrial DNA.* This will generate ultramassive contamination of humanity, and thus unimaginable disease and deformity of humanity—which will be unimaginably profitable for Big Pharma—in addition to unimaginable deformity of the biosphere, such as all human food sources: bee products (anything that is pollinated), animals products, plant foods, etc. These issues discussed in this note will become more relevant later in the book, when I discuss transhumanism and posthumanism, robotics, Morgellons disease, and the Mayan cosmogenesis.

[68] For example, the threat of al-Qaeda.

9. Distraction (inundate the public with pervasive entertainment, games, tabloids, pornography, sports, etc.),

10. Life-long instruction on how to have a slave mentality (this is done principally through public education), which starts at a very young age, and does not cease until death.

11. Various sorts of relentless impoverishment and oppression of the citizens, and

12. Ubiquitous use of torture camps, death camps and concentration camp labor,

13. Make the citizenry believe they are free when they are really slaves: corporatists hide the existence of points 1-12 just listed, and instead, they endlessly tell the citizenry that life could not be better (e.g., poison the citizenry with water by either not informing them that fluoride is in the water, or by telling the citizenry that fluoride is healthy—"vitamin F," as Jeff Rense has joked), that it's the best of times, and that the world is envious of them

All but point 12 have been fully implemented, and the usage of each of them by the corporatists should greatly increase in years to come as the New World Order is set up. As we will see by example in a later chapter, the usage of these tools by corporatists leads to efficient and all-powerful control of the thought and behavior of the American citizenry, whether it's the thought and behavior of a college student talking on her/his cell phone, the retiree managing his/her stock portfolio, the so-called "gang bangers," and so on.

9/11: Towers falling is symbol of the final stage of initiation of the New World Order.

Tower of Babylon: Tower falling is symbol of the commencement of building of the New World Order.[69]

As can be seen from what is being written here, making money is only part of what the corporatists are interested in. Contrary to popular belief, it can be proven that the monopolistic corporatists are *not* most interested in profits. This is perhaps their third-greatest interest. If profits were the foremost goal of the corporatists, then they would sacrifice all things for greater profits; but we can find examples where this is not the case. For example, if the massive media corporations were interested in profit more than anything else, then they'd report on stories that would sell the most news, but they plainly don't do this. If they wanted to sell the most news, then they would report on, for example, the huge fall-off in the bee population that has occurred since 2003.[70] Why doesn't the mass media report on this? They report on Brittany Spears shaving her head as a top story for a week, but not a single story on the bee populations being decimated in ways worse than ever before, which is certainly one of the biggest news stories in history, and certainly would be a massive seller for the corporate media. But the mass media does not report on this, and likewise, they don't report on vaccines, the North American Union, CODEX, epidemics, the ancient pyramids and Tiahuanaco, Morgellons disease, the 9/11 cover-up, the Sirius mystery, Gulf of Tonkin, AIDS in Africa, the conehead skulls found in northern S. America, the daily criminality of the corporatists and the visible government, the fact that the US education system is ranked third-to-last worldwide, and so on. This indicates that the huge corporations that control the mass media in the United States are not primarily interested in profits. What we will see in this book is that, like the other monopolistic corporatists, they are first-and-foremost interested in total humiliating domination over the RP.

---

[69] See Howard 1989, chapter 1, for more information on this earlier Masonic event.
[70] "Bee Decline Threatens Farm Economy," NPR, October 19, 2006, John Nielson.

The Terrorist Hoax: It is Irrefutable
that No Jetliner Hit the Pentagon on 9/11

False flag terrorism is perhaps the most powerful corporatist tool, and currently, it is being used to fully set-up the aforementioned New World Order horror-state right under the noses of the world's citizens, and "as men bus[y] themselves [with] their various concerns," as the world-government advocate, H.G. Wells, wrote on the first page of his famous book, *War of the Worlds*.[71]

False flag terrorism occurs when one group, such as the government or controllers of a country, attack their own citizens and/or infrastructure, and then blame it on a group that the corporatist controllers want to wage war and terror upon, in order to rile up the citizenry to become voracious for revenge and war with that group. There are many examples of false flag terrorism and known history has been shaped out of them. But I will be primarily concerned with 9/11, which was an attack against Americans by the secret corporatist government (the world's most powerful corporatists and the organizations they employ: intelligence agencies, their secret militaries and powerful think tanks, etc.). The secret corporatist world-government exists primarily in corporatist governments of Israel, Britain, the Vatican, and America, but it apparently pervades the governments of all countries that are complying with the move into the New World Order horror-state: China, Russia, the European nations, Iran, and almost any other nation.

Throughout this book, I will refer to people who reject the story of 9/11 told to Americans by the government and the national media as *9/11 skeptics*. If we

---

[71] Most people are under the impression that Wells was merely a science fiction writer. But in reality, he was an agent of the New World Order, and many secrets of the New World Order's plans can be wiggled out of Wells' text. For example, at the end of the Introduction of Wells' book, The Shape of Things to Come, in the last paragraph, written in 1936, Wells' describes that the way to set up the New World Order is by knocking down the skyscrapers in Manhattan in order to move forward in the New World Order setup:

> We begin here with what is evidently the opening of a fresh book in the history, though it was not actually the first paper in the folders handed to me. It reviews very conveniently the course of worldly events in recent years, and it does so in what is, to me, a novel and very persuasive way. It analyses the main factors of the great war from a new angle. From that review the story of the "Age of Frustration", in the opening years of which we are now living, flows on in a fairly consecutive fashion. Apart from this introduction the period covered by the actual narrative is roughly from about 1929 A.D. to the end of the year 2105. The last recorded event is on New Year's Day 2106; there is a passing mention of the levelling of the remaining "skeletons" of the famous "Skyscrapers" of Lower New York on that date. The printing and publication probably occurred early in the new year; occurred—or should I write "will occur"?

are to follow the empirical evidence, we can only find that it is fully on the side of the 9/11 skeptics with respect to the issue that *there was no Pentagon jetliner on 9/11*. If there was no plane at the Pentagon, then the 9/11 story falls into question, and is shown to be a fabrication and cover-up. If the story of 9/11 falls into question, then the stories about the terrorists, Osama, the terrorists' networks and cells, Hezbollah, Iran, and North Korea, *all of it* falls into question and can be seen as fakery (false flag terrorism).

In researching 9/11, there is so much information, that one could spend a lifetime sorting it all out. For that reason, I only focus on the Pentagon. I do not have knowledge of controlled demolitions, the characteristics of planes hitting skyscrapers (if jetliners can bring down buildings, what color the explosion would be when jetliner hits a skyscraper, etc.), and if those sorts of collisions can or should turn skyscrapers into rubble less than two hours after the collisions. I leave that to the experts, and they have given much information on those issues.[72] I instead turn my attention to something that one does not need to have expertise in anything to figure out: *if a massive jetliner traveling at 500 miles per hours hits a wall full of windows, it indeed must break those windows.* I do not need to have expertise in any area—such as the science of collisions, the engineering of the strengths of materials, metallurgy science, civil engineering, and so on—to know that if a 10 ton jet engine hits a window at 500 mph, the engine *must do some damage of some sort to that window.*

We are told that a massive jetliner hit the Pentagon wall on 9/11, but the news and video evidence from those first 25 minutes (before the roof mysteriously collapsed after the initial explosion at the Pentagon on 9/11) shows a wall that was little damaged (e.g., almost all windows were *unbroken*). *Nobody needs to have anything more than the scantest amount of commonsense to know that this is impossible.* Thus, I am forced to conclude that 9/11 was a false flag event, and in this book I focus on the Pentagon on 9/11 to show that 9/11 is not what our corporatist politicians began telling us it was in the morning on 9/11.

The Details of the Pentagon
Before the Roof Collapsed

For those reading this book who don't take 9/11 skeptics seriously, until you can explain how a 60-ton jetliner traveling at over 400 miles per hour can crash into the Pentagon without even taking the wall down, without even breaking most of the windows in the plane's path,[73] and without leaving masses of plane-

---

[72] Incidentally, the experts conclusively show that the World Trade Center towers were blown up on 9/11, and not brought down by the jetliners that hit the towers, as many demolition experts, chemists, engineers, and physicists have shown.

[73] As stated, this was the case before the mysterious sudden asymmetrical collapse of part of the Pentagon 25 minutes after the report of the explosion at the Pentagon.

debris from the over 60 tons of plane material, we who are scientific, empirical researchers *have no choice* but to reject the idea that a plane hit the Pentagon, if we are to obey the empirical prioritizing that a *scientific attitude* involves.

What choice do 9/11 skeptics have *but* to reject the non-skeptics, who ask us to believe that a 60-ton, 125-foot-wide jetliner with two 9-foot diameter 10-ton engines (*each* engine is 10 tons), traveling at over 400 mph:

1. can smack a wall traveling only a few inches above the ground,

2. where upon impact it is claimed to have shrunk down and folded up in order to fit through a 15 foot-hole (that is what the "official story" involves)

3. without doing much more than leaving smoke damage to the part of the wall surrounding that hole,

4. but then turning into *liquid steel* (which has a temperature of 4000 to 5000 degrees Fahrenheit—half the temperature of the surface of the sun) after infiltrating the Pentagon, but

5. without even scorching in the least much of the Pentagon wall around and inside of the impact area (for example, there is the case of the now-famous opened book that is on a table at the damage zone that does not even exhibit pages with the slightest bit of heat damage from the supposed monumental steel-liquefying temperatures)

6. and then cooling down from its incredible temperatures in just five or so minutes at most (a process which, in reality, can only take *weeks*),

7. thus allowing firefighters to walk right up to the damage area without being scorched to the bone in seconds?

Do people really believe this story? How can there be such blatant lack of empirical sensibility, and genuine *loss of sight*, by the non-skeptics?

Attempts to Overturn the No-Plane Pentagon Evidence

There are three methods used in the media and by anybody attempting to refute the fact that no plane was at the Pentagon on 9/11:

I. Claim that there is no pre-collapsed Pentagon.
II. Claim that the windows and wall of the Pentagon were strong enough to repel the plane and remain unbroken.
III. Claim that, somehow, rather than moving forward as one would expect, instead, parts of the plane (such as the wings), moved inward (toward the fuselage) when the plane hit the wall, wherein the 120 foot wide plane (somehow) imploded upon itself right as it hit the Pentagon wall, squeezed through an approximately 15-foot hole, then once inside the

Pentagon the 60-tons of jetliner steel melted and/or evaporated due to the tremendous heat.

I of course can be discarded if one merely watches news footage from September 11, 2001, or if one merely watches a documentary made afterwards (such as the Discovery Channel's *Attack on the Pentagon* DVD). I relies on the fact that many Americans don't remember that the Pentagon collapsed approximately 25 minutes after the explosion there, and it depends on the trust that the public will not check out the facts for their self.

The Pentagon shortly after 9/11. (This is similar to the picture of the Pentagon that is in the *9/11 Commission Report*.) The "official story" of 9/11 delivered to Americans was that the plane that allegedly hit the Pentagon on September 11, 2001 (which was made of 60 tons of steel) melted and/or evaporated upon hitting the Pentagon.[74] But melted steel requires temperatures of thousands of degrees (3000-5500 degrees F), with an evaporation point nearly as hot as the surface of the sun. However, this picture does not reveal such a catastrophic heat event (which would have taken days or weeks to cool down, and firefighters would not have been able to get near the site for a long time, contrary to what Americans saw in the news footage from 9/11). Until it is explained to Americans how a plane melted and/or evaporated at the Pentagon on September 11, 2001, empirically-minded rational and scientific thinkers have no choice but to reject this account as flatly impossible: if we are to accept that 60 tons of steel melted and/or evaporated on 9/11, then we must have some evidence for such an event, such as a mass of melted steel, catastrophic heat damage at and surrounding the crash site, and so on—*none* of which has been observed in any degree.

---

[74] See, for example, Popular Mechanics magazine, March 2005 issue, where they discuss a Purdue University professor's findings that the Pentagon plane melted on September 11, 2001, but where it was not explained in the article how firefighters could approach the Pentagon site minutes after the explosion if there were 60-tons of melted steel.

Opened book. Pages devoid of smoke damage. No evidence of 4000-6000 degree F temperatures at the Pentagon crash site.

II can also merely be discarded also, if, as with I, one merely consults the original footage. If the wall of the Pentagon could be repel a 60-ton jetliner traveling at over 400 mph without damaging most of the supposed "impact zone" of the Pentagon, there would be tens of tons of steel deposited around the crash site outside of the Pentagon, but the original footage shows there was not. There were only some miscellaneous parts found, which the famous film documentaries *Painful Deceptions*, and *Loose Change Second Edition* adequately show do not seem to match up to the plane parts of a massive jetliner (as if the plane parts were planted). But that last point about suspicious or non-matching parts is irrelevant, and I don't want it to be considered as a focal issue in this part of this book. What is relevant is that there just was not tens of tons of debris found at the Pentagon, but only a few strangely unscathed parts that can't be confirmed to be part of a massive jetliner. There should have been coatings, gobs, and heaps of disintegrated and/or miscellaneous amorphous metal all over the lawn of the Pentagon and other places around the crash site. But such a debris field simply did not exist, and thus empirical reasons force the scientific-minded person to reject II.

I will discuss III at length later in this book. There are numerous ways to simply and unquestionably refute III, such as by showing that there just was absolutely no evidence at the Pentagon on 9/11 of the truly cataclysmic sort of heat and fire needed to melt or vaporize 60-tons of steel.

The BBC "Conspiracy Files" episode on "9/11 Conspiracy Theories," which aired in Britain on February 18, 2007, discussed the Pentagon, but did not touch on any of the issues I just raised about the Pentagon before it collapsed on 9/11. This information cannot be revealed (for those who want 9/11 to appear like genuine terrorist attack), since it reveals the truth of the matter: that 9/11 is a lie—a false flag terror event, or what I call in this book, a *corporatist tool* (which is a terror-tool for reorganizing the world and re-educating [brainwashing] the people). This documentary was, however, quick to point out a study from Purdue University, led by an engineer named Sozen, where the team in charge of the study created a film that showed the Pentagon jetliner all fitting through a tiny hole in the Pentagon wall, leaving the windows unbroken on the Pentagon wall, where the plane was so compressed in the process of being squeezed through the Pentagon wall that once inside the pentagon, it reached a liquid and/or vapor state (whether or not it is liquid or gas depends on who is discussing the Sozen work—for example, Fox News has discussed it as being liquid, and Popular Mechanics has discussed it being in a vaporized state).

But this account cannot be correct, for if it were, then we would have some sort of evidence on and after 9/11 that there was over 60 tons of liquefied and/or vaporizing steel—and this would be quite an event, since its heat would be so great that it would be like having part of the sun, or a small star, right in Washington D. C. If this were the case, then nobody would have been able to be within a mile or several miles of the Pentagon. (We feel the heat of the sun intensely while residing on earth, even though the sun is 93 million miles away; imagine how hot the Pentagon would feel to anybody in D.C. if there was the equivalent of a small star in the Pentagon on 9/11.) But there is simply not a shred of evidence for this sort of catastrophic heat-event on 9/11. If you merely open up *The 9/11 Commission Report* that the US government has written and published about the "official story" of 9/11, if one turns to page 313, there is a picture of the Pentagon after it collapsed, but where the picture reveals absolutely no heat-damage from the sort of catastrophic blaze I just described.

How can there be a Mass Media Cover-up of 9/11?

The mass media has and will deliberately confuse issues about 9/11 and the Pentagon. For example, they will report that there are hundreds of eyewitnesses who report to have seen a massive jetliner hit the Pentagon on 9/11, in perfect accord with the official story. But the media will not report that nearly the same number of eyewitnesses to the Pentagon on 9/11 report to not seeing a massive jetliner, but rather to seeing a missile, a small plane, or nothing at all. This one-sided reporting will get the public to believe that the eyewitness accounts are credible and that are the only side of the story.

The mass media carries out this cover-up due to the fact that they are dependent on (via massive profits from advertising) the same corporations that are parts of the secret corporatist government. The secret government profits incredibly from war, increased control of the people, increased military and arms spending, and various other things that have resulted from 9/11. Therefore, all mass media stories about the truth of 9/11 are intentionally filtered out of the mass media before they can be aired or printed, lest the mass media insult and go against their advertising base (which consists of corporations that have profited from 9/11 and the results of 9/11, such as the Iraq War, the setup of the NAU, the setup of the surveillance police state, etc.), which would be like "biting the hand that feeds you." The only way the mass media can involve reports on the truth of 9/11 is if on live television a media celebrity unexpectedly blurts out the information about the truth of 9/11, and before cameras can be turned away from her. This is what happened with Rosie O'Donnell in March of 2003 on the show *The View*.

In this book I am not concerned with clarifying in any way whether or not 9/11 was an inside job. That issue has been settled by empirical evidence, and non-skeptics can only attack 9/11 skeptics by wandering into non-empirical, unverifiable non-information (e.g., "yes I know that there are no pictures of the 'Pentagon plane,' but there were eyewitnesses at the Pentagon who demand that they saw the plane hit the Pentagon!"). Rather, in this book I will only be concerned with *why* 9/11 was an inside job—which is because false flag terrorism is the principal corporatist tactic used when they want to orchestrate change for the world's vassals.

The Secret Government

President Harry Truman to the one of the great Hollywood actors during Truman's time: "You are not the world's greatest actor... *I am!*"[75]
In America, most of the population is either Christian or has been raised with some Christian morality. And when they hear the truth about the secret government, they do not believe that the secret government can be as bad and deceitful as they are... That's their great cover. You tell people about the facts and they say, "Oh come on! Nobody is doing that!"... When you are raised with some morality, you can't believe that people are that diabolical.
—Dr. Lorraine Day[76]

---

[75] This quote of Truman's was discussed by Texe Marrs, former professor at the University of Texas, on the Rense Radio Show (www.rense.com), October 10, 2006.

[76] This is a modified version of a quote from an interview with Dr. Day's on the Rense Radio Show, June 27, 2005.

None of the events of history—from World War II to the Iraq Wars, from the history of oil to the existence of the unseen "al-Qaeda network," from the massacre of Jericho to the massacre of Wounded Knee, from the development of the atomic bomb to the deliberate worldwide depleted uranium (DU), from the polluting now going on to the recent sudden massive decline in the world's bee population,[77] from the so-called "business cycle" to the concept of land ownership, from the fall of the Tower of Babylon to the 109th Congress's HR 6166 (109th Congress, 2006, it was later called the Military Commissions Act), from Morgellons disease/ plague to the fact that humans oddly only utilize a small portion of their neocortex at any given moment, from the fact that mad cow disease currently pervades the US animal food products[78] to the fact that robotic armies are being developed to be run by remote control,[79] and so on— *make any sense until one realizes and understands that the world is (and has been for millennia) controlled by one small group of people that has the following qualities*:

    a. They are the most powerful people in the world (i.e., the corporatists),
    b. They work in astonishing secrecy (which is common for governments),
    c. They have controlling agents planted in virtually all sectors of human institutions (from Hollywood to the universities, from the city governments to the mega-churches, and so on) working to control those institutions in ways that the corporatists desire,
    d. They are unsatisfied with anything but *total* domination of the entire world population, and
    e. They are deeply moved to instill pervasive torture and murder of the world's citizens, in various ways, and to greater or lesser degrees.

In the next section, I will prove that the secret government exists (other proofs will follow later in this book), and in this section and throughout this book, these startling points (a - e) will also be proven. But first, consider the following point, which is perhaps the most important thing I write in this book:

Until one understands these points, and until one understands that there is a secret world-government described by each of these points, the mad nature of the world and world-society will not make any sense. Until one understands these points, the ultraviolent and savage nature of history, the mass suicide of war, the destruction of the family, the

---

[77] This story has remained relatively hidden in the mainstream media, as is not so surprising. Here's one story about it: "Bee Decline Threatens Farm Economy," NPR, October 19, 2006, by John Nielsen, http://www.npr.org/templates/story/story.php?storyId=6326020.
[78] For reasons why, see the footnotes in the section "Total Enslavement of the Citizenry" in chapter 3.
[79] This is covered in detail elsewhere in this book, such as in the section "Machine World" in the last chapter.

corporate servitude that people give their lives to everyday all over the world, all will never make any sense, and consequently, one will never really understand anything about how the social world really works.

Do you have trouble believing that such a secret corporatist government exists? Do you have trouble believing that it could be as well-coordinated, hidden, savage, and tight-lipped as I am describing it? Is it so hard for you to believe a secret corporatist government exists, that you are inclined to reject the entire idea as implausible? Well, if you are inclined to reject the idea, then you have forgotten that this sort of group has manifested all throughout history, with the same level of secrecy, savagery, and well-organized functioning. The Nazis are a perfect example, where Nazi media information, medicine, military, government, and so on, were all perfectly controlled and coordinated by a secretive corporatistic government which, it seems, most Germans were oblivious to. You don't think that is what is going on here in the United States? Well, I will prove in this book that that is precisely what is going on in the United States, and it even involves the same people as the Nazi regime (for example, George W. Bush's grandfather was Prescott Bush, a top Nazi and Hitler's banker[80]).

Hints of the Existence of a
Demented Secret Government

Needless to say, the secret government is not the benevolent group that the mass media portrays them to be, and rather, they are more akin to Hitler and the mad sadistic-hedonism (e.g., "thrill killing") of Caligula. Occasionally news stories or information will surface about the real nature of the secret government, giving us a tiny glimpse of what is going on behind-the-scenes regarding the secret corporatist government that controls the world.[81] And if one looks closely at the mechanics of American culture, there are hints everywhere. For example, the autism epidemic caused by vaccines (this is proven in chapter 5), the fact that anti-depressants ironically increase suicide rates,[82] the fact that the United States now has the world's worst education system,[83] Guantanamo bay and the secret CIA torture-prisons that Bush has

---

[80] I will document this fact in chapter 6.

[81] For example, see these stories: "Three More Former Pages Accuse Foley of Online Sexual Approaches," ABC News, October 05, 2006, Brian Ross, Rhonda Schwartz, and Maddy Sauer; "Naked, Drunk, Surrounded by Sex Toys—It's the Israeli Ambassador," London Guardian, Tuesday March 13, 2007, Rory Carroll, Latin America correspondent. Also see the films of Alex Jones in the bibliography.

[82] See Richards 2006, esp. p. 15.

[83] Strictly speaking, it is ranked third to the last, but when it's that low, who's counting. See Tabor 2006, Introduction and Chapter 1 for more information.

admitted are widespread around the world,[84] H.R. 6166 (the Military Commissions Act) passed by the 109th Congress in fall 2007, and this book is filled with countless other examples. But regardless, Americans have virtually no understanding of what is really going on, even though signs of the twistedness of the secret government are all around them, as the following news story (which is about "al-Qaeda," which is shown in this book is a CIA PMF) from the Washington Post announces:

> The CIA has been hiding and interrogating some of its most important al Qaeda captives at a Soviet-era compound in Eastern Europe, according to U.S. and foreign officials familiar with the arrangement. The secret facility is part of a covert prison system set up by the CIA nearly four years ago that at various times has included sites in eight countries, including Thailand, Afghanistan and several democracies in Eastern Europe, as well as a small center at the Guantanamo Bay prison in Cuba, according to current and former intelligence officials and diplomats from three continents. The hidden global internment network is a central element in the CIA's unconventional war on terrorism. It depends on the cooperation of foreign intelligence services, and on keeping even basic information about the system secret from the public, foreign officials and nearly all members of Congress charged with overseeing the CIA's covert actions. The existence and locations of the facilities—referred to as "black sites" in classified White House, CIA, Justice Department and congressional documents—are known to only a handful of officials in the United States and, usually, only to the president and a few top intelligence officers in each host country. The CIA and the White House, citing national security concerns and the value of the program, have dissuaded Congress from demanding that the agency answer questions in open testimony about the conditions under which captives are held. Virtually nothing is known about who is kept in the facilities, what interrogation methods are employed with them, or how decisions are made about whether they should be detained or for how long. While the Defense Department has produced volumes of public reports and testimony about its detention practices and rules after the abuse scandals at Iraq's Abu Ghraib prison and at Guantanamo Bay, the CIA has not even acknowledged the existence of its black sites. To do so, say officials familiar with the program, could open the U.S. government to legal challenges, particularly in foreign courts, and increase the risk of political condemnation at home and abroad. But the revelations of widespread prisoner abuse in Afghanistan and Iraq by the U.S. military—which operates under published rules and transparent oversight of Congress—have increased concern among lawmakers,

---

[84] See, "Bush: CIA Holds Terror Suspects in Secret Prisons," CNN.com, September 7, 2006. Also see, "The Baghdad Gulag," Asia Times, April 13, 2007, Pepe Escobar.

foreign governments and human rights groups about the opaque CIA system. Those concerns escalated last month, when Vice President Cheney and CIA Director Porter J. Goss asked Congress to exempt CIA employees from legislation already endorsed by 90 senators that would bar cruel and degrading treatment of any prisoner in U.S. custody. Although the CIA will not acknowledge details of its system, intelligence officials defend the agency's approach, arguing that the successful defense of the country requires that the agency be empowered to hold and interrogate suspected terrorists for as long as necessary and without restrictions imposed by the U.S. legal system or even by the military tribunals established for prisoners held at Guantanamo Bay. The Washington Post is not publishing the names of the Eastern European countries involved in the covert program, at the request of senior U.S. officials. They argued that the disclosure might disrupt counterterrorism efforts in those countries and elsewhere and could make them targets of possible terrorist retaliation… Since then, the arrangement has been increasingly debated within the CIA, where considerable concern lingers about the legality, morality and practicality of holding even unrepentant terrorists in such isolation and secrecy, perhaps for the duration of their lives. Mid-level and senior CIA officers began arguing two years ago that the system was unsustainable and diverted the agency from its unique espionage mission… It is illegal for the government to hold prisoners in such isolation in secret prisons in the United States, which is why the CIA placed them overseas, according to several former and current intelligence officials and other U.S. government officials. Legal experts and intelligence officials said that the CIA's internment practices also would be considered illegal under the laws of several host countries, where detainees have rights to have a lawyer or to mount a defense against allegations of wrongdoing. Host countries have signed the U.N. Convention Against Torture and Other Cruel, Inhuman or Degrading Treatment or Punishment, as has the United States. Yet CIA interrogators in the overseas sites are permitted to use the CIA's approved "Enhanced Interrogation Techniques," some of which are prohibited by the U.N. convention and by U.S. military law. They include tactics such as "waterboarding," in which a prisoner is made to believe he or she is drowning. Some detainees apprehended by the CIA and transferred to foreign intelligence agencies have alleged after their release that they were tortured, although it is unclear whether CIA personnel played a role in the alleged abuse. Given the secrecy surrounding CIA detentions, such accusations have heightened concerns among foreign governments and human rights groups about CIA detention and interrogation practices…[85]

---

[85] "CIA Holds Terror Suspects in Secret Prisons: Debate Is Growing Within Agency

The greatest cover that the secret corporatist government has is the fact that very few Americans would ever suspect or believe that such a genocidal group secretly controls the world, and that they are people that really do the sorts of things described in points a - e. David Icke writes: "There is one major reason why the official lies prevail as accepted truth. The alternative is too unthinkable, too unbearable, to contemplate; so most people don't."[86]

Reality Only Makes Sense when One's Theorization About Reality Includes the Secret Government

For those who don't understand the fact of the secret government, they will be compelled to describe reality in terms of all sorts of absurdities—*the sky's the limit*. They will be fooled into believing that it is *helpful* and *good* to give all one-day-old infants an extremely dangerous and poisonous vaccine for hepatitis B (which is a *sexually transmitted disease!*[87]). They will be tricked into believing, for example, that *somehow* the skimpy, ragtag American Revolutionary War "army" was able to defeat the ultra-powerful Masonic British Empire. They will be tricked into believing that the Vietnam War was about "the threat of communism," as Americans were told through the mass media in the 1960s.

To those who do not understand or know about the secret government, it will just appear to them to be a coincidence that children's television involves pervasive content that is ultraviolent, pro-war, and Orwellian,[88] overtly promoting brainwashing in children en masse, including hypnotic, and literally mind-altering material—even to where it can cause *mass epilepsy* in children,[89]

About Legality and Morality of Overseas System Set Up After 9/11," Washington Post, By Dana Priest, November 2 2005.

[86] Icke 2005, 2.

[87] Even the CDC's own documents they give to pediatricians and hospitals to give to parents at the time of shots reveal that Hep. B is only transmitted by sex, blood exchange, or from an infected mother to baby. So, unless a known-to-be infected mother enters a maternity ward, the hospitals must be assuming that the 12-hour-old babies that are vaccinated with the Hep. B vaccine are going to be having sex or doing dope soon?

[88] I say "Orwellian" because so much of children's television involves information about (instruction about) biometrics, military machines, conformity, and other Orwellian issues.

[89] This sort of "mass television-induced epilepsy" was observed to occur, for example, in a famous Japanese case among children in Japan who were watching a *Pokemon* episode in the late 1990s, where literally hundreds of children had to be rushed to the hospital after watching the same segment of the episode. For more information, see "After Flashing Causes Seizures, Japan Re-evaluates TV Cartoons," New York Times, Sheryl WuDunn, December 20, 1997; "Cartoon-based illness mystifies Japan," CNN (Tokyo), December 17, 1997; "Avoiding 'Pokemon' Seizures From TV, Video Games," WebMD.com, Miranda Hitti, September 20, 2005. The last article from

perhaps not necessarily unlike what was depicted in the film *Videodrome*. They will be tricked into believing, for example, that it was a coincidence that Al Gore did not contest (and instead immediately backed down from protesting) the outcome of the 2000 US Presidential election. It will be believed to be a coincidence that the moon landing photos did not involve any stars in the sky, and merely an oddity that the Eagle, when it launched off from the moon, did not exhibit any significant propulsive-explosive emanation to propel it into space. It will be just believed that a 60-ton plane can hit the Pentagon without breaking the windows and then vanish into nothing.

The list is almost endless, and all of these details are patently absurd *if* one has no awareness of the secret government and if one thinks that the events of history are unplanned, random events.

Proof of the Existence of the Secret Government

In this section I will give proof that there is a secret government. This section is only meant to be an introduction to the proof I will present, and in chapter 2 I devote an entire chapter to proving that the monopolistic corporatists comprise a secret government that controls all resources, behavior, information, thought, and all selves.

There are many simple ways to prove that the secret government exists. For example, consider the following analysis, which proves this in just a few words. Washington D.C. is filled with think tanks and lobbyists (this is the subject of chapter 4), and it is no secret that they fund politicians (they *pay them* to create and implement specific legislation) and write policy for politicians. This means that the highest briber/payer can get Washington to do what it wants: the highest briber/payer can get politicians to create and vote for specific laws, and they can have think tanks created to construct various policies or laws. So, this means that the persons in the world who have the most money control Washington—and those people are, of course, *the corporatists.*

> *This means that the US government is controlled, not by the voters, but by unseen (secret) forces that pay off and create policy for Washington politicians. This is proof that Washington is controlled by the corporatists, not by voters. And thus, this is proof that there is a secret group—a secret government—that controls the US government.*

That's how easy it is to prove that the secret government exists.

WebMD.com indicates that this sort of mass epilepsy is something we can expect from children's television perhaps any time, and parents should be aware of how to hopefully avoid it—as if the parents have to take measures to keep things right, rather than the creators of the children's television. .

Many times I have heard people call the ideas that there are (i) secret societies, or that there is (ii) a "secret/invisible government," controlling the US government and the whole world from behind the scenes, *a conspiracy theory*. But that is like saying that the CIA does not exist, that the CFR does not exist, or that Bill Gates, Monsanto, Halliburton, and Fox News do not exist. It is utterly simple to establish, as uncontroversial empirical fact, that the world is controlled by a secret government. Consider the following case in point, involving the CIA, which I will next prove is part of the secret government.

First I will show how the CIA controls the US President and Congress and Supreme Court, and then I will explain how that reveals that the CIA is just the sort of "invisible/secret government" that I just described in the previous paragraph. Establishing these facts will reveal a clear causal connection *from* secret groups ((i) and (ii)) *to* the US government, therein proving that secret societies and a secret government controls the world.

If you analyze the interplay of what we know about, for example, the interaction between the CIA and Congress, or between the CIA and the Presidential Branch of government, we quickly see that *the CIA fully controls each of them*. Let's define the word "control" to mean: group x knowingly or unknowingly forces group y to act/behave or think as x wants y to act/behave. The Iraq War (the second one, that started in 2003), we are told, started because the CIA (suspiciously) gave President George Bush Jr. certain evidence of WMDs in Iraq (which was false information), which, we are told, prompted Bush Jr. to initiate the March 2003 invasion of Iraq ("Shock and Awe"). Bush Jr. discussed this two-step causal interaction of

CIA information on Iraqi WMDs ➔ *Bush Jr. prompted to declare war on Iraq in 2003*

repeatedly in the mass media in 2003 and 2004.[90] That causal interaction determined that the CIA would fully control the actions of the US president on

---

[90] As stated, this was one of the dominant news stories through the second half of 2003 and throughout 2004, and there were countless news items on this issue. Here is one example:

WASHINGTON (CNN) - Facing lingering questions about the nature of the prewar threat from Iraq, President Bush on Friday appointed a bipartisan commission to "figure out why" apparent intelligence failures regarding Saddam Hussein's weapons capabilities occurred. "We're also determined to make sure that American intelligence is as accurate as possible for every challenge in the future," Bush said during a brief news conference at the White House at which he named seven members ... to the commission. He left the door open to appoint two more members. The move comes as Democrats step up criticism of the Republican administration, saying the White House exaggerated the threat posed by Saddam—particularly as it relates to weapons of mass destruction—to bolster the case for a U.S.-led invasion of Iraq ... Bush and top administration figures repeatedly said that Saddam possessed such

the policy (Iraq) that would dominate his presidency for the years following, and up to the time of the publication of this book. That causal interaction determined that the CIA would fully control the US military and the US President, *since the CIA's "information" fully dictated how the US President and US military would act/behave over the course of the next several years.*

What about Congress? Are they controlled by the CIA also? The majority of the Congressional budget since 2003 has been used to finance the Iraq War. (In other words, the majority of the Congressional budget is given to the military-industrial complex [Halliburton, Lockheed Martin, etc.] to create war materials [planes, military bases, soldier's uniforms, trucks, etc.] used in the war.) For this reason, it is clear to see that the CIA dictates how Congress spends money, and thus controls Congress's actions due to the following causal interaction:

CIA and Bush Jr. determine war money is needed
➔
Congress uses majority of its money for Iraq War

The unelected Supreme Court also is controlled, since its members are appointed by the US Presidents (who are CIA controlled), leading to the following causal interaction:

CIA ➔ *US president* ➔ *Supreme Court appointments*

All but one member of the Supreme Court (at the time of the writing of this book) was appointed by Bush Jr., Clinton, Bush Sr., and Reagan—all of whom are warmonger-neoconservatives. These four Presidents have clear CIA ties (e.g., Bush Sr. was CIA director in the 1970s), they all are clearly covertly partnered and working in alliance with one another (e.g., Bush Sr. and Jr. are blood-related, and Bush Sr. and Clinton just "coincidentally" happened to become best of friends after Clinton left office, etc.), and many little-discussed and somewhat hidden news reports have surfaced over how the Clintons and Bushes are covertly close family-friends (for example, even regularly vacationing together), which would be entirely unsurprising, given the close bond seen in the national media between Bill Clinton and Bush Sr.[91] Therefore,

---

weapons stockpiles as they pressed U.S. lawmakers and allies abroad to support military action against Iraq. (From "Bush names panel to review Iraq intelligence: Move comes amid Democratic criticism," CNN.com, Saturday, February 7, 2004.)

[91] There are many such stories, and this provides a good example of how "opposition" in the media and in the US government between the so-called "liberals" and "conservatives" is thespian, to purposely keep the citizenry distracted on irrelevant issues and conflicts (see Pappas 2003 for more information). See, for example, "Hillary Heralds 30 Year Plus Control Of America By Interlocking Crime Family: Pro-war Clinton candidacy success would mean same mob bosses have ruled U.S. since 1980,"

the Supreme Court is entirely constructed out of one CIA-controlled unit, and the most accurate description of the Supreme Court is to label it as a *CIA operation*. And, not surprisingly, it can be seen in their decisions since 9/11 that the Supreme Court is entirely pro-war in its decision-making, indicating that they are also under the spell of the CIA-generated war mania.

We have just seen proof that there is a causal interaction of control that goes *from* the CIA *to* the US government, thus revealing that the US government is not controlled by the people, but rather is controlled by the CIA (and other secret groups I will discuss below), which is a secret organization (secret society). You will see in later chapters of this book that the US government was largely in cahoots with the CIA with the causal connections just described, and, for example, the CIA did not have to twist Bush Jr.'s arm to initiate "pre-emptive" war in Iraq. But the point is that there is a secret higher power over-and-above the US government.

Given the facts I have just given, there appears to be no way to avoid the conclusion that the US President, Congress, military, and Supreme Court are fully controlled by the CIA. This proves that the US government is controlled by a secret society, for the following reasons:

i.   The CIA is a *society*,
ii. The CIA *controls the US government* (as do many other secret societies), and
iii. The CIA *conducts operations secretly*, since, in general, only a handful of outsiders (namely the corporatists) know what the everyday activities of the CIA are.

i – iii are entirely uncontroversial and obvious, and for that very reason I ask you: How do we avoid the simple, logical, and empirical conclusion that the CIA is (part of) a secret/invisible government that controls the US government? Answer: we can't.

What has just been disclosed shows that it is not a "conspiracy theory" to discuss secret groups and societies as controlling the US government (and the world). In fact, the reader should note how astonishingly simple it was to prove that fact. This is the topic of this book: to show that there are secret societies that control the world in secret, and the secret societies have a hierarchy, where the corporatists reside at the top of the pyramid. More specifically, it is the ultramassive, monopolistic corporatists who control the CIA. For example, the CIA is always headed by corporatists [e.g., Bush Sr., Woolsey, etc.], or by people appointed by corporatists [e.g., Gates and Hayden appointed by Bush

PrisonPlanet.com, January 22, 2007, Paul Joseph Watson and Alex Jones. Also of interest are the following stories: "Barbara Bush Calls Bill Clinton 'Son', "Drudge Report, June 17, 2005; "Hillary Clinton defends link with Murdoch," Financial Times, May 10, 2006, by Holly Yeager and Caroline Daniel.

Jr.], and thus corporatists control the CIA. Therefore, there is a secret society of corporatists that comprise a secret society that secretly controls the world from behind the veneer, and thus they compose a *secret world government*. As you can see, this is a simple empirical issue that is very easy to verify, but most citizens of the world have been tricked into having no idea of its existence.

More Proof

There are all sorts of ways, in addition to the CIA example just given, to prove this. For example, it is well-known, that the heads of the biotech industries (such as Big Pharma) are top Congresspersons (e.g., Bill Frist),[92] heads of the FDA,[93] top commanders of the military (e.g., Rumsfeld), and so on. These individuals pose on television as smiling, friendly, helpful politicians and public servants, but if one merely takes a look at what they do when they are not in front of television cameras, one sees that their real daily activities consist of pushing the interests of their industries by helping to write policy and provoke warfare that helps their corporate profits (to the detriment of the RP). This is then, in essence, a secret government: the public face of these politician-corporatists is the inverse of the private face that carries out their daily actions, and since the private face is real (due to the fact that behaviors of the corporatist-politicians are based on the private face), then the public face is a fabrication.

The American public is not aware of the real nature and activities of their corporatist politicians. The idea that they are benevolent, philanthropic people that genuinely want to help the citizenry is a total fabrication created by the mass media; and in reality, corporatist politicians at any level of government resemble something more like a gang of warlords, or Boss Hog from the *Dukes of Hazard*—although the public at large has little awareness of this fact. Even though this image is hidden from view by the mass media, if one looks carefully, one can see the effects of this reality. For example, how many Americans know that a law was passed, due to Congressman and biotech corporatist Bill Frist, that makes it *illegal* for people to file suit against biotech companies for vaccine damage (for creating vaccines that contain mercury, aluminum, aspartame, formaldehyde, and cancer viruses that damage or kill children)?[94] Here is another sign of the real, hidden under-belly of the corporatist politicians: unvaccinated elementary school students are routinely pulled out of school until they get vaccinated, and parents in America are

---

[92] See Angell 2004, Kirby 2005 (esp. see Prolougue, Chapter 1), and Richards, 2004.

[93] See Richards 2004.

[94] I will document these claims later in this book. But this issue is discussed at length in Kirby 2005, Prolougue.

falsely told by school officials, the mass media, and politicians in the United States that they are mandatory by law.[95]

The Corporatists are the New World Order

In this book, I will refer to the highest level of the secret government by the following names: the New World Order, the secret government, world government, and, most importantly, *the corporatists*. I will prove that the corporatists are the real secret group that controls the world in behind-the-scenes, and thus the groups that other researchers usually assert to be parts of the world-controllers (the CIA, the WHO, the WTO, the Trilateral Commission, the FDA, Fox News, the global warming and population control groups, etc.) are not—rather, they are merely employed by, and working for, the corporatists.

There are a large number of groups that fit under the heading of "secret government:" all the New World Order groups that I will discuss later in this book: the IMF, WTO, World Bank, the Federal Reserve Corporation (and any other central bank of any nation that practices fractional reserve banking), the Trilateral Commission, the FDA, the rest of the corporatists of the ultramassive monopolistic corporations that control the basic resources that are used in civilization: the education, printing, media, usury,[96] food, water, clothing, transportation, and energy industries[97] (I will list all of them in a later chapter), and those organizations or groups directly and covertly working for the New World Order groups: lobbyist organizations, special imperialistic think tanks and PMFs, and any of the secret intelligence or military agencies (the NSA, FEMA, the CIA, etc.). These groups compose the secret government, and while Americans rush off to vote for Bush or Kerry (who are cousins, as is not well-known) in a staged election,[98] the secret government conspires to further dumb-

---

[95] As of early 2007, there is no law that forces a person to get a vaccine in the United States, and there are no laws that prohibit students from entering any school. All one needs to do is go to their state government website, and look up vaccines and exemptions, and they will find the laws that very clearly say no students are to be withheld from school because they have not been vaccinated. Usually this is a shock when people find this out, and it clearly shows them that there is something strange going on. Often students of mine ask: How can schools be so out of sync with, and unaware of, the laws? Who told them the incorrect information, and why? My students think this is so bizarre that they are not inclined to believe it. But I just tell them that they are in shock over the absurdity of this issue merely because they do not understand that this is what happens when a corrupt but well-coordinated fascist government is implanted into an existing cultural and social, system, including the medical system.

[96] This industry is illegal, according to the US Constitution.

[97] Except for usury, these are what are called the *legal* industries. There are, of course, other industries that are as large as these, such as the illegal drug industry, human trafficking, and prostitution industries, for example.

[98] See Miller 2005.

down the world population and to further create systems of mass-misery for the citizens of the world.

There are many secret agencies and associations of New World Order that function as training grounds that future politicians, media personalities, and CEOs must attend before entering these fields. These groups are usually so secret that, if their members disclose any information about them, just like with a roving inner-city gang, they are either killed (as is the case with Skull and Bones), or kicked out (as with CFR). These secret organizations include certain Ivy League recruiting societies (such as Skull and Bones), CFR, any intelligence agency (CIA, NSA, MI-6, etc.), secret military organizations, privatized military forces (PMFs), and others that I will discuss in a later chapter. Regardless of where these agencies come from and what their properties are, they are all creations of corporatism and of the most powerful core of the secret government: *the corporatists*.

Many of these societies that control the world are not intentionally secretive, and even have websites with their motives, policies, and tactics published on them. (One good example of this is the think tank named the *Project for a New American Century*, a principal corporatist-created group, which I will discuss at length in later chapters.) But since the public largely does not know of them since the media (news media, school systems, etc.) won't discuss them or report on them, these groups are therefore, in essence, secret and "invisible."

We will see that the corporatists are the most powerful, controlling part of the secret government, and thus are the core of the secret government (this includes the monopolistic bankers, which some people consider the most powerful corporatists, and which are what some call *the illuminati*). These groups have a visible face that they show to the public, and a secret face that they hide. In their hidden mode, they secretly meet[99] and plan the real political, economic, and even scientific events that control the world (via the aforementioned tools and tactics of the corporatists).

The Visible Government and the Invisible (Secret) Government

Plenty of corporatist-government groups are not in a control position, but rather they are secret government organizations that are employed by and controlled by other forces within the secret government or by the corporatists themselves. Although they do not govern, and instead are governed (by the New World Order), these groups must nevertheless be considered part of the secret government, since American taxpayers are unaware of what they are, and/or what they do. Groups such as these include the occupying militaries of

---

[99] Their meetings and meeting events have names such as Bilderberg Group, Bohemian Grove, Trilateral Commission, American Enterprise Institute, PNAC/Weekly Standard, and so on.

the United States (such as the troops in Iraq, where most Americans have no idea at all what these troops are doing in their daily activities in Iraq), most other military organizations, the most powerful think tanks (PNAC, AEI, Hudson Institute, etc.), the FBI, the Wall Street corporatists and their stock trader "puppets," the US government (Congress, President, etc.), for reasons I explained to do with Frist, the Iraqi terrorist militias,[100] al-Qaeda, and Hezbollah,[101] to name a few.

Americans are told that their government is composed of Congress, the US military, the Supreme Court, the Presidential Branch, the "intelligence agencies" (CIA, NSA, etc.) and the supposed "regulating agencies" (the FDA, FCC, EPA, to name a few) constitute the US government.[102] Hereafter, I will call this the *visible government*. Americans, in general, know of the existence of the visible government, such as when they see them in action when they turn on the TV news, but Americans do not know much, if anything, about what the visible government actually does from hour-to-hour, day-to-day, or year-to-year.

---

[100] It is widely known, and admitted by the Bush Administration that the Iraqi police that have been created by US government are to a large degree indistinguishable from the terrorist militias that have been terrorizing Iraq. This was a major news story when it broke in the fall of 2006. See "Iraqi Police Unit Probed for Link to Militias," Associated Press, David Rising, October 4, 2006. And see "Iraq police riddled by Shiite militia," Edward Wong, Paul von Zielbauer (New York Times writers), in San Francisco Chronicle, September 17, 2006. Now if you connect the dots, how do we avoid the conclusion that the "law enforcement" created by the US government in Iraq is identical to al-Qaeda? The idea is that the police are indistinguishable from the militias, the militias are indistinguishable from the al-Qaeda, and therefore the police are indistinguishable from al-Qaeda. But since the police have been created by US military forces in Iraq, that means that certain US military forces in Iraq are indistinguishalbe from al-Qaeda. The situation is illustrated in the following diagram:

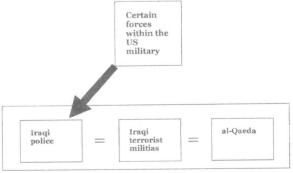

[101] I discuss how al-Qaeda and Hezbollah are parts of the secret government below when I show that they are merely CIA PMFs.

[102] Often Americans seem to believe that things like the Postal Service or the Federal Reserve, for example, are government entities; but this is false. These are private corporations.

So the visible government is partly visible, and partly invisible. On the one hand, the visible government is visible to the world populace, such as on TV, as just discussed, but on the other hand, what I am calling *the visible government* is an invisible part of the secret government. For that reason, what I am calling *the visible government* certainly has invisible qualities: secret government features. For example, Hillary Clinton is prominent in the media spotlight in her purported upcoming 2008 run for President (this is her visible side), but she is also a member of CFR (a key Rockefeller financed, UN-aligned New World Order and world government group that, for example, the oil corporatist and Carlyle Group leader George Bush Sr. is also a member of), and I would guess that less than one percent of Americans are aware of this.

Invisible government ➔   **Visible government ➔**

Corporatists

US politicians financed by lobbyists

➔ "We the People"

Typical American enjoying a
food product, unaware of food
dangers

In other words, what I am calling "the visible government," which is merely what is normally referred to as "the US government" by most Americans, acts in the interests of the secret government, but also acts for the television cameras to fabricate an illusory image of being the governing force of America.

The US Government: The Visible Government
is Only a Made-For-TV Drama

The visible government that Americans see on television every day is, therefore, part of the secret government, but nearly no Americans know this. This issue of television is not to be overlooked: the visible government is not the totality of what is commonly referred to as the US Federal government (Supreme Court, Presidential Branch, Congress, military, regulating agencies, law enforcement,[103] etc.). Rather, the *visible* government is only the parts of the US government that are *visible* in the mass media. For example, Congressman Ron Paul (R, Texas), who is running for President in 2008, is part of the US government, but he is not part of the *visible* government, since Paul is nearly never showcased in the mass media. Thus, there are members of the US government who are not linked to, nor are part of, the secret government of the New World Order, but they are not part of what I am calling "the visible government," since, for all practical purposes, few Americans know of them and few Americans see them in the mass media or hear about them in the classrooms.

Plainly stated: *the visible government consists of corporatists who are members of what is called the "US government" that are featured regularly by the mass media.* In other words, if there is a member of the US government that is discussed frequently on CNN or Fox News or in the New York Times (such as the Clintons, the Bushes, the Kennedys, Obama, Newt,[104] Kerry, Gore, Giuliani, Rumsfeld, Frist, Colin Powell, Condi Rice, and so on), you can practically conclude that they are being covered for a reason: because they are secret government corporatists and you are supposed to, designed to, only have your attention focused on them.[105]

When Congresspersons are meeting and doing "business" with lobbyists at their lavish dinner parties in the evening, they are functioning as parts of the secret government. When American Congresspersons are passing legislation

---

[103] I include law enforcement here because in of 2005-2006 law enforcement largely merged with the centralized Federal military, from being a non-centralized state-run non-military set of conglomerates.

[104] Newt is not actually part of the US government during the time that I write this book, but some might confuse this fact and believe he is, because he is so frequently covered in the mass media discussing government policy.

[105] Similar claims could be made about the biggest corporatists: there do appear to be a few that are not part of the genocidal, Masonic secret government. For example, it appears that Mark Cuban, billionaire, and owner of the Dallas Mavericks, and HDTV cable network, is not part of the corporatist secret government, as evidenced by the fact that he is planning to distribute Loose Change Final Cut in theatres summer of 2007.

like the 109th Congress's H.R. 6166 (the Military Commissions Act), and when they tell the American citizenry it is merely a bill that will help in the "war on terror," they are in that case too, doing things in secret, in the interests of the UN and the New World Order, and thus are functioning as parts of the secret corporatist government. But when the President, for example, gives the State of the Union speech, he/she is functioning and acting only to create a display for the populace, and thus he/she is in that case constituting the non-secret government (i.e., the visible government), which is what most Americans are tricked into believing *is the only American government there is.*

This is because the typical American is distracted with work, entertainment, and petty issues, and therefore knows nearly nothing but the visible face of the visible government (their daily televised press conferences and speeches, their scandals [such as the Foley sex scandal of October 2006], their appearances at major sporting events, etc.) that I just described. Most Americans would be shocked, or would probably go into a state of denial, if they knew about the real activities of the visible government if they bothered to look. (For example, The Space Preservation Act introduced by Kucinich, the massive amount of corporate welfare,[106] Halliburton no-bid contracts for the Iraq War, construction of a massive American concentration camp system that is ready for implementation, denial of health care for over 43 million Americans, etc.).

The Mechanics of the Secret Government

Here is how the secret government works:

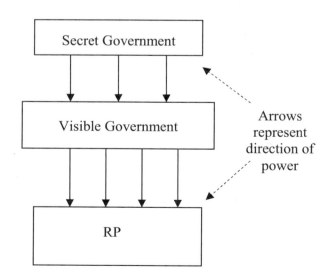

<hr />

[106] See Zepezauer 2004.

The first box represents the secret government, which, in general, controls economics, terrorist events, banking, natural resources, industrial research, education, thought and behavior, war, and almost any other large-scale agencies or events worldwide. There are no arrows leading to the secret government.

A principal purpose of the secret government is to carry out brutal fascism via the visible government *without the people being aware that that is what is going on*, as I will discuss in the next section. This tactic appears to be successful for the corporatist secret government, since most of the denizens of the United States (and most of the rest of the world) are tricked into believing that warfare is unplanned and spontaneous, that economic activity is unplanned and spontaneous, that terrorists are not linked to the controllers of economies, that corporate workaday misery is permissible and inevitable, that torture (i.e., Guantanamo Bay) or prison (the ultramassive profitable corporatist US prison system that holds millions, most of which are held for non-violent crimes) is a normal way to deal with other people, that war is peace, that ignorance is strength, that freedom is slavery (they are tricked into believing that they are "free" even though they are really slaves), and so on.

Planned Failure of the Visible Government

I will next give a few examples of how the secret fascism and torture spread throughout the world by the secret government is implemented onto the world citizenry without the people of the world knowing. In this section, you will see how the visible government is portrayed to the citizenry as a benevolent force, but which is really covertly one of the subdivisions of the secret government that is used to trick the citizenry and to unleash sheer misery.

Every four years, members of the visible government run for President in the United States. Year after year, each of them uses "health care reform," and ideas of "universal health care for all Americans," as principal issues in their campaigning. The mass media pumps these issues up tremendously. Americans are told by the candidates that they will make health care better, safer, more affordable, and available for all. This appears, on the surface, to be a rather benevolent gesture, and these candidates may really seem to be genuine and humanitarian at heart when they tell this to Americans through the television sets. *This is the visible government at work*: endlessly parading in front of television cameras, preaching a similar set of slogans, and appearing to be kind, full of good intentions, and perhaps humble and even desperate to win the election. But, alas, each candidate that is elected somehow just can't get the job done, and the promised health care plan never quite gets accomplished. And year after year, more health care problems emerge (but which are greatly underreported, or are *not* reported, in the national media), and more people are left with inadequate health care, or without health care. *This is the secret government at work*, and it is the real, hidden, but predictable goal of the visible government: the Presidential candidate displays all sorts of good intentions, but unfortunately, conditions were such that she/he could not get the job done on health care due to unforeseen glitches, problems, and other issues, and "coincidentally," the corporatists profited off those failures.

As another way of explaining how the visible government is covertly an instrument of misery used by the invisible government, consider the Vietnam War, the so-called "war on drugs" from Bush Sr.'s presidency, the wars in Iraq, the "war on terror," and Nixon even had a "war on cancer." Do you notice how each of these "wars" "coincidentally" happened to fail miserably, but only after uncountable amounts of taxpayer money was pumped into them and into the hands of the corporatists that control the industries behind these "wars": the "defense" industry and the military-industrial complex, the medical and cancer industries, and so on? Is it just a coincidence that the major policies of American Presidents abysmally fail repeatedly? These "wars" all started off as noble, seemingly benevolent attempts by politicians to help people and to bring "freedom and justice to the world" (to put it in the way that Bush Jr. often does), but by bad luck, these "wars" just happened to be failures. Consider this passage about the so-called "war on cancer" from the very beginning of a famous book on cancer by Dr. Ralph Moss:

> No sooner had the plan been drafted that [the "war on cancer"] came under sharp criticism from scientists within the cancer field itself. The basic assumption of the plan seemed to be that cancer could, in fact, be controlled by existing means. This corresponded to the political needs of President Nixon and the American Cancer Society.. By 1974 the public, which had enthusiastically hoped a cure for cancer was in the offing, was beginning to feel it had been betrayed. The cancer war was Nixon's "other war," and when Nixon resigned over Watergate, this only fueled public suspicion of a double-cross.[107]

This "war" did not even get off the ground, even though countless dollars has been pumped into it. Many Americans probably don't know about, or remember, this so-called "war" on cancer. Now in 2007, cancer rates are *soaring*.[108] I did not know anybody with prostate cancer, for example, in 1990, but now I know five people, and prostate cancer affects 40 percent of men over 50.[109] Every sort of cancer, and some that we have hardly ever heard of before (such as pancreatic cancer), are rising sharply. The medical field tells us that there is no cure, and that cancer victims need to be radiated with chemotherapy (which is a form of torture).

This state of affairs I am getting at here can be illustrated with the following diagram:

---

[107] Moss Page 2002, 5.

[108] See Fagin and Lavelle 1999 (Forward and Introduction). Cancer rates are up over 100 percent in the past century.

[109] Anderson 2004-2006.

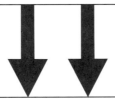

Visible government carries out a policy that appears to be benevolent and full of good intentions

The policy of the visible government sadly fails

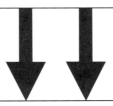

Corporatists "just happen" to profit wildly off of the failed policy, and the citizenry "just happens" to lose money and experience hardship by the failed policy

History proves that the tactic I have just described is a key secret corporatist government maneuver, which can be summed up as follows:

The corporatists covertly create a problem for the American citizenry (cancer,[110] drugs,[111] war,[112] environmental crisis, disease, terrorism,

---

[110] Cancer is caused by the meat and dairy industries (see Anderson 2004-2006).

[111] Drugs are created by the US government and secret government factions creating and having them shipped into the United States, which becomes profitable for the corporatists who sell and ship the drugs, for the medical industry, and for the corporatist

global warming,[113] etc.), and then with the help of the media, the visible government (working for the corporatists) fabricates a reason to tell the American public what has caused the problem, and that they can solve the problem if the American public throws unimaginable amounts of money at the visible government to solve the problem according to some plan that the visible government has concocted. But alas, the problem was so stringent that the visible government could not solve it, even though they tried. The money and the "war" in question are soon forgotten, and the American citizenry never has any idea that the problem was deliberately caused by corporatists for profit and control.

If the secret government wants to carry out a policy, such as invade a country, they invent an issue for the visible government to implement. In the case of invading another nation, the nation that is to be invaded is made to be a threat so that the populace will support an invasion of that nation. The failed policy was, in fact, just a deliberate and profitable policy of the secret government all along, but carrying out their policy under the mask of the benevolent visible government allows the secret government to avoid detection, and to avoid animosity by the citizenry (since the citizenry believes the failed policy was just an honest mistake).

Not all secret government policies are put forth as failed tactics by the visible government. For example, if the secret government wants to poison the citizenry with fluoride, the secret government merely pays for "science," advertising, news footage and so forth promoting the "benefits" of fluoride (e.g., it is good for teeth and bones), and which hides the fact that fluoride is nuclear toxic waste. The point is that the policy was a secret government policy, not a visible government policy.

Icke and the *P-R-S* Thesis

The planned failure of the visible government goes further than just problems being deliberately created by faking the incompetence of the visible government. It *also* includes problems which the secret government deliberately but covertly creates, and then creates a solution to, where the solution consists of rearranging the world and/or money in some way that is desirable for the corporatists. Borrowing from the ideas of others before him, such as the great scholar Jordan Maxwell, David Icke elegantly summarizes this process, which is often called the Hegelian Dialectic:

---

prison systems (see Scott 2003, Herival and Wright 2003, and Cockburn and St Clair 1998).

[112] I discuss how war is created by, and profitable for, the corporatists in several other places in this book.

[113] I show that global warming—at least as being believed to be human caused—is a hoax, in a footnote in a later chapter.

There are two techniques of mass manipulation that people need to understand if they are to begin to see through the game. One I call "problem-reaction-solution" and the other I term the "stepping-stones approach". These have been used for thousands of years to advance the agenda and, together with fear, they remain the two most effective weapons of the Illuminati. The first technique works like this: you know that if you openly propose to remove basic freedoms, start a war, or centralize power, there will be a public reaction against it. So you use problem-reaction-solution. At stage one you create a problem. It could be a country attacking another, a government or economic collapse, or a terrorist bomb. Anything in fact that the public will think requires a "solution". At stage two, you report the "problems" you have covertly created in the way you wish the people to perceive them. You find someone to blame, a patsy like Timothy McVeigh in Oklahoma, and you spin the background to these events in a way that encourages the people to demand that "something must be done". These are the words you wish to hear because it allows you to move on to stage three, the sting. You then openly offer the solutions to the problems you have yourself created. These solutions, of course, involve the centralization of power, the sacking of officials or politicians that are getting in your way, and the removal of more basic freedoms. With this technique you can so manipulate the public mind and they will demand that you do what, in normal circumstances, they would vehemently oppose. The Oklahoma bomb at the James P. Murrah Building on April 19th 1995 was a problem-reaction-solution classic... The two most effective problem-reaction-solutions in the 20th century were the two global wars. They changed the face of the world, as wars always do, and led to a massive centralization of power. The United Nations, like its predecessor, the League of Nations, was an Illuminati creation to act as a Trojan horse or stalking horse for world government.[114]

Some of the relevant examples of this P-R-S programme at the time of the writing of this book are the Iraq War, the impending war with Iran, and World War III which will likely follow the invasion of Iran. As for the Iraq War (the second one), Bush Jr. supposedly received bad intelligence information on the supposed "weapons of mass destruction" in Iraq, and the entire invasion was a "failure" (unless you are a big oil executive, as Bush Sr. is). With the model I am presenting in this subsection, each of these "wars" was *designed* to fail in order that corporatists would profit in various ways; this is the secret government at work. For example, the Iraq "weapons of mass destruction" threat was just staged, and Bush Jr. failed war plan was just a staged policy failure, so that the operations of the secret government could be carried out,

---

[114] Icke 2001, 7-8. Leonard Horowitz (see works cited) also often discusses Icke's P-R-S thesis, but Horowitz calls it "the Hegelian Dialectic."

which were to invade a very oil-rich patch of land that is strategic to hold in order to set up the New World Order. In other words, visible government operations and mistakes can be verified to be *deliberate* operations of the secret corporatist government, behind the scenes, pulling the strings of the visible government, to spread mass death, mass horror, to rearrange borders and nations when and how they desire, to rearrange populations or resources or business partnerships when needed—all while the citizenry believes everything that is happening is doing so spontaneously (not planned). These secret government horror-operations are made to look like benevolent, but failed, policies of the visible government, to "spread democracy," to "create peace," to "help the children," and so on, but that is just a disguise for what is going on underneath the surface and behind the puppet-strings of the visible government.

It is hard to overemphasize the amount of control and knowledge that the secret government possesses. As you will see in this book, they operate in secret, manipulating the world as they wish, all while the world citizenry typically does not even know that there is a secret government. To paraphrase the words of Francis Bacon: the secret government is a society that sees and controls everything, but itself is seen by nobody.[115] While Americans busy themselves with entertainment and petty occupations, falsely believing they are free and not in danger, they have no idea of how they are watched, created, shaped, and perpetually plotted against.

Here is a summary of the points of this section: the world is controlled by a secret corporatist government, and the purpose of the secret government is to fabricate horrific major world entities and events—anything from wars to stock market fluctuations, from epidemics to religions, from drug abuse to history, and from personal thoughts (including mental "disorder") to the spending patterns among shoppers—in order to profit in various ways from those events, and to create literal torment, loneliness, despiritualization, and the feeling of being completely lost in the minds of the members of the world citizenry, even though those citizens are largely not overtly conscious of their misery. FDR said: "In politics, nothing happens by accident. If it happens, you can bet it was planned that way."

Corporatists Control Via P-R-S

Not only is the public unaware of the Hegelian Dialectic used to control world events, but the public is, somehow, still largely unaware that the social world is tied up in the globalist corporatist system—probably because the mass media and the education systems tell the populace otherwise, and the populace mindlessly believes that is the case. But there is no *secret* that a corporatistic structure of the world exists. Consider, for example, a recent passage in the

---

[115] Paraphrased quote from Pinto 2006.

magazine The Economist about a book that a member of Kissinger and Assoc. has written about the corporatists:

> David Rothkopf, a visiting scholar at the Carnegie Endowment for International Peace, argues that these elites constitute nothing less than a new global "superclass". They have all the clubby characteristics of the old national ruling classes, but with the vital difference that they operate on the global stage, far from mere national electorates. They attend the same universities (Mr Rothkopf calculates that Harvard, Stanford and the University of Chicago are now the world's top three superclass producers). They are groomed in a handful of world-spanning institutions such as Goldman Sachs. They belong to the same clubs—the Council on Foreign Relations in New York is a particular favourite—and sit on each other's boards of directors. Many of them shuttle between the public and private sectors. They meet at global events such as the World Economic Forum at Davos and the Trilateral Commission or—for the *crème de la crème*—the Bilderberg meetings or the Bohemian Grove seminars that take place every July in California. Mr Rothkopf makes a fascinating tour of the world of the superclass. He opens the door to the office of the head of Goldman Sachs, Lloyd Blankfein, on the top floor of Goldman's tower on New York's Broad Street. He visits the factory that customises Gulfstream jets (every year nearly 10% of Gulfstream's clients attend Davos). He calls on the Carlyle Group where financiers and former presidents get together to make each other richer. And he offers a tour of the weird proceedings of the Bohemian Grove meetings, which Richard Nixon described as "the most faggy goddamned thing you could ever imagine."[116]

It is quite stunning to see who is included in this superclass of corporatists, that Rothkopf's book describes—for example, the Pope, Osama bin Laden, and others are included:

> Rothkopf announces that he and his researchers have identified "just over 6,000" people who match his definition of the superclass -- that is, who have met complicated (and vaguely explained) metrics designed to determine "the ability to regularly influence the lives of millions of people in multiple countries worldwide." These include heads of state and religious and military leaders -- even the occasional pop star, like Bono -- but the core membership is businessmen: hedge fund managers, technology entrepreneurs and private equity investors… The pope is a member of the superclass, as is Osama bin Laden, who can undoubtedly claim influence over current international affairs, even if he sometimes lives in a cave. The Russian illegal arms dealer Viktor "Merchant of

---

[116] From "Billion-Dollar Babies," The Economist, April 24, 2008.

Death" Bout is a member, as are Rupert Murdoch and Bill Clinton, who, while no longer commander in chief of the world's remaining superpower, nevertheless heads the Clinton Global Intiative, a brand new dynamo in the area of international philanthropy.

This shows us how there is a secret "world" of government that stands behind the visible governments, and which controls the world without the world citizenry having really any idea—this is an invisible government: *unseen and thus unknown*. Many of these global corporatists are stated in the mass media as being "enemies" of one another (e.g., Osama bin Laden vs. Western global corporatists), but where they actually *are not*, which shows that many of the "conflicts" that world leaders have are not really genuine conflicts, but rather are staged conflicts, which lead to more control over world populations—similar to how out of the staged conflict of World War II a "reason" was given for the creation of the United Nations (from the League of Nations), which was a big step in the increasing of power for global corporatism. All world conflicts (natural disasters, plagues, economic activities, wars, populations changes, etc.) are of this nature: deliberately planned struggles among unknowing ordinary humans, where the corporatists enter to provide a "solution", which involves some agenda they wanted to have in place all along: the invasion of a specific oil-rich nation by the US military, terrorist threats and attacks, increasing the amount of Prozac humans ingest, instituting a new education reform, crime waves and the consequent building of more prisons, etc.

The Core of the Secret Government: The Global Corporatists

There is a lot of talk in various intellectual circles on scholarly internet radio,[117] in a blog and book publishing, and lately, to some degree even academics have caught on (though they are very late in the game), about the emerging world government, which, of course, is admitted to already exist in its beginning stages by those who are setting it up.[118] According to many involved in this discussion, such as Alex Jones (an activist filmmaker) and Zbigniew Brzezinski (a key neoconservative that I will discuss at-length later), the world government will be a *corporatist* government,[119] and therefore, we will see that it will be *fascist*, and it will be the most dramatic sort of horror-state one can imagine. I am intending this book to be about America, but most of the Fortune 500 has moved off shore, and the corporatists do not follow the borders that the rest of the world pays attention to (the borders of cities, continents, nations, etc.)—they are global, and their domination is *world*-domination.

---

[117] For example, infowars.com, rense.com, nprlive.com, nutrimedical.com, among others.

[118] See Slaughter (2005), who is a CFR member, for an example of such an admission by a New World Order advocate/agent.

[119] Brzezinski discusses this in his famous book, *The Grand Chessboard*.

The corporatists are the heads of the secret government because they create all elements of the secret government: intelligence agencies, PMFs, visible government(s), lobbyists and think tanks, the UN, various secret societies (e.g., Skull and Bones), militaries, New World Order organizations (World Bank, IMF, and others discussed below), and so on. For these reasons, the corporatists control the entire world, even though very few people know this. The ultramassive monopolistic corporatists all, to some degree, work together,[120] and organize themselves via their secret agencies just listed. Corporate competition is mostly an illusion. Corporate monopolization and domination is the real nature of government.

Conclusion: The Family and Corporatism

I have found that it is hard for Americans to understand that they are controlled and brainwashed, and that the fundamental cores of their lives are entirely manipulated by the secret government. It is easiest, however, to see the fact of this deep control if we merely look at what has happened to *the family* in the United States during the 1900s. The family appears to be a primary anthropological unit, and deliberately breaking it apart would be no small feat by a set of corporatists who control thought and behavior. But if one looks at what the family has become, one sees that the corporatists have succeeded.

Consider the average day for the average American child. He will be roused from sleep, likely too early (without enough sleep, which can cause *real* irritation all the rest of the day in a young child), in order to be rushed off to school (or daycare) very early in the morning. Then he will be forced to sit through hours of non-education in the public "education" system learning boring non-facts, and during these hours he will be forced to endure what can often be considered overt humiliation by the "teacher" (giving the student failing grade for not understanding the right facts [which will be nonfacts in most cases, though the teacher does not know it[121]], teachers talking down to children, or not caring genuinely about children [which leads to mistreatment of children] and perhaps even yelling at children, or requiring that the child sit still and be quiet, etc.). Then after school (if he is lucky enough to go right home, rather than have to attend an "after school program") he will likely spend much of his evening watching television (i.e., being brainwashed) and/or playing videogames (i.e., being prepared for military combat[122]). Throughout his day, this child has eaten poisonous food filled with MSG (brain toxin), aspartame (brain toxin), pesticides, herbicides, steroids, hormones, antibiotics, viruses (via

---

[120] See Bagdikian (2004) for an example of how corporations "work together" rather than compete.

[121] See my section at the start of this chapter about how American education does not contain, in general, any empirically verifiable ideas and facts.

[122] See Halter 2006 for information on how video games are often covertly attempts to train children for military activity.

GMO food and direct spraying of viruses on the food), and heavy metals (and this is food that his teachers and parents are tricked into telling him is "good food"), he drinks fluoridated water (a known carcinogen and neurotoxin[123]), and there is likely a high concentration of heavy metals, hostile antibodies (due to antibody biomimicry), and other catastrophic toxins flowing through his body from the vaccines he is regularly subjected to. It is safe to say that this child is literally harassed, tormented, brainwashed, and humiliated throughout his day of being drugged, poisoned, forced to sit in silence (in school). Not only have Americans abandoned their children, they have resorted to torturing them daily, because their corporatist government has tricked them into doing it. As Jim Keith writes:

> The populace has been drugged, shocked, irradiated, made ill, manipulated, and even killed in the efforts of the military and intelligence agencies and their psychiatric dupes to devise the most effective and invisible manacles for the containment of members of our "democracy."[124]

Americans are a group of people who, in general, do not spend their lives in or near their home. They are *home-less*. They spend it at the corporation. When an American meets a person who has a job from home, they are shocked, and stunned with jealousy. Americans have come to believe that it is normal to live this way: to spend the moments of life away from family and home. Spending considerable time at home is something that is considered a luxury (for those who have reasonable domiciles), rather than as a standard human trait, as it has been for thousands of years. Without home there is no family structure, and without family structure, Americans are closer to living in a Brave New World than they appear to realize. Americans are, for these reasons, apparently living in homelessness and the non-intimacy of the state of broken familyhood.

---

[123] See the article: "Determination of Fluoride in Water Residues by Proton Induced Gamma Emission Measurements," by AKM Fazlul Hoque, M. Khaliquzzaman, MD Hossain, and AH Khan, published in 2002 by the journal, *Fluoride*, vol. 35, no. 3, pages 176-184. Also see Bryson 2004.
[124] Keith 2004, 31.

2 Corporatism

I see in the near future a crisis approaching that unnerves me and causes me to tremble for the sake of my country… Corporations have been enthroned and an era of corruption in high places will follow, and the money power of the country will endeavor to prolong its reign by working upon the prejudices of the people until all wealth is aggregated in a few hands and the Republic is destroyed.

—Abraham Lincoln, November 21, 1864[125]

In this chapter I will prove that the United States is a corporatist nation. (These arguments also show that the entire world is corporatistic as well) To do this, I will analyze the structure and nature of America, where the details I point out verify that America is corporatistic. I will prove this in three different ways, and by looking at three different facets of American corporatism: (1) as tyranny by the corporatists over the *resources* that people depend on to live, and as consequent tyrannization over the *behavior* of people (since resources determine behavior, as you will see); (2) as tyrannization by the corporatists over the *daily lives* of people, and consequently over the structure of the *minds and feelings* of people (i.e., the *consciousness* of people); and (3) where corporatism is an *idea* of a nonexistent entity that people create that leads to the full tyrannization of human culture and life. I call each of these, respectively: (1) structural corporatism, (2) lived corporatism, and (3) abstract corporatism.

The Corporatist Structure of the United States (and the World)

The first account of corporatism that I give is what I call the *structural interpretation* of corporatism (which can also be called *structural corporatism* or the structural aspects of corporatism). The resources that humans depend on in order to live—food, water, medicine, homes, health care, genuine education, etc.—all derive from monopolistic corporations that are controlled by corporatists in the contemporary world. Americans have little or no power over the nature of these resources. For example, Americans have little or no choice but to drink dangerously polluted—more specifically, *fluoridated*—water that corporations charge customers to use. On planet earth, humans generally cannot drink water "for free" nowadays, but rather they must pay for it, and to be able to pay, they must have a job (usually a very low paying job), *at a corporation*. In other words, in the contemporary world, to live is to be a slave.

---

[125] Cited in Caldicott 2002, 24; and in Korten 2001, 64. Notice that Lincoln uses the word "republic," not the mob-rule term, "democracy." Although Lincoln himself was a savage tyrant (see Thomas Dilorenzo, 2003, *The Real Lincoln*, Three Rivers Press), executing Indians and so forth, he was aware of the set up of the state of domination by the corporatist banks which was taking place in the United States (finalized in 1913) and his measures to stop it are what many believe were caused his assassination.

I will next show that this dependency that Americans have on the resources that are controlled by the monopolistic corporations is the primary reason why the structure of the United States is a *tyrannical-communist* structure. To arrive at this *structural* interpretation of American corporatism, I will have to give three consecutive arguments that build upon one another, and which in precise detail lay out the corporatist mechanics of America. I will call these *step 1*, *step 2*, and *step 3*, and I will cover them in order before proceeding to discuss lived corporatism and abstract corporatism.

Structural Interpretation - Step 1

Here is the first argument in the trio of arguments that I will give:

1.   Corporations control resources and wealth.

2.   Resources and wealth control human behavior.

Therefore, Corporations control human behavior.

I will discuss the details of this argument shortly, but first notice how I have written the argument. This argument involves the following "argument form:"

1. A is B,

2. B is C,

Therefore, A is C.

(A= corporations, B=resources, C=behavior)[126]

Whatever comes before the word "therefore" is evidence for, and support for, the conclusion, and for what comes after the "therefore." I will make use of this specific *argument form* at various points in this book. Lines 1 and 2 are terse, simple premises and pieces of evidence, which are meant to build up to and

---

[126] More technically put, the "is" in this *argument form* functions like an "=" sign, and thus this argument form involves mathematical precision. The way I wrote the argument above, and before I discussed the symbolization of it in the argument form, does not exhibit the word "is." But the "is" is nevertheless there, since in critical thinking jargon, there is an item that is describable in two ways: A is B, B is C, but then A is C. In other words, the first premise, *corporations control resources and wealth*, can be rewritten with the "is" (the "=" sign) present: a set of corporations *is* system that controls recourses and wealth. Therefore, though I did not need to write the argument with the "is" exhibited in it above, it can however be rewritten as follows, where "is" is exhibited, thus being shown to obey the strict logical argument form A is B, B is C, therefore A is C:

1.   A group of corporations *is* an edifice that controls resources and wealth.
2.   An edifice that controls resources and wealth *is* a group of things that controls human behavior.
Therefore, a group of corporations *is* a group of things that controls human behavior.

prove the third line, which is the conclusion. This is one of the ways that students are taught to express arguments in a basic college critical thinking class. Expressing reasoning in simple points that provide evidence for a conclusion is a productive and intellectual way for one to prove what they want to get across.

The first statement—*corporations control all resource wealth*—is not meant to imply that corporations *possess* all resource wealth that exists. Rather, what I mean by the first statement is that, ultimately, corporations in the United States, in one way or another, logistically dictate the activity of nearly all resources and money. In other words, they oversee and dictate the use of all resources used by Americans, and Americans have little or nothing that they can do about it.

For example, Americans seem to *believe* they have choices (and power) because they are consumers, where they believe they can choose between ESPN1 and ESPN2, between Kerry and Bush, between Coke and Pepsi, between one low-paying-job versus another, between bottled water or tap water, paper or plastic, sitcom or soap opera, CNN or Fox News, the University of Texas or Purdue University, and so on. But in these sets of choices, Americans cannot decide which two options they could choose from in the first place. Therefore, choice is an illusion. For example, what if you want ESPN4, or what if you want a new big name cola, or what if I want

an anti-war presidential candidate that is not a corporatist (and who has been given equal and fair media coverage or ballot space compared to the other candidates), or what if you want water that is not polluted (for example, with fluoride,[127] perchlorate, and Prozac[128])? There is no choice, due to the fact that you can't have any of these.

Furthermore, what is the real difference between the choices just listed? For example, how are ESPN1 and ESPN2 really different? One may have basketball on tonight, and the other football, and thus there may seem to be a

---

[127] See Bryson 2004.

[128] Yes, it is true, the water supply is largely polluted with large amounts of Prozac. This is not a secret, and this made national headlines in the corporatized mass media in early 2008. See "Prozac in Drinking Water? Likely So," on WebMD.com (http://www.webmd.com/content/Article/92/101794.htm), which reads as follows:

> August 10, 2004 -- Scientists in Great Britain have found levels of a common antidepressant in the water. It begs the question: What about the drinking water in the U.S.? Should we be concerned? The exact quantity of the antidepressant Prozac -- found in river systems and groundwater used for drinking -- was not specified. However, the British report says that it could be potentially toxic. Similar problems have been discovered both with prescription and nonprescription drugs in the U.S. and throughout Europe, albeit at low levels. Many have questioned whether even low levels of these medications could affect human health and reproduction.

choice, but what if you want to watch tennis, and there is none on? And suppose you don't want to watch any sports, and none of the 900 cable channels (that are only owned by a five or six media corporations), have what you want to watch, since most of it contains tabloid material, sports, or quasi-intellectual "educational television" (which is really just an ultra-powerful brainwashing tool; I will discuss this in the future in another book I am writing)?

Fluoride is an example of the way in which Americans are secretly poisoned. There are no scientific studies or publications that show that Fluoride helps build strong bones and teeth.[129] Toothpaste tubes contain warnings that inform users to seek immediate medical attention if more toothpaste than what is normally used is swallowed. Why are there such warnings if it is all so safe? The type of fluoride inserted into consumable food products (which is *sodium fluoride*, which is different from *calcium fluoride*, which is found in nature, but the corporatized media often hides the difference between the two, thus fooling people), is actually a product of nuclear weapons production, and other toxic industrial processes.[130] Dentists are not aware of the researched fact that fluoride is one of the most toxic items in the American food and water supply, and that it is a sedative.[131] Tap water in America is often fluoridated, and often super-fluoridated water is aimed at use for children, where defenseless parents are uknowningly giving them a nuclear waste product to consume.

What if you want to watch a scientific show on quantum entanglement (which, to my knowledge, has never existed for cable television, even though entanglement is one of the big topics in quantum physics since the early 1980s)? What if you want to watch an informative documentary about pollution? Or about the CIA? Or about 911 skeptics discussing the issues of the Pentagon that I discussed in chapter 1? *You can't*; these don't exist. In fact, very few choices on television exist, since it's literally all tabloid information, sports, and news (which, you will see, is not really news, it is thought control).

---

[129] See the first few pages of Bryson 2004 for discussion of this absence of research.

[130] See Bryson 2004. It is no secret in the nuclear weapons industry that fluoride is a chief product used in the process. For example, here is one of the countless articles published on fluoride as a key element in the nuclear industry: "Concept of a closed nuclear fuel cycle with fluoride reprocessing of spent fuel," published in *Atomic Energy*, vol. 78, no. 4.

[131] See Bryson 2004 for more information on these issues.

Even the so-called "educational television" channels (The National Geographic Channel, The History Channel, etc.) are owned by the same bellicose military-industrial complex as the other 900 cable television channels, and consequently only involve shows that are thought control, rather than education.

Corporations have control of dictating how resources are used, how they get split up, sorted out, and sold. For example, American consumers may imagine that they are free to buy any product they want, as if they control resources and the products made from them. American consumers may imagine that they can buy and sell automobiles in almost any way they want, where anybody can buy almost whatever automobile they wish, so long as they merely can afford it. But American consumers do not seem to consider how little choice they have, as seen by the following questions, all of which have "no" as their answer: Can I buy a solar car? Can I buy an electric car (the so-called "EV"[132])? How about a car that runs on water? Can I buy *any* sort of non-gasoline-based car? Can I buy a car that does not pollute, that is silent, and that does not have a tracking device in it (a transponder)? Can I buy a car that will last for 10 or 20 years without having to replace the engine and most other parts and without spending an-arm-and-a-leg on repairs? Can I buy a car that is not so expensive that it takes up a significant portion of my monthly income? Can I buy a car that is run by a free energy generator? *No* is the answer to each question.

Many Americans travel a significant distance to their jobs each day, and due to the fact that there is no decent community transportation system in America (which is suspicious in itself, as if such an industry would take profits away from the oil and auto industries[133]), they have little choice but to own autos. The auto industry is largely monopolized by all the same players, decade-after-decade (Ford, Honda, etc.), all of which offer basically the same sort of car (a gas-powered metal car with a tracking device built into it), and thus Americans may believe they have all sorts of choices in their purchasing of cars, but in fact they have only one, since they buy only buy one sort of car: a clunky, metal, dangerous, multi-ton, stinky, low-tech, noisy, gasoline-powered, big-brother automobile that gives off an incredibly large amount of exhaust.

Another good example (another one of nearly countless examples that could be given) of the lack of choice American consumers have, due to their living under monopolistic corporations, is the way *land masses*, whether big or small, are split up and handed out for use to families, cities, corporations, and so on. Land ownership is a large subject, so I will only briefly touch on it. It is widely believed that many families and individuals in America *own* land, but we will see in chapter 3, that this is false. As for corporations, land-masses are often basically *given* to corporations. Zepezauer discusses how the US government,

---

[132] This automobile—which exists and was selling well in the early 2000s—has been made illegal. See Paine 2006.

[133] See Black 2006.

which is comprised of corporatists, is fond of giving all sorts of handouts to corporations (land is just one of many), where taxpayers are the ones who suffer for this, in multiple ways:

> Welfare for the rich takes five basic forms. The first two are tax breaks and direct subsidies.[134] ... The other three forms of welfare for the rich are more subtle than handouts or tax breaks. One is when Uncle Sam sells off properties belonging to We the People at a fraction of their true market value.[135]

Consider the oil drilling going on in northern Alaska, which takes up truly massive amounts of land. There were, of course, Native Americans living on that land just recently. Here are the questions: Why do oil companies now "own" and control these huge expanses of land? How did they acquire all this land when there were people recently living on it? Answer: only by the government (which is full of "oil men") creating "policies" and "programs" to remove groups of people by various means, in order to hand land over to oil corporatists.

Premise 1—*corporations control resources and wealth*—is about corporations "controlling" resources and wealth, but that is really a rather nice way of putting it. What typically occurs is corporations *usurp* (steal) resources and wealth—anything from land, energy, and water, to our very lives (our daily lives), including our behavior or the power of our cognition and mental problem-solving skills. The basic issue here is grasped by a quote from Elaine Bernard of Harvard University, in a comment about not past or present taking of land from American Indians, but rather of the present-day "acquisition" of resources from all Americans in order to put it into the hands of the corporatists.

> With deregulation, privatization, [and] free-trade, what we're seeing is yet another enclosure, and... private taking of the commons. One of the things I find very interesting in our current debates is the concept of who creates wealth? That wealth is only created when it's owned privately. What would you call clean water, fresh air, a safe environment? Are they not a form of wealth? And why does it only become wealth when some entity puts a fence around it and declares it private property? That's not wealth creation, that's wealth usurpation."[136]

As for the second premise in the argument—*resources and wealth control human behavior*—it is pretty easy to show how resources and wealth control virtually all human behavior in America. Humans are all presented with similar

---

[134] Zepezauer 2004, 4.

[135] Zepezauer 2004, 6.

[136] This quote is from Achbar and Abbot, 2004.

problems in their ordinary day-to-day tasks of life: How do we acquire food and water, raise children, keep our homes warm, stay safe, keep a stable income, get all our tasks finished each day, and (hopefully) find small amounts of time to enjoy ourselves in various ways in the meantime (where in contemporary America, it seems most Americans carry out the last one—entertainment—primarily with television)? Given the environments humans find themselves in, certain ways of solving these problems are optimal. It only makes sense that people will adapt to use the best tactics to solve and deal with daily-life issues each day. In other words, if two people need to get the berries from a tall and thorny tree in order to have some food to eat, it is likely that they will each learn to use some of the same tactics for solving this problem, and thus their behavior will be similar, not diverse. This is one reason why human behavior tends to be so similar all over the planet.

For example, one of our main problems is, How do we acquire food? It is pretty clear that some strategies are better than others and similar choices will be made among people in solving or handling these issues: eating carrots is better than eating rocks; eating tofu will be chosen far less than eating something fatty or ultra-sugary in flavor, since sugars and fats are addictive "narcotic food." Therefore, the behavior of people is not as diverse as it is similar when there are similar environmental situations. When humans are hungry, humans will all seek food, and in doing this, they will all seek out what they believe is their best food-acquisition opportunities (they will seek the tastiest food they are in the mood for and which they can get their hands on). Other examples of the commonality of human behaviors in everyday life are easy to find; the point is that there are optimal ways to solve these problems given the options available in the environment one finds oneself amid. Humans have been made to find simple solutions through these optimal ways. In other words, people almost always behave in quite similar ways in similar environments, but these actions are always limited by, and governed by, which resources are present, and the characterization of the environments.

All base human behaviors (i.e., necessary survival behaviors) ultimately involve, and are controlled by, *resources,* such as food: humans have no choice but to seek food, and they typically have little choice but to be compelled to seek the optimal (which usually means, *the tastiest*) food available, and thus human behavior is a prisoner to these drives. Resources control behavior, and behavior does not control resources. But as stated above, resources, including money, are controlled by corporations, and thus *corporations control virtually all human behavior.*

Structural Interpretation - Step 2

The first argument in the trio only shows that corporations control *behavior*. But more is needed to show that, without question, the United States is a corporatist nation. Thus, I will proceed to the next argument, which builds on the last one, which also uses the same argument form as the argument in Step 1, and which thus moves us closer to seeing how the structure of America is a corporatist structure.

In this next argument, the conclusion of the argument in Step 1 is the first premise:

1. Corporations control human behavior. (Conclusion of argument 1 in Step 1.)
2. Human behavior is culture.
3. American culture is what the United States is.

Therefore, Corporations control what the United States is.

As with argument #1, this argument also follows the same sort of argument form:

A is B,

B is C,

C is D,

Therefore A is D

(A= corporations, B=behavior, C=culture, and D= the United States)

With respect to the second premise, here I am using the anthropologist's definition of the word "culture:"[137] culture is interaction among living creatures, where that interaction results in the living creatures learning and copying behavior from one another. This social interaction is ultimately a behavioral interaction, for reasons I discuss next.

If I did not move parts of my body in various ways (my eyes, lips, legs, facial muscles, hands, etc.), I could not have any social interaction with others. Only by my behavior (or, more specifically, by moving and twitching muscles) when I am communicating with others in various ways, can I create a display (facial expressions, "body language," etc.) for others to see, and which will have the power to generate *social interaction* behavior.[138]

---

[137] It seems best to use theirs, since they are specifically the group that studies and works out the definitions of culture.

[138] Culture may be believed by some researchers to be primarily a mental and subjective phenomena, since it may seem to have to do with the mind, but that seems to be incorrect, since that model of behavior leaves out the basis of the social interaction required for culture, which is the behavioral (muscle twitching) interaction I just described. Behavioral and social interaction does not occur by people seeing each others' minds (unless a culture is primarily telepathic, which the United States does not seem to be, unless the PEAR group [Princeton Engineering Anomalies Research group] can show otherwise), but rather it occurs with their faces: facial movements, facial muscles. When you look at me, you see a face, not my thoughts. When I look at you, I

As for the third premise of the second argument—*culture is what the United States is*—while the United States might be believed to be many things (its land, its history, its corporations, etc.) more than anything, it seems that the United States is best defined as *the people* of the land (which currently exist in a corporatist setting): the people which make up the corporations, and the people who have created America's industry and history, regardless of whether or not they have been shaped by the secret corporatist government.

Structural Interpretation - Step 3

To this point, we have indeed found that corporations command and govern the United States, thus showing that America is a corporatist empire. I will however give one more argument that is critical in developing proof that the United States is a corporatist nation. Using the conclusion of step 2, the next argument goes as follows:

1. The United States is under the control of Corporations (paraphrase of the conclusion of argument #2).
2. That which is under the control of corporations is under fascist control.

Therefore, The United States is under fascist control.

In other words, the United States is a corporate dictatorship. America is not a dictatorship in the sense that literally just one person rules all people (but, as will be explained below, I don't think any of those sorts of dictatorships have ever existed, and any of the societies that Americans commonly refer to as "communist" and "tyrannical," such as Nazi Germany, Red China, etc., which did not have such a one-ruler structure). Instead, the United States has perhaps 1000 or 2000 top corporatists (in this book I will not be concerned with ascertaining an exact number, as only approximate numbers are needed for one to analyze and understand corporatism) who answer to nobody, but who have full control over the resources that the citizens of planet earth depend on for their daily survival.

As for the second premise—*that which is under the control of corporations is under fascist control*—it is evident that corporations are not democratic institutions. If they were, then the workers would elect their corporate leaders (if corporate leaders were deemed necessary in a truly democratic corporation, which they are not in the aforementioned *anarchistic* corporatism), the rules of the corporation would be created by the workers, payment would likely be high enough to be sufficient (or as sufficient as possible) and uniform among all workers, community decisions would be made among all workers about what

---

can't see into your subjectivity (i.e., your consciousness), I only see your face and body. This is why culture is manifested with behavior (twitching of muscles), and thus culture is defined in terms of behavior alone, even though subjectivity may run the show.

the corporation's activities and structure should be like, and so on.[139] But this is not a reality in corporatist America. Rather, corporations are tyrannical in their top-down power structure. The worker is expected to follow orders, *period!* The worker usually cannot choose her hours (which tend to be very long, anywhere from 35-90 hours per week), her payment (which is typically astonishingly or even humorously low), what she does while at the corporation (which is usually work that she hates and which makes her miserable, desperate, uninformed), and if she makes mistakes, it is not unusual that they will result in her getting a good old fashioned "ass chewin" from the boss, even if her mistake is caused by "the boss" (due to poor communication, training, for example).

Some conditions in corporations are better than others, with respect to how cruel and unusual the circumstances and treatment are. Roofers, for example, tend to evoke enormous pity, such as when they are working ten or more hours per day in 86 degrees Fahrenheit temperature in humid Michigan air. This sort of a situation would seem to be, quite literally, analogous to some of the lower-levels of Guantanamo Bay "interrogation" (i.e., torture). On the other hand, university professors often seem to be looked upon as having an enviable situation, where they can get paid big bucks to be radicals if they want, to read books, and where they often only have to work a few hours per week. But is this an accurate picture of professors? This is sort of the picture of American professors that David Horowitz, author of the widely read book, *The Professors: The 101 most Dangerous Professors in America*,[140] wants to convince us pervades the American universities. Certainly there are cases where this is so, but nowadays, most university professors do not resemble anything like this, and they, in fact, conduct some sort of *corporatist research*: they work in some sort of *extremely* specialized science or technological area (where a truly *huge* percentage of the research is for corporate purposes—pharmaceutical research, military research, biomedical research, psychological and behavior modification research, and so on[141]—as if the universities in America are little more than taxpayer-financed military and corporate research centers), under a truly massive amount of pressure to conduct research in a very narrow research area (which means that they have only expertise in that area—if they can even attain that—and likely have no reasonable knowledge whatsoever about the rest of reality). Further, university professors can often make reasonable salaries if they are at the high-end schools (Big Ten schools, for example), but at most universities, the salaries of professors are in fact mediocre at best (often even significantly below $40,000.00 per year), and they are controlled not by their academic merit, but rather by what I called the visible government in chapter 1.

---

[139] These are the traits that are observed in real-world examples of anarchistic corporations, such as the sorts of corporations documented in Lewis, 2004.

[140] 2006, Washington, DC: Regnery Publishing, Inc.

[141] Caldicott (2002) and Angell (2005) discuss these issues in detail.

So the professor is certainly in better circumstances than the roofer by most standards I would imagine, but the professor is nevertheless also living under corporatistic (tyrannical) oppression. And if one talks to, for example, your average science professor—let's say a professor in agriculture—you can see the results of this tyranny in her/him: you likely won't see a master researcher, who has discovered the secrets of reality, in the way Einstein, Tesla, Buddha, or Thoreau did; rather, you will most likely see somebody who can tell you everything you want to know (except perhaps safety standards) about, for example, Monsanto genetically modified soy, but they will not know what the Federal Reserve is, they will not know about the ancient city of Tiahuanaco in Peru (or what its significance is), they will not know the Bill of Rights or what the Gulf of Tonkin incident is, or what the negative health effects of Monsanto bovine growth hormone are when people drink it in milk, and they will have no idea how unhealthy soy is—especially genetically modified soy.[142] She/he will likely merely be as lost and confused as any other American has been manufactured to be, even if the professor has more money and social status than the rest of the lost tribe of people, called Americans.

Americans often hold the idea that going to college gives a person an ability to choose their fate and control their career—in short, to choose what they want to do with their life. But even if an engineering student chooses her career by going through a deliberate and well-thought-out process of deciding to be an engineer, for example, she still will likely not have much choice in where she works and what she does at that job. Those critical issues depend on who's hiring at the time she is looking for work, and what the corporation she works for wants her to do on the job and in her 35-90 hours per week that she will likely be ordered to work. Corporations, from this perspective, are better described as a home-away-from-home for most Americans—or, in other words, they are forced labor camps.

Regardless of the situation, little argumentation is needed to verify that corporations are fascistic in their power-structure, and thus I will move on (although this issue will come up again later in this chapter). What has been shown so far in this chapter appears to prove a quite simple idea: American culture is fully shaped and dominated by corporations, but since corporations are fascist, then American culture is fascistic. Next I will move to the second of the three accounts I give in this chapter that show that the United States is a corporatist empire.

Lived Corporatism: The Tyrannized Experience of Everyday Life

In the last section we found that the *structure* of the United States is a *corporatist* structure. In this section, I will show that the daily experience of Americans under corporatist rule is *tyrannized experience*. Therefore, not only

---

[142] See Daniel 2006.

is the structure of the United States corporatistic, but the daily *experience* of Americans is *corporatized* (tyrannized). This is because Americans are under the control and dependency of corporations, which are tyrannies, and therefore the daily life experience of Americans is that of tyrannized creatures.

For example, when Americans go to their jobs, stocking Wal-Mart shelves, writing accounting reports, flipping burgers at McDonalds, creating engineering plans, running the cash-register at 7-11, selling used cars, moving boxes in the warehouse, mopping floors, writing memos, and so on, they have little or no power, little or no choice, little or no respect, and little or no enjoyment coming to them. They will be told that the corporation cares for them, and that they are lucky to have a job, but if one looks at the moment-to-moment dynamics of their lives, it can be pointed out that the corporation merely causes mass torment in people. Consider what David Icke writes on this issue:

> ...most people are told what to think, where to go, what to do and how to do it... [W]here do you get your 'information' that leads you to reach the conclusions about yourself and the world? Who decides what time you get up every workday? Who decides where you go and what you do when you get there? Who decides how you do it? If you are like the overwhelming majority of people currently resident in this dreamworld, those decisions are not made by you at all; they are imposed by the 'system', the spider's web of control that dictates its will upon your 'life'.
>
> You get your 'information from the mainstream media that sells you the daily falsehoods on which you decide what to think and believe. You have to get up at a certain time because you have to report for work and you can't be late. You go where your bosses tell you to go and you do what they say. If you rebel you get fired and if you don't get paid you can't afford a home or enough to eat... To meet all these perceived needs and responsibilities, you have to spend every day keeping other people happy. In turn, the bosses are also slavishly following the impositions of those who control *them* and *they* dare not step out of line either.[143]

Workers typically have little or no appreciation for, and little or no camaraderie with, their bosses, who, as I show elsewhere in this book, typically could not care less about the workers.[144] This, in general, is true everywhere: in small businesses, in the massive monopolistic corporations, in government jobs,

---

[143] Icke 2005, 1.

[144] I will verify in later chapters that the highest-level bosses—the corporatists—appear to relish when their workers are hurt, tortured or killed.

service jobs, in the teaching profession,[145] and among university professors.[146] What industry or profession is exempt from corporatism?

To understand the significance of this *lived tyranny*, consider the following issues. First, from the reasoning given in step 2 of the structural interpretation, we have the following equation,

the United States = We the People.

Now, from this equation we can derive another equation. If, as I will discuss throughout this section, the American people, in general, live in a tyrannized state, then another equation follows:

United States = life in a tyrannized state,

which occurs by substituting "the people" in the first equation with "life in a tyrannized state" in the second. This substitution seems justified since what people are, is their state of being and their state of consciousness: what a person is, is their mind and their subjectivity. Without our mental life, without our states of mind, filled with love or hate, anger or happiness, boredom, personality traits, dreams, memories, self-identity, and hope, we cease to be human. This also indicates that what people are is a product of the nature of their daily lives, since one's immediate surroundings from moment-to-moment is the primary factor that goes into shaping a person's subjective self. Therefore, a person is what their feelings and thoughts involve, and what people identify themselves with *in their daily occupation*. A person is what their daily work and toil causes the person to *be*, *feel*, and *think* in that situation. This is a basic tenet of social science: what a person is, is largely defined by their world and environment that they find themselves in. So, if a person is subjected to perpetual tyranny from the world around them, then their feelings, actions, and thought can only be *tyrannized*.

So what does this mean for Americans, who endlessly exist in a tyrannized environment and in a corporatized state of consciousness? The answer is, of course, that their consciousness and their self is tyrannized: *tyrannized experience*.

---

[145] In the case of elementary teachers, for example, as far as I know, they do not choose their hours, their students, nor their curriculum. and often do not choose their classroom. They do not choose to go attend countless meetings after school that they are nowadays ordered to attend, nor to accept Bush's 'no child left behind.'

[146] As stated above, professors are often portrayed as people without rules and who can be radicals. This idea is a media fabrication, and, in reality, the university is largely a domain of thought control and social engineering. For example, who can forget that when Rumsfeld resigned as head of the DoD just after the 2006 mid-term elections who took his place: William Gates, who came from being the head of Texas A&M University, and before his job at Texas A&M, Gates was the head of the CIA!

Moment-to-moment, year-after-year, the American lives a tyrannized, corporatized life. If we add up all this experience for each individual person, adding up all the tyrannized experiences and lives, we will get a sum of all experiences of Americans. What would the sum of that experience be? It can only be, of course, *tyrannized experience.* If we take all the people, and add up the moments of their lives, with all this adding, we are only adding tyrannized states, and thus we don't ever get out of it: no matter how many tyrannized states of consciousness and states of tyrannized life you add up, you never come to anything but tyrannized life-experience.[147]

Consider all the millions and millions of people in the United States, all working and living under a corporatized state. Consider the millions and millions of parents, working and spending their days in a corporatized labor camp (a corporation) amid tyrannized job-settings. Consider their children, spending umpteen hours in day-care, for example, since their parents must both work long hours, spending less and less time with them, fooled into focusing their energy and attention on the corporation and on their corporatized state of existence (rather than on their self or their children), largely because they have been tricked into believing that they have to "buy shit [they] don't need," to again quote the film *Fight Club.* They have been fooled into giving their lives not to exploring themselves and finding out what their passions and dreams are, but rather to slaving away for somebody else's dreams—namely, the corporatists financial dreams. So this is the average tyrannized situation for the average American: a tyrannized life of tyrannized experience.

Media in America (both the education system and the newsprint and televisual media) perpetually attempts to convince the citizenry that their corporatized lives are good lives, perhaps the best of anyone in the world or in history. I often hear politicians utter through the cable news channels: "Americans have the best standard of living and the best health care of any group of people in the world." (This, of course, is not true, and I will disprove it at many places in this book.) But in the American corporatized/tyrannized state of existence, a *huge* percentage of people in the population are severely oppressed (which is virtually never discussed in the mass media) for many reasons. In their corporatized state of existence in America, the people are forced to work at jobs that they despise, in a fascistic power structure that doesn't pay enough to reasonably raise children. For example, they cannot

---

[147] If somebody wanted to imagine that the United States is an *oligarchical* state rather than a *tyrannical* state, as some researchers do, I don't see how we can reach that conclusion, given the reasoning of this discussion of lived corporatism, or tyrannized experience. It seems that if we are considering America from what it seems to be its very core, namely "We the People" and their daily lived experience, if that experience is corporatized, then we can only get to the conclusion that the United States is a massive state of tyranny. If, in general, all experiences of Americans are tyrannized, then the United States is a state of tyranny, not a state of oligarchy.

purchase health care (and if they can, the health care system is only a deceptive and worthless corporatist ruse), or they must resort to the government mandated and UN-controlled public education system that keeps children needlessly separated from their families and from becoming well-educated.[148]

Abstract Corporatism: A Corporation is Only an Idea

Round and round it goes, this circle of dependency and imposition of will. One man's slave is another man's master; one mans' sheep is another man's shepherd. This is the way the world is purposely structured. The system wants everyone controlling everyone else and this is done in a billion different ways. What we call 'free societies' are Gulags by any other name. The system doesn't serve us—we serve it. We are slaves who delude ourselves that we are free because we don't want to face the reality of our plight.

—David Icke[149]

Above, we have seen that the *structure* of the United States is corporatistic, and that the *lived experience* of the Americans that make up the United States consists of a corporatized/tyrannized way of life. I will next discuss the last of the three reasons I give in this chapter for why the United States is corporatist empire, and this last reason is what I call the *abstract* interpretation of American (and global) corporatism.

To get an idea of what I will be getting at in this subsection, consider an excellent passage from Professor Korten:

Less widely recognized is the tendency of individual corporations, as they grow in size and power, to develop their own institutional agendas aligned with imperatives inherent in their nature and structure that are not wholly under the control even of the people who own and manage them. These agendas center on increasing their own profits and protecting themselves from the uncertainty of the market. They arise from a combination of market competition, the demands of financial markets, the efforts by individuals within them to advance their careers and increase their personal income. Large corporations commonly join forces to advance shared political and economic agendas. In the United States, they have been engaged for more than 150 years in restructuring the rules and institutions of governance to suit their interests. Some readers may feel uneasy with my anthropomorphizing the corporation, but I do so advisedly, because once-created corporations tend to take on a life of their own beyond the intentions of their human participants. Corporations have emerged as the dominant governance institutions on the planet, with the largest among them reaching into virtually every country of the world and exceeding most governments in size and power. Increasingly, it is the corporate interest rather than the human

---

[148] See Tabor 2006 for discussion of related issues to do with the education system.
[149] 2005, 2.

interest that defines the policy agendas of states and international bodies.[150]

The idea that Professor Korten illustrates for us, and which I will build upon in this section, is that the ultramassive monopolistic corporations are like an ant colony or an ocean: *the individual constituents/members/units* (in this analogy I am giving, these are the ants or water droplets, which represent the individual workers of a corporation) cannot individually control the overall activity of *the whole* (in this analogy, the whole is the entire ant colony or the ocean, which represent the entire corporation). The entire structure is beyond the control of the individual constituents.

Abstract corporatism involves two critical illusions that workers must be fooled into believing:

A. That a corporation is not just the activity of the workers, but is something greater than that, something beyond and far more powerful than any worker is—namely the corporation itself. But what, exactly, "the corporation" is, is never defined for the worker (or for anybody else), and how a corporation can be more than the workers, and the worker production that makes it up, is never explained. But it does not matter—as long as the worker is merely fooled into believing that she/he is small and inconsequential next to the corporation, which is somehow greater than, and supervenient upon, the workers, the worker will not think of questioning her smallness, and she will never gain her innate autonomy and power.

B. The worker cannot control the abstract idea of the supervenient corporation discussed in A, so the worker should submit and give in to the corporations, and should devote her servitude to whatever the abstract supervenient corporation may need of her.

A and B compose a dreamworld: a picture of non-reality, a picture of that which *does not exist*. Without worker behavior and activity, there is no corporation—not one single bit of it is left—and thus, "the corporation" can only describe the activity of *the workers*, no more, no less. And the abstract corporation—the idea that the corporation is something that is greater than the workers and the production of the workers—is only an idea of something that does not exist.

It is critical to the controlling corporatists that the workers not awaken from this dream. They could awaken if they were merely given reason to question, and to examine their life and their circumstances. Questioning is an act of sobering up, waking up—it is raw realization—and that is, it seems, why politicians and Big Media ridicule "the skeptic," which they often describe with derogatory language. In the acclaimed BBC documentary, *The Century of the*

---

[150] Korten 2006, 59-60.

Self,[151] which is all about case studies of how corporations have carried out deliberate and secret plans and programs to brainwash entire nations of people so that the people will spend money in the specific ways that corporations want them to, a person who spoke in the documentary named "Countess Erziekarolyi" discussed society in the late Victorian Age in Europe (which is in some sense similar to the society of helpless, non-questioning workers I have just described, who are engineered and trained to follow, to not question, and do not develop or focus on themselves and their passions—for if they did, they could not continue to be the thoughtless, soulless cogs that I have just described). Countess Erziekarolyi eloquently elaborates on what happens to the ideas one has if one begins to *examine* them:

> Of course you were just not allowed to show your bloody feelings, you just couldn't... But it was Freud that put that thought very much into question, because, you see, to examine yourself, you would have to put a lot of other things into question, your society, everything that's around you, and that wasn't a good thing at that time... because your self-created empire you've created would have fallen into bits.

Thus, workers must be fooled and brainwashed, with various sorts of tactics that I discuss at various places in this book (fear, distraction, busyness, TV, desperation, entertainment, illusory beliefs that their predicament is wonderful and inevitable, etc.), in order to keep her/him in control: not skeptical, not scientific in spirit and mind, dejected and the owner of a crushed soul.

It is just by the worker's *ideas* that a corporation exists; and the corporation is an abstract *idea* that tyrannizes the mind of the worker. In other words, corporatism is *abstract tyranny*.

When people gather together to form a corporation in a corporatist empire, in that corporatized environment, the workers assume specific tyrannized behaviors when they are at the corporation, such as often acting against their feelings or denying their feelings,[152] typically performing work that, to some degree, they do not like, often wearing clothes they do not want to wear, putting up with oppressive conditions for *low* pay, often discussing issues and topics

---

[151] This aired on the BBC in 2002, created by Adam Curtis. I learned about this documentary from Alex Jones's web site, and the documentary was posted on his website:
http://www.infowars.com/articles/science/psychology_freud_was_used_control_the_m asses.htm.

[152] To my knowledge, this has become standard, "normal," and expected behavior among people in the United States, to the extent that the person who allows their self to just feel however they feel (or, as the Buddhist, Alan Watts said in his classic text, *The Way of Zen*: "the way you feel is the right way"), for example, letting oneself feel sadness without Prozac, is a sign of somebody who is now viewed to be deranged or disturbed for simply letting those feelings flow, without resorting to some sort of "therapy."

they are not genuinely concerned with and which they might be discussing merely out of boredom, and so on.

Worker Against Worker, Fighting for the Corporatists

Now combine this with the fact that workers are taught in various ways to not cohere and unify with one another while on the job in a way that develops camaraderie between them. For example, workers are paid different wages, they are treated more as slaves or children than as adults, and that makes them tend to treat one another as such also, due to the fact that they are given positions that have different levels of prestige and income, and they are favored or disfavored in different ways by bosses. (Similar issues exist in schools and in families, where teachers and parents will unknowingly spread their approval to children in a differential rather than uniform way, which generates rivalries, competition, spite, approval-seeking, and general lack of confidence that can often last a person's entire life.) These and other issues often generate spiteful competition between workers rather than a sense of togetherness. While workers are generally told by corporatists that they should "work together" when at work at the corporations, this however will not happen when the worker who earns minimum wage and has little prestige, will, for example, tend to be jealous and spiteful of the worker who earns more money and has more prestige (but may do less work, such as in the case of a manager). For these and other reasons, "working together" can only tend to be a strident affair among the laborers: order out of chaos.

Combining these two points about workers, we can see why workers do not form strong alliances, and, for example, they are largely unable to form well-organized non-violent or even Thoreauvian/Gandhistic boycotts or labor unions. Furthermore, for the reasons just given, we can see why the American worker is, in general, alone, isolated, and powerless—unable to control the reality of her/his world (i.e., of her/his corporatized existence). These issues show us how readily workers can be tricked into sacrificing their rationality and their power (i.e., their "strength in numbers") to a mere idea: that there is something over-and-above them, something greater than the workers—namely the corporation—but where this idea is just an illusion, since there are, and always have been, only the workers that power economy.

Corporatized Existence is the End of Life

It is staggering how much the worker will sacrifice her spirit and her passion for this *idea*, called "the corporation, that she somehow imagines is over-and-above her. *Think about it*, the worker will give up his/her family, leisure time, and consciousness in order to spend nearly all of her waking hours at an occupation that she most likely does not even enjoy, or likely even bitterly hates. Is this any sort of a life?

In her corporatized state of existence, the worker is endlessly pushed around by the forces of her corporatized life, unable to change her destiny, and the worker likely will gain the idea that the corporation is a force beyond her or him, and thus some degree of helplessness is all that is left. This is what the lifestyle of the average American is rooted in, and its end result is the TV-culture that pervades America: Americans are helpless, with unfulfilled passions, with no time to figure out who they are or what is happening in the world around them—they are lost, and only the TV is left for them—their nightly best-friend. To paraphrase what Leuren Moret once said about television and media: by filling their minds with television, Americans fill their homes with their own mind-control devices. It is the corporatized, helpless, slave-like existence of the American laborer that helps make the televisual addiction so catchy. When there is little hope and little enjoyment, addiction is a luxury, since seeking out and delving into one's passions is impossible, and only a desperate *escape* from life seems practical.

From the reasoning just given, we can see that Americans are tricked into going along with tyrannical treatment, sacrificing their time, their families, their passions, their peace of mind, their consciousness, and even their safety, for "the corporation" and for the Orwellian-corporatized life. We can see why Americans so often give up so much for corporatism if we analyze a principle from science and which I just touched on: *the world creates a person's thoughts and behaviors*. A setting or environment one exists amid determines their thought and action,[153] and thus an environment of tyrannization leads to the aforementioned life of corporatized experience, where even something like family, for example, is fully sacrificed.

When I enter a football game, I suddenly may start screaming, or when I go to a funeral, I may act sullen and/or quiet. When my students come to class, I never fail to see them behave "appropriately," transforming right before my eyes from garrulous and smiley students, for example, as they enter the room, into studious people who sit straight, look forward, don't talk (at least most of the time, and depending on how interesting my class is), keep a deadpan face, and so on. The *action*, and the carrying out of certain *behavior*, of gathering in a certain way (such as going to a funeral, to a football game, or gathering and sitting in a college classroom), gives rise to an *idea* in a person's mind (e.g., I am a student), which causes behavior (e.g., I am supposed to be studious). This is how *environment creates thought, which creates behavior*.

---

[153] This is in line with the idea from social science introduced above, where it was discussed that a person is considered to be a product of their environment, not of their own free will—this is the *scientific* perspective of a person, rather than a metaphysical account. This does not indicate that a person does not have any degree of freedom (though it may lead to that), it merely means that most persons spontaneously evolve to be persons that are endlessly thrown around hopelessly by the forces of life, rather than to developing and learning autonomy.

This becomes more poignant when we consider a situation where an environment is one of corporatism, such as with the United States and the global economy, where people are oppressed into becoming thoughtless flesh, where their limbs move around without purpose or choice, where their minds are crushed into dust, and where they can be tricked into becoming supporters of the madness and irrationality of a no-family state, of despiritualization, of war, of pervasive Orwellianism, and of a situation where people can be tricked into devoting their selfhood and most of their dynamism to an unsatisfying, death-star life.

The Rise of Anarchist Corporatism

"Own nothing! Possess nothing! Buddha and Christ taught us this, and the Stoics and the Cynics. Greedy though we are, why can't we seem to grasp that simple teaching? Can't we understand that with property we destroy our soul?

Own only what you can always carry with you: know languages, know countries, know people. Let your memory be your travel bag. Use your memory! Use your memory! It is those bitter seeds alone which might sprout and grow someday. Look around you—there are people around you."

—Alexander Solzhenitsyn

It is the *ideas* in the minds of people that give existence to the fascist corporations. All that workers need to do is change their perspective about their environment, recognizing that a corporation is *only the workers*, is fully and only powered by the workers—if workers only knew this, their behavior and their lives would cease to be corporatized.

In such a scenario, the corporations would become the anarchistic corporations discussed in chapter 1, rather than the fascistic corporations I have been discussing in this chapter. This is essentially what Gandhi taught when he helped workers liberate India when they pushed the British out: do not participate in fascistic corporatism, do not invest in it, do not put your money or energy into it, and if that is done then it ceases to have power and it will cease to exist (and anarchistic corporatism will rise in its place). In other words, fascistic corporatism (where the people are powerless and corporatized) would spontaneously transform into anarchistic corporatism (where the people genuinely have the power).

It starts by small, incremental movements, when a citizenry gradually begins to, for example, return to the idea of acquiring food themselves, or from local farmers who have healthy crops and grass-fed undrugged livestock (for those people who consume animal products) that are free to run about on a pasture, rather than the vegetables and meat from Wal-Mart, which is poisonous, irradiated, and is a product of a eugenicist-corporatist food industry. Then after that, another step is made, where one builds a water well, or one recognizes that continuing to support US government taxation is robbing them, and is supporting child murder in Iraq (via depleted uranium poisoning, for example), and so on.

The Helpless, Infantine Workers
of the Abstract Corporatist Death Star

When workers "go along with the system," and when they give their energy and spirit to the corporation (rather than to their family or their own interests or self-sustenance), and when they agree to abstract corporatism by forming the idea that the corporation is an "entity" that is above them, controlling them, rather than being an instrument of *their* control, in that situation, bosses are all-powerful.

In the case of abstract tyranny, concepts like "Dupont," "FDA," "Halliburton," "Federal Reserve," "Thomson-Wadsworth," "Carlyle Group," "US Postal Service," "Merck," "CIA," "Monsanto," and so on, are themselves unflinching, tyrannizing forces, subduing all members of the corporation (except the corporatists controlling them) to their force, where it is imagined that the person is nothing, and the corporation is everything (i.e., the corporation is the only worthwhile or real thing, and the worker is insignificant to it and must serve it). In reality, it is the other way around: there are only the workers, and there is nothing over-and-above them.

In this situation, when the worker-power, worker-autonomy, and worker-camaraderie is obliterated and not known to the workers, the possibility of anarchism (anarchistic corporatism) is destroyed, and "bosses" are imagined to be needed to help the workers understand how to work. The bosses help the workers work not for themselves, but for the abstractum ("the corporation").

Under this system, workers will be taught that they are cogs, not brains; expendable, not soulful; despiritualized, rather spiritual and literally electrical flesh. They will thus learn to imagine themselves as incapable of, or uninterested in, investing in the corporation (due to their being so little reward or fulfillment for doing so), and thus they will have to work by force, and they assume a demeanor where they take orders and learn to be followers of orders, where they just seek to be "taken care of," rather than to assume some level of assertiveness. These sorts of patterns emerge among the behavior of despiritualized, corporatized workers because there is no self-investment in corporatism (fascistic corporatism). When such factors are present, corporations—whether they are big or small—contain a tight top-down power structure, *from* the most powerful member(s) of the corporation, down *to* the mass of menial laborers and office vassals, due to the fact that despiritualized workers will be so often unmotivated, and must be forced to carry out the tasks of their toil. More specifically, corporations involve a *tyrannical* power structure. They involve a cold, feelingless, empty, plastic communistic, and often fandangle-filled aura—like a perfumed, Huxleyan version of Vader's Death Star—replete with bored denizens who only know the veneer of life and the veneer of their own self (if even that), and who are lost, since they have been tricked (via the education and media systems) into not understanding what reality involves or what their self is, since they've undergone a lifetime of brainwashing.

Americans live under full corporatized experience everyday, and it touches every part of them, but oddly, it is an idea that typically does not enter their conscious awareness (even though they are conscious of it at some level), since they are tricked into believing they are free—*freedom is slavery*, as the Orwellian party slogan goes.

Ultimate Corporatist Power: Basic Life Needs are Monopolized by Corporations

Abstract corporatism is the ultimate reason that corporatism is successful. People become imprisoned by corporatism, and they are tricked into letting their food, water, fuel, labor, health care, clothing, homes, education, minds, and any other basic life needs *go into the control of the corporatists.* Under this communistic domination, the corporatists are given the power to sell (for profit), tax, and incrementally inflate the prices of, and control the flow of, the basic items that the people need to live. In such a system as this, if a person is to live at all, they must comply and obey fascism, lest they not have basic life necessities, and they die. Therefore, the RP will not only go along with corporatistical oppression, they will even learn to actually defend and fight for it, and they will protect it and sacrifice everything for it—they will give their lives to the very corporations that have eclipsed their humanness and dissolved their consciousnesses.

A simple way to discuss this issue is as follows. A large percentage of Americans do not like their jobs, but despite this fact, they typically will *fight* to keep them and perform well at them, lest they risk putting their survival in question. It can be predicted that in this sort of a system, one will do what is needed to acquire basic life resources, and thus the masses will become unquestioning, unflinching soldiers for, and defenders of, the corporatist horror-state. Therefore, each day, in America, there will be swarms and hordes of people who travel to despiritualized, passionless occupations that they despise and which take them far away from their inborn lust for life and self, and from their families, and instead they will invest their time and kismet into building up the corporation they are entrapped by, working often in a state of desperation to "please the boss" so as not to be "terminated." For the most part, this will hold true from the bottom all the way up to the top. Each person locked in the pyramidal social system is usually afraid of losing their positioning, and that fear keeps the system in place. People are tricked into believing that they must work at a *corporation*, rather than a personal *farm*, to, for example, acquire food (which is extremely inexpensive if one uses indigenous farming techniques, and additionally, it is much more healthy, and it only takes about the same amount of time weekly that it takes to make a few trips to the grocery store that is loaded with Monsanto products). Thus, people are tricked into believing that the corporation is all there is for them, and thus they are tricked into believing that it is their life-force, when that is clearly not the case. This is how abstract tyranny tricks the citizenry into fighting for their own corporatized experience: the citizenry is fooled into believing that there is only the corporation, and nothing else.

For a member of the RP in this network, what their personal feelings say about what they must do while in this hierarchical pyramid, is irrelevant. For example, if a person's positioning in the corporate-communist hierarchy involves oppression, humiliation, misery, too much time away from their families, and so on, they will simply have to "deal with it." They cannot rock the boat lest they risk termination. Thoughts, appearance, behaviors, work practices, and opinions that appear in the bosses eyes to be far enough outside acceptable range, can get worker "terminated." Imagine the burger-flipper at McDonalds trying to tell her boss the following: "I don't think my wages are enough to support a family," or "these burgers are not healthy and thus we should cook something else for people to eat." Even though these comments are empirically verifiable, they will likely be considered humorous, irrelevant, offensive, or even those of a troublemaker, and they almost certainly won't be considered to be true, by "the boss."

Only the *top-down power structure* of the corporation matters, and this is a basic issue in how the corporation remains truly fascist, regardless if a specific corporate setting is a somewhat placid or reasonable situation, or is a "Death Star."

USA-Style Tyranny

Having discussed the three ways that the United States is a corporatist system, I will next discuss a few more specific details of corporatism.

Typically when Americans think or talk about dictatorship or tyranny, they appear to imagine that dictatorships and tyrannies are primarily found in the contemporary third-world regimes, or past regimes like Nazi Germany, Caligula's Rome, Soviet Russia, Red China, or Saddam's Iraq. And Americans usually believe that a tyranny is a system where there is literally one all-powerful ruler. Webster's dictionary gives three definitions of "tyranny," and the second one involves this *one-person-rules-all* idea:

> **1** : oppressive power <every form of *tyranny* over the mind of man -- Thomas Jefferson>; *especially* : oppressive power exerted by government <the *tyranny* of a police state>
> **2 a:** a government in which absolute power is vested in a single ruler; *especially* : one characteristic of an ancient Greek city-state **b** : the office, authority, and administration of a tyrant

3 : a rigorous condition imposed by some outside agency or force (living under the *tyranny* of the clock -- Dixon Wecter)

Considering definition 2, tyranny as the "single ruler," we can easily discover that this is simply an incorrect definition of the word "tyranny," if we merely take a look at the examples of tyrannies that exist today and that have existed through history, such as those just mentioned. All one has to do is look at the structure of the Nazi regime, for example, wherein one would see that Hitler surely possessed all-powerfulness, *but so did a few other tyrants in that regime* (Himmler, etc.). Hitler did not truly dictate everything in Nazi Germany, and he did not dictate everything that his immediate commanders did, and therefore, Germany did not involve "a single ruler," as Webster's Dictionary would have us believe. For example, Goering, a top commander right next to Hitler in the Third Reich, rather autonomously created the Gestapo (secret police) that was so influential in the way the entire Nazi regime's reign of terror played out. Goering's very act of creating this institution reveals that he had some all-powerfulness, and that he was not in servitude to Hitler. The "single ruler" idea of tyranny is a fabricated, unrealistic description of the tyrannies that Americans glom on to, and it has very little or no basis in empirical reality.

The following diagram illustrates the real power structure in a corporatist, tyrannical state, where there are a *multiple* heads that have all-powerful control, rather than "a single ruler" holding that power. In this diagram, the circles represent persons in the corporatist system, the arrows represent a direction of power (notice that the top circles do not have arrows that lead to them, designating how they are all-powerful tyrant-corporatists), and the arrows of power only go one way: top-down.

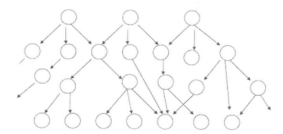

For reasons given above, the surprisingly widely held idea that tyrannies involve a single ruler is unfounded and is to be rejected. Instead, it is more appropriate to define "tyranny" as a system where there are multiple all-powerful savage leaders, and *not* "a single ruler."

The accurate definition of tyranny just given is precisely what corporatism involves: multiple all-powerful governing heads that control and terrorize the citizenry. This definition of tyranny and corporatism is more about the control of resources, the oppression of the people, and the dejection of the citizenry under the corporatist and/or tyrannical state—which is precisely what I have outlined in my three accounts of corporatism I have given in this chapter: the structure of corporatism, lived corporatism, and abstract corporatism.

The arrows in the diagram represent the one-way power-relationship of control from the top to the bottom—a one-way channel of authority from corporatist down to the lowliest vassals. The diagram roughly exhibits four rows, which resemble four layers of power, the top being the most powerful and the second the second-most powerful, and so on. The top layer represents the corporatists (the "board of directors," the members of the secret society, the owner(s), the top shareholders, the unseen bankers pulling the strings behind-the-scenes, perhaps the CEO, and so on). As we will see in a later chapter, the second layer is the lobbyists and think tanks, or any person or institution that acts as a go-between or a line of communication between the invisible-secret corporatist government and the visible government. Therefore, the visible government is the third row of power. The fourth row represents "We the People," and it includes the smaller corporatists (so-called "small business" or "mid-sized business") who are, for the most part, not influential, powerless, not in control of resources, and who are pushed around by the all-powerful monopolistic corporatists just as much as anybody else in the fourth row (which includes anyone from homeless people to non-masonic Hollywood stars), even though the smaller corporatists also function as a corporatist governing body, mimicking their distant ultra-massive monopolistic relatives.

This is a very different picture of the power structure of the United States that people are used to considering, where they imagine, for example, that George W. Bush is the power-person, and he is acting autonomously and spontaneously. It may seem that George W. Bush is acting on his own when he decides to carry out an action autonomously, such as signing what political activists have called "the torture bill" (H.R. 6166 of the 109th Congress, which was later passed as S3930, the Military Commissions Act; Bush signed this "legislation" in fall of 2006), or setting a record for not vetoing bills from Congress, as he did in Spring 2006.

One of the principal reasons that Americans do not understand, and will not consider as possible, the empirically verifiable idea that there is a secret corporatist government that controls the world, is because George W. Bush and other members of the visible government are astoundingly good actors: professionally trained liars, as Alex Jones has said.[154] The average American is distracted by television and the education system, they are very busy working heavy hours each week, and they are taught from a very young age—via the education system—to trust government and politicians, and to not be critical, skeptical, shrewd thinkers and observers, and thus they do not look carefully at a politicians' real activities from day-to-day, week-to-week, year-to-year. They only look at the façade, which is, for example, Bush's smiling face and what his

---

[154] Infowars.com radio show, May 16, 2007.

CFR partner, Hillary Clinton, once referred to as his "charm."[155] The average American does not live in a secret world of deceit, and since the face/actor side of a politician they on see CNN or FOX News reminds them of an ordinary person, it is extremely difficult for them to believe politicians are working as low-level agents of a secret, Machiavellian, masonic cult that controls the world and pleasures in terrorizing the world-citizenry.

Objection: Consumers Control Demand, and Thus Control Corporations.

Here is a common objection I have received to what has been written in this chapter: consumers' choices determine which product the corporation creates, and thus the control is in the hands of the consumer, not the corporation, since the consumer controls the corporation's interests, not the other way around.

This objection involves the widespread illusion that consumers are making the choices about which products they buy. This idea is against the very basis of marketing, which is a means of usurping consumer choice, and is a way of manipulating the consumer to buy product x, which is often a product they don't want or need, and also to manipulate the consumer to specifically buy product x rather than product y, even if x is an inferior product. The consumer is therefore not free to choose, but instead is fooled into believing he can choose, and instead she/he has been controlled. Brainwashing expert, Taylor, writes about this issue:

> Advertising is not coercive, but it is a deliberate attempt to change minds. Companies do not promote their products by accident, and their aim is primarily to increase their profits by removing money from customers... Advertising certainly aims to change belief. The advertiser wants to alter your cognitive landscape such that your previous indifference, aversion, or total ignorance vis-à-vis Brand X is replaced by a more favorable attitude toward it.[156]

This is a basic marketing issue that business students are taught in their college business classes: to sell product x, the seller must not merely sit back and let the consumer tell them what they want, but rather the seller is to influence and change the mind of the consumer (which is to prohibit their free choice in favor of the interests of the seller). This is the basis of marketing: don't let the buyer buy what she wants, but rather what the marketer/seller wants her to buy, where the superiority, quality, or necessity of the product is typically a secondary or tertiary issue.

---

[155] See "Stubborn Facts on the Ground," ABC News, May 10, 2006, by March Halperin, David Chalian, Teddy Davis, Jonathan Berger, Sarah Baker, and Emily O'Donnell.
[156] Taylor 2004, 52-53.

It is common that a poorer quality product will out-sell a superior quality product to the point that the superior quality product will become extinct. To verify this, all one needs to do is make note of the many examples where products flooded into American households that were products of lower quality than other competing products out on the market. A good example is Monsanto: Monsanto foods, which are shockingly poisonous, and are surely responsible for many of the cancer and other epidemics spreading around the nation, have virtually replaced most of the healthy foods that once existed in the grocery stores.

Also consider the VHS tape, which is a famous case that is often referred to in college marketing classes. It dominated the home movie market when that industry took off in the 1980s, but it was far inferior to its competitor, the so-called *Beta tape*. For a while, one could buy each product, but soon Beta disappeared, and one could only buy VHS tapes.

Other examples are easily found: EVs (electric cars) were replaced by oil/gas powered cars, chemotherapy replaced amigdalyn-based (i.e., nitrilocide-based) diet as cancer prevention (chemotherapy, however, causes cancer, and there is no evidence that it cures it[157]) paper money replaced precious metals as monetary exchange,[158] and so on. Why are battery-powered portable radios filling the store shelves, but solar powered portable radios are hard to find in stores? Why did dangerous non-stick Teflon cookware and cooking pans[159] largely replace the safer old-fashioned pans to the store shelves? Why are pollutive, noisy gas-powered scooters used world-wide in the nations that rely on scooter transportation (Italy, many Asian countries, etc.) rather than silent, ultra-non-pollutive fuel-cell scooters used (such as the one that the New Mexico company, Manhattan Scientifics, has patented and has won numerous top awards for)? Why are dubious, error-filled, vacuous, and *incredibly* expensive "textbooks" being used in universities, rather than relatively cheaper research books that professors publish by the thousands each year on every topic one can imagine? The list is almost endless, and it seems to me that the RP hardly seems to notice.

Before moving on, I will consider a few more examples of how inferior products make it to market and superior products go unnoticed. One of the very largest and most widely used consumer goods is *media*. As mentioned above,

---

[157] See "The Nitrilosides (Vitamin B-17)-Their Nature, Occurrence and Metabloic Significance (Antineoplastic Vitamin B-17)," *Journal of Applied Nutrition*, 1970, by Ernst T. Krebs Jr., Vol. 22, No 3/4. Also see *Cancer Doesn't Scare Me Anymore*, a DVD lecture by Dr. Lorraine Day, where she discusses these issues" (available at www.drday.com), Rockford Press, Thousand Palms, CA. Lectures were given and recorded in early 2000s.

[158] See Smith 2001.

[159] See "Harmful Teflon Chemical To Be Eliminated by 2015," Washington Post, January 26, 2006, Juliet Eilperin, page A1.

the media has become a "rich person's media," where the non-rich person's interests are not addressed in the mass media, and they are perpetually ignored and are deliberately covered-up. So the consumer has no choice but to accept their media as being the corporatists' media (unless they use the internet, which for the moment is still *somewhat* controlled by the people). Similar arguments could be given about other items that Americans purchase. For example, war, secret government, senators, prisons, government policymakers, and military, are items that Americans pay unimaginable amounts of money for (via taxation), but like the media, it's also the case that military, war, secret and visible government, and prisons, are things that are completely beyond the control of the average person (e.g., did Americans vote on the troop increase of Iraq in January 2007, which occurred just after the Democrats took control of Congress?). Media, government, and military are corporatist entities that come into being and exist far beyond the volition and consciousness of the average individual American citizen.

There are no better examples of the inferior product coming to market than in the drug industry (Big Pharma). Dr. Angell, formerly of the *New England Journal of Medicine*, writes: "What's true of the eight-hundred pound gorilla is true of the colossus that is the pharmaceutical industry. It is used to doing pretty much what it wants to do."[160] In her book about the pharmaceutical industry (Big Pharma), which so few people know about (since it is not discussed in the national media, since the media is largely financed by Big Pharma, as you will see if you turn on Fox News and see an ad for Merck, maker of the death-drug, Vioxx), Angell writes:

> The real pharmaceutical industry… over the past two decades has moved very far from its original high purpose of discovering and producing useful new drugs. Now primarily a marketing machine to sell drugs of dubious benefit, this industry uses its wealth and power to co-opt every institution that might stand in its way, including the U.S. Congress, the Food and Drug Administration, academic medical centers, and the medical profession itself. I witnessed firsthand the influence of the industry on medical research during my two decades at *The New England Journal of Medicine*. The staple of the journal is research about causes of and treatments for disease. Increasingly, this work is sponsored by drug companies. I saw companies begin to exercise a level of control over the way research is done that was unheard of when I first came to the journal, and the aim was clearly to load the dice to make sure their drugs looked good. As an example, companies would require researchers to compare a new drug with a placebo (sugar pill) instead of with an older drug. That way, the new drug would look good even though it might actually be worse than the older one. There are other ways to bias research, and not all of them can be spotted, even by

---

[160] Angell 2005, 3.

experts. Obviously, we rejected such papers when we recognized them, but often they would turn up in other journals. Sometimes companies don't allow researchers to publish their results at all if they are unfavorable to the companies' drugs. As I saw the industry influence grow, I became increasingly troubled by the possibility that much published research is seriously flawed, leading doctors to believe new drugs are generally more effective and safer than they actually are... Instead of investing more in innovative drugs and moderating prices, drug companies are pouring money into marketing, legal maneuvers to extend patent rights, and government lobbying to prevent any form of price regulation.[161]

Control of Resources is Control of Thought, Behavior, and Life of the RP

Members of the RP like to think that they are free and autonomous, and that their behaviors, thoughts, and the overall structure of their lives, are the product of their own free will. They don't want to believe that they are controlled, shaped, and created for the purposes of being slaves and cogs for the corporatist system. But what has been shown in this chapter, and which will be further shown throughout the remainder of this book, is that thought, behavior, and life are dictated by resources, but since resources are dictated by the corporatists, then thought, behavior, and life are ultimately dictated by the corporatists. Here's a diagram illustrating what has just been spelled out so far in this chapter:

---

[161] Angell 2005, xxv - xxvii.

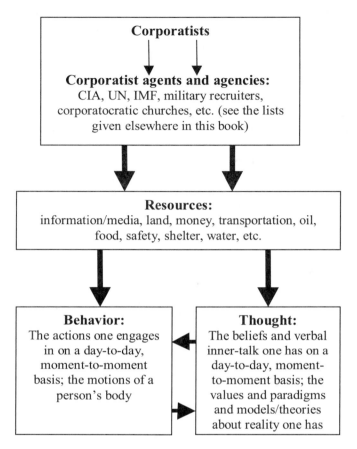

As with other diagrams in this chapter, the downward-pointed arrows indicate the direction of control and power. One can plug different values in for each of the boxes, and see how they fit into the diagram, and thus see how thought, behavior, and life is controlled by the corporatists and by corporatism.

For example, if we place the basic life resource, "information,"[162] in the middle box—the "Resources" box—we can see the following causal chain emerge:

---

[162] Information is a basic life necessity/resource because, ultimately, it is language, and without language, the human cannot function—analogous to how a human cannot function if they do not have food, water, or safety.

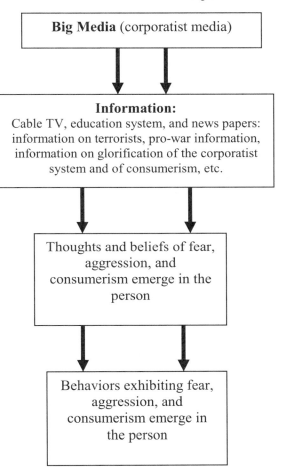

Conclusion

In this chapter I have proven that a group of monopolistic corporatists controls the entire world, from the resources human use, to how much money they have, to the very thoughts they possess or the behaviors they exhibit. For that reason, I have proven that a secret corporatist government exists, and controls the entire world. I have also shown that this secret government is eager to psychologically, socially, and physically torment the citizens of the world. The corporatists who control the entire world in secret have various tools and techniques they use to exercise their control: lawmaking, money, banking, lobbying, war, poverty, entertainment, consumerism, stock markets, false flag terrorism, monopolization, vaccines, fear, media control, public education systems, disease and contamination of people, pervasive surveillance, communism, and religion, among others (all of these will be discussed in later chapters).

This book is about how the corporatists push into every part of a person's life—everything from how a person talks, to how they dress, to how much time and what kind of time they have with their families, their thoughts and actions, and so on. The typical American has their mind inculcated by politicians, media personalities, and often educators, with repetitious conditioning: "you are free!" "you live in a democracy!" "the United States is the freest country!" "democracy is the only legitimate form of government!" "the standard of living of an American is the best of any people in any country in the world!" "the American health care system is the best in the world!" "We need to get those terrorists."

But we have seen many examples so far in this book that show that the freedom so often discussed in America is very hard to find anywhere, in any person. There is no shyness of employers to impose anti-family tyranny on the lives of workers. Consider this example of boss-worker discourse, which is from the film, *The Matrix*, but which is so realistic that it could be the sort of sermon that many workers in America will receive tomorrow at work:

> "You have a problem with authority Mr. Anderson. *You* believe that you are *special*, that somehow the rules do not *apply* to you. Obviously you are mistaken. This company is one of the top software companies in the world, because every single employee understands that they are part of a *whole*. Thus if an employee has a problem, the *company* has a problem. The time has come to make a *choice*, Mr. Anderson: either you choose to be at your desk on time from this day forth, or you choose to find yourself another job. *Do I make myself clear?*"

Notice how the way this is put makes it appear that the employee is not being reasonable with the tyrannical circumstances of this fascist/non-democratic situation, and notice that there is the ever-present attempt to put forth the illusion that people have choices and freedom ("The time has come to make a *choice*, Mr. Anderson…"). The *ownership* that an employer has over a worker's life and a worker's time is so natural to American culture, as if it were a normal and natural part of reality, that Americans have largely lost the ability to see that it is fascism pervading their lives. Americans have learned to believe fascism is freedom—*that freedom is slavery*.

3   Corporate Communism

People in the Midwest do not understand—this is a Socialist country. —Dwayne
Andreas, Chairman of Archer Daniels Midland Corporation[163]

If you stop paying the taxes on your property, you will find out very quickly that you
don't really own that property.

—George Whitehurst-Beery, economist, on the Rense Radio Show, May 11, 2006

Your commie has no regard for human life, not even his own. And for this reason, men,
I want to impress on you the need for extreme watchfulness. The enemy may come
individually, or he may come in strength, he may even come in the uniform of our own
troops. But however he comes we must stop him... Trust no one! — From the Stanley
Kubrick film *Dr. Strangelove*

The Mechanics of a Corporatist Nation

To understand American corporatism, it is essential to understand the clear
and simple reasons why the United States is a *communist* nation. That is the
goal of this chapter. Understanding this will help readers of this book to more
fully understand the circumstances and destiny of their lives while living in the
corporatist horror-state. In describing American corporate communism in this
chapter, I will first discuss a few more details about corporatism that will help
in understanding American communism, and then I will use the majority of this
chapter to thoroughly discuss American communism.

The Systems of Government

It is no longer very controversial to assert that the idea that the United States
is a "democracy" is unfounded. Democracy is the scenario where the
conformist RP—the "mob," or "we the people"—have control: the majority of
a population of a nation (which tends to be the poorer groups) holds the power
and structures the culture. It is quite obvious that the United States is not a
democracy, and that very few genuine democracies have ever existed.

Democracy is different from oligarchy, which is a societal structure where
only a few people hold power. Many researchers (e.g., Tarpley 2006) hold that
the United States is an oligarchy, but for reasons I gave in chapter 2 (especially
where I discussed *lived corporatism*), it seems that oligarchy is not an adequate
description of America since nearly all Americans live under tyrannization and
exemplify corporatized experience and crushed selfhood. Oligarchy and
corporatism are indeed very similar, but oligarchy only involves a description
of culture as a state where small groups or a few people rule. Thus, oligarchy is
a description of the political world that does not go far enough: it does not
emphasize that government is always an instrument of terror, war, torture, and

---

[163] Cited in Thorn 2003, 217.

general horror, which is the essence of *corporatism*—which is a *fascistic* system (unless it is the aforementioned anarchistic corporatism, which is not typically included in the definition of "corporatism"). Thus, descriptions of oligarchy must always collapse into descriptions of corporatism.

A fascist society is similar to oligarchy in that a small group of people hold the control, as discussed in chapter 2. The point of defining a nation as oligarchical is to point out that there is a huge difference between how many people are controlled versus how many people are the controllers. This is different from fascist governments, which are defined as those which possess strictly Orwellian characteristics, which is why I have referred to fascist nations as *horror-states*. As discussed, this is why America is *fascist*, and not oligarchic.

A corporatist societal structure is one which is composed of more than one fascist government. More specifically, a corporatist nation is comprised of two or more fascist regimes within the nation that are each

1. Largely autonomous
2. Interrelated and collaborating with one another
3. In control of resources and behavior,
4. Create misery for the citizens (the RP, the workers) in the regimes.

For these reasons, in a corporatist system (such as the current global American and global corporatocracy), "nations" do not exist, and they are merely fabricated ideas that the RP latches on to but which have no foundation in reality. What exists are, rather, the Orwellian-monopolistic corporate dictatorships, which supplant nations, and thus which render the entire world fascistic.

If there is Government, then Government Oppression is *Inevitable*

The reader who has a grasp of history knows that it is not just corporatism and fascism that involve tragic oppression of world citizens. It is nearly impossible to find examples where democracy or quasi-democracy (e.g., contemporary Brazil) does not involve severe oppression by a government against the citizenry. Likewise, fascism, corporatism, and oligarchy appear to always involve oppression of people. There is a reason for this: all systems of government involve oppression by rulers against the people due to the fact that if one person or group has power and/or authority over another person or group, the group in power cannot be trusted to keep that power in check; and there are nearly no instances that show that it is *ever* kept in check.

(The only one I can think of is the Tibetan Buddhists, who now live in exile outside of China, and have a largely quasi-fascistic power structure, but where oppression among their leaders has for centuries remained peculiarly low or non-existent. Therefore, strictly speaking, Tibetan Buddhists are not fascists since they are not savage oppressors, and thus they might be better described as having a non-violent power structure.)

Fractal Corporatism

We have seen in chapter 2, and we will more clearly see in this chapter, that the United States is corporatistical: it consists of pods of fascist assemblages, which in turn consist of fascist elements, wherein the nation is a fractal-like fascist plexus, from the lowliest slave to the wealthiest corporatist-banker. Consider the diagram below that illustrates the fractal corporatist structure of the United States.

Notice that the diagram only consists of *circles*. In other words, the whole nation (which is a circle) resembles the corporations (which are also represented as circles) and the departments of corporations (which are also circles). The nation fits the definition of corporatist system, but so do corporations and parts of corporations. From the ground-up, and the top-down, all layers and levels of the United States are fascist-corporatist, where the part and the whole are nearly indistinguishable. In other words, everywhere one looks there is corporatism: corporatist misery creeps into and pervades all of culture—from the family to the classroom to the doctor's office to the workplace. Icke lucidly discusses this fractal corporatism, where he uses the word "illuminati" to denote the monopolistic corporatists:

> The Illuminati have created a pyramid structure throughout society that allows them to operate a global agenda that only a relative handful of people know exists. It is like those Russian dolls with one doll inside anther with the biggest one encompassing all of them... Every organization today is a pyramid. The few at the top know what the organization is really about and what it is trying to achieve. The further you go down the pyramid the more people work for the organization, but the less they know about its real agenda. They are only aware of the individual job they do every day. They have no idea how their contribution connects with that of other employees in other areas of the company. They are compartmentalized from that knowledge and told only what they need to know to do their work. These smaller pyramids, like the local branch of a bank, fit into bigger and bigger pyramids, until eventually you have the pyramid that encompasses all the banks. It is the same with the transnational corporations, political parties, secret societies, media empires, and the military. If you go high enough, all the transnational corporations (like the oil cartel), major political parties, secret societies, media empires, and the military (via NATO, for instance), are controlled by the same pyramids and the same people who sit at the top of all the pyramids. In the end there is a global pyramid that encompasses all the others...[164]

---

[164] Icke 2001, 5-6.

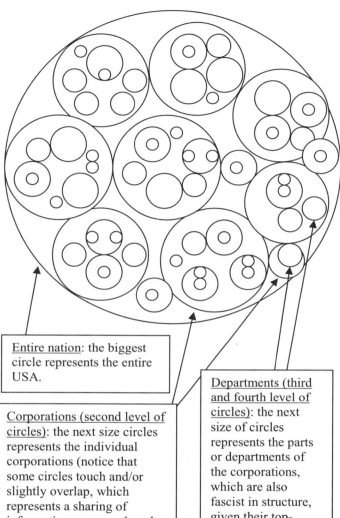

Entire nation: the biggest circle represents the entire USA.

Corporations (second level of circles): the next size circles represents the individual corporations (notice that some circles touch and/or slightly overlap, which represents a sharing of information, personnel, and etc. from corporation-to-corporation.

Departments (third and fourth level of circles): the next size of circles represents the parts or departments of the corporations, which are also fascist in structure, given their top-down authoritarian power structure.

Progressing from Weak Corporatism to Strong Corporatism

Stage 1: Weak Corporatism (1870 - September 11, 2001)

From the 1870s to 1970, corporations had full control of the United States,[165] but interestingly, outside of the corporations (and in school, family-life, church, etc.), and even within some of the more placid of the corporations (e.g., universities, etc.), the United States lacked many fascist elements: free speech existed to some degree, there was only a fragmentary rather than pervasive concentration labor camp system,[166] there were rare but occasional traces of a free press and information system, the US Constitution occasionally proved to be powerful in court and was largely believed to be an esteemed document (even though FDR postponed the Constitution during World War II, and even though corporations have blatantly violated the Constitution every day from 1870-1970), and so on. The United States had only the rudiments of a corporatist structure, but it nevertheless was a corporatist nation, and thus it could be called a *weak corporatist nation* compared to, for example, Nazi Germany, slave-era America, or Soviet Russia.

The corporatist structure of the United States strengthened between 1970 and 9/11, due to the increasing power of corporate-financed think tanks and lobbyists.[167] But the United States still lacked many of the elements of a genuine or full corporatist state from 1970 to 9/11.

Stage 2: Moderate Corporatism (September 11, 2001 – 2007)

It is 9/11 that has catalyzed the United States to quickly race down the path to becoming a fully corporatist state, or what can be called a strong or pure corporatist state. This state has not been fully implemented yet, since martial law, mass population reorganization into concentration camps, mass population reduction,[168] and so on, have not been yet fully put into place; rather, they are being set up to be put into place. This is what I will call moderate *corporatism*,

---

[165] See Korten 2001 and Nace 2003 for thorough analysis of this.

[166] See Herival and Wright, 2003.

[167] Korten 2001; Nace 2003.

[168] From 1970 to the time of publication of this book, what can be called *moderate population reduction* has been mainstreamed into society. This occurs with the meat diet (and consequent heart disease and other ailments), human-made diseases (like AIDS), or cancer treatments, vaccines, war, and so on. I call these moderate population reduction programs because the US population has been increasing amid these hidden genocide programs, and since the rate of mass killing is too low to be considered full-fledged genocide.

which is the state that the United States is in at the time of the publication of this book.

The principal issue in this moderate stage is this: all traces of weak corporatism have been eliminated by the corporatist controllers in favor of full corporatism, but those controllers have not begun to *fully implement* and *enforce* their state of full corporatism.

This trajectory from weak to strong corporatism can be seen in the bills Congress has passed (e.g., HR 6166 in fall 2006 [the so-called Military Commissions Act], the Patriot Act, etc.), the multiple American invasions of oil rich countries, talk of more invasions at the time of the publication of this book (such as Iran), the huge ramp-up of tracking and surveillance of the citizenry,[169] the secretive and careless behavior of the Federal Reserve (e.g., wildly increasing the money supply) in 2006 and 2007, and so on. These issues have to do with preparation for Stage 3: full corporatism.

Stage 3: Full or Genuine Corporatism
(estimated to commence some time between 2008-2014)

We will see in the last chapter of this book that US politicians, think tank members, and military generals have been announcing that if there is "a second 9/11," America will be changed into a martial law dictatorship. This has been announced and "predicted" by Newt Gingrich since 1994 (but since he is a member of the AEI, which involves many members that will be proven in a later chapter to have been complicit in 9/11, we will see that Gingrich and others have such "clairvoyance" merely because they are creating these Orwellian-style false flag events that have occurred before the publication of this book [9/11, the 2/22/06 mosque bombings in Iraq, Oklahoma City, USS Cole, etc.], and which will occur after it has been published).

The "next 9/11," to put it how Gingrich does, will bring on the start of the full stage of corporatism, and it could begin any time after this book is published. The full corporatist-Machiavellian military state could however commence by other events fabricated by the secret government, such as an

---

[169] It is possible that the government is not actually ramping up surveillance, but it could be the case that Americans have been watched for decades, and what is different *now* is that the visible government is deliberately using the corporatist media to announce that all citizens are being watched, as if to place next to all citizens the continuous conscious knowledge that they have a giant watching-eye, a big brother face, always looking at them. It is likely that this is really what is behind the media blitz since 2003 about the "secret spying" on Americans that has been going on, since we know that the government has been watching Americans for decades (Begich 2005), and there is nothing essentially new going on accompanying the new announcements of the government tracking all Americans. Therefore, what other purpose could these announcements involve than to create fear and to create the removal of the feeling of anonymity that Americans have?

attack on the American people by the secret government involving a "burst of the debt-bubble," to put it in the way that economist George Whitehurst does, in a deliberate collapse of the US dollar, a deliberately placed pandemic of weaponized bird flu or Ebola, a military-aided speedy set-up of the North American Union, and so on. All that is known is that the military state is coming; how or when is speculative.

A *full corporatist state* involves all the standard fascist elements: standardized and pervasive death camps, secret police, preemptive warfare, glorification and normalization of torture, mass poverty, tightly controlled mass-media, Orwellian-level surveillance and thought crimes, unfree speech, one-party rule, soma, forced labor (slavery), a military draft, never-ending war, unseen enemies, and so on. Many of these are already in place in the United States, and all of them can be implemented immediately, at a moment's notice, by the secret government. 2007, the year this book is published, is the final moments of what has been known as *America*.

Communist America

Now on to American corporatist communism.

A corporation is a group of people working together, most of which are underpaid, many of which might be mistreated to some greater or lesser degree, and all of which give the brunt of the time and energy of their lives to strive not primarily for their own dreams, but for the dreams of the person or persons at the very highest ranks of the corporation (the corporatists: the owner(s), the secret society members, the board of directors, etc.). Consider how Professor Korten puts the issue:

> The marvel of the corporation as a social innovation is that it can bring together hundreds of thousands of people within a single structure and compel them to act in accordance with a corporate purpose that is not necessarily their own. Those who revolt or fail to comply are expelled and replaced by others who are more compliant.[170]

The control of the corporation resides with very few people who are unelected, and who own and control the labor of all others working for the corporation. The controllers enforce certain acceptable ways of thinking and behaving, while rebuking or punishing unacceptable ways of thinking and believing. These are "thought crimes," or "behavior crimes." Working conditions are fabricated, "plastic," Orwellian, and often harsh or abusive, where the majority of workers are impoverished (since, for example, minimum wage is far below the poverty line, and even rather "well paid" workers cannot earn enough to support a family, wherein two parents must work outside the home for a living).

---

[170] Korten 2001, 74.

The corporatist that hires an employee is believed to *own* that employee's time, behavior, or even her/his thought to some significant degree while that employee is at work (and perhaps also to some significant degree outside of work, such as if the corporatist urges the worker to get enough sleep [rather than, for example, staying up late to read and to get informed about society and the world], so as to be rested for the long workday at the corporation).

Before I continue, the reader should notice something interesting here about how these details I am giving about corporations are unfolding: corporations, can be shown to have properties that are indistinguishable from the famous and haunting communist dictatorships of history (Nazi Germany, Soviet Russia, Totalist China, etc.), and corporations are even very similar to a miniature Orwellian society, such as was described in the novel, *1984*. There will be no doubt by the end of this chapter that *corporations* are communist assemblages, and they have therefore turned the United States into a communist nation.

Orwellian America

Surveillance cameras are common in many cities, monitoring tough street corners to deter crime, watching over sensitive government buildings and even catching speeders. Cameras are on public buses and in train stations, building lobbies, schools and stores. Most feed video to central control rooms, where they are monitored by security staff. The innovations could mean fewer people would be needed to watch what they record, and make it easier to install more in public places *and private homes*. (Emphasis added)
—Associated Press and Fox News, February 25, 2007[171]

Corporations have a fascist structure due to the strict top-down power arrangements that they exhibit, and due to the fact that corporations have unelected leaders who dictate commands, rather than engage in democratic power-sharing. In other words, if, for the sake of discussion, a corporation can be considered to be a nation or society, then when Americans are at work, they appear to be participating in, and they are inhabitants of, *an Orwellian-communist society*.

It is very important to note that this communistic Orwellian society that Americans participate in and devote their lives to when they are "at work" has the most extreme features of an Orwellian and communistic reality: the absence and nonexistence of family, the absence of diversity of speech, dress, behavior, total surveillance, terrorism and genocide and ultraviolence (this will be clarified below), the absence and nonexistence of reproduction and romanticism, the absence of intellectualism and critical thinking, thought crime and face crime, extreme control, and repression and restriction of the emotions, creativity, spontaneity, and movement—and that is just the beginning of the Huxleyan, Orwellian, Death Star features. (These very same features are often

---

[171] "In-Development Security Cameras to Detect Suspicious Actions," Associated Press, February 25, 2007.

what describe the home- and family-life and the neighborhoods of America also.)

The reader may be surprised by some of what I am writing there, such as how corporations can be committing mass genocide. But if that is the case, then that reader is not clear on these issues because the terrorism and genocide committed by corporatists are done in a somewhat hidden or invisible fashion: hidden in plain view. For example, vaccines are touted as being safe and helpful, but they are really instruments of genocide; also, workers are told work environments are safe, but in reality they commonly involve pollution that is lethal, as I will discuss below.

American Ideas of Communism

As we will see, this Orwellian-communist influence that the corporation has on people's lives also fully affects them outside of work-time, in more ways than most Americans realize. For the reasons just given, and for many other reasons I will point out in this chapter and the rest of this book, the structure of the United States, ironically, appears to be *communist*—the very antithesis of the way we have all been told for decades by politicians, educators, and media channels.

I am, of course, not the first to notice this similarity between corporations and communist societies. Professor Gar Alperovitz of the University of Maryland has written that

> the difference between a system dominated by General Motors and Exxon and one based upon the individual landholding farmer may very well be greater... than the difference between a system based upon large private bureaucracies in the United States and public bureaucracies in socialist nations.[172]

Words such as 'fascism" or "communism" tend to have only one sort of meaning to the typical American. As Felton writes: "'Fascism' has become such a meaningless epithet of contempt that a person cannot discuss the subject rationally, lest he be scurrilously accused of condoning the Third Reich's atrocities."[173] What Felton appears to mean is that when Americans conjure up ideas about fascism, tyranny, dictatorship, or communism, it appears that they are equating these concepts with what they know as being the most horrific regimes that they have been told about in school or on TV: Nazi Germany, Soviet Russian, Saddam's Iraq, Red China, and perhaps a few other regimes. In the academic world communism is studied in a broader fashion, and it involves study of several different sorts of political activities, taking on somewhat different forms when and where it has appeared around the world (Cuba,

---

[172] Quoted in Korten 2001, 75.
[173] Felton 2005, 130.

Ancient Rome, Vietnam, Germany, Luxemburg, etc.). But I will not be concerned with the academic accounts of communism in this book, and instead I will primarily be concerned with the "loose and popular definition" of communism used by Americans, and how that loose and popular definition of communism or fascism that Americans tend to have is identical to an Orwellian reality, such as that which was described in *1984*.

The basic features that Americans tend to believe that fascist and communist nations have according to their "loose and popular" way of believing communism exists are: the absence of private ownership, mass poverty, pervasive thought-control, disintegrated family structure, mass terror, perpetual and pervasive fear and irrationality, genocide, the absence of mass consumerism, and a single irrational ruler portrayed as being all-powerful. Again, these are primary Orwellian features. These features can be shown to be identical to the features that comprise the American corporation.

Typically when Americans think or talk about a communist nation, one thing they appear to often do is develop a picture of communism with a lot of emphasis on how the communist nation is believed to be an empire of horror, full of lost citizens who are subjected to endless torture, manipulation, terrorism and mind-control—all perpetrated by a single all-powerful dictator administering an empire of revulsion. Professor Halberstam gives us a spirited and relevant description of what non-democratic states[174] evoke in the mind of the typical American:

> The idea of totalitarianism conjures up the image of the sorcerer's apprentice, of social and political forces spinning out of control, of a world gone awry just when it was thought that humanity had made strides toward political maturity and intellectual independence, had begun finally to liberate itself from the idols of the past and was ready to assume responsibility for its own destiny.[175]

Americans typically believe that all non-democratic states are communist, and that communist states are almost always spooky realms of horror, concentration camps and/or impoverished condensed cities, brainwashing, state-ownership of all goods, and a diminished family structure. But we will see by the end of this chapter that the spooky communism that Americans have been taught to hate, disdain, and fear *is the very government system they live amid in the United States*: The United States is a corporate communist nation.

As implied above, the loose and popular definition of communism involves all sorts of horrific features in the minds of Americans, and that is perhaps why

---

[174] Halberstam uses the word "totalitarian" rather than "communism." I will show below why I am treating them as if they are interchangeable, and how they mean the same things to the typical American, who holds the aforementioned loose and popular view of communism.

[175] Halburstam 1999, 2.

Americans use each of the terms "fascism," "communism," "dictatorship," "tyranny," and "totalitarianism" interchangeably, as if they are synonyms. (Since that is how Americans tend to use these words, then I will also do that in this book, and I show in this chapter that corporations are identical to these sorts of communist horror-states.)

How American Ideas of Communism are Created

The loose and popular concept of communism just described is advocated and created in the media. To see what I mean by this, I will next give a few examples of news stories and politicians' comments about communism. In these we can get an idea of how Americans form their ideas of what communism is, and why they are so spooked by it.

First, consider the way the following *Associated Press* news article portrays "dictatorship" and "communism" in one of the countless news articles about North Korea that was released during the early July 2006 media frenzy (which was abruptly postponed when the Israel-Hezbollah DU-war emerged very shortly after in July 2006) over North Korea launching a rocket (pay specific attention to the italicized words: "ruthless dictator," "communism," "starving his people" "terrorist," etc.):

> SEOUL, South Korea (July 5) - At home, North Korean leader Kim Jong Il is *hailed* by state-run media as a prodigious general, an ace film director and the "Lodestar of the 21st Century." To the outside world, he is a *ruthless dictator* seeking *weapons of mass destruction* while *starving his people.* Kim, 64, has often alarmed the world with his *saber-rattling.* On Wednesday, he brandished one of his strongest cards by test-launching seven missiles, including a long-range Taepodong-2 that some analysts say could be capable of reaching the U.S. mainland. Kim took power after his father and North Korean founder, Kim Il Sung, died in 1994 at the age of 82 in *communism's* first hereditary transfer of authority. Activists estimate that up to *2 million North Koreans died of malnutrition or related ailments* in the mid- and late-1990s, when North Korea's chronically inefficient farming industry was beset by a series of floods and droughts... The West's demonic image of Kim is based in part on suspicions he *masterminded* a 1983 *terrorist bombing* in Myanmar that killed 17 high-ranking South Korean officials and the 1987 bombing of a South Korean airliner that killed all 115 people aboard.[176] (Itals mine)

Now consider a BBC article in which the author presents a flurry of explicative words ("socialist," "communist," "dictator," fascist," even

---

[176] This story was taken from, "N. Korea Leader Seen in Several Lights," July 5, 2006, by Jae-Soon Chang, Associated Press.

"atheistic," among other words), which are all keywords in the American lexicon of the dreaded communist-Orwellian nightmare:

> It's not often you hear a paean of praise to the Spanish fascist dictator General Franco these days. And you certainly don't expect to hear it in the European Parliament. So members were shocked when Polish MEP Maciej Giertych got to his feet. He was speaking in one of those debates that seem rather pious and pointless, to mark the 70th anniversary of the beginning of the Spanish civil war—full of MEPs condemning a regime that is long dead and buried, already reviled by most. Now Mr. Giertych is not some marginal figure. He was a presidential candidate and his party is a coalition partner in the Polish government. His son doubles as deputy prime minister and education minister. This is what Giertych senior said: "Thanks to the Spanish army and Franco the communist attack on Catholic Spain was thwarted. The presence of such people in European politics as Franco guaranteed the maintenance of traditional values in Europe and we lack such statesmen today. Christian Europe is losing against atheistic socialists today and this has to change." He says today's assumptions are "historical revision". How do you think the history of Europe would have been different if the elected socialist government and their communist allies had won in Spain?[177]

Now consider another story, which uses the word "tyranny" to describe Cuba (which is also universally referred to as a communist nation[178]), which also depicts Cuba as a tyranny of lawless horror, whose citizens are starved and mistreated, and it is assumed in the article they are starved and mistreated because of the tyranny.

> MIAMI (AP) - A boat overloaded with *Cubans being smuggled* into the U.S. tried to ram a Coast Guard vessel in rough seas early Saturday, and a woman aboard the boat died, authorities said. The 36-foot, go-fast boat ignored orders to stop when the Coast Guard tried to intercept it 4 miles south of Boca Chica around 6:30 a.m., said Petty Officer James Judge, a spokesman for the Coast Guard. Coast Guard crew then fired two shots into the vessel's engine to disable it, he said. "The boat was bouncing around like crazy. It was very rough, choppy waters," Judge said. "They repeatedly attempted to ram the vessel more than five times, but they never made contact." The boat carried 31 Cubans and three people authorities said were smugglers. The woman who died suffered a head injury and severe bruising to her face, and an autopsy was scheduled

---

[177] "Europe diary: Franco and Finland," by Mark Mardell (BBC Editor), July 6, 2006, BBC News, http://news.bbc.co.uk/2/hi/europe/5151504.stm?ls.

[178] One of countless examples that could be given to show how Cuba is commonly described as communist, is: "Castro Brothers' Plan: The Party Must Go On," Miami Herald, by Jaime Suchlicki, July 12, 2006.

Sunday. Judge said three men on the boat were treated for minor injuries. Authorities said none of the injuries was caused by the Coast Guard gunfire. *A pregnant woman also was hospitalized*, but her condition was not immediately known. The remaining migrants were still aboard the Coast Guard cutter and will be processed as usual, he said. Under the "wet foot/dry foot" policy, most Cubans who reach U.S. soil are allowed to remain, while those intercepted at sea are generally sent home… "The people who are culpable are those who engage in the *smuggling of humans*," said Alfredo Mesa, the group's executive director. "At the same time, we call upon the U.S. Coast Guard to remember that these are *human beings fleeing tyranny*."[179] (Itals mine)

Now consider this passage from George W. Bush's 2006 State of the Union Address, on January 31, 2006, which also makes synonyms of the words "tyranny," "dictatorship," "radicalism," and "terrorism:"

Abroad, our nation is committed to an historic, long-term goal—we seek the end of tyranny in our world. Some dismiss that goal as misguided idealism. In reality, the future security of America depends on it. On September the 11th, 2001, we found that problems originating in a failed and oppressive state 7,000 miles away could bring murder and destruction to our country. Dictatorships shelter terrorists, and feed resentment and radicalism, and seek weapons of mass destruction. Democracies replace resentment with hope, respect the rights of their citizens and their neighbors, and join the fight against terror. Every step toward freedom in the world makes our country safer—so we will act boldly in freedom's cause. (Applause.)

Next, consider the remarks by Vice President, Dick Cheney, which equates tyrants with terrorists, while he is talking to troops in Norfolk Virginia about the multi-year mission in Iraq.

We are going to keep at this mission until it is completed—because we have given our word, and because freedom's victory in Iraq is vital to our own security. If the *terrorists* were to succeed, they would *return Iraq to the rule of tyrants* and make it a source once again of *instability* in the Middle East. And if that region remains a place of *tyranny and resentment*, we can expect more *violence directed against the United States and other free countries*. Yet if people are given a say in their own affairs, and the Middle East is allowed to grow in liberty and freedom, then *tyrants and terrorists* will lose their appeal. And if

---

[179] "Boat Carrying Cubans to U.S. Tries to Ram Coast Guard Vessel, Authorities Say; Woman Dies," July 8, 2006, by Kelli Kennedy, Associatd Press.

freedom and democracy take hold in that part of the world, we'll have a better chance for a future of security and peace.[180] (Itals mine)

And here is a passage from a *wildly* popular online magazine, which involves three political theorists talking to a student named Jamie:

The Left has a long, depressing, ugly and blood-stained record of worshipping the most vile and barbaric tyrannies of the 20th century, including Stalin's Soviet Union, Mao's China, Ho Chi Minh's Vietnam and Castro's Cuba... No one on the Left apart from Communists believes in a classless society and there are hardly any Communists left. If I were to advocate higher taxes on the American rich and propose using the proceeds to, say, improve the lamentable quality of public schools would you seriously argue that I was taking the first steps on the road to the Gulag? ... ...Jamie, you say you have spent many years in academia, my advice is to get out before your thinking deteriorates any further. Naturally, I accept that being surrounded by a bunch of post-modern theorists is enough to drive the most level-headed men and women quite mad, but your comments show in miniature why America is losing. Here you are up against a psychopathic totalitarian ideology. You ought to have the sympathy of democrats around the world. But if you, like the Bush administration, refuse to understand that there are different currents in democratic thinking and say with no self-consciousness of what a fool you sound that 'the Left has been totalitarian throughout its history' you alienate your potential allies. Democracy is a little more than one notion of the free market from America which in practice America follows more in theory than in practice.[181]

These passages are filled with overly broad generalizations, charged language and name-calling, non-analytic accounts, and non-empirical discussion. Overall, this is how the loose and popular American definition of communism is created, and how it consists of Death Star features: forced concentration camp labor, absence of passion and family, and the other spooky characteristics mentioned above. Passages like these would appear to fuel Americans' biases in their beliefs and perceptions about non-democratic societies, fueling fear and hate, even though the passages do not give any real empirical, impartial information, and even though it can be shown that the communistic environments are identical to the circumstances Americans devote their lives to at the corporation throughout their lives.

---

[180] "Remarks by Vice President Cheney at a Rally for Expeditionary Strike Group 8," July 7, PR Newswire.
[181] These are the words of Nick Cohen, in an article by Jamie Glazov, "A New "New Left'?," in the hugely popular *Frontpagemag.com* (July 14, 2006), http://www.frontpagemag.com/Articles/ReadArticle.asp?ID=23339.

The Characteristics of Communism

Now that I have given a basic account of communism, we can find out why America is a communist nation.

What Americans typically believe communism is, is a cultural system that has the following set of characteristics:

- **Dictatorship**. There is a single unelected tiny group (board of directors, etc.) or a single unelected single person, not answerable to the people, that dictatorially controls everything about society: all production, resources, behavior of the workers, media and, information, and, as we will see, even the very inner thoughts of the people of the population
- **Cultic allegiance**. There is blind, unquestioning, and irrational allegiance to "the Party" (as in Orwell's *1984*)
- **Impoverishment**. Citizens do not have much wealth or opportunity, and they often do not have the material possessions that they should have and which are essential for their survival
- **Labor intensive**. There is intensive focus on industrialization and controlled labor
- **No private ownership**. The production enterprises are said to be government owned. All citizens, and citizens' goods, are government owned
- **Absence of capitalism**. It is believed that in a communistic society, capitalism does not exist, or it is greatly subdued
- **One party rule**. There is a single party regime over a classless society, and there is far less wealth differentiation and hierarchy as compared to, for example, America
- **Economy does not involve competition**.
- **Terrorism**. Frequent deranged military activity, including death camps
- **Renunciation of free speech**
- **Atheism**
- **Brainwashed citizens**
- **Endless imperialist war**. Preemptive warfare that often appears to have no purpose
- **Classlessness**.
- **Massive, nationwide, death camps and/or labor camps involving unfathomable atrocity**

I will discuss why *all* these communist-fascist principles *also* describe the Orwellian monopolistic corporations, and their top-down power structure. In doing this, I will prove that America is a communist nation. (Not all of these characteristics of communism just listed will be discussed in this chapter; a few will be discussed in the next few chapters.)

Corporatist Genocide and Terrorism

First I will discuss the way that corporations are engaged in mass genocide and terrorism. Above I eluded to the way that so many people die each year from corporate pollution—anything from the more significant pollution (e.g., asbestos), to the ultimate population damaging chemical weapons/pollutants, such as DDT, aspartame, *Serratia marcescens*,[182] perchlorate, thimerosal, bovine growth hormone, whooping cough bacteria chemically sprayed on Americans (likely via chemtrails),[183] GMO food, Morgellons fibers,[184] nutricidal food,[185] and the military industrial complex's greatest genocidal weapon, DU. Corporate pollution kills more people than wars do, and this is done is fully known by controlling corporatists.[186] But there are many sorts of corporatist genocide, and what I wish to do is to briefly discuss one example here: economic population control.

Consider an interesting quote from Professor Chossudovsky about this issue, which is a key ingredient to setting up the New World Order of the corporatists, which involves their earnestness to set up worldwide poverty and labor camp plantations:

> Structural adjustment[187] is conducive to a form of "economic genocide" which is carried out through the consciousness and deliberate manipulation of market forces. When compared to previous periods of colonial history (e.g., forced labor and slavery), its social impact is devastating. Structural adjustment programs affect directly the livelihood of more than four billion people... This new form of economic and political domination—a form of "market colonialism"—

---

[182] See Cole 1988, 6. This is usually touted by military officials as not being a dangerous chemical when it is sprayed on humans, but see Cole for refutation of this.

[183] Cole 1988, 18.

[184] I have heard some researchers, such as Doctor Bill Deagle, assert that they do not believe that the US military or the secret government could have created Morgellon's as a bioweapon due to its oddness, sophistication, and its seeming unearthliness. This may be true, but the issue appears to be open. Morgellon's fibers are clearly associated with chemtrail spraying, as Clifford Carnicom has shown, and also because it is clear that the secret government has their hands on secret technologies that are *far beyond* the imagination of the American public, and clearly into the domain of the sophistication of something like a Morgellon's bioweapon. The typical American just has no idea how sophisticated the secret technologies of the world have become, and thus I believe it is too early to tell whether or not Morgellons is not a secret government creation.

[185] See Afrika 2000. Also, copious information is available at www.healthfreedomusa.org.

[186] Winslow 2003, 46.

[187] Chossudovsky is referring to the IMF, and other New World Order "lawmaking" agencies, that create policies and laws for the world so that things are made easy for the corporatists to set up their global monopolization. I will discuss these "agencies" at length later in this book.

subordinates people and governments through the seemingly "neutral" interplay of market forces.[188]

New World Order organizations, such as the IMF, the UN, the World Bank, the WTO, and others, create economic policies that are touted as being helpful to the world's citizens, but in reality they are merely ways to cripple economies, thus leading to mass death and poverty. Joseph Stiglitz, Nobel Prize winner in economics, was "terminated" from the World Bank for disclosing that this is what the World Bank deliberately does in order to set up more "favorable" conditions (such as mass slavery) for corporatists and in order to allow money to be gravitated into the hands of the corporatists. Corporate terrorism will be discussed at great length in later chapters.

Atheistic Corporatism

Moving on to the next point, some readers may be questionable about the idea that the average corporation is atheistic. But is Christianity preached in the average corporate setting? It does not seem so. In fact, in my boyhood jobs I held, working at factories, in offices, in fast food chains, convenience stores, warehouses, and package delivery companies, and now in my teaching career as lecturer at IUN and PUC, I never was preached to or proselytized to in any way, and many of the people I worked with were crass, perverse, foul-mouthed and seemed to not have much to exemplify in terms of the fruits of the spirit.[189] They were concerned with beer more than Christ, and with television more than the Bible. In the office settings I worked in, however, many people were Christians, some very energetic Christians, but never once did they preach to me, and I would say that if they did, it would have been frowned upon by management and perhaps most other workers. For these reasons, it seems to me that my office and job experience in corporations has been non-religious, and to assert that they were even slightly religious ordeals in the way church is would be completely false.

---

[188] Chossudovsky 2006, 20.

[189] I use these terms, "crass," etc., not because that is what I thought of my fellow workers, but only because that is how many of the workers—such as the warehouse crew—was labeled by the more "upper class" members of the companies I worked at.

The three anti-heroes in the film Office Space smash a photocopier.

The classic film, *Office Space*, illustrates many of the ideas in this book, including the impossibility that a person can live a religious or spiritual life when all of their time is fixed on serving the corporation, rather than on cultivating their consciousness. Under corporatism, the human spirit is crushed, and scientific and religious pursuits are replaced by wrath, addiction, masochism, and petty concerns.

What has just been written applies to Americans when they are at work, in the corporatist environment. But what about outside of work? As has been implied above, the influence of the corporatism in America does not only reside in the corporation environment, but it reaches out to all levels of society, into everything: into our minds, religious organizations, our families, and so on. If this is the case, it should be expected that the corporatistic government system in America should influence society on every level, and in every dimension, including church on Sunday. And that is precisely what is the case for religion in the corporatist world—regardless of what religion one espouses: Buddhism, Hinduism, Islam, Christianity, and so on—as I will explain next.

If a person is truly religious, that religious person must have time and energy available so that she/he can prepare and carry out her/his religious practice. Americans spend most of the time of their life at work, in school, sleeping, taking care of children, watching television, or doing other daily tasks. Notice that in this list, practicing religious rituals, contemplating, carrying out religious reading and research, are not listed. Work and school take up so much time for the typical American, that their entire life, it could be argued, becomes off-balance: the brunt of their efforts go into attempting to succeed at the corporation, or at school, and insufficient energy is left over to tend to the other things just mentioned, such as religion. The majority of a person's hours are spent at the corporation, and thus the remaining time outside the corporation is often a time when the worker is worn-out, hurried (since they have many basic life tasks to get accomplished in the scant remaining time away from the corporation), and it is vegetative time: the worker is exhausted, and when the kids are in bed, and the groceries are put away, lawn mowed, dog in the garage, and so on, there is little more energy left, one can do little more than relax in front of the television. In this way, American life is spent either at the corporation, or it is spent outside the corporation watching television or hurrying through basic life chores. In America, it is rare—*extremely* rare—that we find a person who spends more than a few tired and rather unfocussed minutes each day carrying out some sort of religious practice. What everything I am saying in this paragraph leads to is this: the corporatism in the United States *prevents* people from being religious, and if they are not religious, they are irreligious, and irreligiousness is akin to atheism. Corporatist America is atheistic.[190]

Americans have grown accustomed to understanding religion as a mere belief, and something one carries out in ritual form once per week, if even that. For the American Christian, or the American Buddhist, it is nowadays typically considered normal to spend the majority of the day involved in ungodly activities at the corporation, and only spending scant time carrying out meditations or prayers, that are often of a trivial nature, asking for petty security and wealth of various sorts. Religion has become "easy religion," to paraphrase what I once heard Bill Moyers once say: religion without religious consciousness or religious depth, where an extremely insignificant amount of a person's life is spent carrying out religious practices, prayers, meditations, and so on. This is "religion" that is little more than a belief in something invisible; religion as a loose membership in a group or club, such as church. Easy religion is considered normal in American society, but if one studies comparative religion, getting a grasp of all religions all over, one soon sees that the easy religion of the United States is anomalous indeed.

From what I have written here, America would appear to be best described as an entirely atheist nation. Experts who have written and lectured on the development of the emerging world government (New World Order), such as

---

[190] If the reader believes this paragraph condemns atheism, or shows that atheism only exists when corporatist and communist societies exist, then those readers do not understand that atheism has many varieties. The corporatist atheism I have just described is not a philosophical or scientific sort of atheism, which espouses atheism for noble reasons. Rather, corporatist atheism is merely the result of the fact that citizens in a corporatist society do not have time or energy to be religious, and likewise, they do not have time, energy, or the educational background to espouse any sort of profound philosophical or scientific atheism. The citizen in the corporatist empire only has enough mental space for entertainment and distraction, given the soullessness that their rat-race life involves, and which they are conditioned to accept, from birth to death.

Professor Michael Coffman in his work concerning the UN,[191] have shown us how the breakup of family and religion all over the world has been part of a deliberate plan[192] put forth by the Masonic corporatists. These experts have also shown us that the New World Order corporatists have a goal to set up a world religion—a "New World Order religion"—that is somewhat like a degenerate form of Hinduism. It is not difficult to see that the atheistic nature of corporatist nations could facilitate the entry of such a religion, under the right conditions (such as with the fear caused by false flag terrorism).

Big Pharma and Soma: Corporatized Religion and the Creation of Super-Cogs

For some time I have believed that the religion of the New World Order will have something to do with claims other experts who have researched and lectured about regarding the emerging New World Order have made concerning the theory that the New World Order will be a world society that involves *pervasive medicating*, where all citizens will continuously deluge themselves with pharmaceutical drugs in order to "feel good." One can see that the first stage of this "Soma world" already exists, due to the fact that a *huge* percentage of the US population is tricked into taking Prozac, Wellbutrin, lithium, Ritalin, Lipitor, Viagra, and countless other drugs on a daily basis.

But this is just the first stage, and soon the United States, if not the world, will be a Soma world, as described in Huxley's *Brave New World*. Consider the following news story from the very popular neoconservative magazine WorldNetDaily:

> President Bush plans to unveil next month a sweeping mental health initiative that recommends screening for every citizen and promotes the use of expensive antidepressants and antipsychotic drugs favored by supporters of the administration. The New Freedom Initiative, according to a progress report, seeks to integrate mentally ill patients fully into the community by providing "services in the community, rather than institutions," the British Medical Journal reported. Critics say the plan protects the profits of drug companies at the expense of the public. The initiative began with Bush's launch in April 2002 of the New Freedom Commission on Mental Health, which conducted a "comprehensive study of the United States mental health service delivery system." The panel found that "despite their prevalence, mental

---

[191] Professor Coffman's work is plentiful, but I have found his lecture, "Final Countdown to UN World Government," to be an excellent summary, which is available on DVD from www.cuttingedge.org.

[192] This is, of course, not hidden, and is totally admitted by the corporatists and New World Order. For example, see Brzezinski's book, *The Grand Chessboard*, such as on page 40.

disorders often go undiagnosed" and recommended comprehensive mental health screening for "consumers of all ages," including preschool children. The commission said, "Each year, young children are expelled from preschools and childcare facilities for severely disruptive behaviors and emotional disorders." Schools, the panel concluded, are in a "key position" to screen the 52 million students and 6 million adults who work at the schools. The commission recommended that the screening be linked with "treatment and supports," including "state-of-the-art treatments" using "specific medications for specific conditions."[193]

American culture is a culture of "mental health," meaning that it is widely believed that people can have something called "mental illness," that needs to be cured, and that any behavior that is believed by, for example, school officials, to be slightly "irrational"—such as a seven-year-old boy having a hard time sitting still in his chair for hours and hours in an elementary school classroom listening to what is most likely a boring, uninspiring teacher— warrants "corrective" "medication," such as Ritalin, to "fix" the child.

With new programs, such as "The New Freedom Initiative," mental health programs and pervasive drugging of Americans with pharmaceutical "prescriptions" will only skyrocket. Big Pharma will make unimaginable amounts of money, and America will be indistinguishable from the society discussed in Huxley's *Brave New World*. In the society in Huxley's book, all citizens are endlessly drugged with a euphoric, mind-numbing, drunkenness-inducing pharmaceutical drug called "Soma" (which is sort of like a super-intense Xanax, Ritalin, or Prozac), which turns all citizens into semi-drunken, sedated, happy and giggly, obedient, sex-crazed party-goers and gullible, malleable factory workers. Soma is used to replace genuine religious experience (which, I am guessing, very few Americans have had, let along enjoy on a daily basis) with degenerate pseudo-religion (i.e., mindless inebriation, rather than an experience of explosive religious experience). It is not hard to see that America's culture of "easy religion" (which is really just corporatistic atheism) is really just a few steps away from becoming a Brave New World.

But I often hear something like the following objection to what I have just written:

> *My friend was so depressed after she had her second baby. She couldn't even take care of her family, but then she started SSRIs (antidepressants) and she got all better and could take care of her family... How's that a bad thing?*

---

[193] "Bush to screen population for mental illness," WorldNetDaily.com, June 21, 2004.

This example embodies the standard way I hear people discussing SSRIs in a positive light. In contemporary American, *culture* is never blamed for causing a person's problems (such as their so-called "mental illness"); rather, the *individual person's brain* is always blamed, where the person will be told by "professionals" that they need to "fix" their "mental imbalances," and they need to take billion-dollar blockbuster pharmaceuticals for the rest of their lives (or until the problem is fixed) if they have "mental health" issues.

But I will next show that the following is true:

> *In any case where SSRIs are introduced because of some perceived "mental illness," I can argue that in reality, there is a cultural issue and dysfunction that has actually caused the problem, not a "brain imbalance" or "brain disorder."*

The individual is not sick—it is that the individual is forced to fit into the sick culture.

In the aforementioned case of the mother not taking care of her family, the natural cultural phenomena causing the depression is *busyness*. The picture of a Western woman who is a stay-home mom, and who does not use television to a large degree as a "babysitter" (in an above chapter I showed how any amount of television is harmful to young children and babies), is one where she is trapped in her suburban cubicle of a house, radically overworked in caring for the children (which is often done all alone), especially when there are multiple children. This Western woman has absolutely no time to think, or have a moment to herself, with this overload, and this can feel as if the self is dead, to some degree, and it certainly is not a situation that will always lead to a feeling of well-being.

If we look at hunter-gatherer and primitive cultures—the cultures that we came from (either by evolution, creation, or intervention, which are the three most popular theories of human origins), we see that women were largely congregative: grouping together, helping each other, with kids playing together and taking care of one another, and the unreasonable work-load of the aforementioned Westernized stay-home mom did not exist. Therefore, a significant percentage of stay-home moms in the Western world will inevitably develop panic, depression, or anger to some degree, due to their being out of sync with their evolutionary heritage.

Difficulties in life are inevitable, and there is no question that they always make people grow. Sadness is a normal, inevitable part of life, since hardship is a normal part of life. While it is good to try to avoid physical injury (such as not trying to fall off a bike), and while it is obvious that people will try to avoid mental hardship, Prozac, for example, is a way of merely drugging the self rather than learning from the hardship—the psychiatrist might as well prescribe cocaine, rather than an SSRI. Like addictive "street drugs," the SSRI drugs are toxic, addictive, depression-inducing, and deadly,[194] and like the bodily diseases (cancer, heart disease, diabetes, etc.) the so-called "mental illnesses" are problems that are found exclusively in Western and Westernized cultures.[195] Therefore, "mental illnesses" are cultural issues, and SSRIs and other "mental health drugs" are not a solution, but are a problem.

Difficulties are inevitable in life. Is it better to

(a) find the causes for our mental distresses, and to face them and learn how to handle the problems of life, rather than be blown over by them every time a big hardship comes our way (which is often)? Or should one

(b) learn an addiction, such as Prozac, and cover up learning experiences about life, and thus not learn how to handle the inevitable hardships that come our way?

It seems that (a) is a more sensible option. It seems that (b) is, simply put, running from a problem, or drinking a problem away, by analogy. Furthermore, (b) is a way to serve the secret government, since the secret government is all about getting the public addicted on the secret government's substances (in this case, Prozac-soma, but other examples are television, alcohol, oil, junk food, milk and meat, and so on). (b) facilitates addiction and dependency on the secret government, whereas (a) facilitates autonomy.

Given what has just been discussed, it appears that "mental illness" does not exist, and perhaps Professor Szasz's commentary from the first lines of his book *The Myth of Mental Illness* is appropriate to cite here:

> Psychiatry is conventionally defined as a medical specialty concerned with the diagnosis and treatment of mental diseases. I submit that this definition, which is still widely accepted, places psychiatry in the company of alchemy and astrology and commits it to the category of pseudoscience. The reason for this is that there is no such thing as "mental illness." Psychiatrists must now choose between continuing to define their discipline in terms of nonexistent entities or substantives, or redefining it in terms of the actual interventions or processes in which they engage.[196]

---

[194] See Richards 2006.

[195] See Hansen 2000 for an excellent example of how primitive cultures do not involve the "mental illness" and criminality of a Westernized culture. Walsh (1990) also shows how many primitive cultures revere what would normally be called schizophrenia in Western psychiatry. Gowan (1975) also holds that position, and he describes how the shaman's "madness" was often viewed as a religious trance that contained a helpful religious message for the tribe.

[196] Szasz 1974, 1.

Classlessness

Some readers may wonder about the idea that a corporation is a classless society, since obviously there are different strata of a corporation arranged by the different incomes and positions people have in the corporation. But the idea that communistic societies are classless in this way is flatly false. Most readers of this book probably remember how, in the film *Schindler's List*, the corporation owner, Oscar Schindler, had workers, but he in turn was far beneath the social status of the core of the Nazi party and the top Nazi corporatists. Referring to the film *Schindler's List* offers a simple way to show that the American idea that the communist-fascist states involve economic classlessness is not correct.

It is interesting how badly Americans have misrepresented actual communism by believing it to have economic classlessness. Even our dictionary definitions include this misrepresentation of economic classlessness. Consider what Webster's says:

> Main Entry: **com·mu·nism**
> **1 a :** a theory advocating elimination of private property **b :** a system in which goods are owned in common and are available to all as needed
> **2** *capitalized* **a :** a doctrine based on revolutionary Marxian socialism and Marxism-Leninism that was the official ideology of the Union of Soviet Socialist Republics **b :** a totalitarian system of government in which a single authoritarian party controls state-owned means of production **c :** a final stage of society in Marxist theory in which the state has withered away and economic goods are distributed equitably **d :** communist systems collectively

And consider what Dictionary.com says in definition 2.a. for the word "communism:"

> 1. A theoretical economic system characterized by the collective ownership of property and by the organization of labor for the common advantage of all members.

> 2. a. A system of government in which the state plans and controls the economy and a single, often authoritarian party holds power, claiming to make progress toward a higher social order in which all goods are equally shared by the people. b. The Marxist-Leninist version of Communist doctrine that advocates the overthrow of capitalism by the revolution of the proletariat.[197]

The real classlessness of citizens in a communist regime is found not in their having similar economic situations, but in their having minds that have been created by the state, and where those minds are all virtually identical. This is

---

[197] All entries from Dictionary.com come from The American Heritage® Dictionary of the English Language, Fourth Edition, *Copyright © 2000. Published by Houghton Mifflin Company.*

not an economic classlessness, but rather a human or mental classlessness—a classlessness of the human spirit—where the spontaneity and diversity of humans is stripped, and the people all become very similar to one another, in their desires, dreams, thoughts, language, preferences, appearance, education, and so on.

If one watches the excellent films, *The Island*,[198] *1984*,[199] or *Brave New World*,[200] one will likely be instantly struck by how the people in these films all seem identical: they are all entirely complacent, dressed nearly identically, they talk nearly identically, they act almost exactly alike, and one even gets the feeling that they are all thinking the same thoughts. But interestingly, it is as if none of the denizens of these worlds are aware of any of these details, and they actually believe they are quite unique and quite different from one another. Americans overall exhibit this conformity, and it reaches to the core of nearly all of them, even though nearly none of them realize it. Americans believe the same snake oil account of reality (due to how it is delivered to them in education and the media), they have uniform fears (they fear terrorists, side effects from pharmaceuticals, car crashes, long waits at restaurants, their team losing on Sunday, power outages that would prohibit them from watching TV, cell phone calls being dropped, bad coffee, stock market crashes, and so on), they have the same interests (shopping, cable TV, cell phones, new computers, church, voting, and so on), and that is only the tip of the iceberg. If one looks at this issue carefully, it is actually difficult to find an issue that Americans are *not* almost perfectly uniform about. For example, it is difficult to find two people that don't like the same television shows (it's even harder to find people who don't own televisions), that do not both like the same sorts of food (e.g., pizza, MSG filled bread-like food, etc.), or that don't just talk about the same old things (e.g., the Democrats vs. the Republicans, global warming, war and "terrorists," weather, TV, and all the rest).

The classlessness of consciousness that I am describing, and which is found pervading Americans corporations functions very much like communistic economic classlessness just described. American corporatist classlessness involves the idea that Americans are taught, and urged to believe that, "we're all equal:" the black, the white, the rich, the poor, the Arab and the Jew, we're all just equal people—so long as we all think alike, and think permissible thoughts (such as believing that corporations are virtuous institutions, that taxation is fair and inevitable, that there are invisible terrorists that could "strike at any moment," and so on). Few ideas could sound more Marxist or communist than this sort of classlessness. An interesting comic book, called

---

[198] Bay, Michael (director), 2005, *The Island*. Studio: Dreamworks Video. ASIN: B000BO0LH2.
[199] Radford, Michael (director), 1984, *1984*. Studio: Polygram. ASIN: 6304362498.
[200] 1988. Studio: Universal Pictures. ASIN: B00004S32U. This is a "made for TV" film.

Introducing Chomsky (by Maher and Groves), puts the matter like this: for corporatists, "[i]t's extremely important to make ... people, the ...population, believe that there is no such thing as class. We're all just equal. We're all just Americans. We live in harmony. We all work together. Everything is great."[201] Here is how Professor Howard Zinn puts this classlessness issue:

> Our political leaders like to pretend that there are no classes in this country, that all of us have the same interest: Exxon and me, George Bush and you. But we're always had classes in this country, class conflict, class struggle,... the poor against the rich,... like Shay's Rebellion, which put the Founding Fathers on edge.[202]

This is a tricky issue. Above I have showed a few of the ways that Americans are taught to distrust, compete, and nit-pick one another, so that they don't form deep brotherhoods with one another, since strong alliances among the people are dangerous to the secret government. Yet Americans are also taught to believe "we're all in this together," so that they have enough of a low-level veneer of camaraderie that we can work together at the corporation. So, the people are taught two contradictory things: everyone's a possible enemy,[203] and everyone is like you. It's sort of like having a next-door neighbor that you are jealous of because they have a better car than you, or which you are leery of because they hold different view or television shows tastes, but if you need to borrow a cup of sugar from them, you are able to put on a smile and go over and knock on the door to ask for some.

In America, political leaders attempt to make it appear that they "relate" to the populace, or that they have the same interests as the populace, as if they all have the same sorts of interests as the citizenry. (For example: George Bush Jr. will attempt to act like a cowboy in front of television cameras, wearing a cowboy hat, talking with a cowboy accent—when nobody else in his family seems to have the same accent.) There is a huge push for this sort of classlessness of the human spirit through media and the education system, Americans are taught about this idea that "we're all Americans with common interests," "we're all in this together." The carefully planned and fabricated image and demeanor of George W. Bush for the TV cameras, where he is portrayed as a likeable, friendly, ordinary guy, with simple ideas and who talks like a good-ole cowboy, and who's tough enough to go and chop wood (Bill

---

[201] Page 144.

[202] Zinn 2004, tape 1. Zinn comments on the conflict between the rich and the poor. I will show in later chapters that that conflict may be the least it has ever been in the current landscape of America, primarily due to what I sometimes refer to in this book as "the rich man's media," where the rich own the media, and make it appear that the views of the rich are good for everybody, or are the only views (e.g., Iraq, Osama, Iran, oil is good, etc.).

[203] This is especially prevalent in the "war on terror," where politicians routinely tell us that "terrorists are among us," and the like, thus getting us to all be leery of one another.

O'Reilly on the Fox News Channel also tries to portray himself as just another "ordinary guy."), may give people the feeling that they can identify with him, as if he is an "ordinary guy" that is on their level, and not a haughty, intellectual, or elitist. The only catch is that this "ordinary guy" is a gazillioniare, the PNAC spokesperson, whose friends are the CEOs of the oil industry, and, as of summer 2006, who has the US military and Congress by the spurs.

Through the messages of the corporatist media, Americans are often tricked into believing that the CEOs of Wal-Mart, Exxon, Lockheed Martin, Disney, Dupont, and most other corporatists, are kind and ordinary people, interested in their workers' lives and needs, where we are "all in this together." As we will see, there is no empirical evidence to support the idea that corporatists are really like this, and later in this chapter and in the next chapter, we will see evidence that reveals that they actually are eager to oppress their workers to the point of removing the items they need to fulfill their basic necessities, even if it kills them. For this reason, one of the primary functions of the rich media is to make the corporatists look like friendly ordinary people, and to make corporations look like the best thing the world has ever seen. If the rich media did not do this, it is hard to imagine that corporations would be so eager to pay the rich media extraordinary amounts to place advertisements on their networks and in their newspapers.

The Myth of Private Ownership in the United States

Some readers of this book may object to the idea that corporations are nearly indistinguishable from a communist dictatorship, since they may believe that American culture involves private ownership and private consumption of goods. But it is so easy to show that there is no significant private ownership in the United States that it is quite amazing that Americans have actually believed that there *is* mass private ownership of goods and/or land in the United States— a testament to how gullible a citizenry can become, and/or a testament to how powerful social engineering and mind control of a citizenry can be.

When the typical American is at work, at the corporation, it seems that the typical scenario is that most of the goods and items are owned by the corporation: the stapler, the desk, the forklift, the building, the computer, and almost anything but the clothes and sack-lunch that the corporate worker brings with her to the corporation. This is certainly identical to the situation that exists in the communist state (according to the loose and popular definition of corporatism), where the corporatists "own" (i.e., control) everything, and "the people" own nothing. For these reasons, there is no sense in imagining there is any private ownership among workers in the corporate setting.

That's the case for the inside of the corporation, when the citizenry is at the corporation. What is more interesting is to consider the typical American person when she is not at work, but rather when she is in the domain of homes, Chucky Cheese, malls, public education, neighborhoods, apartment complexes, church, and so on. When the typical American worker is not at work, there is a whole lot more government ownership going on than most Americans tend to acknowledge. The vast majority of Americans who "own" homes and/or land do not have them "paid off" (they still have a bank mortgage payment), and that means that even if the homeowners or landowners only owe $1 on the house and/or land, the bank can take it under the right circumstances (such as late payment). In this scenario, is a person really the *owner* of her home, if it can be taken from her, and if she only has control over it under the right circumstances (such as during times that the she has money to pay the mortgage and the taxes)?

Would you say you *own* a car if you borrowed money from your boss (who controls your income, and thus your stability and perhaps your family peacefulness, or stress-level) in order to pay him back over the course of three years, with interest? What if after paying your boss back with interest over two-and-a-half years, your boss decides to terminate you from work, wherein your income is disturbed to such a degree that you cannot continue paying the payments, and thus you are forced to turn the car over to your boss in a repossession of the car? Think of how well off your boss makes off here. Not only does he get the car for nearly no cost, but he also had you paying him, with interest, for the past two-and-a-half years. Your boss would obtain a free car and nearly the cash amount price of the car also, since over that time of making payment, you would have paid interest in addition to the payments, which would approach the amount of the car originally (if not even more than the original price). Not a bad deal for the boss! This is indistinguishable from a situation where you pay your boss more than the amount of the car in order to take the car from you. What if, instead of being fired, you die after two-and-a-half years of payment? Another great situation for your boss.

In these examples, your boss represents the interconnected banking community worldwide, that controls and fabricates economics as needed to prevent accumulation of capital by citizens through phony concepts and fabrications like "supply and demand," "interest rates," and "natural inflation." Not only did you never really own the car, but you can be tricked into giving it up, and into giving another group/person money for it in the meantime. Very few people drive cars that are paid off, and live in homes that are paid off; and the examples just given show that there is no ownership in such cases. Private ownership in America is an illusion.

As for land and home, an American *does not* fully own their house and land—they only can live in it as long as we can keep paying the mortgage payment, most of which is often just a payment to cover interest and taxes.

Ownership is an illusion, which usually amounts to massive usurpation of land and goods by corporatist banks—who are, in some sense the strongest corporatists of all, the corporatists who control all the other corporatists (often to the detriment of the rest of the massive corporatists). A similar situation exists for most of the cars and boats, businesses and major business equipment (e.g., the printing press in the printing company) in America. Americans only fully "own" major items after years of paying them off, and such ownership is quite rare. One might be reminded of Thoreau's quote from *Walden*: "And when the farmer has got his house, he may not be the richer but the poorer for it, and it be the house that has got him." Even in a situation where a person owns a house, for example, the "owner" can still be shaken loose from the house if they cannot pay taxes in, for example, a time of "recession."

Ultimately all the "loan money" in the United States, including the loan money for business and major business equipment, comes from the Federal Reserve (which is a private, for-profit corporation, even though few people know it), ultimately in some sense, cars, boats, educations, homes, media, and businesses are government/corporatist-owned in the USA. In other words, if you have a car payment, for example, then your car is really owned by the massive Federal Reserve Corporation, which is perhaps the most powerful corporation of all. So, to some degree, and from a certain perspective, there is *a whole lot* more corporatist ownership going on in the USA than it seems the typical American citizen believes there is, and I do not see how I am to avoid the conclusion that the United States resembles a communist nation where the corporatist controllers own goods, labor, and land, and the RP really doesn't own anything at all.

In Corporatist America, Ownership = Government Ownership

The financial power and global reach of the corporatists of the New World Order removes and destroys local economy, usurps, removes, and destroys the power inherent in small-level industrial research and invention (which is a real threat to monopolistic corporatism), and literally supplants city-level economics. Professor Chossudovsky writes:

> In this system, state power has deliberately sanctioned the progress of private monopolies: large capital destroys small capital in all its forms. With the drive towards the formation of economic blocks both in Europe and North America, the regional and local-level entrepreneur is uprooted, city life is transformed and individual small-scale ownership is wiped out.[204]

There often are attempts by media personalities in the United States to show that the United States is not communistically corporatist, but is capitalistic and "free." But what we are seeing so far in this chapter is that such ideas are

---

[204] Chossudovsky 2003, 10.

unfounded. From what has just been shown above, widespread private ownership of major items (rather than insignificant ones, such as a cup, a dress, or a roll of toilet paper), which are the critically important ones (homes, cars, etc.), is rare in corporatist America. But oddly, virtually no Americans have awareness of this fact. Consider how this passage from an article from the wildly popular *FrontPageMagazine.com*, tries to uphold the illusory idea that America is not socialist since, according to the article, America is all about private ownership of possessions:

> What is corporatism? In a (somewhat inaccurate) phrase, socialism for the bourgeois. It has the outward form of capitalism in that it preserves private ownership and private management, but with a crucial difference: as under socialism, *government guarantees the flow of material goods*, which under true capitalism it does not. In classical capitalism, what has been called the "night-watchman" state, government's role in the economy is simply to prevent force or fraud from disrupting the autonomous operation of the free market. The market is trusted to provide. Under corporatism, it is not, instead being systematically manipulated to deliver goods to political constituencies. This now includes basically everyone from the economic elite to ordinary consumers.[205] (Itals original)

This is the standard way that members of the RP in America are indoctrinated: they will be merely told that the United States involves extensive private ownership, and thus the RP will unthinkingly believe it, even though there is, in general, no evidence for private ownership anywhere in the United States.

Also, this passage starts from the assumption that the United States government is in charge, and corporation owners answer to *it*. Only with that unargued for assumption does this passage succeed. But I show explicitly in this book that this assumption is entirely unfounded (and thus this passage is absurdism), and that American politicians are entirely irrelevant, since they are merely implementers of policy for the all-powerful corporations. All one has to do to show that the assumption in this passage is wrong is go and see who controls Big Pharma, Big Media, Big Agra, the FDA, the FCC, the EPA, the USDA, the meat industry, and the pesticide industry, and you will see that it's all the same people (e.g., controllers of the EPA = controllers of Monsanto) controllers of the FCC = controllers of Big Media). Government and industry are indistinguishable, and this is precisely what corporatism is, which the frontpagemag.com passage merely ignores, in order to put forth the nonempirical idea that America is owned by "We the People" (the RP).

---

[205] "What is American Corporatism?" by Robert Locke, *FrontPageMagazine.com*, September 13, 2002

The Mythical Idea that One Owns "Their" Thought and Behavior

It is important to note that corporatism does not just involve the monopolization of, and the government ownership of, land, labor, and goods; but rather, corporatism also involves the monopolization of, and government ownership of, *thought and behavior* of all members of the RP

In a particularly straightforward passage, Professor Halburstam writes that

(1) Totalitarianism is rule by force not by consent. Totalitarianism eradicates political freedom, democratic process, and legality as such, by setting up the daily pronouncements of the ruler and of the party as an omnipotent force with unchecked powers to exercise control over the institutions of the state as well as all other social institutions. (2) Totalitarianism violates the freedom of conscience. Totalitarianism forcibly disseminates an ideology that is total and claims to be authoritative for all areas of individual consciousness. (3) Totalitarianism violates the boundaries between the public and the private spheres by politicizing all areas of the life of the community, including those that, according to liberalism, are neglected to the private sphere and regarded as the domain of individual freedom of choice.[206]

In this subsection I will discuss (1) ((2) and (3) will be discussed later), and (1) involves the corporatization of experience and consciousness that I discussed in the last chapter. If we compare the structure of a corporation to the first point in Halburstam's passage, what could be a better account of a corporation than the description he gives? For example, if in Halburstam's point (1), we replace "state" with the word "corporation," "totalitarianism" with "corporatism," and if we replace "social institutions" with "part of the corporation," it seems we have a perfect description of what occurs at a corporation and in a totalitarian-corporatist society (such as the totalitarian Nazi Germany, Soviet Russia, or the contemporary United States), without changing in any way the meaning of Halburstam's overall passage, due to the fact that corporations involve totalitarian structure. Here is Halburstam's passage with those substitutions:

(1) Corporatism is rule by force not by consent. Corporatism eradicates political freedom, democratic process, and legality as such, by setting up the daily pronouncements of the ruler and of the party as an omnipotent force with unchecked powers to exercise control over the institutions of the corporation as well as all other part of the corporation.

Halburstam's point (1) involves the unfreedom of the human in corporatist America. Now ask a simple question: If a human is unfree, what is it,

---

[206] Halburstam 1999, 5-6. Halburstam discusses two other characteristics on page 6, but they get rather abstract and thus I won't put them in here.

specifically, about a human that makes them unfree? Above we saw that what a human is, is *consciousness*: the subjective life of feelings and thoughts. Therefore, the unfreedom of the corporatized human person involves the unfreedom of consciousness, and that can only involve the domination and imprisonment of thought and behavior.

If one works at McDonalds, for example, one does not fully *own* their behavior or their thoughts when they are "on the clock" at the corporation. One typically does not decide when they will work, what tasks they will or will not perform, their pay, what is appropriate to say or wear or look at[207] and so on when at the corporation. Rather, employees of corporations are *ordered* by others who are "higher" in social-corporate status in the corporatist one-way power relationship, and they may even be warned that if they do not unconditionally cooperate, they can be "terminated."

For these reasons, under the corporatist system, the human spirit is *owned* (controlled), rather than spontaneous. As I showed in chapter 2, this is a tyrannization of consciousness and of the human spirit. In such a system, workers lose the awareness of the power they hold, and thus virtually all the power in this scenario lies with the corporatists. The worker is expected to have blind slave-like complicity and allegiance, and is not expected to question the circumstances of her corporatized world and existence. This leads to totalist subservience on the part of the workers, to such a degree that the most notorious and corrupt military generals and slave-masters might nod in approval of it.

Professor DiLorenzo discusses this ownership of the human spirit, in a passage that adequately describes a corporation (if one merely interchanges the word "state" with the word "corporation" in the passage):

> From an economic perspective, fascism meant (and means) an interventionist industrial policy, mercantilism, protectionism, and an ideology that makes the individual subservient to the state. "Ask not what the State can do for you, but what you can do for the State" is an apt description of the economic philosophy of fascism. The whole idea behind collectivism in general and fascism in particular is to make citizens subservient to the state and to place power over resource allocation in the hands of a small elite. As stated eloquently by the American fascist economist Lawrence Dennis, fascism "does not accept the liberal dogmas as to the sovereignty of the consumer or trader in the free market.... Least of all does it consider that market freedom, and the opportunity to make competitive profits, are rights of the individual."

---

[207] For example, it is typically not appropriate for a person to daydream, to "stare off into space," while at the corporation. One must not revel in moments of self-absorbed freedom, but rather one must keep their mental energies away from such moments of unproductive poet-behavior, and on the wishes of the corporatists.

Such decisions should be made by a "dominant class" he labeled "the elite."[208]

The corporatized human in the corporatist society is successfully tricked into not asking what she can do for herself, and how she can help herself. Rather, she is tricked into giving her personhood—her consciousness and subjectivity—to the corporation. This is evidenced by her daily sacrifice of her time to the corporation, where the bulk of her day goes toward it, rather than to any of her own interests (children, hobbies, art, education, farming, community, etc.). This is a mindless, familyless, passionless, artless, helpless and totalist devotion to the state (the corporation) that is right out of Orwell's *1984*

It seems that the spooky communism Americans so often dread and disdain is precisely what they live under daily while they are at work at the corporation (and outside of the corporation). This is perhaps the best way to illustrate that Americans are jailed within what some theorists call the most successful sort of enslavement: *where the slaves do not know they are slaves, and the slaves believe they are free and happy.* Americans have seemed to imagine that they are free of the tyranny of communism, and that their American way of life is not communistic (they seem to primarily believe this because they have so many cheap consumer products to play with). Even American academics, who very typically believe they are not brainwashed, that they are exempt from the enculturation that the population undergoes, typically tell their students that America is not a communist state, and instead, academics often seem to believe in concepts which are devoid of evidence, such as the concept that the United States is capitalistic, democratic, non-communist, or the idea that it is a republic.

The Ownership of the Subjectivity of the Corporatized Person

What about Halburstam's second point? Are people pressured and tricked into obtaining a certain belief or thought system, or even a total ideology, while at the corporation? If they do, does it make up their ideology while they are outside the corporation, such as when they are at home after work watching television, taking care of children, mowing the lawn, and so on?

Let me begin to answer these questions with another question: Have you ever gone to the bathroom at Target Department Store? If you have, perhaps you noticed the employee entrance that is often back by the bathrooms. There will likely have been a sign on the employee door, but it did not say, "Employee Door;" rather, I have noticed that it says, "Team Player Entrance." I noticed this at the two Target stores I visited very few times in 2005 and 2006, and I have seen very similar sorts of things going on at other stores, such as Subway. Now ask yourself another question: Have you ever had an interview for a position at

---

[208] DiLorenzo 1993.

a corporation where it was *not* expected that you will be a "positive thinker" or a "positive contributor" ("positive team player") to the corporation? Of course not. Have you ever been at work at a corporation and told your boss repeatedly, "I don't want to be here," and had those natural feelings accepted as being normal feelings to have in such a situation? I could go on with other examples, but I think what I have written in this paragraph starts to reveal how thought is pervasively controlled by corporations. It typically does not end with being a "team player" (i.e., working well with others), being "positive," and so on, Usually it goes much further, and one is "urged" or "persuaded," for example, to not complain about what the level of pay one receives (which is almost always insufficient, in the case of America), to not complain about not having health care provided for by the corporation, to not complain about poor or inhumane treatment, not to be in any way a questioner of the corporation or of corporatism, and to not say certain "inappropriate" things or wear "inappropriate" clothing. And very typically, employees of a corporation will be pressured to have similar views as the corporatist himself/herself (such as the ideas that corporatists inhabit a higher level on the food chain than laborers, that stratified pay is natural and inevitable, that it is natural and good to spend most of the week at the corporation rather than with family, that labor unions are bad, and so on), as if the ideas and ways of life of the rich are good for the non-rich.

It is critical to understand how belief and thought among the members of the RP is *created* by the corporations, for the corporations, and to the detriment of the average citizen in communist America—all while most citizens will go a lifetime without ever knowing that any of this has happened. The real purpose of corporatist culture

> is to instill, by intimidation, in the people of a society the uncritical conviction that corporations are omnipotent. People learn that a prayer is slow to reverse what a law, a classroom, a jail-cell or bullet can do in a short order of time. Thus, a person trained in a religious and family environment for the first eighteen years of her/his life can, by the instrument of the government (corporations), be broken down, purged of her/his fantasies, passions, and delusions in a matter of mere months. Once that conviction is instilled, all else becomes easy to instill.[209]

The corporatized human does not shape her self and subjectivity; it is constructed for her. For that reason, she does not own herself; rather, the state owns her. She is an instrument of the Brave New World.

---

[209] This is a modification of a passage from "The Draft" section of the famous document, *Silent Weapons for Quiet Wars*, which is a document dated May 1979, found on July 7, 1986, in a former military IBM machine that wound up at a surplus sale, as the legend goes.

Brainwashing and the Unison
of the Big Media Agenda

One of the points of the loose and popular definition of communism was that communist and fascist states involve *mass brainwashing* of the citizens. This is perhaps the most important issue in the study of corporatism and American communism. The descriptions I just gave about how thought is controlled by corporations starts to hint at how subtly and pervasively Americans are brainwashed. They have been taught that a horrific existence, of devoting life to drudgery in the corporation (rather than to family at home), working in soulless Orwellian corporate settings, is natural, normal, and good. If one reads anthropology and studies the way of life of non-Western, "pre-civilized" humans (such as the classic but rigorous scientific text, *Foraging Spectrum*, by Robert L. Kelly[210]), one will be awakened to the fact that American life and culture is not the way humans naturally and spontaneously live, and normal human life involves centeredness around farming and children, rather than TV and slave-like Orwellian labor, around knowledge and religiosity in the profound sense, rather than brainwashing and despiritualization.

Americans have nearly no idea of what ordinary human life is like, that it is a way of life dedicated to family, philosophy, intimacy, and spontaneity. It is the inverse of the culture of America, which unfortunately can be shown to be a conglomerate of brainwashed supporters of corporatism, who have gone along with the destruction of the family, the enslavement of behavior and the mind, and the injury of virtually all American children (via vaccinations, low-quality diet, public [government mandated] education, etc.). It is no small feat to corral an entire population into specifically doing what makes them unhappy and enslaved. This takes years of planning by the secret government. But it is all made a rather straightforward project by the secret government, since they have control of all American media, in order to turn American into a massive military brainwashing camp.

Nearly all media information of any sort in the United States is controlled by a dozen supermassive corporations that all have similar militaristic, Orwellian interests (Viacom, the Carlyle Group, Hearst Corporation, Disney, GE, News Corp. Tribune Company, Gannett Company, Clear Channel, AOL, the McClatchy Company, the New York Times Company, etc.), all of which are controlled by people who work together behind the scenes,[211] who are proven to be extremely interested in war, and are able to financially profit enormously when there is war. Aurora Wallace, Professor, New York University, Communications Department, has said: Why would companies like GE and Walt Disney want to own the largest media corporations, like NBC and ABC

---

[210] Smithsonian 1995.

[211] Bagdikian 2004.

respectively? To keep a check on the information that is going out of them.[212] As was seen before the invasion of Iraq in 2003, when reports of weapons of mass destruction were played every minute on the news stations, these corporatists are able, over time, to fully dictate what appears on "the news."

I imagine that millions of Americans would probably doubt my claim here that the entire news media could be so tightly streamlined, as to function as a mass brainwashing mechanism, even to the extent that the mass media can be considered to be working for the secret government, all in order to deliberately convey false information to the world (e.g., vaccines are safe, fluoride is nutritious, WMDs are in Saddam's Iraq, a jetliner hit the Pentagon on 9-11-01, and on and on). I believe most Americans would find this *preposterous and ridiculous*, and I believe they would imagine this all to be something only for dark times, under dark regimes, like Nazi Germany, but not the USA. But if that were the case, and if the media is not so carefully orchestrated and choreographed, fabricated, unified, and planned, then why do all the media networks act in unison, reporting on all the same stories for roughly the same amount of time, not following up on them after they fade away, without any sense of closure or completion? We can all verify this cohesion in the media for ourselves since it is something we have all seen. At the time that I write this paragraph (May and June 2006), all the corporate news agencies (including NPR, to some extent), are devoting *extensive* news-time, day-after-day, week-after-week, to reporting on an unproven claim that a few members of the Duke Lacrosse team have raped one or two women. There are surely many rape accusations going on around the United States right now, so why report endlessly on this one speculative story, and ignore all the rest? And why are all the aforementioned mainstream news agencies paying attention to this story and ignoring other rape cases all over the country in the same way? Are any other college athletes mentioned in rape cases? Or being merely accused of rape? Don't you think at least *one* of these major news media corporations would have decided that this story is not really "news" and would have started reporting on something else, or would have decided to report on another rape case, or would have at least reported on *something* different, rather than perfectly emulate each of the other news agencies? Also, remember all the incredible coverage all at once about Martha Stewart, Michael Jackson, and Coby Bryant in 2002 and in the summer of 2003? How about Brad and Jenn? or Brad and Angelina? Bill and Monica, Bruce and Demi, Robert Downy Jr., T.O., O.J., and the list is nearly endless? Why such uniformity on over-reporting on these petty and often tabloid stories? Again, why wouldn't at least *one* of the major networks have ceased coverage, avoided coverage, and reported on other things?

The Duke Lacrosse team did not even contain any celebrities or celebrity sex scandals. And why are all corporatist media conglomerates covering just the

---

[212] This quote is from Pappas 2003.

same stories? Certainly there is some variety possible, some variety in the sex scandals, celebrity gossip, war news, "terrorist threat" news, government scandal news, and so on, that could be reported on. It is easy to verify that this uniformity of the corporatist media is *not* principally profit-driven: it is not working primarily in the interest of good business. For example, why on 9-11-2001 did *all* the major mainstream corporate news networks, including *NPR*, report that Osama bin Laden was responsible for the attacks when precisely zero evidence or proof had been presented?[213] If the media is not in unison, why has there been virtually no coverage of the recent warfare in Congo/Zaire and Angola, which is one of the most deadly wars since World War II, killing millions and millions of people? Why has there been virtually zero coverage on Brazil, who in 2006 was refining radioactive material in order to make nuclear bombs—the same thing the media has been utterly preoccupied with in North Korea and Iran throughout 2006.

It may be difficult for the average American to believe that entire media apparatus is a secretive and tightly streamlined mass brainwashing mechanism of the secret government, unleashed upon the people in order to deliberately convey false information to the world and to create a false view of reality in the minds of world citizens, perhaps not unlike the false reality portrayed in the film *The Matrix*. But this is what Rampton and Stauber have shown is the case, where media is corporatist controlled, carrying out secret agendas of "perception management,"[214] where the

> PR [public relations] industry has turned to the social sciences for help in developing techniques... Psychologists, sociologists and opinion pollsters work in tandem with computer programmers to develop complex databases so refined that they can pinpoint prevailing "psychographics" of individual city neighborhoods... Today's public relations industry has become so pervasive that part of its invisibility stems from the fact that it is, indeed, everywhere—from T-shirts bearing product names to movie product placements to various behind-the-scenes efforts at "issue management," "perception management," or "crisis management" (to use just a few of the currently fashionable buzzwords).[215]

The Media and 9/11

Imagine that in 1999 you told a friend that politicians and the US media as-a-whole will fervently tell the world that a plane hit the Pentagon on September 11. 2001, but no plane parts will be found at the crash site (which has never

---

[213] It has been well established by those who question the 9/11 events, that the Osama bin Laden confession tape that was later released was a fake. See Tarpley 2006 for copious discussion of the nonexistence of evidence that Osama bin Laden had something to do with 9/11.

[214] Rampton and Stauber 2002, 22-30.

[215] Rampton and Stauber 2002, 26-27

happened before in any other plane crash),[216] no pictures of this plane will be shown the public as it crashes into the Pentagon and thus no person could visually prove that it was a plane that hit.[217] You would probably be embarrassed to say this to a friend. Then imagine that in 1999 you told your friend that *all* politicians and corporatist news media personalities were ubiquitously and unquestioningly telling the world that a massive jetliner *did* hit the Pentagon, never even suggesting that there were confusing issues and many absurdities, involved with the plane-hitting-the-Pentagon story. Would you not be afraid and embarrassed to tell your friend that story out of fear of sounding like a crackpot or a conspiracy theorist?

If it is hard for you to believe that the news and information media are in such unison as I am suggesting above, then why has not one single news organization at least *once* reported on the discrepancy of the size of the hole in the pre-collapsed Pentagon (the Pentagon before the roof collapsed 25 minutes after the explosion there on 9/11/2001) compared to the plane's width?[218] Why has not a single news agency *ever once* pointed out the obvious madness in suggesting that a jetliner can hit the Pentagon at 400 m.p.h. without breaking nearly any of the windows (and the Pentagon wall is full of windows)? I even took the time to specifically call (more than once) in May of 2006 my local TV station, WLFI, in West Lafayette, Indiana, and I even emailed them information and pictures on these stories about the Pentagon, and I told them that they could go and see the evidence for themselves if they merely looked at Pentagon crash footage from September 11, 2001. You'd think that the news agency would be dying for this *huge* story—a story which could be one of the biggest ones of the last 50 years. But not only did WLFI in West Lafayette, Indiana, *not* report the story, they did not even want to talk to me about it, as if the story was a waste of time.

The Pentagon issue is extremely simple, and merely comes down to merely comparing the sizes of things: object A (plane wing span) is over 120 wide, and thus does not seem to be able to fit into object B (15 foot hole in the Pentagon wall). This simple comparison is something we all learn to do when we are about one or two years old playing with blocks and tinker toys and so on: it is the simplest of empirical issues, like comparing the size of the hole in the opening of my gallon of milk with the size of the hole in the bowl of cereal I pour the milk in to: one hole is bigger than the other: the round hole at the top

---

[216] What was found were only a few, mostly unscratched, and oddly uncharred pieces of plane debris, which strangely were found very far from the crash site, out on the Pentagon lawn near the road, these parts did not clearly appear to be plane parts.

[217] There should be a huge number of pictures available since the Pentagon is perhaps one of the most intensely surveilled buildings in the world.

[218] You can verify that there never has been one mainstream corporatist news agency reporting on this by doing a search on something like newslibrary.com, which searches newspapers for text keywords.

of the milk container is a smaller hole than the big round hole that the bowl has. Simple stuff, but no reporting on it in the national media whatsoever in the half-decade since the 9/11 "terrorist" event. I also emailed several senators about this, but there was never a report that showed up in the national media, and not even one email response back from any of the Senators. I even called the "liberal" senator from Nevada, but he did not take my call, or respond to the email I sent him.

Big Media Uniformity

It seems that the idea that the corporatist media *cannot* be in the miraculous unison is wrong. The corporatist news media *must* be in astounding unison. The idea that the corporatist media is in perfect unison is not just possible, it is *provable*, by the few examples I have already given in this book. Here are a few more examples. Near the start of the Iraq war, it was caught on film how the US military attacked and killed members of the Arab news agency, Al-Jazeera.[219] This story was widely reported on outside of the USA, but this story was not reported on in the United States. In the famous "Battle of Fallujah" in 2004 during the Iraq war, Americans used chemical weapons against the Iraqis.[220] In other words, the US Administration accused the Iraqi government throughout 2002 and into 2003 up to the March 2003 invasion of having ready-to-fire weapons of mass destruction, which they did not, but instead the US administration used weapons of mass destruction *on Iraq*. This is an example of the inversion of what the typical American is led to believe in their news media. This story of the chemical attack in Fallujah was widely reported on outside of the USA, but was virtually never reported on in the USA.

And here's another example: US Steel, which is near Indiana University Northwest, where I taught at until June 2007, is pumping out hazardous chemicals all over Lake Michigan, and downwind are all sorts of towns (Kalamazoo, Holland, Benton Harbor, Ann Arbor, etc.), and it is virtually never reported on. Given the catastrophe that mercury can cause to children and fetuses, this story may contain as much murder and slaughter as a typical Iraq war story might have, but no news coverage on it can be found.[221] Here's

---

[219] For more information, see the film, *Control Room*. 2004. Director: Jehane Noujam. Studio: Lion's Gate.

[220] There are many news stories covering this outside of the United States. For example, see "White Phosphorous: Weapons on the Edge," by Paul Reynolds, November 16, 2005, *BBC News*. The only news coverage I know of associated with a US news agency was the *Washington Post Foreign News* Service: "U.S. Forces Battle Into Heart of Fallujah Units Meet Scattered Resistance; Attacks Continue Elsewhere," by Jackie Spinner, Karl Vick and Omar Fekeiki, November 10, 2004, *Washington Post Foreign Service*, page A01.

[221] Interestingly, America is also undergoing an autism epidemic, where in just a decade autism went from being a not-so-common ailment among children to being one of the most frequent among children. Mercury is, to my knowledge, a top candidate for being

another example of the way the media is always in unison. Why in November of 2000, deep into the night after the day of the Presidential election, did *all* the networks start calling the election for Bush, when obviously no such claim could be made yet given the fact that there was no evidence and all the votes had not been counted? Why have all the networks virtually ignored talking about PNAC (discussed in a chapter below), a non-secretive, but virtually unknown, organization (think tank) that claims it seeks global military dominance for the USA, and claims that this can only be done in the proper amount of time if the citizens of the United States are energized by a Pearl Harbor sort of event to shake them into preparing for battle, and which includes members like Dick Cheney, Donald Rumsfeld, Jeb Bush, Steve Forbes, to name a few?[222] Examples of the unison of the news media are nearly countless. Here is another story that has literally never been reported in the United States: US-led sanctions on Iraq that started in the early 1990s and which, without reason or justification, were never lifted, and this resulted in, at the very least, 1 million Iraqi civilian deaths.[223] 300 millions Americans have no idea that this happened, because of the amazingly well coordinated and synchronized news media. Also, it is amazing that almost no Americans know what the over 150,000 American troops in Iraq have been doing from day-to-day from 2003 to 2006, since it is never reported.[224]

This discussion makes it appear surprising that anybody ever assumed the media *was not* fully uniform. There is no reason to hold that assumption, and the uniformity of the mass media shows how successful of a brainwashing tool the mass media is. When one looks at the media corporations in more detail,

---

the cause of this epidemic. Yet, no news media coverage of US Steel, one of the leading mercury polluters. See the Introduction of Kirby 2005, which appears to prove that the autism epidemic is caused by the mercury in vaccines.

[222] I will discuss PNAC, The Project for a New American Century, in detail in a chapter below, including documenting their eagerness for a 9/11-like Pearl Harbor event that would ready the nation for preemptive.

[223] For more information see Brohy and Ungerman 2001; Felton 2005, chapter 13.

[224] Here is a sample of what they are doing. They are practicing old-fashion (and what could even be called Nazi-style) intimidation tactics: trying to act intimidating to make their forces look bigger than what they are. Another thing they are doing is, without exaggeration, breaking into homes during the middle of the night, often which are occupied, and very commonly breaking into peaceful family homes, often barging right into small children's' rooms, pulverizing them with fear, then rummaging through their belongings. For footage of this, see Olds and Scott 2005, and Langan 2003. I have had students that are soldiers that have been in my classes at three of the universities I have taught at also confirm with me that this breaking-and-entering is a dominant part of what the troops are doing in Iraq on a daily (and nightly) basis.

one finds they are really one big company collaborating in business and profit.[225]

Media Absurdity and Control

The information in the corporatist mass media is meant to give the *appearance* that it comes in all different flavors, colors, and from all different views and sources. But this is an illusion,[226] and it is all corporatist-friendly, only conveying one sort of information: corporatist pleasing information. A person is subjected to this information throughout a lifetime, and the net effect is a massive *education* in corporatist-approved views, political positions, and so on.

> Television can... be planned so as to teach social values and social behavior as well as academic and cognitive skills. It can be designed to mobilize viewers to take certain actions and it can be used as a forum for airing socially controversial topics.[227]

Only the simplest of examples are needed to establish the idea that mass media influences and/or structures thought. For example, if a person sees a sexy television commercial she may have more sexual thoughts in the minutes after. And here is another example: on 9-10-2001, Americans seemed to be not overly concerned with terrorism, but on 9-12-2001 it was the hottest topic in town, *any* town. The idea that mass-media affects consciousness, and can affect society-at-large, seems to be utterly straightforward, but interestingly, it seems it is something that I could more easily explain to my 6 year-old niece than I could to most adults.

The famous books, *Brave New World* and *1984*, also involve societies that have completely controlled media that is run by the controlling powers of a nation. Also, like American media, the media depicted in those books consists of the same constant and repeating phrases of propaganda, which, like American mass media, is also replete with absurd ideas ("war is peace," work is fun", "are you a weekend warrior?" "freedom is slavery," etc.), and it also spreads fear, deifies war, glorifies enslavement and corporatism, denigrates family, contains nearly no fact (see chapter 1), and portrays life as being shallow and artificial: as being only full of youth and joy, of forced and fabricated "fun" and "happiness."

---

[225] See Bagdikian 2004 for more information on this huge one-corporation media monopoly that exists.

[226] See Rampton and Stauber 2002, chapter 1, and Bagdikian 2004, for more information on how the mass media is meant to give the appearance of being diverse, consisting of a competitive set of corporations, but where this is however a facade.

[227] Huston, Donnerstein, Fairchild, Feshbach, Katz, Murray, Rubinstein, Wilcox, and Zuckerman 1992, 63.

Many Americans are familiar with these famous books and the controlled media they involve, but those same Americans ubiquitously fail to see how, by analogy, the American mass media operates in precisely the same way. Perhaps the most overt similarity is the *repetition* in American media and the media in *Brave New World* and *1984*. The same messages endlessly beat the same mantras and doublespeak into the minds of Americans: "Iraq is a threat," "Iraq has weapons of mass destruction," "Hezbollah are terrorists," "they hate us because we are free," "stock trades for only $8 per trade," "Iran may soon nuke you when they get a bomb," "America is a democracy," "we need to get the terrorists," "are you getting the best out of your wireless plan?," "you are free," "terrorist cells have infiltrated American society," "a lot of guys over 40 need Viagra," and so on. Just like the Orwellian or Huxleyan worlds of *1984* and *Brave New World*, these ideas are nonsense: they are based on ideas of a reality that *does not exist*, and they involve hidden contradiction (it is actually in plain view, but is hidden for those who do not see it). There are so many ideas that Americans hold that are about things and events that do not and did not exist, and which involve contradiction, such as the idea that Iraq was a threat, the idea that 911 and Pearl Harbor were a surprise to all American politicians and corporatists, that Christopher Columbus was the person that discovered North America, the idea that George W. Bush was elected democratically in 2000 and 2004, and that vaccines are safe, just to give a few of the nearly countless examples that could be given.

It seems that most Americans are not aware of how absurd the bombardment of the unified corporatist media information is. Pervasive absurdity of the media information is a fundamental characteristic of a corporatist-controlled media in a communist-fascist setting. This is precisely the sort of media we find in the worlds described in Orwell's *1984*, or the news media of the entertainment world of Huxley's *Brave New World*. We are all familiar with the non-logical statements in American media, since we have all heard them throughout our life: "only with war (pre-emptive strikes) can we be assured of peace," "we think Osama bin Laden is in the rugged mountains of Afghanistan, but we cannot capture or locate him." And who can forget these utterances by Rumsfeld, on February 12, 2002 at a Department of Defense news briefing:

> As we know, there are known knowns.
> There are things we know we know.
> We also know there are known unknowns.
> That is to say we know there are some things we do not know.
> But there are also unknown unknowns,
> The ones we don't know we don't know.

It seems that the majority of Americans do not notice the utter absurdity and careless reporting that pervades the media, and rather they get accustomed to this sort of imprecise and absurdist information flow. This has the effect of dumbing down the entire world population, who cease to demand or even expect high-quality, verifiable, scientifically-oriented information from their media (including the information delivered to them in schools and universities). In other words, the media can be replete with absurdism, but who's really even clear-minded enough to notice?

Controlled, Implanted, Repeating Language in the Mass Media

In such cultures as ours, and as the Huxleyan *Brave New World* and the world you can read about in Orwell's *1984*, from early in life, the mass media, education, and religious systems of the nations are primarily devoted to constructing unscientific citizens who are not analytical or critical thinkers, and who are not taught to value the evidential and logical modes of thought. Instead, citizens are taught that *belief* (defined as a thought or statement that is devoid of evidential backing) is knowledge, and that *evidence* is, quite literally, to be disdained. Citizens who speak in terms of data, and only make claims in terms of empirical data, are considered pests, and often even fools!

It may be the case that some people have sayings from the mass media swirling through their heads for years, and even some of the sayings that they were inculcated with as children may be swirling through their minds as adults: "Where's the beef!," "GE, we bring good things to life," "Heeeeeeer's Johnny!," "Take the Pepsi Challenge," "snap, crackle, pop," "they're grrrrrrrreat!," "Coke is it!," "they make money the old fashion way, they *earn* it," "kid tested, mother approved," "I *love* this place," "trickle-down economics," "Read my lips: *no new taxes*!, "I *did not* have sex with that woman," "Power E-trade," "That's the wayeee theyeee became the Brady Bunch." It often appears that our minds are like a tape recorder, where implanted phrases such as these flash through our minds and we have no control over them. Regardless of what media channel or media stream one watches, listens to, or reads, there are times (such as 2002 and 2003, with phrases like, "Iraq is a "threat to peace"[228]), that you may hear specific phrases

---

[228] Consider this discussion from George W. Bush, October 7, 2002, from Cincinnati:
Tonight I want to take a few minutes to discuss a grave threat to peace, and America's determination to lead the world in confronting that threat. The threat comes from Iraq. ... Eleven years ago, as a condition for ending the Persian Gulf War, the Iraqi regime was required to destroy its weapons of mass destruction, to cease all development of such weapons, and to stop all support for terrorist groups. The Iraqi regime has violated all of those obligations. It possesses and produces chemical and biological weapons. It is seeking nuclear weapons. It has given shelter and support to terrorism, and practices terror against its own people. ... We also must never forget the most vivid events of recent history. On September the 11th, 2001, America felt its vulnerability -- even to threats that gather on the other side of the earth.
Now Bush uses this identical phraseology targeted on Iran: "Iran is a threat" such as he did from the White House, January 13, 2006.

over and over, even hundreds of times in a single hour on a news channel, for example, and you may see them dozens of times on the front page of a news paper, or hear them hundreds of times in an hour on a radio show. Then you will go to work, talk to others, where you will likely hear others talk about all the same things, perhaps over and over. The nationwide debate in America is established and created by the mass media, and it is amplified throughout society. We will see that this leads to a situation where America takes on the characteristics of being a huge and efficient mass brainwashing camp, created and managed by the corporatists.

Indirect Rule

It seems that Americans usually imagine a tyrannical state to involve governing by what is called *direct rule*, where citizens are forced to live in endless and pervasive forlornness and poverty, because they are *forced* with guns to work and behave in horrific ways. But the persuasive shaping of thought and behavior not by force, and without the people knowing—which is called "indirect rule"[229]—has been a dominant feature of many of the dictatorships and communist states (e.g., Nazi Germany), and it is recognized by tyrants as being a far less messy way for tyrannical control over a citizenry than direct rule. For a fascist, indirect rule is better than direct rule in many ways. With direct rule, once you dominate the citizenry by direct force, you become dependent on direct force for control, and rebellion is perhaps always a threat. Force is expensive, and thus seeking control by information and indoctrination is far more sustainable and economical, and revolt is far less likely since the people don't know they are being mentally enslaved and controlled.

If the controllers of a nation can shape the desires, emotions, beliefs, and selves of the citizens at will, they likely will be able to maintain much tighter control than they could with martial law. For example, if a citizen can be told tens of thousands of times about how free she is, and how much of a threat another country is to that freedom, and she sees everyone around her also believing the same things, why would she believe anything else? It might even seem *crazy*, from her perspective, to believe anything else.

Thought, Behavior, and Self
Created by Corporatism

The claim that mass brainwashing pervades the "free" Western world may sound a bit too extreme even for many of the readers of this book. But if my claim, that Americans are thoroughly brainwashed is extreme, then how else do we explain, for example, why in March of 2003, and for over 13 years before that, Americans firmly believed that a leader of another nation (Saddam

---

[229] Chang 2005b, xviii.

Hussein) who was a threat even though he was really a non-threat? And why do so many Americans believe that the American medical system provides the best treatment of people in the world, when over 20 percent of the US population can't even get that treatment, due to the fact that over 40 million people in the United States don't have any health care, and when those who do have health care are abused and not helped by the medical system?[230] How can we think America has the best health care system in the world when there are never cures developed for any diseases within the orthodox medical system?[231] Why did millions of working class Americans, at the time of Ronald Reagan's death, come together by the millions to celebrate what they were labeling as one of the greatest presidents in American history—when he was, in reality, the epitome of the super-rich man's president, who deliberately initiated a horrific recession in the early 1980s specifically to put more wealth into the hands of the rich (the program was officially called, "Voo-Doo Economics") and out of the hands of the non-rich Americans? Do Americans really believe that the DVD is *really* a better technology than the VHS tape? An improvement over DVD?[232] Did polls *really* show right in the war fever that inundated America after 9/11 and around the time of the invasion of Iraq ("Shock and Awe") (this war fever faded in 2004) that the majority of Americans supported nuclear weapons to be used against Iraq?[233] Do giant pharmaceutical companies *really* produce new drugs? (Amazingly, we will see in a section below that they *do not*!) Is Iran *really* a threat to the safety of Americans? Do many Americans really believe that bottled water is healthy? How many Americans know that one of the first discoveries of the very dangerous and insidious pollutant perchlorate was in bottled water? Did, not millions, but *billions* of people around the world instantly believe on 9-11-01 that a massive jetliner hit the US Pentagon Building, even though it was not even seen in a replay on the news?[234]

---

[230] See chapter 5 below for more information. Also see Richards 2006, Court and Smith 1999, and Angell 2005 for more information.

[231] This includes the diseases, like polio and smallpox, which Americans (including American medical students) are told were eradicated by vaccines. See chapter 5 below.

[232] DVDs are often three to five times more expensive than VHS tape movies, they freeze up all the time (which I don't think many of us were warned about before purchasing them, and freeze-ups do not occur with a VHS tape *nearly* as often), they scratch very easy, they break, you often can't make copies as easy as you can with a VHS tape, and so on. But Americans were told the DVD is "so much clearer" and "better" to watch on DVD than VHS. But is that really true? And isn't most of that dependent on numerous other issues, such as on the clarity of the television screen (HD versus non-HD), and etc.?

[233] A Fox News/Opinion Dynamics poll from March 11-12 2003 revealed that 65 percent of Americans were in favor of using weapons of mass destruction in Iraq if Iraq used them against American soldiers. This poll can be viewed at pollingreport.com.

[234] Official surveillance footage of this from Pentagon surveillance cameras was not released until May of 2006 by the US government, and the tiny film showed no conclusive information (and that's an understatement), or, in the words of Bill O'Reilly

These are the sorts of situations where millions or billions of people are tricked into believing *without a doubt* that an absurd and false reality is the true reality:

what is real is believed to be not real, and what is not real is believed to be real.

This brainwashing is remarkably powerful, and citizens are so thoroughly tricked that they will even be fooled into doing absurd things, such as fighting wars in Iraq and Afghanistan without objection, and parents may willingly support their sons and daughters to fight in these wars. More recently, billions of people around the world were tricked into believing that the Hezbollah-Israel conflict of July 2006 was a real, spontaneous event, rather than ultimately a synthetic, pre-planned, secret government fabrication (I discuss why it was a fabrication elsewhere in this book). In other words, the world was fooled into believing that x was true and real, but what actually is real is *not-x*. Furthermore, x is usually, to some degree, comically absurd, in the eyes of the non-brainwashed—as was observed how so many Americans were dumbfounded by the absurd actions of the soldiers who went off to fight in Iraq.

The Muslim philosopher, al-Ghazali (1058-1111 C.E.), commented on how all the boys in one culture will believe in their God, and all the boys in another will believe in another God, and each culture will reject the other's God—often to the point of coming to violence over the issue. This illustrates the power of culture's shaping of belief and thought, and when a culture is corporatistic, thought and behavior will be shaped in such as way that it will be *crushed* under the tyrannizing force of the slave labor system and the education thought control system. The nature of the American citizen *is to be a destroyed person*, who believes she is free: she thinks she has freedom when, for example, she goes home and supposedly "does what she wants" after work (which usually involves watching TV). She may be fooled into thinking she is in control, and that she is exercising her free will. But she has no idea that she was injured from birth by vaccines that crippled her brain and consciousness, and that she was then tricked into drinking fluoridated water throughout life (which is a daily dose of a powerful neurotoxin, further crippling cognition and consciousness), and the motivational parts of personality,[235] and then she arrives at adulthood, after a lifetime of television watching and forced schooling that involves an education of unverifiable "facts" (which can be called an *Orwellian education*), to work at a job she does not like for low pay that destroys family, where in the evening all there is time and energy for is not

---

of *Fox News*, "all I see is an explosion."(He said this on "The Factor" on *Fox News*, May 18, 2006)

[235] This was discussed in detail on the Rense Radio Show, www.rense.com, March 23, 2007.

the family, but rather television, which is the government mandated in-home mind-control system that virtually all homes have and use extensively in America. Hence, the American person is crushed and destroyed, with injured consciousness, while believing that they are free.

The uniformity of the media, such as with the examples I gave above (and countless others could be given) show that it is corporatist culture, more than free will, that *causes* people to have the thought and belief that they do, to feel the feelings they do, to be the selves they are, and so on. Typically denizens of cultures around the world do not notice these patterns of belief and thought that show up in cultures, where people in cultures evolve in such a way where they think, feel, and behave uniformly. Instead of noticing that selfhood is usually the product of a person's placement in a culture, many people seem to imagine that these traits are the product of the free will of the people of the culture, rather than the culture one is immersed within every moment from birth and after.

It is difficult to tell a person who is in a dream-state that they are in a dream since they will most likely not see the dream. How would the fish know that there is water all around when the water is invisible to the fish? I am sure if any of us could go back in time to tell the "Manson women" that Charles was merely brainwashing them, they too would harshly object. Similarly, it is difficult to show an American the empirical data that shows that they are destroyed creatures, who do not even own their thoughts and feelings and actions.

Brainwashing involves getting masses of people to believe in a false and absurd reality, not by putting a gun to their head, but rather merely by controlling the information they take in. Professor Kathleen Taylor has written that "[b]rainwashing in fiction is often depicted as a coercive torture, but its conceptual heart, the deliberate and manipulative changing of belief, need not require force."[236] As in Orwell's *1984*, the citizenry never knew of anything about reality except for the picture of it given to them by the state-controlled, state-produced mass-media. How many people in the United States also, on a daily and hourly basis, gather nearly all of their information from the national corporatist media (which of course includes information from church or school, since, as mentioned above, I am using the word "media" to refer to all information in a nation)?

Televisual "Education"

Brainwashing appears to be most successful when it is in the form of a government mandated "education system" and by use of "the telescreen"

---

[236] Taylor 2004 , 52. Also see Taylor pages 53-54. On 54 she discusses how "the idea that the environment effects of advertising and the media are shaping our minds in subtle ways which we do not recognize."

(televisual information), to put it in Orwellian terms, as we have here in America. Radio talk-show scholar, Jeff Rense, has commented that television is the greatest weapon unleashed onto humanity *ever*.[237] Consider the following passage by a number of leading scholars discussing televisual brainwashing media:

> Scholars and social critics [who research national media issues have] … some basic assumptions on which [they] all agree. First, as a former commissioner of the Federal Communications Commission once said, all television is educational television. Although television is often used for entertainment, it is always more than mere entertainment. Even when it is not intentionally designed to teach, it carries messages about social interactions, and about the nature and value of groups in the society that can influence attitudes, values, and actions among its viewers. It serves as a source of information about the world, whether viewers seek entertainment or enlightenment.[238]

Changing one another's minds seems to be a natural part of human interactions and human culture. For example, when I teach, I try to use empirical (scientific) evidence to change the minds of my students on various issues and as I attempt to teach the students about reality. I will tell them, "it is up to you if you want to follow the evidence." In doing this, I am not attempting to brainwash them: I am not attempting to *force* their minds to change and to be structured in a different way, I am not attempting to trick them into believing in something that does not exist, and I am not attempting to *replace* their subjective selves with a new self that I deliberately implant into them for coercive measures. When a professor, or a politician, or a media personality talks in front of people, they use various words to try to convince people of things. Trying to convince other people of things, and to *change* their minds, is a pillar of human life, few things could be more expected and normal. Furthermore, if people did not have the desire to change the minds of others, we would not have endeavors like science, we would not have libraries, and so on.

Brainwashing is different than this, and involves pervasive, ubiquitous, forceful, totalist thought re-arrangement and self replacement that occurs in the masses of the citizens. Like in the classic film, *The Invasion of the Body Snatchers*, it is as if someone has taken the self and replaced it with an alien or foreign self—with some sort of freakish foreign identity: your self is removed or destroyed, and a new self is implanted in a person's nervous system. The United States involves education from the moment of birth in the form of faces, sounds, and feelings, and then later through guilt, dejection, duty, thought

---

[237] Rense said this on the Alex Jones Radio show December 1, 2006.
[238] Huston, Donnerstein, Fairchild, Feshbach, Katz, Murray, Rubinstein, Wilcox, and Zuckerman 1992, 6.

control, and so on. On all fronts, the function of this "education" is to obliterate the person, and replace it with corporate property.

Brainwashing Versus Science

In other words, it seems that what *brainwashing* is, is something that is aimed at robbing a person of their selfhood to some significant degree, raiding their subjectivity and identity. Consciousness and selfhood are crushed into nothing, and a false, immature, murderous self is implanted in the person in place of the genuine self that has been destroyed.

In the case of American brainwashing, there is a deliberate implantation of an illogical, irrational, scared self, and that's what constitutes a brainwashing event. Usually if I try to convince my students of something, their autonomy remains in place while I do, and do not forcibly remove the bedrock of their thought-structure or their subjective self in the process, therein implanting a totally new self that does not at all resemble the original self (which is literally what occurs in classic, textbook brainwashing). Also, out in the open, I present my students with some bit of data or information that serves as *evidence*, which is the essence of the scientific process, rather than the brainwashing process, which is secret and covert, and which usually is forced on a person without evidence.

A brainwashing event is a covert trick to persuade to the point of removing and replacing the self. It is not open, curious, and empirical, in the way my teaching is, and in the way that science is. It does not test counterpoints, or present ideas and then attempt to challenge all ideas, as a scientific pursuit does. Brainwashing is not skeptical and evidence-based, as a genuinely scientific pursuit is.[239] If I were to deliberately try to trick my students, rather than merely present them with straightforward empirical evidence of some sort, purposely taking measures to try to fool them into accepting false and even absurd information so that I can get them to believe irrational things, and even resulting in my students consequently acting in irrational ways, well, that's more like classical totalist brainwashing. Brainwashing involves a situation where a person's spontaneous and natural ability and proclivity to analyze and think about *empirical reality* is removed, due to the fact that approximately all thoughts are hijacked in a person's mind. A brainwashed person's mind consists of destroyed and irrational thoughts about unreality, wherein a person lives in a dream state. As mentioned, this is done by uniform control of the mass media. We will find in this book that virtually all Americans are subjected to a totalist "re-education" (outright, textbook, Orwellian brainwashing) on a

---

[239] If there are persons who assert that they are scientists, but who do not follow the criteria of what I am listing here (which are the defining characteristics of science), they are in reality not scientists, no matter what they want us to believe. For that reason, many of the people in the world today who tell us they are scientists are not.

daily basis, and the "re-education" takes over their consciousness, supplants consciousness, and *becomes* the new corporate (corporatized and communistic) consciousness.

Case Study: Big Pharma and Brainwashing

I would like to further explore the topic—brainwashing—with another example: Big Pharma. Big Pharma is another example—in addition to those given in previous chapters—of the contamination of humanity. As also discussed above, the corporatists from Big Pharma are perhaps some of the most powerful corporatists there are. They have tricked Americans into believing that the only medicine is orthodox medicine (drugs and surgery), and that "natural" medicine is inferior: it is witchcraft. The Big Pharma corporatists have transformed the United States into a pharmaceutical corporatist state—or what could be called a *pharmatocracy*.

Americans are taught that the massive pharmaceutical companies are involved in intensive research in order to create new pharmaceutical drugs for Americans. The massive pharmaceutical companies create the illusion that they are pioneers in drug research. This message is sent primarily through (I) the mass media, and it pervades the mass media since Big Pharma has an unfathomable wealth store to dip into order to create endless advertising that soaks the American public, and (II) with their overwhelming financial power that they use control medical schools and doctors.

I often teach a class called *Biomedical Ethics* at Indiana University Northwest. Each semester we have a unit of the class where we study Big Pharma. I always start this part of the class in the exact same way, with the following question:

Can any of you guess how many new drugs the big commercial drug companies create each year?

The students—who, you should note, tend to be nursing students, pre-med, and so on, and thus are familiar with the biomedical industry—always make the same predictable responses:

"100," says one student.
"1000," says another student.
"30," says another student.

Then, purposely, I abruptly interrupt them curtly:

"7!"

Then I explain to them that it is often even less than that.

Needless to say, the students violently object. Being biomedical students, they quickly begin listing the technical names of drugs that they "*know* for a fact are new drugs!" So what is going on here? How could a *philosophy* professor be telling a group of *biomedical* students that something so simple as the number of new drugs put out each year by Big Pharma is dramatically incorrect? Is this just more philosopher's mish-mash?

Drug Companies. The basic issue with drug companies (the biggest ones are known as "Big Pharma", BP hereafter), is that they maintain that they must continually boost the prices of drugs in order to support (1) their incredibly expensive R and D, and (2) their incredibly expensive process of bringing new drugs to market. But we will find these are both bogus claims.[240]

Developing new drugs *is*, indeed, costly, and not a sure thing. Also, drugs that are in development could fail after they are far into the costly development process, thus rendering all that research and money in the development process a waste. For that reason, we can presume that Big Pharma may take measures to make money in ways that avoid the costly drug development process. One way to do this is to modify existing drugs that are *already on the market*, and that are already proven successful sellers—merely *copying* existing drugs—in order to sell them under a *new* name and with new media and advertising fanfare. This sort of copy-cat process is cheap, profitable, and it is a sure-thing—it involves far less risk than the original drug development process.

The copy-cat drugs are called "me-too" drugs.[241] Angell writes:

> The real pharmaceutical industry… over the past two decades has moved very far from its original high purpose of discovering and producing useful new drugs. Now primarily a marketing machine to sell drugs of dubious benefit, this industry uses its wealth and power to co-opt every institution that might stand in its way, including the U.S. Congress, the Food and Drug Administration, academic medical centers, and the medical profession itself.[242]

The capitalistic/corporatist monopolization of industries and resources of the world by the corporatists dictates that the drug industry seeks "profit drugs." Angell writes that "For the many more 'me-too' drugs—minor variations of drugs already on the market—the R & D process is much faster, since a great deal of it has already been done."[243] Big Pharma will pour its incredible wealth into getting me-too drugs on the shelves, marketing them, and getting them sold.

The capitalistic-corporatist system, by its very nature, prohibits a massive pharmaceutical company from pouring all its wealth into new drugs that are unknown and risky and very costly. The mere quest for profit prohibits Big Pharma from doing much but producing me-too drugs. Big Pharma tries to

---

[240] See Angell 2004.

[241] Angell 2005, xxiv

[242] Angell 2005, xxv - xxvi

[243] Angell 2005, 21-22

conceal this, and tries to not let people on to the fact that there is no large-scale R&D going on at their corporations, and tries to give the impression that it is creating all sorts of new drugs. Keeping their real image secret is very profitable. For example, by keeping their dishonest operations covert, they can hide the fact that from 1980-2000 the sales of drugs manufactured by Big Pharma skyrocketed, but the nature of the drugs, and the quality of them, was very little changed, and if anything degenerated.[244]

Two "Laws" from the 1980s. How did this all happen? This all started with the passage of two laws from the 1980s, and it is these laws that have virtually led to the disappearance of R & D in Big Pharma (and which are doing other things, such as corrupting university research, for example). Here is information on the two laws:

> The Bayh-Dole Act (1980): This "enabled universities and small businesses to patent discoveries emanating from research sponsored by the National Institute of Health (NIH), the major distributor of tax dollars for medical research, and then to grant exclusive licenses to drug companies. Until then, taxpayer-financed discoveries were in the public domain, available to any company that wanted to use them.[245]

What this amounts to is that taxpayer supported items get turned over to private industries, where they can be dictated by corporatists, and where corporatists can jack-up the price unjustly, and not give a portion of their profits to the public, even though it is the taxpaying public that has largely financed their development. This leads to serious questions, such as why there is no public voice in what gets done with the drugs that they have paid to have developed, and how can these drugs get charged back to them at stratospheric prices.

> The Hatch-Waxman Act (1984):
> These laws extended monopoly rights for brand-name drugs. Exclusivity is the lifeblood of the industry because it means that no other company may sell the same drug for a set period. After exclusive marketing rights expire, copies (called generic drugs) enter the market, and the price usually falls to as little as 20 percent of what it was.[246]

It may seem that if x invents y, then x should be in control of y and should be able to be the faction that makes profits from it, and can monopolize the product. Why did this not happen before the two laws just described came into existence? The answer is: because x was not allowed to have full control over y before these two laws, even though x created y, and this was simply because it

---

[244] Angell 2005, 4.

[245] Angell 2005, 7.

[246] Angell 2005, 9.

was recognized that x was funded by others, and it was recognized that monopolization of y by x prohibited maximum people from benefiting from y.

Interestingly, the scenario just described helps the American consumer, by preventing what happened when this was overturned (price jacking, quality decreasing, disappearance of innovation, etc.). *This scenario helps keep drugs cheap, innovation high, competition intact, and so forth. But these laws totally undercut public power of the drug innovations, and stop the cheap pricing of them.* This is a great example of how lawmakers and congress do not act in the interests of the people but only the interests of the corporatists.

Angell writes that

> [t]hese laws mean that drug companies no longer have to rely on their own research for new drugs, and few of the large ones do. Increasingly, they rely on academia, small biotech start-up companies, and the NIH for that... One of the results has been a growing pro-industry bias in medical research... Faculty members who had earlier contented themselves with what was once referred to as a 'threadbare but genteel' lifestyle began to ask themselves, in the words of my grandmother, 'If you are so smart, why aren't you rich.' Medical schools and teaching hospitals, for their part, put more resources into searching for commercial opportunities.[247]

Non-Regulation of Big Pharma. Angell shows[248] how Big Pharma is not regulated, and how their profits are so unbelievable that they are really of the strongest of any monopolized secret government industry by far. Also, she discusses[249] how Big Pharma wants us to think that they are spending their profits on R & D, but if we merely take a look at Big Pharma it will show us that most of their massive profit goes toward "administration and marketing," where what these expenditures involve is often unprestigious to criminal.

Angell tells us[250] that there are massive criminal investigations underway. Then she gives a nice summary:

> Instead of being an engine of innovation, it is a vast marketing machine. Instead of being a free market success story, it lives off government-funded research and monopoly rights. Yet this industry occupies an essential role in the American health care system, and it performs a valuable function, if not in discovering important new drugs at least in developing them and bringing them to market.[251]

---

[247] Angell 2005, 8.

[248] Angell, 2005, 10-11.

[249] Angell, 2005, 11-12.

[250] Angell, 2005, 18-19.

[251] Angell 2005, 22.

Big Pharma is all about "image creation," with its massive marketing campaign. This is exactly what Big Pharma does not want you to know.

> So learning about the disease or condition is usually the beginning of the "research" part of R & D, and it can take a very long time—sometimes decades. There is no question that this is the most creative, and the least certain, part of the R & D process. Contrary to industry propaganda, it is almost always carried out at universities or government research labs, either in this country or abroad.[252]

Getting a drug approved and going through clinical trials takes a long time, eating into the company's wallet. So BP is always hyper-rushed to get the process of drug-approval going.[253] BP even has companies that they have created and that they have hired in order to help rush the drug-approval process along.

Of course the "regulating" FDA is advertised as being protection for the RP. But if it is aligned with the corporate tyrants, and made up of them, then it too will be unregulated, as with the above examples. Here's how Winslow puts the issue:

> The Food and Drug Administration had an annual budget of only $1.4 billion in 2000 to regulate pharmaceutical drugs that produce 50,000 to 100,000 deaths each year from overdoses and improper use, while government agencies spend $30 to $40 billion a year to fight the illegal drug trade, which produces 8,000 to 10,000 deaths from drug overdoses...[254]

BPs tell us

> Drugs are too expensive because they need to cover their very high research and development... costs. In 2001, they [BP] put these costs at $802 million (in 2000 dollars) for *each* new drug they bring to market. [my itals] (Later, the consulting firm Bain & Company upped that to $1.7 billion per drug, but they included marketing expenditures.) Implicit in this claim is a kind of blackmail: If you want drug companies to keep turning out life-saving drugs, you will gratefully pay whatever they charge. Otherwise you may wake up one morning and find there are no more new drugs.[255]

BP says it costs $802 million to bring a new drug to market.[256] All costs, including research, "are in a black box, hidden from view."[257] We don't know

---

[252] Angell 2005, 22.
[253] Angell, 2005, 28.
[254] Winslow 2003, 42.
[255] Angell, 2005, 37.
[256] Angell, 2005, 38.
[257] Angell, 2005, 39.

what activities are included in "R & D."[258] But Angell and others have done their own calculations of how much new drug development costs are, and they get to $170-270 million, far less than the black box number of $802 million.[259] The media has accepted the $802 million number "at fact value", "uncritically,"[260] and has accepted anything else BP tells them. So the media's uncritical thinking is perpetuating this whole BP image creation. The studies that BP carries out, and that they pay university researchers to do, are utterly meaningless.[261] The public, and the media, not being scientific, do not understand this, and thus do not have the ability to understand the scam. So, clearly, BP is not an R&D industry. Rather, they take publicly funded research, create poisonous products, and overcharge Americans who use BP drugs for on what we already paid for.

Just as is shown elsewhere in this book, like other massive corporations, BP gets massive tax breaks.[262] This issue, in addition to other issues that Angell writes about, show that there is a partnership between BP and Congress. This is, of course, the trademark of American corporatism.

Furthermore, we are told by Angell[263] that the government gives handouts to BP if they have losses (as if they did not have enough money to handle the losses). BP pays other corporations to deal with Congress for them on issues such as these, thus functioning roughly like a think tank. One such corporation is quoted on page 53: "Voters do not want to jeopardize the miracle of life-saving innovation in modern medicine." This is a good example of how think tanks have specific motives to only help corporatists at the detrimental expense of Americans.

Here is an actual email I sent to my students in April of 2006 where I was addressing their complaints that my lectures were wrong, due to the "fact" (according to them) that there *are* specific examples of new drugs that they knew about that Big Pharma created. The following information disproves their claims:

> The drugs you presented to me in class clearly DO NOT offer competition in that they are better (or worse) treatments than other existing drugs currently on the market. It appears that Caduet and Vytorin could have advantages over other drugs (I have to confirm this however, it is hard to find studies that are clearly non-biased, and/or which are not 'hidden' studies done by the companies themselves), but what is important about Vytorin and Caduet is that they each are combination drugs, but are not composed of new ingredients, and thus in some sense they are not drugs that are the result of the arduous process

---

[258] Angell, 2005, 39.

[259] Angell, 2005, 40.

[260] Angell, 2005, 41.

[261] See Angell, 2005, esp. 42.

[262] See Angell, 2005, 45, p. 46 gives specific dollar amounts.

[263] Angell, 2005, esp. 50-51.

of bringing new drugs to market, which, as we've said in class, is what BP endlessly tells us is all they are doing. So, in sum, NONE of the drugs you told me about can clearly be called NEW drugs.

I will go over all this information in class, but here are my results:

1. Seasonale: this appears to only use already existing drug ingredients but which are only released in the body in a different way, here is the FDA report:

Click here: FDA Approves Seasonale Oral Contraceptive

Since it offers virtually no ingredients other drugs don't, I am not sure how it could be considered competition against other drugs, from the perspective of what the drug does to the body. To say it does would be like saying that Jello is competing against *generic* gelatin because generic solidifies much quicker, even though the ingredients are identical, each tastes the same, affects the body the same.

2. Vytorin:

Here is a news story that talks all about how well Vytorin is selling, but interestingly it is never stated why it is, or what difference it has from other cholesterol drugs.

Click here: Vytorin rockets to No. 3 top-selling cholesterol blocker - Jul. 26, 2005

3. Caduet:

This is a combination drug, so it could offer competition over existing drugs for the same ailment if it can be shown to really perform better (which I did not check out). But at any rate, Caduet is not a new drug in the sense that it involved the toil of new drug development, since it is merely existing drugs combined.

4. Boniva:

This one confused me. I was not sure why any of you were suggesting that this was a new or a competitive drug. This drug is not new at all, and it is so old that it already even has a whole string of generics (copies). Remember, as we said in class, a drug that exists for a long time has generics, so if Boniva has generics, it is not new at all. Here is a link to FDA webpage of one of the generics:

Click here: Ibandronate Sodium (marketed as Boniva): Consumer Information Sheet

So any of you who were telling me that this is competition since it is a new drug and/or has alterations that offer competition, it appears that Boniva is a good example for our class since it is an example where it appears you have been fooled by the BP'ers!

Here is another site that talks about all the groups of copies (generics) of Boniva (I don't know how credible this site is, but it appears to have been written by a doctor or something):

Click here: Boniva (ibandronate) for Osteoporosis - audio medical podcasts on MedicineNet.com

5. Fosamax:

Like 4, this is also not a new drug. My page on the web I looked at on Google showed me that this drug has been around for at least almost a decade. Here is the FDA page (which, interestingly, is a page that involves an FDA-posted letter from a scientist in 1996 writing about its side-effects, which apparently, and interestingly, were missed (?) during FDA approval?):

Click here: MedWatch Safety Summaries - Fosamax
I did no more research on this drug than just this, since it is not an example of a new drug, and it is not an example of a new drug offering competition against existing drugs, as I think some of you were implying.
6. Cialis vs. Levitra vs. Viagra:
These are truly blockbuster drugs! Some of you were asking me about this. I did very little research on this one, but on page 87 and elsewhere Angell talks of how they are all copies of one another. Also, here's some FDA information on how they are all lumped together, given their identical status:
Cialis (Tadalafil) Information Page

Total Enslavement of the Citizenry

Citizens are made to be fully dependent on the corporatist system. Fewer and fewer backyard gardens and water wells exist in America. Citizens become dependent on corporatists, for food and water, and the corporations give them poisoned food and water. Citizens stop using supplements, herbs, good diet and nutrition, and home remedies for medicine, and they instead use the products and services from the medical industry and the big pharmaceutical companies, which are widely known to be deadly, ineffective, and Nazistic in origin.[264] Citizens stop learning basic survival skills, such as wilderness skills, farming, home maintenance, hunting skills, and so on. All basic life knowledge and skills are relinquished, and the citizen instead gives all her time and mental energy to working for the corporation, and then indulging in the superficial entertainment and distraction systems that the New World Order corporatists have deliberately and carefully set up in order to distract citizens.[265] But there are two tricks involved with this:

1. This dependency makes persons completely enslaved and dependent on the corporatists, and
2. The products and services that the citizenry must purchase from the corporatists are all (yes, *all*!) harmful to the citizens.

It is not a secret that points 1 and 2 are gradually and *deliberately* put in place by the secret government in order to enslave and poison the citizenry, and to do whatever they want to the citizenry. For example, Catherine Bertini, Executive Director of the U.N. World Food Program said: "Food is power! We use it to change behavior. Some may call that bribery. We do not apologize."[266] Professor Chossudovsky eloquently writes about how the malls, grocers, and

---

[264] See Angell 2005, Horowitz 2001, Richard 2006, Tenpenny 2005, Matsumoto 2004, and to see how this is tied to food, the CODEX, and nutricide, see Pawlick 2003 and Afrika 2000.
[265] It is no secret that this setup of an entertainment system to distract citizens, and to, in other words, keep them essentially dumbed down and uncritical thinkers. The New World Order discusses this in many documents, such as Brzezinski's book, *The Grand Chessboard*.
[266] Cited in Thorn 2003, 213.

the massive globalist corporatist food production is meant to remove local farms and economies, thus rendering citizens helpless:

> At the local level, small and medium sized enterprises are pushed into bankruptcy or obliged to produce for a global distributor. In turn, large multinational companies have taken control of local-level markets through the system of corporate franchising. This process enables large corporate capital (the franchiser) to gain control over human resources, cheap labor and entrepreneurship. A large share of the earnings of small local level firms and/or retailers is thereby appropriated by the global corporation, while the bulk of investment outlays is assumed by the independent producer (the franchisee).[267]

Point 2 may surprise some readers, but it is not a secret that the water supply is poisoned,[268] and in addition to that, medications, vaccinations, furniture, cookery, soap, textiles, air, plastics and petrochemicals, and so on, which are the products that are all created by corporations for use by the world's humans in order for them to survive, are utterly *toxic* and deliberately made to be poisonous.[269] These items are *covertly* laced or filled with, for example, pesticides, mercury, lead, herbicides, steroids, aluminum, anti-biotic remnants, manmade neurotoxins, bizarre things like masses of Prozac (which are, for example, in the water supply, as mentioned in chapter 2), just to name a few.[270]

The covertness of this broad and pervasive poisoning of the world citizenry by the secret corporatist government is startling. For example, things like vegetables are devoid of nutritional value due to genetic engineering.[271] A tomato on the shelf at the grocery store may look nutritious, but it has vastly fewer essential and critically important nutrients than tomatoes in the past. Medicines, such as psychiatric medicines[272] and vaccines,[273] among others, are literally poisonous and deadly. Americans are also routinely sprayed with bioterrorist weapons and chemical weapons by the United States government,[274] and amazingly, this spraying has been made *legal*, even if it causes mass death among Americans, since it is in the United States Code of law.[275] Americans are dependent on, and give their weekly earnings to, grocery stores and other corporatist edifices, that ensicken and kill them.

---

[267] Chossudovsky 2003, 9.

[268] Bryson 2004.

[269] See Simontacchi 2000.

[270] See Fagin and Lavelle (1999) for interesting information.

[271] See Pawlick 2006.

[272] See Breggin 1991; Richards 2006.

[273] See chapter 5 below, and see the Introduction of Kirby 2005. Also see Tenpenny 2006.

[274] Cole 1988. Also see chapter 5 below.

[275] See US Code Title 50, chapter 32, Sec. 1520a, paragraph b.

The idea is that corporatists take over the government, create and make the populace dependent upon poisonous food, clothing, water, air, furniture, and so on that weaken and sicken the entire population, wherein some of the corporatists (Big Pharma) will therein create the medications to treat these deliberately caused plagues. For example, if cancer is caused by fooling the American citizenry into eating *meat* and animal products every day, as if that is what humans have always done, cancers from this will be blamed on, for example, aging, lack of exercise, or something else, but not on the corporatists' products.

Americans are told that the products they use in their daily life are safe and good, and most Americans, it seems, use them and consume them without worry. Americans are told that the long life-expectancy of Americans is the best it has ever been; but they are tired, lazy, imprisoned to countless medications and mind drugs (Prozac, etc.), with broken hips, osteoporosis, brain tumors, repeating cancer, diabetes, allergies, asthma, MS, irritable bowel syndrome, acid reflux, Alzheimer's disease,[276] autism, by-pass and other surgeries, pneumonia, and so on. They need heart transplants, liver, kidney and bone marrow transplants, but they are fooled into believing it is the best of times, and that no culture on earth has it so good, and is so healthy.[277]

There is no Capitalism in Corporatist America (Except for the Corporatists)

You can't foment, you can't create, *yourself*, an impression that a stock is down, but you do it anyway because the SEC doesn't understand it... This is blatantly illegal, but ... I think it's really important to foment... These are [the issues of] what's really going under the market that you don't see. But what's important when you are in a hedge fund mode is to not do anything remotely truthful, because the truth is so against your view, that it's important to create a new truth [in order] to develop a fiction, and the fiction is developed by almost anybody who is down two percent here six percent there... Who

---

[276] Most cases of Alzheimer's are most likely mad cow disease (mad cow and Alzheimer's have identical symptoms). It is no secret that the US government has been hiding cases of mad cow (see "USDA Suspected of Hiding Mad Cow Cases," United Press International, Steve Mitchell, February 9, 2004), and has ceased widespread testing right when mad cow in the meat supply in the USA entered the news (see "Government to Reduce Mad Cow Testing," Associated Press / CBS, March 14, 2006.). This theory becomes more plausible when one considers that in the 1920s, Alzheimer's was basically non-existent, but now, in 2007, there are over four million cases in the United States alone (100,000 – 400,000 new cases per year), and that Alzheimer's is often diagnosed when what a patient in fact has is a prion disease (i.e., mad cow). (These statistics come from the Rense Radio Show, www.rense.com, January 2, 2004, interview with Dr. Michael Gregor, MD.)

[277] For more information on the issues discussed in this paragraph, see Angell 2005, Tenpenny 2005, and especially Anderson 2004-2006.

cares about the fundamentals. The great thing about the actual market is that it has nothing to do with the actual stocks... It's just fiction and fiction and fiction.

—Jim Cramer[278]

The last characteristic of American communism that I will discuss in this chapter is perhaps the most illuminating since it sheds light on how the overall mechanics of a society are controlled, so that the corporatists can profit wildly, and remove money from the non-corporatists.

In a corporatist nation, where thought and behavior are not the property of the RP, the people can therefore be made to believe anything that the corporatists desire, no matter how absurd, and no matter if it is as outlandish as the ideas that humans are meat-eating creatures, America is a democracy, that the builders of the great Egyptian pyramids were primitive farmers, and perhaps the most outlandish idea of all: that American involves capitalism and private ownership.

If the United States is capitalistic, Americans would have evidence that they could simply point to that supports this. Americans would, for example, see the populace accumulating and owning some level of significant wealth and property.[279] At various places in this chapter I will show that there is no wealth (capital) or private ownership among non-corporatists in the United States. I will also show that this is so obvious that to believe the opposite is like believing the sky is green.

It is interesting how widespread these illusory ideas are within the corporatized America. Consider this thesaurus entry from Thesaurus.com, which actually involves the erroneous idea that communism is state control, and the opposite capitalism:

Main Entry:	communism
Part of Speech:	*noun*
Definition:	government
Synonyms:	Bolshevism, Marxism, collectivism, dictatorship, socialism, state ownership, state socialism
Antonyms:	capitalism

---

[278] This is part of a long, excellent interview with Jim Cramer on Wall Street Confidential, where Cramer was interviewed by Aaron Task late December 2006, and where Cramer candidly discusses how the stock market really works. As of March 2007, this interview was located at http://www.youtube.com/watch?v=ZTt7IQB9rc0.

[279] And this should be wealth and property that they really *own*, and which can't just have it taken from them in the event that the economy goes into recession or depression in the fabricated "economic cycle."

It is also interesting to note that Thesaurus.com's entry for "capitalism" holds that "democracy" is a synonym for "capitalism:"

Main Entry:	capitalism
Part of Speech:	*noun*
Definition:	system
Synonyms:	commercialism, competition, democracy, free enterprise, free market, industrialism, laissez faire, mercantilism, private enterprise
Antonyms:	collectivism, communism, socialism[280]

Academics very often inform the citizenry that communism is the antithesis of capitalism, that capitalism is a widespread phenomenon throughout America, and that supply and demand is the primary determinant of the market activity of their American world. But these points, which are presented without evidence, appear to be contradicted by the empirical data I present at various places in this book.

Money is the Ultimate Weapon and Tool of the Corporatists

The RP generally thinks of money as something they need to get more of, something that they are lucky to have when they have it (especially when they have surpluses of it), and when they do get a surplus of it, very often spend it on unneeded items. This is *not* how the corporatists view money. To them, they have and control the world's money and resources, and there is no reason to seek money or feel lucky they have it. The corporatists merely see money as a shaping tool, out of which they create the social world in the way they want it.

Money, in various forms (gold coins, cash, computer bookkeeping entries, etc.), is a primary weapon and an ultimate tool of the corporatists. It is what they use to shape culture, to move resources in specific ways, and to control people and their consciousness. It is most effective when it is relatively or severely scarce—or at least when it appears to be that way in the eyes of the RP. If there is scarcity, people can be made to do anything for it, and that is powerful for the corporatists, who hold the capital (surplus money) of a nation. Money is also an all-powerful effective tool and weapon when people are fooled into believing that money is the most important thing in life, and that petty possessions are what creates a person's happiness and status in culture. In that situation also, people can be made to do nearly anything for money, even

---

[280] Entries from Thesaurus.com are from Roget's New Millennium™ Thesaurus, First Edition (v 1.2.1)

finance the murder of children, as is happening currently in Iraq via taxpayer financing.

Money shapes and steers everything about culture and thought. For example, if corporatists want universities to shape students' minds in specific ways, then certain corporatists, via the Rockefeller Foundation, for example, can financially support certain professors and academic programs they approve of, and withdraw funding for others that they do not.[281] This activity would shape a university entirely, and thus would entirely shape the learning of the students, which controls the ideologies that students will acquire in the university.

Every aspect of corporatist culture involves this sort of financial domination, even things that are falsely described in the media and by politicians as untainted by financial influence, such as voting. This financial domination is deliberately, and secretly planned. For example, presidential candidates are deliberately created, and presidents are carefully chosen (and the public falsely believes they are elected) by this process,[282] and this is done by making some candidates prominent in the mass media, and others not—which is done with money, as I will discuss in the next chapter. In June 2006, Vermont officials tried to put campaign spending limits on their state elections—which would have ended, to some extent, the fraudulence of elections—but Washington intruded and prohibited this. Consider what was written about these events in an article from the *Boston Globe*:

> States are the laboratories of democracy unless someone in Washington doesn't like what's in the test tube. Yesterday, the US Supreme Court struck down a Vermont law that attempted to bring some sanity to the financing of political campaigns. It was a disappointing decision, especially at a time when the corrosive effect of money on politics is apparent in headlines nearly every day.[283]

NPR also covered this story on "All Things Considered" on June 26, 2006:

> A divided Supreme Court throws out Vermont's limits on campaign contributions, ruling that the law constitutes a restraint of free speech, in violation of the First Amendment. Vermont's limits on campaign spending and fundraising are the lowest in the nation.[284]

American Communism

Often Americans will invent juicy details about the communist nations (Nazi Germany, Soviet Russia, etc.) that they have learned to fear and loath via the media (including the education system), such as imagining that communist

---

[281] See Simpson 1994 for more information.
[282] See Miller 2005.
[283] "Saying 'No' to Vermont," June 27, 2006, Boston Globe, Globe Editorial.
[284] "High Court Throws Out Vermont Campaign Limits," by Nina Totenberg, *NPR*.org, June 26, 2006.

states don't involve any capitalism, and that their economies involve non-competition, whereas American economics is replete with competition and capitalism. To view America this way is so radically backwards that it is absurd to the same degree as if one were to claim that the sky is green, not blue. And as for the communist states viewed as being non-capitalist, Americans may believe communist nations do not involve any capitalism because they have not been educated about the real nature of the famous communist nations (Russia, Nazi Germany, etc.), and Americans will even hold this position if they have seen the extremely famous film, *Schindler's List*, which involves the story of a German Nazi *capitalist* earning a wad of capital.

For the remainder of this chapter, I will show specifically how corporatist America is not a capitalist nation, does not involve any sort of capitalism (except for the sort of capitalism that exists in the famous communist regimes, namely: *capital only for the corporatists*), and how there is no private ownership or capital for all other members of society (the non-corporatists). As Alex Jones said on his radio show on February 7, 2007: capital is the enemy of the monopolists; they want it all!

In America, corporatists accumulate wealth and capital, but nobody else really does. This is equally true for America as it was for, say, Nazi Germany or Soviet Russia. What we will see in this subsection is that the American economy consists of a system of monopolies (this is the essence of corporatism), devoid of any competition of any sort, and where economic events are pre-planned and fabricated for the stratospheric profit of the corporatists, but where the non-corporatists (the RP) suffer while believing that "the business cycle" is spontaneous rather than rigged and staged.

Corporatist Economy is Monopolistic Non-Local Economy

Professor Chossudovsky writes:

> Survival of the fittest: the enterprises with the most advanced technologies or those with command over the lowest wages survive in [the] world economy... While the spirit of Anglo-Saxon liberalism is committed to "fostering competition", G-7 macroeconomic policy (through tight fiscal and monetary controls), has, in practice, supported a wave of corporate mergers and acquisitions, as well as the bankruptcy of small and medium-sized enterprises.[285]

We have all seen this process in action, where, for example, Wal-mart moves into a town, powered by its unfathomable illuminati-based financial all-powerfulness, and where this invasion causes most of the local business (the farms, small local grocers, clothing stores, and all the rest) in the community to

---

[285] Chossudovsky 2003, 9.

be removed, since citizens—being not fully aware of the detriment and imprisonment they set upon themselves by going to Wal-mart for "low prices"—abandon their local economy in favor of the non-local Chinese-based Wal-mart economy. In other words, as Chossudovsky might put it: globalist economy replaces local economic networks: "large multinational companies have taken control of local-level markets through the system of corporate franchising."[286]

Professor Zinn's passage above describes how the wealthy American education system and news media each make it appear that the world created by the monopolistic corporatists is good for everyone, and that the perspectives and belief-systems demonstrated by the wealthiest corporate controllers is a sound view, and the best or the only real view to see reality through. In other words, non-rich Americans are told by the rich corporatists (via the ultra-rich media) that the world and the philosophy of the ultra-rich is good for the non-rich, and they should desire and cherish the world of the rich, they should emulate it, adopt its opinions and philosophies, and if anyone rejects this, they are terrorists. (Recall Bush at the 2002 State of the Union Address, shortly after 9/11: "You are either with us, or you are with the terrorists.")

Monopolization of the World's Industries and Resources Involves the Creation of Artificial Scarcity

The bedrock of the communism of American corporatism is gained by the corporatists through *monopolization* of resources, industries, and thought. The critical issue involved in corporatist monopolization is to make the citizenry, and the entire world, *dependent* on the monopolized resources that the corporatists control, and then to fabricate shortages or surpluses in order to control the people in desirable ways, and in order to maximize financial profit. For example, by having monopolistic control over resources, the corporatists can, if needed, create artificial shortage and scarcity, where the phony and unverifiable supply-and-demand philosophy will be cast upon the citizenry through the national media, to be used to create the false idea that supply is low and demand is high and thus that prices can only be high also.[287]

---

[286] Ibid.

[287] In Black 2006, it is shown how through all of recorded history (i.e., the account of history taught to kids in schools and colleges), there has been total monopolization by a few corporatists of the energy resources needed for basic survival. Black points out how the first fuel known in the standard account of history is wood (fire wood), which was "more valuable than gold." With such a scenario, scarcities can be fabricated in order to control the people, or booms can be fabricated in order to create wealth that can gravitate toward the corporatists (such as when the banks get so much of the land and resources of a nation during a depression or recession). For example, in medieval

There are countless examples of this occurring through history, since this is the standard way that corporatists have dominated and terrorized world citizens for thousands of years. The recent escapades with oil from 1998 to 2007 offer an excellent example to cite, as I will at various places in the remainder of this chapter. What has happened is that oil, which is very plentiful worldwide (there is no shortage at all, as revealed by Cornell University's huge oil field discovery,[288] among other discoveries, and even Bush Jr. has commented on how much oil is in the Alaskan Wildlife Refuge—but where Bush also says that environmentalists won't let him touch that oil[289]), has been however largely dominated by the United States and some of its "allies" via the US military, where the existence of most of this oil is kept hidden. Instead, the citizenry is told (via education and big media, as always) that there is only a small amount of oil available, which is of course a lie, as I discuss elsewhere in this book. The resource that the world depends on is deliberately governed into a shortage, by hiding supply and limiting production. For example, not a single oil refinery has been build since the early 1970s, even though supply has dramatically increased in the meantime.[290] Prices of the one resource that the world depends on, and which is undergoing "shortage," can be made to skyrocket, when needed, so that corporatists profit wildly, and non-corporatists are held prisoner. Usually, corporatists will tell Americans (via the mass media) that it is the "Arabs" and "OPEC" or something that is holding back production of oil, which allegedly increases the price, and thus that Americans should be angry at *them*. But this is just another way to get world citizens to rise up against each other for more war that is profitable to the corporatists, which decimates the citizens in the given nations that a war involves, and which leads to unimaginable profit for the corporatists, who, secretly, have fabricated everything from behind the scene, in their banks and board rooms,[291] news studio back rooms and university seminars.

England, it was illegal to own wood; the king owned it all (control of fuel, and power to create scarcity, etc.).

[288] See "Sustainable Oil?", WorldNetDaily, by Chris Bennet, May 25, 2004.

[289] See "Senate Rejects Drilling in Alaska Wildlife Refuge," AP./MSNBC, Dec. 21, 2005; "Senate Rejects Oil Drilling in Alaskan Wildlife Refuge," AP/CNN, March 19, 2003; "House Drops Arctic Drilling From Bill," AP/Washington Post, by Andrew Taylor, November 10, 2005.

This is what is really behind all the wealthy environmentalist groups: keeping the population primitive and low-tech, so that they cannot sustain population increases, since resources and land are tied up in environmentalists' interests, and wherein people die since they cannot sustain themselves.

[290] This was discussed on the Nutrimedical Report, www.nutrimedical.com, May 31, 2007, hour 2.

[291] See Rampton and Stauber 2002 (chapter 1) for information on how media is *directly created by corporations*, even at their corporate facilities, and is given to the mass media to look *as if* it is news. Most Americans are unaware that this is going on, and they appear to believe that all media is created only by the big media corporations.

This is the primary issue that has governed economics for thousands of years. Which resources are dominated by the corporatists—whether fire wood, oil, water, food, money, stone, consciousness, metal, or whatever—is irrelevant, and all that matters is that the corporatists control it, that the people are made to think they absolutely need it, that it's the only resource that will allow them to live, and if they do not get it they will die. So, for example, rather than grow their own healthy food, Americans are fooled into believing they must "pay through the nose" to acquire nutricidal and carcinogenic grocery store food.

If the dependent group (the non-corporatists: the RP) needs to be blackmailed or manipulated by the corporatists in some way, then that dependent group can be withheld oil, the corporatist-created food (i.e., grocery store food), or anything else they are fooled into thinking they *must* have and cannot get on their own, until they comply with the corporatists and do what the corporatists want. For example, as I write these words in 2006, Americans are largely against the war in Iraq (an oil war), but if they revolt, they will be crushed, and the war will likely go on because the people will not understand that they must *boycott* oil in order to have any real influence on the situation. If the corporatists gain enough wealth off of the monopolization of oil, for example, or any other resources they monopolize, the corporatists can build massive militaries and technologies to gain even *further* control over the citizenry, as is currently occurring in the United States.

What has just been described is how culture is controlled by *addictions*. A corporation will create an addiction (in this case oil, but other examples are unhealthy meaty or sugary food ["junk food"], pharmaceutical drugs, nicotine, MSG, video games, cable television, etc.), and then the citizen will be fooled into making huge sacrifices in order to accumulate it—even, for example, to the extent that parents will neglect children, and children will lose their minds, where SSRI's will be used as a dependency, and taxation will voluntarily be paid so that the corporatists can further perpetuate their child-killing wars.

It is no secret that the world is utterly exploding with usable oil.[292] A world oil shortage—the so-called "peak oil"—is seen as an absurdity and a ruse when one understands this. Rather, the corporatists have developed a world which is utterly dependent on oil, and in order to implement the aforementioned control, Americans are told that the only usable oil is in the Middle East and a few other scattered places—and they are told that these supplies have various time-limits, as if they will run-out someday in the not-too-distant future. Full control is therefore implemented with this sort of addiction and monopolization of a resource, and political anti-war activists will be fooled into believing that Bush invaded Iraq due to the need to control "the world's remaining oil."

---

[292] See the note above about oil in Alaska and the Gulf of Mexico; also see Williams, 1980.

In understanding the monopolization of the world's fuel supply and resources, we can start to see that only the wealthiest of people ever can accumulate wealth (capital), and thus capitalism is only for the corporatists, not for the rest of the population (RP). This is precisely the sort of capitalism that existed in communist Russia, for example. But calling it "capitalism" is not appropriate, since a nation made up of 300 million, but which only has a few ten or hundred thousand capitalists (if that), is not a nation of capitalists, and thus is not a capitalist nation. Rather, it would be a *communist* nation, where people do not own much of anything (except, perhaps, petty goods, like videogames and televisions, but a lot of these are just bought with credit cards in America, and thus are not even owned in that case).

The Fabricated Business Cycle

In addition to artificial scarcity, other concepts, like "supply and demand," "the business cycle" and the "stock market," are also fabrications that are designed to prevent the RP from gaining capital, and thus they keep the RP fully communistic (in debt and without wealth).

One of the best ways to discover how there is no real capitalism within communist-corporatist America (except the capitalism that exists for the very few corporatists), is by studying the fabricated "business cycle." Americans are all somewhat familiar with the story of "The Business Cycle," and it usually goes something like this:

> In what is accepted as the "normal" scheme of things, the economy oscillates between periods of inflation and deflation, or between growth and recession. The government tries to reduce the volatility or amplitude of these cycles, to prevent the hardship caused by extreme swings. For example, we noted in chapter 6 that our government learned, through the experience of the Great Depression and similar events, that the way to deal with an economic slowdown is to stimulate growth with a fast infusion of cash.[293]

This account from a supposed "expert" named Leeb, who is a very famous and popular Wall Street "expert," and this account represents what is, in his words, "the accepted view." This is the view that is taught to students in high school and college, and it is the view portrayed through the rest of the national media. This view involves the idea that economic cycles are normal and inevitable (unplanned), that the government tries to minimize these swings, where the swings are largely accidental, meaning that nobody causes them and no group deliberately plans them out in order to benefit from them (if you know what the market is going to do, you can really make a killing).

---

[293] Leeb 2006, 91.

We will see that there is virtually *not a shred* of evidence for this picture, and instead, it is astonishingly simple to prove that the business cycle is controlled, planned, and fabricated, and it is surprising that Americans do not understand this, due to the fact that the fabrications are not even secret: they are easy to spot for anybody who just takes a few moments to think critically about the US and world economy.

The US business cycle is associated with, and controlled by,

I. the rate at which the Federal Reserve "creates" debt-money (out of nothing), and with

II. the rise and fall of interest rates, which is also controlled and planned by the Federal Reserve.

Both of I and II are controlled by the Federal Reserve, and both combine to drive the rise and fall of the stock market and the business cycle. Economists often want us to believe they are not predictable, and that they are spontaneous, difficult to predict, and where big changes come without warning. Since the Federal Reserve fully controls both I and II, and since I and II are the primary engines behind the business cycle, one can only conclude that the business cycle is fabricated by the Federal Reserve.

The stock market is a weapon inflicted upon non-corporatists in America, where by accumulating wealth (wealth "on paper") for a short time via stock market increases, the non-corporatists who take part in stock market investing gain the illusion that they are capitalists (they have the illusion that they are persons who have accumulated *real* wealth: actual capital). But through "unpredictable" market and cycle downturns, these non-corporatists more often than not lose their "earnings," due to the fact that the business cycle is fabricated to turn downward without warning, since the stock market is controlled by the corporatist bankers who control the Federal Reserve and the interest rate "cycle." By having control of the Federal Reserve money production and the interest rate "cycle," "bankers" at the Federal Reserve have full power to steer the economy and business cycle in whatever way they wish, and thus they can see and create the financial future in order to profit from the market fluctuations, and from investors who invest before a market and a business cycle are crashed.

More specifically, the systems works like this:

The Federal Reserve deliberately increases the money supply, which leads to inflation (i.e., goods require more "dollars" [i.e., paper Federal Reserve notes] for purchase). Americans are told that inflation is harmful. (Americans are never told *why* it is, and economists often argue that it is not harmful unless it is runaway inflation.). Bankers create situations where credit (loans) are harder to get access to (usually by raising interest rates) in order to slow down the economy is an antidote to inflation. (Americans are also never told *why* this is the case either, and they are never told what inflation and interest rates, for example, have to do with one another. As the economist George Whitehurst has discussed,[294] it appears that it is actually impossible to show that inflation and interest rates are related in any sort of mathematical, scientific, or predictable way.) After a rate increase, very predictably, business activity slows and often even crashes, since bank loan activity slows when there are sufficient interest rate hikes. But before the crash occurs, the corporatists dump their stocks near the high point of the business cycle, when stocks are the highest, and then after the crash, at the low point of the market, they buy back in, in order to get stocks at the lowest rates. And, most importantly, during the slumped economy, members of the RP will often be unable to pay their bills, and via foreclosures and repossessions, banking corporatists will collect their land, possessions, resources, and money that the RP supposedly "owned."

The usury corporatists fully control the business cycle, and they use that control to manipulate the business cycle so that it periodically and predictably "crashes" (as it did in 1929, the early 1980s, 1987, the early 1990s, 2000, among other times), wherein the non-corporatists (the RP") typically lose all or much of their investment "wealth," in addition to property and resources. Stock market wealth accumulation is an illusion, and it is mainly a way for corporatists to remove money from non-corporatists, which is fitting for this chapter on American communism since the stock market and the business cycle are the keys to keeping ordinary Americans from accumulating wealth and becoming non-communistic by acquiring capital.

The Repeating Big Picture of Society: Crash then False Flag then War and Plague (C➔FF➔W/P)

Interestingly, there is a very interesting repeating pattern that has existed within the "business cycle" over the past 100 years: there are repeated stock market crashes (C), and while the market is down, a false flag (FF) terrorist event occurs, and then a war (W) follows, and often a plague (P) accompanies the war. This is a pattern that has repeated through history:

$$C➔FF➔W/P$$

First, there's a stock crash, then a false flag event, and then a war and a plague. The pattern of course implies that these major patterns of events have been engineered by the secret government throughout history, and the evidence of this book verifies that. And it is no secret among many major historians that the major wars, holocausts, and stock crashes of the last 200 years have been carefully engineered by them.

---

[294] He discussed this on the Rense Radio Show in several appearances in 2006.

The American stock markets roared upward during the late 1990s and up until spring of 2000, where at the beginning of March of 2000 they suddenly and abruptly crashed. This was especially the case for the NASDAQ stock market, which lost approximately 80 percent of its value, falling from a high of well over 5000 to a low of near 1000. At the bottom points in the markets, both 9/11 and the invasion of Iraq occurred, and there is a reason they happened at those low points. I will next explore the mechanics of this intricate secret government process.

A common story that bankers—speaking through the media—tell to the RP, is the vague idea that "psychology can dictate the market."[295] In other words, the RP is told that if negative political events happen, like a "terrorist attack," they can negatively affect the markets since they will lead to a shortage of stock

---

[295] This is common discourse in Wall Street propaganda. I will give an example here to show how it works. Consider the following passage from the wildly popular Motley Fool web site, which is about the so-called "short-term" effects of "negative psychology" on the market (both long- and short-term are regularly cited by Wall Street "experts" '[i.e., bankers and market makers] as affecting the market), and it involves the idea that "negative psychology" can affect and drive the market (this article also involves another key propagandistic issue that I will discuss later, which is that of "buy and hold" concept):

> The amorphous long term is a philosophical point well worth pondering. A five- to 10-year time frame (or more) certainly isn't out of the question, although some investors might prefer just a few years. I recently read Common Stocks and Uncommon Profits and Other Writings by Philip Fisher, and his views on long-term investing really resonated with me. The late Mr. Fisher proposed finding well-managed, growth-oriented companies with large market opportunities and holding positions in those stocks for years -- maybe even forever. The power of holding for the long term is evident in David and Tom Gardner's Motley Fool Stock Advisor scorecard. *Stock Advisor* debuted in 2002. If you look at all the picks from that year, every single one has double- or triple-digit percentage gains. For example, as of this writing, Marvel Entertainment, picked in July 2002, has a 670% gain. And Moody's, which was recommended in the April 2002 debut issue, has appreciated 250%. Investing for the long term does require the ability to be honest with one's self as to whether the future of a given company is still growth-oriented. These are not decisions any of us should take lightly, since we could leave big money on the table if we misjudge and sell our shares too soon (not to mention if we sell at a loss, only to find out that the negative sentiment was far from the truth). In his writings, Fisher also addressed the fact that sometimes short-term negative psychology on Wall Street may suppress a stock, regardless of whether that psychology is warranted or prescient. Such negative sentiment may come from bear markets, macroeconomic concerns, fears that a company's future growth isn't bright, or a misinterpretation that a stock's valuation has outpaced future growth. Blindly following such short-term and often emotional sentiment can, of course, be dangerous to your portfolio. (From "Long Haul, Giant Gains," Motleyfool.com, Alyce Lomax, January 30, 2007)

buyers, since buyers will be afraid that the negative event will make the business cycle slump and consequently the stock market will go down.

Of course there is little data to support this thesis. For example, 9/11 and the invasion of Iraq both occurred at the low point of the market during the 2000-2003 slump, but they were followed by a market *rally*, which is still going on as this book goes to press. So, the overall point I want to disclose is this:

> *If the Federal Reserve is to fabricate the business cycle, they must coordinate it with the activities (wars, terrorist attacks, population decreases and rearrangements, and so on) of the rest of the secret government, so that the catastrophes that the secret government fabricates don't occur anywhere but at the low points of the business and stock market cycles.*

For these reasons, events like terrorist attacks, wars, and other things mentioned elsewhere in this book, are deliberately planned at the low points in the fabricated cycles, since bad things can't happen during the high points of the market if, as we are told, "psychology" is supposed to be a factor.

One can see this process at work for themselves. For example, in 2000, literally all the stock market "experts" featured in the big media on CNBC, CNN, and so on (typically these featured "experts" are really just employees of the banking industry), told the world that the markets are going *up up up*, and that they should *buy buy buy* without worry. The "experts" repeated this mantra with tremendous zeal, and with an unparalleled din, *right into the huge NASDAQ crash in spring of 2000*. Interestingly, these "experts" were specifically telling investors to buy NASDAQ "tech stocks," which were the stocks about to be hit *by far* the hardest, but the experts nevertheless relentlessly preached this "buy! buy! buy! buy tech!" mantra literally *the night before the huge crash started in 2000*.

Now let me repeat all this, since it very clearly proves how the stock market is rigged and how it merely is set up to remove capital from the RP in order to keep the United States fully communistic (to shape the nation so that there is no capital in existence except for the few monopolistic corporatists). As stated, in 2000, optimism was continuously flowing from the "Wall Street gurus", *right up to the crash*, literally to the evening of the day before it started. So the question is:

> *How could all these "experts" uniformly all be so wrong?*

How could literally not a single person in the big financial media have had absolutely no idea of what was imminently coming? Answer: they had to have known, so therefore, they can only have been lying and acting for the cameras and reporters of the mass media. The issue I would like to emphasize is:

> *It seems impossible that right up to and on the eve of such a massive crash, that literally nobody profiled in the big media would have had*

any idea that even a slowdown in the rise of the stock market was coming, let alone a massive crash.

Abbey Joseph Cohen

Abbey Joseph Cohen, supposed stock market "guru," but who is in fact merely an employee of the big banks (Goldman Sachs), predicted on CNBC in 2000 to a pageant of fanfare, that the DOW Industrial Average stock market was going to soar to nearly 15,000, and that investors should invest in Dell Computer since Dell apparently was going to acquire an increased stock price due to the upcoming DOW bull market. Almost immediately after she made this claim, what was to become a massive stock and economic crash began, Dell Computer lost much share value, and before the crash was finished, the NASDAQ Stock Market lost the vast majority of its value.

This is the standard scenario on Wall Street: all the "gurus" are mysteriously often all wrong, and all these "experts" strangely never can get it right. They never predict a crash, even though crashes are periodic and inevitable due to the fact that the United States is a reserve debt money system: it is as if they just never can see it coming, even though few things are simpler to predict. All the "gurus," who are just employees of the usury industry and of Wall Street, are always all wrong in predicting downturns in the market and "business cycle" when they make their predictions on CNN, CNBC, FOX, in the Wall Street Journal, and so on.

The Communist Economics of No-Capital: The Debt-Money System

As discussed elsewhere in this chapter, capital is nearly non-existent in the United States, except for the corporatists. This is because the United States economy is a debt-money system: big-ticket products (homes, cars, businesses, and so on) are acquired not by wealth, but by debt. Many younger Americans have no idea that only a few decades ago, this economic system of debt largely did not exist in the United States, and the United States was a wealth system—ask your grandparents about it.

Few people understand that every single unit of money in the United States is a *debt*. Let me explain this with an example. If I loan you forty dollars, that you must repay me with later, and you use that money to pay your monthly cable television bill, it may look like you have some wealth since you were able to pay your cable television bill, but in fact you are not any richer. You still owe me money, and thus your level of wealth actually decreased, even though it felt like it increased, and even though you had some buying power in being able to pay your bill. But it is as if I merely paid your bill since you were just an extra pair of hands in the way of the money going from me to your cable company. But in the meantime, you have gained a debt of $40 that you are responsible for. So, you will feel like you have gained some money, but you have not; you gained a debt.

Now imagine if I could merely create the $40 I loaned you by, for example, simply taking a blank piece of white paper and drawing the number "40" on it, wherein I claim that this is real money, and low-and-behold it works, since the cable television company recognizes it as currency and accepts "your" payment. This is how the Federal Reserve functions, and this is the nature of all—yes *all*—money in the United States. Every single cent ever "created" is a debt to the Federal Reserve (which does not have any reserves). The Federal Reserve writes a check, but there is no checking account, to put it the way that Edward Griffin once did. There is only the check. The check turns into a bookkeeping entry on a computer somewhere, but it is based on nothing—and therefore it is nothing. All US money is nothing.[296] David Icke lucidly discusses these issues:

> When a bank makes a 'loan' it is loaning *nothing*. They simply type into your account the figure they have agreed to 'loan' you against your house, business, or land. They don't create money, they create *debt* by tapping the keys of a computer program and from that moment you have to pay them back the non-existent 'money' they have 'loaned' you, plus interest! If you don't do that they can take your property—*for loaning you nothing*. Governments borrow 'money' in the same way and taxpayers become responsible for 'paying back' the banks the non-existent money that has been 'borrowed' on their behalf by governments controlled by the same forces that own the banks. If you

---

[296] Interestingly, this statement is a contradiction, since there are no things that can "be nothing." That would be like saying that there is a thing that does not exist, or, in other words, there is an existent item that is nonexistent. This reflects the pure absurdity of the US "money" system.

wrote this as fiction they would say it was too far-fetched to be credible...[297]

I believe that it is appropriate for me to give a long citation from an excellent passage from Craig R. Smith, President of the Swiss American Trading Corporation, on this issue. In this excellent passage, Smith describes how the US economy system was hijacked in order to badger, impoverish, and enslave Americans:

Imagine for a moment that you have the ability to create any amount of money, without ever having to produce anything. Is there anyone or anything you couldn't buy? Probably not. Sound impossible? It should be, but it isn't. Just ask your local Federal Reserve banker—they do it every day. The folding, spindling and mutilating of America's monetary system became legitimized in 1913, when the Federal Reserve was formed. Long ago bankers discovered a nasty little secret referred to as "fractional-reserve banking" which is fueled by credit and debt creation out of thin air. The modern American monetary system is the result of an incestuous relationship between the federal government and the private banking cartel, deceptively called The Federal Reserve System... The fundamental misconception today is that America's paper or electronic currency, denominated in Federal Reserve Notes, is that a dollar actually has any intrinsic value. In the words of former Fed economist John Exter, "Today's U.S. dollar is nothing more than an IOU-nothing."... As difficult as it is for honest, hard-working Americans to fathom, the lifeblood of the American political and economic system is legal plunder. The 19th-century economist Frederic Bastiat summed up the tendency of central governments to embrace plunder in this way: "There are two ways to acquire the niceties of life: to produce them or to plunder them. When plunder becomes a way of life for a group of men living together in society, they create for themselves in the course of time, a legal system that authorizes it and a moral code that glorifies it." In short, "We the People" allowed the Federal Reserve, with the full cooperation of the federal government, to replace the "Puritan work ethic" with a "pagan blunder plan" and now the chickens are starting to flock home to roost. To achieve this massive wealth distribution plan required a shift in public values from hard work and responsibility, to hardly working and gambling. This dramatic change has occurred gradually over the past two or three generations... History has proven... neither bankers nor governments possess the discipline needed to limit the amount of credit (or paper money) to equal the true supply of gold and silver coins. So the supply of paper money (credit/debt) must continually rise. The result is always disastrous in the long term because the economy suffers through cycles

---

[297] Icke 2005, 9.

of inflation, deflation, artificial growth, recession and depression. Because the U.S. citizens did not protest the use of trust money, our economic system then began to degenerate into untrustworthy or *fiat* money… Fiat money abandons any promise whatsoever to redeem the paper currency in any physical commodity… The Federal Reserve and the federal government are banking on… that the public will not become aware of this insidious process… until it's too late… The facts are that popular delusion and public confidence are the only two forces that uphold our present fiat money system.[298]

The "Unpredictable" Business Cycles Occur Predictably

The so-called "business cycle" is, Americans are told, random, unpredictable, and the product of unplanned and spontaneous world events, such as wars, resource shortages, changes in consumer spending habits, and so forth. But the truth is quite different: the business cycle is merely a product of how available the banking cartels (which are controlled by the Federal Reserve) make credit to consumers. In times where credit is restricted, recessions or depressions ensue, and in times when it is not restricted, inflation and prosperity ensue. This can be verified if one merely studies when business downturns happen, and they will find that they always happen after credit restrictions. For example, just before the Great Depression, the Federal Reserve massively raised interest rates. The most popular way credit is restricted is by claiming that inflation is a problem, and then mysteriously raising interest rates to "solve" that problem. But raising interest rates puts the idea in consumers' minds that they should wait to get loans until rates go back down, and that amounts to a planned restriction of credit (and a consequent downturn in economic activity). There are other tactics that are used to restrict credit, but raising interest rates is a primary tool.

For some reason, professional and academic economists don't notice these patterns, and they perpetually preach the unverified assumption that market cycles are unpredictable and spontaneous. This is another way that academia so radically overlooks simple patterns and events, bases their research on assumptions and theories (which are oftne first publicized in the mass media and by politicians). Not surprisingly, this sort of shoddy "research" leads to absurdities and nonsensical findings. For example, economists (especially those working for the big banks and those who are featured in the mass media, i.e., CNBC) will tell us that the business cycle is too difficult to predict, but also that we can predict that there will be upswings, for example, in the markets (and thus you should all invest in the stock market now!). This is a contradiction: we can, and can't, predict the market trends.

---

[298] Smith 2001, 2-7

I will next give a quote from a popular university economics textbook, written by a Harvard professor, that is used at many American Universities, such as Columbia University, and which tells us that economic fluctuations are *not predictable*. It is standard for economists to however literally never tell us why they are (and we will see below that it is astonishingly easy to see that they in fact *are predictable*). Here is what he has to say in this textbook:

> Fluctuations in the economy are often called *the business cycle…* The term business cycle is somewhat misleading, however, because it seems to suggest that economic fluctuations follow a regular, predictable pattern. In fact, economic fluctuations are not at all regular, and they are almost impossible to predict with much accuracy.[299]

Amazingly, three pages past this quote in this same textbook (on page 685), Mankiw tells us that economic cycles and the business cycle *are regular*! "Describing the regular patterns that economies experience as they fluctuate over time is easy. Explaining what causes these fluctuations is more difficult."[300] Within these pages, Mankiw tells us that the business cycle is entirely unpredictable, and that it is predictable. This is like saying that the sky is blue and not blue.

Needless to say, the reader of this textbook (who are, unfortunately, the "best and the brightest" of many American Universities) will have a difficult time figuring out which is the case: Whether business cycles are "impossible" (page 682) to figure out, or whether they are "regular" (page 685), and thus rather easy to predict. As I've shown elsewhere in this book, this sort of sophistic and contradictory writing floods the college textbooks.

The truth is in fact this simple:

> Business cycles are caused by inflation hikes and interest rate hikes, both of which are fully controlled by the Federal Reserve, and both of which are always preventable since the Federal Reserve can merely stop the money-printing (which stops inflation) and thus can prevent the need for interest rate hikes.

The Federal Reserve does not take measures to prevent these events from happening, and that is because—contrary to what virtually all Americans are told—the Federal Reserve is not attempting to prevent the business cycle swings, but is deliberately creating them in order to profit off of them. The business cycle is one of the easiest things in the world to predict, all one has to do is watch the rate at which the Federal Reserve creates money, and how they create too much money, which causes inflation and prompts the Federal Reserve to then raise interest rates (or takes some other measures to cause a "credit crunch," where it is much more difficult for people to get loans and

---

[299] Mankiw 1998, 682.
[300] Mankiw 1998, 685.

more debt), which in turn leads to slowdowns in the economy since it removes the very vehicle that keeps the debt-money system moving, namely the ability to go more in debt by taking out loans to purchase big-ticket items.

It is easy to predict the business cycle, due to the fact that it is fabricated, and due to the fact that each cycle downturn is fabricated with the same strategy: print and create money at too fast of a rate, announce through the media that there are inflation problems, increase interest rates as a purported way to solve the inflation problem, watch and wait for the business cycle turn downward, then watch the corporatists collect the homes, businesses, buildings, land, and etc. of the RP, who are having trouble making payments in the "slow" economy.

Therefore, the quotations from the economics textbook I just gave that was written by a Harvard professor, is merely another classic example of the blatant lying that goes on in university textbooks by prestigious "academics." I have often been astonished at how much of this I have come across through the years. According to that textbook, we are asked to believe that the business cycle is difficult to predict (page 682) (which, as I have shown, it is not) and that it is not difficult to predict (page 685). This is classic Orwellian doublespeak.

There are corporatists who control the stock markets via controlling the money supply and other factors, and if anybody out there believes they would never be tempted to control, or deliberately plan, stock fluctuations for their own benefit, then such naïve people need to use a little common sense and realize they are wrong. Ben Bernanke, Chairman of the Federal Reserve, ambiguously said at the celebration of Milton Friedman's 90th birthday in Chicago on November 8, 2002: "Regarding the Great Depression. You're right, we did it. We're very sorry."

Monopolization and the Myth of "Supply and Demand"

Another fabrication used by the corporatists is the concept of "supply" and "demand." We are told in our universities, and in the media, that the economy is controlled by supply and demand, but it is easy to show that this principle does not describe anything that really exists in reality. Rather, it can be verified that monopolization and usurpation of markets and resources by monopolistic corporatists is what determine prices, and where it can be assumed that corporatists price resources and goods as high as they can get away with. The passage from the article given above about oil attempts to get the reader to believe that rising oil prices are not necessarily a thing to be dreaded or avoided, but rather they are as natural and inevitable as death and taxes. This rise in oil prices, is, however, shown by Tarpley[301] and many others to have

---

[301] Tarpley 2006, 100-120.

nothing to do with supply and demand, and to actually be the result of a premeditated and carefully executed plan by corporatists, which gives incredible amounts of money to them and to various oil controllers, as has been widely publicized.[302]

Furthermore, we don't need PhDs in economics to know that the story about supply and demand being the reason oil prices have escalated is bogus. This is because from 1999 to 2007, oil rose over seven times (700%). In that time, we are ubiquitously told by "experts" that supply has not fluctuated anywhere near as much as decreasing by seven times, in order to change the market as to where prices would rise 700%. And in that time demand did not increase nearly enough to account for such a rise in oil prices. Additionally, I have discussed above how there is copious oil all over the planet, and thus there is no supply shortage—rather there is a huge supply overabundance. So the thesis that supply and demand are the cause of oil's rise in price is simply untrue.

Hikes in energy costs are very hard on the non-wealthy. Americans have not been given a choice about which sort of fuel they would like to use in powering their civilization. That choice was made for them by oil men, who chose not to have civilization's transportation and society powered by non-oil energy sources (e.g., nuclear powered cities, trains, EVs, etc.). Therefore, oil price increases are not the choice of Americans, and Americans have had no choice but to pay several times more for gas than they did not too long ago, due to the monopolistic control of oil energy, and which surely will radically alter society in the near future.[303]

Supply and demand are believed, it seems, by nearly everyone, to be the principal issues driving what are assumed to be non-communistic, capitalistic economies. But we are seeing in this chapter that the corporatist nations are actually communistic and non-capitalistic, and as with the example being discussed here (oil monopolization), it is more the case that wealth, resource, and intellectual property is usurped by supermassive corporations in order to dictate prices and what products people do or do not have the opportunity to purchase. Therefore, it is not the case that supply and demand, in this example, have any relevance whatsoever.

Other examples of the monopolization and non-competition are entirely easy to find in corporatist American. For example, who are Microsoft's competitors for developing a rival to Word? Why are all the giant media corporations collaborative partners rather than competitors?[304] Why do Monsanto and just a few other ultramassive corporations utterly dominate the food, seed, and

---

[302] For example, see "Exxon Mobil Posts $10.49B Profit in 3Q," *Associated Press*, October 26, 2006.
[303] See Ruppert 2004; Deffeyes 2003, Simmons 2005, and Greene 2004.
[304] See Bagdikian 2004, 4-10.

pesticide industry,[305] and actively and illegally crush even their non-threatening and/or small-time "competitors?"[306] Examples like this can be given for all the industries—Big Pharma, oil, mail, automobiles, energy, water, etc.—where in each case, there is no real competition, but rather, there is raw monopolization.

If the ultramassive corporations are fascist, as I show in this book, then we should expect to find that communistic and non-capitalistic economic practices and policies pervade American economics. For that reason, we should expect all sorts of deceit, lies, scandals, and shenanigans to be observed among the corporate-government leaders. This is indeed what we find when we look at issues of economics, where all that the American citizen is told about economics is entirely fabricated, absurd, and a comical joke. Consider the following excerpt from an LA Times news article, that, in contradiction to the last article about supply and demand, *instead* tells the reader that the massive run-up in the price of oil is being contributed to, not supply and demand, but rather, by tensions in the Middle East *with Iran*. But the USA does not get oil from Iran, and thus Iran cannot affect the supply side of the supply and demand for United States' pricing:

> Worsening geopolitical strife drove the price of oil to a new high Thursday and sent stocks plummeting worldwide, threatening a replay of financial markets' spring turmoil. Crude oil futures in New York soared $1.75 to $76.70 a barrel, topping the previous record of $75.19 reached last week, *on fears that escalating violence between Israel and Hezbollah militants in Lebanon could deepen tensions with Iran and spill into other energy-rich Mideast countries.* Oil continued to rise in after-hours activity on the New York Mercantile Exchange late Thursday, reaching $78.40. On Wall Street, the Dow Jones industrial average tumbled 166.89 points, or 1.5%, to 10,846.29, its third triple-digit loss in five sessions. Although the Dow and most other U.S. indexes held above their June lows, the technology-dominated NASDAQ composite fell to its lowest level since October. Stocks also were broadly lower in Asia and Europe. Financial markets this year have appeared to mostly shrug at the violence in Iraq and saber-rattling by North Korea and Iran over their nuclear programs. Many investors' main worry has been the upward trend in inflation and interest rates. But the Israel-Hezbollah conflict seemed to add one more geopolitical concern than investors could handle, analysts said. *"Fear is starting to take over,"* said Dan McMahon, chief trader at brokerage CIBC World Markets. Investors, he said, are thinking that "there are a whole lot of reasons to be selling stocks, and not a lot to be buying." What's more, as oil climbs relentlessly, it complicates the outlook for interest rates and for global economic growth. Many investors expect the Federal Reserve

---

[305] Thorn 2003, chapter 30.
[306] See Garcia 2005.

to soon halt its two-year-long credit-tightening campaign, perhaps at the policymakers' Aug. 8 meeting. But a further surge in oil prices could fan inflation fires and put pressure on the Fed and other central banks to keep raising rates. Energy expert Daniel Yergin said that the oil market's jitters "are outweighing the fact that the market fundamentals are actually improving." *Global crude inventories are in good shape*, said Yergin, chairman of consulting firm Cambridge Energy Research Associates. Nonetheless, he said, "another event could well send oil over $80, even though the fundamentals don't justify it." Crude futures contracts for March, April and May 2007 all closed above $80 a barrel Thursday, illustrating traders' nervousness about oil supplies as far out as next spring. The stock market had managed to rally in the first four months of the year even as oil rose above $70 for the first time. Wall Street and equity markets worldwide began to sink in mid-May only after Fed officials made clear they were concerned about inflation and would continue to tighten credit. The blue-chip Dow slumped from a six-year high of 11,642.65 on May 10 to 10,706.14 on June 13, a drop of 8%. Broader stock indexes, and many foreign markets, suffered deeper declines. But stocks had rebounded in recent weeks as investors once again bet that the Fed was nearly done lifting rates. A key concern now, some analysts said, was that the Dow and other indexes could fall below their June lows. That could stoke worries that the spring sell-off was the start of a bear market rather than a brief pullback.[307] (Itals mine)

Notice how in this news article, we get an entirely different explanation for the skyrocketing price of oil than the article above which claimed supply and demand was behind the rise. In this article, mysteriously, and very vaguely put, the rise is blamed on the assertion that "fear is starting to take over" (this has to do with the supposed "psychology of the market," that I discussed above), and I guess the author of the article expects the reader to find this to be a clear and precise enough account to sum up why oil is rising the way it is. But of course, in reality, this concept of "fear ... taking over" has no meaning whatsoever, and this article contains no informational content.

But add to this that, contradictorily, the article says that there are supply concerns, but then the article also mentions that supply is just fine: in the exact words of the article, "inventories are in good shape." This is classic Orwellian doublespeak, since the article is saying that there are supply concerns and there are not supply concerns. But aside from that issue, this article does in fact tell the reader that supply and demand *are not* the reason for the soaring oil price, during the summer of 2006, which is in *direct* contradiction to the first article quoted above about supply and demand.

---

[307] "Mideast Violence Lifts Oil to New High: Crude soars to $76.70 a barrel on rising anxiety about supply. Stocks tumble worldwide," July 14, 2006, By Tom Petruno and Elizabeth Douglass, Times Staff Writers, *Los Angeles Times*.

I think we can see that there is no real information being conveyed in this article. This is the standard operating procedure for the mass media. Not only is this merely another good example of how the corporatist media has no informational value and instead is merely a brainwashing instrument, but furthermore, it verifies the uniformity of the corporatist media that I discussed above. Specifically, the two articles I have quoted about oil in this section, along with virtually all other reports on oil by the big media, uniformly *do not* tell us the real cause for the oil increase: oil is monopolistically controlled.

It is interesting to note how far-and-wide the explanations go in fabricating reasons why the price of oil is skyrocketing, but none of the reasons given are ever the right one: *monopolization*. Consider the following *Associated Press* article:

> Oil prices rose Monday after Saudi Arabia's oil minister said OPEC might cut output when it meets next month. There were few other geopolitical or weather factors driving prices, which stayed within the range of the last eight weeks. Light sweet crude for January delivery rose 50 cents to US$59.74 a barrel in electronic trading on the New York Mercantile Exchange. Brent crude was up 27 cents to US$60.30 per barrel on the ICE Futures Exchange in London Monday afternoon. Trading was light last week, with floor trading closed for two days due to the U.S. Thanksgiving holiday. Oil prices have fallen by about 23 percent since hitting an all-time trading high above US$78 a barrel in mid-July. They haven't settled above US$62 a barrel since Oct. 1, despite the Organization of Petroleum Exporting Countries' announcement in mid-October that it would reduce output by 1.2 million barrels a day. Skepticism that OPEC members are committing to production cuts, as well as milder-than-normal U.S. temperatures this fall, have moderated prices. London-based newspaper Al-Hayat said Saudi oil minister Ali al-Naimi had indicated the organization would evaluate the effect of October's decision when it meets next month in Abuja, and if necessary authorize another cut. In other Nymex trading, heating oil gained 21 cents to US$1.6860 per gallon, unleaded gasoline rose half a cent to US$1.5935 and natural gas rose 19.7 cents to US$7.915 per 1,000 cubic feet.[308]

In this article, we are told that, rather than monopolization being the factor for the rise of oil, instead, it is 1. OPEC, 2. geopolitical factors (whatever that might mean), 3. weather, and 4. atmospheric temperatures (4 is apparently not identical to 3.). What we can conclude from these issues is that

> many of the economic principles Americans are told about in school and college, and in the national corporatist media—such as the concepts of

---

[308] "Oil prices rise despite lack of news to drive prices," The Associated Press, November 27, 2006.

supply and demand—are vacuous, for the simple reason that they cannot explain empirical events and empirical circumstances (in this case, the philosophical concepts of supply and demand cannot explain a 700% increase in the price of oil). It is as if these concepts are endlessly paraded in front of the faces and minds of Americans in order to cover-up the *real* monopolistic nature of American economics—which are the aforementioned "fascist pods" (i.e., monopolistic corporations)—in order to inculcate their minds with false ideas of how America is a competitive free market that is working in the RP's interests. I am of course not the only academic to note how it is an illusion to believe that capitalism in American only exists for the very few ultra-wealthy corporatists.

Although Americans are told that supply and demand are the drivers of the oil market, it is not entirely a secret that this is not true. Consider what Senator Byrd (D-WV), talking on the Congressional Floor about pre-emptive warfare in Iraq, has apparently admitted is the motive behind the Iraq war, and which leads to *American interests controlling the price of oil*:

> There's no debate. There's *no* discussion. There's *nothing. Nothing…*
> This administration has turned the patient art of diplomacy on its head…
> into labeling and name-calling... Labeling whole countries as *evil*?
> Denigrating powers, European allies as *irrelevant*? … Will we seize
> Iraq's oil fields, becoming an occupying power, which controls the price
> and supply of that nation's oil for the foreseeable future? … [M]any of
> the pronouncements of this administration are *outrageous*! There's no
> other word. And yet this chamber is hauntingly silent. *Silent!*[309]

Senator Byrd—somewhat of an outsider to the neoconservativism that has inundated Washington—made this comment while acting as one of the only dissenting senators. Just before this quote, the narrator in Karel (2004) said that there was so little resistance and debate about the Iraq situation that the US government resembled" a single-party system."

Big Oil: An Example of a Fabricated "Supply and Demand" Market

When one understands that the business cycle and the stock markets are part of the secret government's tool-chest, one can start to understand how business and the big markets work, and how they are fabricated and controlled, in order for the New World Order corporatists to profit. A great example is the skyrocketing prices of oil and gasoline from 1999 to 2007, but especially in 2005 and 2006, as just discussed.

Firstly, it is interesting to take a look at the propaganda that goes into defending the oil price increase. For example, Americans are actually told by

---

[309] Quote from Karel 2004.

big media that skyrocketing prices, which remove money from their pocket and gives it to just a few ultra-rich oil monopolists, *is good for them*. Americans are told that it is part of a natural and inevitable process, and there is no real reason to blame anybody for it or to be upset with anybody for it. Consider a passage from an *Associated Press* article, which has the rather Orwellian title, "Big Oil Executives Say Fuel Is Relatively Cheap,"

> Americans paying $3 per gallon at the pump have it relatively cheap when compared with prices globally, say oil and gas company executives who defend their record profits as essential to maintaining supplies... "This is a global business, and it's not only that we need to add to supply, but we need to reduce demand," Mulva said. "In the United States alone, we have about 2 percent of world oil reserves, 5 percent of the population and yet we use about 25 percent of the world's consumption of oil." Mulva and two other executives who appeared on NBC's "Meet the Press" said they are optimistic about keeping a lid on domestic prices, unless their fears come true about the potential for damage to U.S. energy production from the hurricane season that began June 1.[310]

In addition to telling Americans that they should be happy about how the skyrocketing price of oil is progressing, this passage is concerned to some degree with the old economic principle of "supply and demand," which is widely assumed to control the prices of goods worldwide. This is another concept that is often spoon-fed to Americans via the national media. For example, William Clay Ford, in a supposedly pro-ethanol commercial for Ford in July of 2006 that aired daily on news channels (such as the *Fox News Channel*): said that "...we can't control the price of gasoline..."

Americans are taught to believe that supply and demand control the price of oil. Few Americans realize that there is no world oil shortage, and there is no need to invade Middle Eastern nations in order to secure oil. Americans are endlessly told that there are worldwide supply concerns regarding oil,[311] and

---

[310] "Big Oil Executives Say Fuel Is Relatively Cheap," by John Heilprin, June 18, 2006, *The Associated Press*. The reader should note that this article does not cite any data to support the claims about supply and demand being made.

[311] For example, in the days before this book went to the publisher, there was continuous talk in the big media about how oil was rising due to supply shortages. See, "Oil Breaches $60 On Supply Concerns," Reuters, by Barbara Lewis, February 9, 2007. Also, consider this passage from an October 25, 2004 article from MSNBC entitled "How Long Will the World's Oil Last?"

> No one is suggesting that the world oil industry is close to pumping its last drop. But the question now being raised is whether new reserves can be discovered fast enough to both replace depleted oil fields and keep up with growing demand. Some argue that the world is rapidly approaching the point where the pace of oil depletion overtakes the growth in new supplies. "The

therefore some Americans (including many activists) believe Iraq was invaded in order to secure their oil, as the PNAC document says. But there is no oil shortage of any sort, and supply and demand are not the engines of the pricing of oil, but rather, they are fabrications of, and effects of, the monopolization of resources and industries by the secret government. Like the concepts of "inflation" and "the business cycle," "supply and demand" is another snake oil: a market-fabricating tool that is used by corporatists to manufacture market activity to their liking and their profit.

Conclusion: America:
Communism with Lots of Distractions

In this chapter I have shown that America is a purely communistic nation, in addition to being a corporatistic nation. Democracy, private ownership, worker-power, freedom and autonomy of thought, and a healthy and wealthy population, *simply do not exist*. Americans are told they are free, that they live in a democracy, and in general they are too busy and distracted to take notice that this is obviously not true. Americans, therefore, do not realize that they are largely indistinguishable from the citizenries that they pity of other nations. Icke sums up this and all other issues in this chapter in a powerful passage (and this passage follows from the passage I gave from Icke early in chapter 1):

> Once you have the herd mentality policing itself, there is a third phase in this entrapment of human consciousness. You create factions within the herd and set them to war with each other. This is done by creating "different" belief systems (which are not different at all) and bringing them into conflict. These belief systems are known as religions, political parties, economic theories, countries, cultures, and "isms" of endless variety. These beliefs are perceived as "opposites" [but]… they are

---

worry is whether there is something worse than the Great Depression of the 1930s waiting for us — particularly that the United States gets heavily hurt because we burn a quarter of the world's oil," said Princeton University geologist Kenneth Deffeyes. Deffeyes is perhaps the leading proponent of the work of the late M. King Hubbert, a Shell Oil geologist who accurately predicted, in a controversial 1956 paper, that U.S. oil production would peak in 1970. Deffeyes has applied Hubbert's work to global oil supplies and has come up with his own projection for peak global production. He expects world production to peak around Thanksgiving of 2005, give or take a few weeks. See Williams 1980. Also see Williams' interview in the archives at the Rense Radio Show, www.rense.com, from February 7, 2005. The American citizenry has been flogged with fearmongering about oil running out since at least the 1970s (and it is interesting and not surprising how that faded away through the 1980s and 1990s, only to reemerge in the past few years), just after the alleged US "peak oil," which is really just a time when the United States began using Saudi and Middle Eastern oil. (Of course, it is no secret that America has a rich oil supply in Alaska and the Gulf of Mexico, and Canada is a Saudi-level oil-rich nation in itself.)

opposames. The vision of reality and possibility within the pen is so limited that it contains no opposites. So the elite have to create the perception of them to manufacture the divisions that allow them to divide and rule... The Far Left, as symbolized by Joseph Stalin in Russia, introduced centralized control, military dictatorship, and concentration camps. The "opposite" of that was the Far right, as symbolized by Adolf Hitler. What was he into? Centralized control, military dictatorship, and concentration camps. Yet these two opposames were set at war with each other amid propaganda that claimed they were opposites. The only difference between the Soviet Union and the so-called "West" during the Cold War was that the Soviet Union was openly controlled by the few and the West was secretly controlled by the few. And when you get to the capstone of the pyramid, you find they were the *same* few controlling both "sides". The same force operating through Wall Street and the City of London funded all "sides" in the two world wars and that's provable.[312]

The only reason, I think, that Americans believe that Soviet Russia, for example, was communist, and that the United States is non-communist, is because Americans have more distractions: entertainment, cheap goods (video games, televisions, Wal-Mart clothing that is made by slave-children in China), ESPN, and so on. Often it is these very things that Americans will say define Americanism, and they are not the sorts of things found in Soviet Russia. But if you remove these, Americans would quickly sober-up and see that they are living in not only a Soviet state themselves, but much worse, they are living in a *1984*-like state.

It is interesting to note how tyrannical control and dictatorial behavior can wiggle their way into nearly all domains of society. They are, in fact, *the* standard tools through which social interaction of almost any sort occurs, and the primary ways that control is grasped in almost any institution in American society. For example, consider what the child psychologist, Jane Nelson, writes in a passage about how disciplining children by parents is usually on the order of the behavior of *a tyrant*, rather than a loving and supportive friend:

> Many people feel strongly that strictness and punishment work... [But] [w]here did we ever get the crazy idea that in order to make children do better, first we have to make them feel worse? ... Parents and teachers don't like excessive control or permissiveness, but don't know what else to do... They try excessive control until they can't stand themselves for sounding so tyrannical.[313]

Americans shutter and feel their stomach turn when they think of tyranny. But acting like a spooky tyrant is, to some degree, how parents often deal with

---

[312] Icke 2001, 4-5. For more information on these issues, see Horowitz 2001; Stinnet 2000; Sutton 2002; Tarpley 2004.
[313] Nelson 1996, 13-14.

their children, and is also how teachers often deal with their students, how restaurant frequenters often interact with waiters and waitresses, how prison guards interact with prisoners, how professors interact with students, and, of course, how corporatists deal with employees. Totalitarian behavior is such a "normal," accepted, and pervasively used mode of behavior for Americans that they typically do not even know that there are other modes of behavior that exist and that can be carried out. It is almost as if tyrannical control is so natural and normal in the eyes of the typical American that she/he cannot imagine any sort of institution (including the institution of the family, which hardly exists in the United States, which is a sort of a "daycare nation") managed in any other way. It seems that most Americans would have no idea how to discipline a child without a tyrannical top-down fascist activity of pain-inducing punishment. The fascist pattern of social interaction is so ingrained that it is considered normal, inevitable, and perhaps even reasonable.

4 Secrecy, Terror, Theft, and Destruction: Corporatist Strategies, Tactics, and Economics

"Behind all the lies and deceptions that accompanied all these wars, was one basic motive: expansion, power, economics, *business*."

—Howard Zinn[314]

[On the telescreen,] the Eurasian soldier... seemed to be advancing, huge and terrible, his submachine gun roaring and seeming to spring out of the surface of the screen, so that some of the people in the front row actually flinched backwards in their seats. But in the same moment, drawing a deep sigh of relief from everybody, the hostile figure [on the telescreen] melted into the face of Big Brother, black-haired, black-mustachio'd, full of power and mysterious calm, and so vast that it almost filled the screen. Nobody heard what Big Brother was saying. It was merely a few words of encouragement...

-*1984*, p. 15-16, Signet Classics Edition

"All warfare is based on deception."

—The great Chinese philosopher, Sun Tzu[315]

In this chapter, I discuss the tools and tactics of the corporatists (how they control the world, and what means they use to do so). More specifically, I show how the ruling corporatists control the courts, wars, the military and police, and all of the visible government, in addition to all labor, consciousness, terrorism, and even life and death. This is a critical discussion, since it concerns the very details and mechanics of how the real secret rulers of the United States (and the world) in fact do their ruling.

The information in this chapter is virtually nonexistent in American schools and colleges (which, we will see, are also corporatist controlled). Americans have virtually no knowledge of how corporatists operate, and thus how the world operates. For example, I have conducted polls in my classes with my students every time I have had a group of them to poll, asking them if they know what lobbyists and thinks tanks are (these are key corporatist entities that the corporatists use to create and rule the world), what they do, and if any other teachers or professors have ever informed them about what they are, and year-after-year, class-after-class, I never get a single student answering in the affirmative. Even though the very fate, livelihood, and consciousness of humans are dependent on and controlled by lobbyists and thinks tanks, their existence is largely a big secret.

---

[314] Quoted in Mueller and Ellis, 2005; itals original.
[315] From Sun Tzu's *Art of War*, I, 18.

And this chapter is about all the mostly clandestine ways that the corporatist secret government creates, steers, and controls culture. I will specifically discuss some of the tactics and tools used by corporatists that I do not devote much space to elsewhere in this book: poverty, war, secret military activity, corporate terrorism, creating "terrorists" (al-Qaeda, Savak, etc.), false flag terror, wealth usurpation, resource usurpation, inadequate education, monopolization, consumerism, and what I call "the economics of destruction," among other topics. (There are other tactics and tools used by corporatists—brainwashing, domination of resources and basic life needs, tyrannization of consciousness, deliberate corruption of the food, water, and medical industries, widespread slavery, banking and the so-called "business cycle"—that I discuss at length in other chapters in this book, and thus I will only discuss them to a small degree in this chapter.) These corporatist tactics have the possibility to teach us about our current state of life in America—about our American psychology, about our confusions and problems that emerge for us on a day-to-day basis, and about how we have been created and shaped by our culture around us. Also, these corporatist tactics have the possibility to teach us about the upcoming Orwellian horror-state—which will certainly include the emergence of mass-death camps and/or labor camps created and controlled by the corporatists for the purpose of instilling neofeudalist slavery of a global scale.

Wealth-Power, the New World Order, and Think Tanks: The Mechanics of Corporate Tyranny

It's reminiscent of the Wizard of Oz where both sides are doing the dirty work of a hidden figure that is lurking behind the curtain. And although these individuals may disagree on the particulars, they all want the same end, so they use a variety of different means to attain it. Two of these tactics are distraction and disinformation. The Controllers keep everyone fighting each other instead of focusing their energy on the real enemy. They do it by clandestinely financing each opposing group, then standing back to watch the aftermath as they fight like cats and dogs.

—Victor Thorn, *The New World Order Exposed*, page 83 (Sisyphus Press, 2003)

While discussing the Iraq war, during the Sunday December 17, 2006 edition of the *Beltway Boys* on the Fox News Channel, one of the co-anchors, Fred Barnes,[316] informed the Fox News Channel audience that a member of the American Enterprise Institute (an ultra-powerful, militaristic think tank) had developed the new plan for the Bush Administration to execute in the failed

---

[316] Barnes is also the executive editor of the Weekly Standard, which is an organization that is identical to PNAC (Project for a New American Century) (See Caldicott 2004, xxi). Later in this book, it will be shown that PNAC was responsible for carrying out 9/11. (We know that PNAC and the Weekly Standard are identical because the public is told that they involve many co-members, and because they both had the same physical address up until 2007: 1150 17th Street, NW, Suite 505, Washington, DC 20036)

Iraq War. The plan called for a massive troop build-up in Iraq, even though opinion polls in the United States had shown for years that the vast majority of the population did not support the war or keeping troops in Iraq. What is important is this: a person who was not a member of the US government (i.e., the visible government) created this war policy that would be implemented by the US government, and the public did not vote on whether or not this policy was to be implemented. And even more importantly, the policy was not to end the war or bring troops home, but rather it was to bring forth a massive troop buildup in Iraq. This example shows how misled most Americans are when they believe that their votes matter (or are counted), and when they believe that they are the controllers of the nation. Americans can venture to as many voting booths as they would like, but until they understand think tanks, lobbyists, and all other corporatist organizations and tactics for controlling the world, they will continue to be utterly powerless (even though they will believe they are free), as shown in this example about a member of the AEI creating war policy for an American public that wanted no more war. And most importantly, an entire new war for the war-tired American public (the war with Iran, which will be World War III) is also being planned by policy-writing think tanks (such as PNAC[317]) for the war-tired American public. And as this book goes to press in early 2007, the imminence of this new war is being *openly* announced.[318]

Think tanks (PNAC, AEI, Hudson Institute, etc.)[319] and the New World Order organizations (CFR, IMF, WTO, and several others which I discuss more below) are created by, funded by, and exist because of the corporatists, and they deliver the laws, infrastructure, personnel, programs and policies for the militaristic and monopolizing corporatists, regardless of whether by means that are legal or illegal, secret or non-secret, or terrorist, medieval, or Nazistic. It is conducive to lump think tanks and New World Order organizations into one group, as I am doing here in this chapter, since they all involve a similar specific function:

> to act as an intermediary between both (i) the corporatists on the one hand, and (ii) the RP and the visible government on the other.

In other words, a principal feature of think tanks and New World Order organizations is that they provide a very structured, detailed, and specific process of communication *from* the corporatists *to* the visible government (Congress, President, Supreme Court, parts of the military, etc.) and to the citizenry.

---

[317] 2000 (see the bibliography for full information).

[318] "U.S. Weighs Military Buildup to Warn Iran," by Pauline Jelinek, Associated Press, December 18, 2006; "US naval war games off the Iranian coastline: A provocation which could lead to War?" Globalresearch.ca, by Professor Michel Chossudovsky, October 24, 2006.

[319] Think tanks are often called "public interest groups," "political action committees" (PACs), "coalitions," "education institutes," and so on.

Think tanks and New World Order organizations have only one principal purpose:

> *To use corporate money to get power, and to use that power to influence Washington, where that influence is so strong that it overpowers all other interests and voices, and where that influence is used to create laws, policies, military, and deregulation that is intended to help the corporatists—and which seemingly always has the result of not helping "the people" (the RP).*

Setting up the corporatist New World Order has been a project in the making for hundreds of years, if not thousands of years, by the same secretive group of freemasons,[320] and the illuminati at their core.[321] But the activity in this set-up has dramatically escalated since 1913 (the year the Federal Reserve was created and the first year Americans were forced to pay taxation on their labor), but it has reached a fever-pitch since World War II and then also the late 1960s and the early 1970s—which are two eras of history replete with deception. Over the past ten years, the activities have begun to near a finalized state. Events such as the first Gulf War ("Desert Storm"), the pollution of the earth with depleted uranium, 9/11, the second Iraq War, the upcoming war with Iran, the blatant transhumanist interests of the corporatists (as elaborated by the inventor, Ray Kurzweil, who is on George W. Bush's "technology panel"[322]), the appearance of Morgellons disease, among other events, all are indications of an approaching ultramassive world-shift that will bring in the full implementation of the corporatist world government which will be a move into a global Orwellian way of life, and will likely involve a transition of all humans into a new state of global consciousness, as I discuss in later chapters, which will perhaps be a more titanic shift in consciousness than the one that apparently occurred with the rise of philosophy and inchoate science world-wide around 450 B.C.E.

Think Tanks

Corporate interest in think tanks expanded around 1970, which is also the time that they greatly increased in number.[323] This is why, in discussing President Ford, Professor Zinn informs us that "Ford's closest friends in Washington were corporate lobbyists."[324] (I will discuss the connection to lobbyists later, but for now, you can consider them to be similar to think tanks: they are people or groups that create the activity of the visible government, and who ultimately create the shape of thought and action among "We the People.")

---

[320] For more information, see Howard 1989, Pinto 2006.
[321] See Maxwell 2000, Jones 2005.
[322] See Kurzweil 1999.
[323] Rich 2004, 49-50.
[324] Zinn 2003, 546.

This expansion was centered around the so-called Business Roundtable, which is discussed by Nace, Rich, and most researchers who study the mechanics of think tanks. Rich writes:

> ...by 1972, with the formation of the Business Roundtable, the CEOs of many Fortune 500 companies became personally involved in Washington policy making. The Business Roundtable acted to advance and protect the shared interests of business.[325]

Rich points out that there was deliberate planning by neo-conservatives to specifically be rulers of *ideas*: "Avowing that ideas were the only weapons able to overturn the establishment and working diligently to build an establishment of their own, conservatives founded and strengthened scores of institutions."[326]

The entire political landscape in Washington turned to a "conservative" focus in the 1970s and 1980s and up to today,[327] which primarily means that Washington honed its corporatist alliances—although in the 2000s Washington has metamorphosed more into neo-conservatism, which is marked by the principles outlined in PNAC (2000, see bibliography): totalistic control of information, preemptive warfare on a *global* scale, domination of oil, implementation of race-specific bio-weapons, and so forth.[328] This shift to conservatism and then neo-conservatism occurred precisely because of the aforementioned refocusing in the late 1960s and early 1970s, as Nace discusses,

> [In] [t]he late 1960s and early 1970s... [p]ublic attitudes toward businessmen were in a free fall... Perhaps it could have been foreseen that the success of the environmental and consumer movements would trigger some sort of backlash by big business, but the scale of the corporate political mobilization proved to be unprecedented.[329]

Before going on, it is worth correcting Nace on his comments about "environmental and consumer movements." Culture is socially engineered, and

---

[325] Rich 2004, 50. Interestingly, later on this page, Rich implies that the social protests, and thus apparently the whole "60s atmosphere," was what the neoconservative think tank eruption was largely about*--almost as if that time of media-created, corporatist engineered "rebellion" was helpful to setting up the final phase of the New World Order.

[326] Smith 1991, 182.

[327] Rich 2004, 10, 18-25..

[328] These issues are all clarified in PNAC 2000, which the reader is strongly recommended to read. "Race-specific bio-weapons" could mean Morgellons disease or AIDS, given that these are each man-made bio-terrorist weapons that have been implemented in the past few decades. For information on AIDS, see Horowitz (1999, 2001), and for information on Morgellons, see chapter 5.

[329] Nace 2003, 137-138. Rich also points out how 1970 was the time that the numbers of think tanks exploded, and how that explosion was dominated by the conservative think tanks (see Rich 2004, page 28, and other places in chapter 1).

as FDR pointed out, if a political event happens, it was planned.[330] Therefore, there are no accidental events: basically all major political events that shape social reality are generated by the corporatists. Given this revisionist view of history, the question then is: What good did the 1960s "countercultural" movement and "environmental movement" of the 1970s (and the effects of which largely extend to the present) do for the corporatist secret government? The 1960s countercultural movement helped to spark protest against the obvious atrocity of the Vietnam War which helped to break down American jingoism and nationalism—which was integral to setting up a corporatist New World Order.[331,332] And in late 2006, the filmmaker and Internet radio scholar, Alex Jones, of Infowars.com, pointed out that environmentalism is just a cover for "land-grabbing," where the citizenry is tricked into putting land aside in the name of "environmental protection," but which is later usurped by the corporatists, as Jones has pointed out has happened in many instances in Texas. It is difficult to tell how much of the 1960s revolution was genuine, and how much of it was staged (but if we take FDR's maxim literally, then we can look at virtually all of the 1960s as being staged). But what is known is that the 1960s helped the corporatists' secret government and New World Order interests in many ways: it increased the drug movement (which the corporatists control and profit from[333]), it removed a sense of American nationalism (which is in some ways a good thing, since it makes the US more multicultural, but the corporatists don't have benevolent or non-Orwellian motives in mind with this breakdown of nationalism), it de-Christianized America, it hurt the education system and put the education system more in line with UN-style education,[334] and the 1960s involved an attack on intellectualism, which is always good for corporatists who want to dominate an unthinking public.

Returning to the discussion of think tanks, and specifically, the *neoconservative* think tanks, it can now be seen in 2007 that the surge in corporate reorganization via think tanks after the 1960s was a well-organized program to use the resource- and wealth-base of America to build up the military and wealth of the United States in order to prepare for the next world war: the upcoming World War III, which will surely be catalyzed with an

---

[330] The exact quote is: "In politics, nothing happens by accident. If it happens, you can bet it was planned that way." —Franklin D. Roosevelt

[331] See Epperson 1985, chapter 3; Perloff 1989, chapter 1.

[332] There are perhaps some other, speculative bits of evidence for the idea that the 1960s were fabricated by the corporatist secret government: we know that key members of the movement were Skull and Bones (John Kerry), New World Order agents, such as Aleister Crowley (Pinto [2006] maintains that Crowley could have been one of the principal catalyzers of the 1960s movement). Perhaps it is not a coincidence that the peace symbol adopted for the 1960's countercultural movement is one of the principal occult symbols.

[333] See Ruppert 2004a, 2004b, Scott 2003, and Cockburn and Clair 1998.

[334] See Tabor 2006, chapter 1.

Israel-Iran or US-Iran conflict, but which will quickly turn into a US-China and/or US-Russia conflict (since Iran contains much of the oil that China and Russia use), which will fully set up the New World Order. Nace goes on to discuss how the use of the ultra-"conservative" (i.e., *neoconservative*) think tanks was specifically planned out, and initially heavily funded by, for example, the brewer and ultra-wealthy corporatist, Joseph Coors,[335] among others. The rise of the neoconservatives, and the increased use of neoconservative think tanks by corporations, were coincident in time, and they enabled the initiation of a fuller takeover of American militarism, media,[336] thought, and behavior, by the ultra-wealthy, CFR-based, neoconservatives, from 1970 to the present.[337] The neoconservatives are a group of CIA-link, well-organized, secretive, Dostoyevskian (two-faced), neo-Machiavellian corporatists who constitute a significant vein of the global New World Order, and who specifically have openly set up imperialist world war plans centered around usurpation of the world energy.[338,339] They include the corporatists George Bush Jr., George Bush Sr., Dick Cheney, Steve Forbes, Rumsfeld, and James Woolsey, to name a few.

Washington has always been loaded with imperialist oil-usurpers, but the neoconservatives appear to be a class of them that behaves somewhat differently than the old crowd—such as the Nixon- or FDR-era politicians/corporatists/imperialists—since the current neocon crowd is certainly Hitleresque in their drive to set up their New World Order (which was also Hitler's motive, but Hitler just called it "World Order," rather than "*New World Order*"). In the early 1970s, somewhat humorously, the early neoconservatives of that time that would later gain totalist control over Washington were purported to be *anti-communist!*[340]

Think Tank Solecism

Think tanks are described and discussed in Washington and the media as if they are impressive, prestigious academic organizations. Their descriptions often involve an academic ring (e.g., "intellectual research organization"), and their descriptions often involve academic sorts of terms to describe their

---

[335] Nace 2003, 143. Coors is a founder of AEI, another think tank that, below, I will show could have, with PNAC, have masterminded 9/11.

[336] See Bagdikian 2004.

[337] Rich 2004, 49-53.

[338] PNAC 2000.

[339] But, as stated in a previous footnote, the real motive is more likely a planned defeat of America in an ultramassive war between China and the United States, where in the defeat, the wealth and power of the United States will be more fully transferred to the Chinese economy than it already has by the American Fortune 500 recently moving overseas (especially to China, as with Dell, Boeing, Wal-Mart, etc.).

[340] Rich 2004, 50.

members: "senior fellow," "emeritus," "researcher," and so on. But there are problems and deceptions involved in these academic-sounding terms.

To start with, when one looks at the members of the most powerful neoconservative think tanks, the intellectual description often seems unfounded. For example, PNAC is replete with members that are primarily news commentators, businesspersons, and politicians, and there are few real academic researchers or professors. For example, Jeb Bush, Donald Rumsfeld, Dick Cheney and Steve Forbes, and several others that could be listed certainly do not seem to be academics, and they do not have the sorts of properties that university and college professors have. For example, these and most other PNAC'ers do not have Ph.D.s, academic publications, or teaching positions, but these properties define academics, so they do not have similarities, and they seem to be the inverse of one another. Similar claims could be made for many other ultrapowerful neoconservative think tanks.

I am not the only person to be suspicious about the "intellectual" and "academic" character of think tanks. In discussing the (often dubious) research put forth by think tanks, Professor Rich writes,

> ...as more think tanks have emerged whose missions include advancing clear ideologies rather than neutral research, the substantive value of their research is increasingly viewed with a skeptical eye by policy makers who are overwhelmed by scores of studies on similar topics, all with different evidence and conclusions. That which is better promoted might get more of their attention.[341]

The *promotion* that Rich mentions in the last sentence of his passage appears to have to do with the *wealth power* I discussed in the previous subsection, which is the ultimate tool and weapon of the corporatist, due to the fact that spreading around information requires money, and the more money the more information spreading there can be. For these reasons, only militaristic corporatist interests will be *actually manifested* in reality, and in the government policymaking.

Secret Power Via Corporatist Wealth

The existence of think tanks and the New World Order organizations is for one purpose: to set up a one-way relationship of control and power *from* corporations *to* the citizenry (through the intermediary of government [politicians, police, education systems, courts, media, military, CIA, FDA, NSA, corrupted Christianity, etc.]). Princeton economist, Gene Grossman, puts the issue rather pointedly in the very opening of an article where he disdains the romantic idea of pure democracy, as if it is just an idea sold to the commoners by the corporatist-financed politicians, and where in the real-world, power-

---

[341] Rich 2004 , 25. Also see Felton 2005, chapter nine.

politics are controlled by the financially-backed special interests (think tanks and New World Order organizations):

> In the idealized democratic society, economic policy is determined by "one man, one vote." But in all real societies, special interest groups play an important role in the process that determines economic policy. Pressure groups represent relatively narrow interests, for example of peanut farmers, auto workers, or shareholders of firms that produce semiconductors. They also represent broader interests, such as those of retired workers, capital owners, and those with special concerns for the environment.[342]

When workers are blinded to the power they have—which is the power of *the people*—the all-powerfulness is handed over to the corporatists by way of *their own* think tanks and New World Order organizations. This is how corporatists control the visible government, and it seems that most Americans do not even know that these think tanks and New World Order organizations exist, and thus the citizenry latches on to this romantic and vacuous idea that *voting*, or "writing their Congressperson," gives them control of the United States. This is a blatant loss of critical reasoning and skeptical awareness by the American citizenry, due to their inability to see the obvious fact that politicians are not acting in the interests of the people, and this is verified each day, even in the mainstream national media. It is difficult to understand how they cannot see they are being used to set up the New World Order via a military holocaust to be carried out around the world (i.e., World War III) that will rearrange the social world far more than World War II did.

I take this blatant loss of sight and loss of self-preservation activity by the typical American to be a product of the aforementioned corruption of the American person's mind through the education system, which does not teach the person to be a critical thinker, a scientist, and a poet. I take this blatant loss of sight and loss of self-preservation activity by the typical American to be because America is a land of poisons (fluoridated water which depletes brain activity,[343] mercury in food and medicines that destroys parts of the nervous system (see chapter 5), poisoned food and air also do the same thing, etc.), where the average person inhabits a damaged nervous system and they typically do not even know it. I take this blatant loss of sight and loss of self-preservation activity by the typical American to be a product of the life-long "education" in television and video games that Americans receive, especially American children, often from infancy onward. The end product is a land full of

---

[342] Grossmann 2000. These are the first sentences of his article, which can be read at http://www.nber.org/reporter/.

[343] See, "Determination of Fluoride in Water Residues by Proton Induced Gamma Emission Measurements," by AKM Fazlul Hoque, M. Khaliquzzaman, MD Hossain, and AH Khan, published in 2002 by the journal, *Fluoride*, vol. 35, no. 3, pages 176-184. Also see Bryson 2004.

Americans who typically are without mental, spiritual, or psychological depth or stamina, without conviction and direction, and who merely embody a semi-zombic state, from moment-to-moment thinking about little more than their cell phone activity, what to watch on television, going out to the club, chit-chat, the boredom of their jobs, and the information in the news paper. This is not meant to be a cantankerous diatribe against Americans, but rather it is meant to be an empirical but lugubrious analysis of what I see in the faces of my fellow human beings on the streets and campuses in America. The corporatists wanted a Brave New World of unquestioning workers, and they have succeeded.

Returning to the think tanks and New World Order organizations, Caldicott lucidly describes the power they have in their process of shaping the visible government and the consciousness of Americans, and she describes the way money is the weapon used by the corporatists to do this:

> In the seventies leading international corporations jointly organized and endowed a series of think tanks—their own "battle management organizations"—whose primary purpose was to sway popular and political opinion in directions useful to the think tanks' corporate sponsors. These think tanks are staffed by erudite researchers who produced editorials, TV news pieces, papers, media releases, and legislative material, which are well-conceived, well-researched, well-written, easy to understand, and very acceptable to the media and Congress... Mostly Washington based, these think tanks also have a pervasive presence in the media, their spokespeople being regular political commentators on the Sunday-morning talk shows and in print...
>
> This broad-reaching, sophisticated, high-level manipulation of the so-called free, democratic media and legislature... has been extraordinarily successful for the sponsoring corporations and the points of view they espouse. Such an approach effectively controls government agendas in many countries—certainly including the United States—and is more effective by far than grassroots organizing, for all but the very few issues around which millions of concerned citizens can be mobilized...
>
> But these think tanks are neither free nor democratic. They are nonelected, private bodies controlled by wealthy and powerful corporations. In effect they are advertising agencies acting for the corporations that founded and fund them. They represent the corporate philosophy of "economic rationalism," which favors the corporate takeover of all public enterprises, for health care and education to water and electricity, and an agenda that includes decreasing or abolishing government regulation of big business, decreasing corporate taxes and taxes for the rich, destroying the unions, and increasing corporate

profits… The IMF, the World Bank, GATT, NAFTA, APEC, FTAA, and WTO have all taken their cues from these think tanks.[344]

The reader should consult Caldicott's excellent book to read the next few pages after this passage, where Caldicott goes on to explain how there are specialized think tanks and New World Order organizations hired by the biggest and most powerful global corporations (e.g., GE, Exxon, etc.), many of which are the huge military weapons-making corporations (TRW and Lockheed Martin, in addition to GE). This secretive arrangement that corporatists have with the military corporatists and the visible government of the United States, which has the autonomous power it does due to the wealth that exists in the hands of the corporatists, ensures that only corporatist and military-industrial complex interests are served in the District of Columbia and the stratospheric military and monetary power of the District of Columbia.

And, as stated, Rich comments on how it is the conservative think tanks that flourished because of the all-powerful corporate finances behind them,[345] and thus it can be concluded from that, that only the firmly corporate-aligned, corporate-minded think tanks that had the corporate leaders' interests as *their* interests were the ones that were influential. Rich discussed how these corporatist think tanks specifically wanted to disrupt the nation for the benefit of the corporatists, in order to even more effectively dominate the culture:

> For scholars of modern conservatives, the emergence of conservative think tanks… is attributed to the efforts of conservative intellectuals along with corporate and ideological patrons, who formed think tanks and other organizations in order to disrupt the political status quo.[346]

In the same fashion as Caldicott, Nace goes on to discuss[347] how the think tanks and New World Order organizations of the 1970s that held views most similar to the neoconservatives were the most adequately funded, and thus became the most powerful and influential think tanks and New World Order organizations.[348] As is still the case, the ultra-powerful think tanks were clandestine ("under the table," as Nace puts it), and they have sought to cement

---

[344] Caldicott 2002, 24-26.

[345] Rich 2004, 32. In this quote, we can presume that by "conservative," Rich really means to say "neoconservative."

[346] Rich 2004, 32.

[347] Nace 2003, 143-147.

[348] This sort of reminds me of what is discussed elsewhere in this book w hen I discuss the manufacture of consent, of how in a similar way, the news media also evolved over the centuries to become only a *corporate* media, since corporate money was able to make other papers extinct by putting so much power into the minority fringe papers that just happened to be in agreement with what corporate leaders like. This also reminds me of how Pappas (2003) says that whenever there is a means of communication that is invented, whether a think tank, the internet, television, etc., it's always only a matter of time before corporations gain full control over it.

into minds everywhere that corporatist-interests are good for the RP. (This is similar to how we saw in the last chapter that big news papers were writing articles that informed the American citizenry that high oil and fuel costs are good for them.)

As shown in chapter 2, the mass of America's resources and wealth resides in the hands of the corporatists and the think tanks, New World Order organizations, and the visible government (all three of which specifically work for the corporations, even though they deceivingly tell the world that they work for the people). The wealth-power of these three comes from corporations, and thus it is so much wealth-power that all other wealth and money become meaningless. This reveals a principal issue of corporatism:

The weaponry and machinery of the corporatist is money.

Nace writes:

> Foundations, think tanks, coalitions, litigation centers, PR agencies, publications, judicial education—all these contributed to the corporate political comeback [in the 1970s]. But there was one final old-fashioned ingredient to add to the mix: *money.*[349]

This is still the same assault that the corporatists carry out on American and world citizens today. The equation of the mechanism and the money-power and chain of influence looks like this

Corporatists➔think tanks & NWO org.➔visible government➔citizenry (RP).

This process shown in the figure above is possible because the government is replete with money-stuffed and money-drunken businesspeople who have exclusively corporatist interests. This is a critical issue; the issue that makes corporatism possible in the first place. And it is also not an accident, for reasons I will explain next.

The Key to Corporatist Power: Domination of Washington, D. C.

As is now well-known, elections in the United States are not fairly or legitimately won by candidates. Rather, the way American national "elections" actually work is as follows:

> Through the power of money and controlled media, a few ultra-wealthy corporatists that the secret government carefully chooses are brought

---

[349] Nace 2003, 147. Nace discusses how various laws and actions took place in the 1970s to allow for more free-flow of money and communication between corporations and government, to the point of being virtually unrestricted, as it is now, and which lead to things like Enron (2003, 147-151).

forward to be candidates. They are most often CFR-trained puppets[350] (also, they are occasionally Hollywood actors, as was the case with Reagan and Schwarzenegger). The media focuses on the candidates that are hand-picked by the secret government, and ignores or pays little attention to any others. Americans are told that the candidates getting the most media attention are the ones that the polls show have the best chance. An election is held, which is utterly replete with fraud and corruption,[351] but it is standard that nearly none of it is ever reported in the national media,[352] and thus Americans do not know that it exists and they erroneously believe that the election is fair and accurate.

Most presidential candidates in the United States curiously *do not even make it on to the ballot* in the United States, as if they are eliminated before election time. And since the only way a candidate can be seen and heard by the American people is via the corporatist media, when election time comes, most Americans do not know that there are other candidates other than Democrat or Republican candidates, and/or they are made to think that they are inferior to the Democrat or Republican candidates. A candidate will be allowed on the corporatist media if they are chosen by the secret government, if they have money to advertise on their corporatist media networks and channels, and if the candidate's ideology is approved by the corporatist media and the secret government.[353]

Since *free* campaign advertisements and air-time of *any* sort for persons running for office has (somehow) been made illegal in the United States,[354] this means that only very few people can run for office *and* get the needed publicity and press-time while doing so. Also, the national media will only allow material in their media channels that will be approved by their corporatist sponsors, and if the corporatist sponsors start to become unhappy with information being presented in the national media that they are sponsoring, they may complain and/or cease sponsorship. This assures that only air-time for corporatist-friendly messages, corporatist political candidates, and pro-war and pro-military messages will fill the 900 cable channels. (Some of the war and

---

[350] See Perloff 1988, chapter 1.

[351] See Miller 2005.

[352] An exception to this was the 1999 Presidential election for the 2000 Presidential position between Bush Jr. and Gore, where for a few weeks there was some reporting on the corruption going on in Florida, and where for at least a day after the election, a President was not chosen due to the questionable nature of the Florida circumstances in the election. In the end, Al Gore merely bowed out without a fight, the Florida Supreme Court informed the nation that they would not consider any sort of recount, and the state official, Katherine Harris, declared Bush the winner before an adequate recount was carried out.

[353] For fuller treatment of this topic, see Bagdikian 2004 and Pappas 2003.

[354] This is discussed by Professor McChesney, by Pappas, and by others in detail in Pappas 2003.

military coverage on television may seem to be antiwar, but it is not. John Kerry ran in 2004 for the Presidency of the United States on what he purported was an anti-Bush approach to Iraq, as if that meant Kerry was antiwar. But Kerry was for keeping the troops in Iraq for a long time, just like Bush. Hillary Clinton is going to run for the 2008 Presidency, and now in 2007 as this book goes to press, she frequently and aggressively discusses "ending the war in Iraq."[355] Many believe she is putting forth an antiwar message, but she is actually putting forth a pro-war message: *Keep the troops in Iraq for war activity for three more years.* Consider the following passage from a story titled, "Clinton Promises to End War if Elected" (Associated Press, February 2, 2007, by Nedra Pickler):

> "Believe me, I understand the frustration and the outrage," Clinton said in a speech to the Democratic National Committee meeting that brought the party's nine White House hopefuls together for the first time. "You have to have 60 votes to cap troops, to limit funding to do anything. If we in Congress don't end this war before January 2009, as president, I will.

This is the same message Bush has put forth: "keep the troops in Iraq until it's time to bring 'em home!" Also, as is well-known, Hillary Clinton voted for the Iraq war.[356])

The conclusion of what I am discussing here is this:

> Only corporatists and those they choose to hold power positions for them, can hold influence in Federal government offices in the United States.

As Hertz puts it, in discussing the candidates for the 2000 American presidential election, "their very ability to run depended upon their securing corporate funding. Al Gore's campaign war chest was $33 million; George W. Bush's $191 million,... with Enron and its executives among Bush's biggest donors."[357] Consider Professor Grossman's theorization of these issues:

> [C]ampaign contributions (of time and money) [are]... the tool by which interest groups might influence the policy process... [There is] strategic interaction between interest groups and policymakers on the one hand and the strategic interaction among the interest groups on the other...

---

[355] See "N.H. voters want clarity on Clinton's Iraq views," CNN, February 12, 2007, http://www.cnn.com/2007/ POLITICS/02/12/2008.campaign.trail.ap/; and see "Hillary Clinton Vows to End the Iraq War," Agence France Presse., February 2, 2007.
[356] See "Hillary Clinton: No Regret on Iraq Vote," CNN, April 21, 2004, http://www.cnn.com/2004/ALLPOLITICS/ 04/21/iraq.hillary/.
[357] Hertz 2003, 10-11. Readers who are interested in numerology and the secret government might find these financial numbers (33 and 191 [911]) rather interesting in this passage from Hertz.

[T]rade policies can be viewed as objects "for sale," with the policymaker as seller and special interest groups as buyers... [T]he policymaker covets political contributions, which can be used to finance a bid for re-election. [P]olicymakers [are rendered]... "common agents" of the special interests. Special interest groups are assumed to represent industry interests in an economic model in which those with (human or physical) capital invested in an industry stand to gain from protection or subsidization of their sector. In [this] model, every organized interest group makes a bid for influence. These bids take the form of "contribution schedules" that link the amount that a group will contribute to the policymaker to the collection of trade policies that the policymaker adopts. We impose no restriction on the design of these offers, except that no group can contribute negatively... Each group understands that the others also will be bidding for influence and that, ultimately, the policymaker will set trade policies to maximize a political objective function that includes aggregate welfare and aggregate contributions as arguments. The groups design their contributions to maximize the welfare of their members, assuming that other groups will be behaving similarly and that the policymaker is politically motivated... The rate of protection to an industry is the product of two components: the first component, common to all industries in a polity, reflects the weight that the policymaker attaches to aggregate social welfare and the fraction of the population that is represented by an organized interest group. This can be regarded as a summary of the political environment. The second component varies by industry according to its economic characteristics. It implies that more protection will be provided to politically organized industries with a high ratio of output-to-imports and to those industries for which the demand for imports is relatively inelastic.[358]

With only corporatists holding and demonstrating actual power in Washington, that means that only corporatist culture, and things friendly to corporatist culture (such as war, profits for corporatists, and so on), will be created by the visible government, and other aspects of society that are not friendly to corporatist interests and profits—such as the existence of a middle class, quality education, reasonable pay and health-care, cures for diseases, and so on—will suffer or be destroyed. If something is owned or controlled by the visible government, it is actually corporatist controlled. Many things, like roads and bridges, are often believed to be controlled or owned by the visible government or by American citizens, but which are not, and are in fact owned by corporations.[359] Thus, the corporatists will make decisions based on

---

[358] Grossman 2000.

[359] I discussed this in detail in chapter 3. See Korten 2001 for more information. Alex Jones also repeatedly discussed these issues in his infowars.com radio broadcasts in November and December of 2006.

corporatistic monopolistic interests, no matter how much poverty, war, sadness, horror, slavery, and literal human dementia (brain/mind breakdown) results. If wars in Iran or Iraq, or if false flag terror attacks are good for a profit, then the visible government corporatists will proceed to implement and engineer them by any means necessary.

According to Homeland Security, Americans are al-Qaeda

Corporatists fund New World Order organizations and the think tanks they are partial to in order to have policy created that is in accord with their interests. And then when the corporatists are in need of policy to implement, the visible government *will merely seek and use policy from the New World Order organizations' think tanks that the corporatists have created in order to execute their corporatist plans and thus to bring in wealth control, power, and sadomasochistic domination to the corporations and corporatists.* For these reasons, it will be virtually impossible to find real examples of cases where the corporatist politicians create policy and laws that actually benefit the citizenry. If a law is created that has the appearance of being of some help to the citizenry, it is typically the case that there is deception involved, and it really does not help. A good example is the so-called Patriot Act, or the creation of Homeland Security, both created right after 9/11, and which have resulted in creating a Nazi-like, Orwellian surveillance/Big Brother infrastructure, created by corporatists in the biometrics, communications, and other profitable industries. Now, years after 9/11, there is no display of a search for Osama bin Laden being carried out by the US government, and there is hardly any search for any "terrorists" being carried out; instead, Americans are now harassed endlessly at airports,[360] in highways,[361] on computers,[362] in schools,[363] at

---

[360] See the following stories: "Phoenix Airport to Test X-Ray Screening," Associated Press, December 1, 2006; "Air Travelers Stripped Bare with X-ray Machine," USA Today, May 15, 2005, Thomas Frank; "Nice Bombs Ya Got There," Associated Press, June, 26, 2003; "Massive Terror Screening Draws Outrage: Lawmakers and Businessmen Object to Terrorist Screening of American International Travelers," The Associated Press, Michael J. Sniffen, December 1, 2006; "Iris Scanning To Begin At Orlando International Airport," Associated Press, May 11, 2005; "Fingerprint, Iris Scans for Airport Employees: Canada To Use First Biometric System in World; National system to boost security in wake of 9/11," Toronto Star, Kevin McGran, December 7, 2005.

[361] "Is the US Becoming a 'Nation of Snitches?'" WorldNetDaily, Barbara Ferguson, July 19 2004, "Speed cameras fail to halt a rise in fatalities on the roads," London Telegraph, February 12, 2007.

[362] See, "IMs Being Monitored at Home, Work," CBS News, October 31, 2006; "Big Brother Isn't Watching - Google Is," Christian Science Monitor (CSMonitor.com), Tom Regan, February 01, 2006, http://www.csmonitor.com/2006/0201/p16s01-cogn.html.

banks,[364] and everywhere[365] by Homeland Security and their Patriot Act. This is because there never were any terrorists, and the plan has only been to conquer the American people and the world citizenry.

Corporatists Control Government, and Therefore Corporatism *is* Government

A Key issue brought up in this chapter is that the government policymakers in Washington cannot, and do not, control the corporatists and their corporatist interests. It is important to point this out since so many people imagine that government controls and regulates business. Since the corporatist position in society is far more powerful than the government/policymaker level of society (and, as discussed, corporatists occupy, or chose inhabitants for, most of the Washington policymaking positions anyway), that means that government/policymaker authority is always inferior to corporatists authority. In other words, since enforcement or control of a stronger group by a weaker power cannot exist for long (if it ever exists in the first place), then government cannot regulate, govern, or enforce law (or punishment) on corporations, and thus corporations are not accountable to anyone or anything.[366] Hertz writes that:

> Each new merger gives corporations even more power. All the goods we buy or use—our gasoline, the drugs our doctors prescribe, essentials like water, transportation, health, and education, even the new school computers and the crops growing in the fields around our communities—are in the grip of corporations which may, at their whim, nurture, support, or strangle us. This is ... the world at the dawn of the new millennium. Governments' hands appear tied and we are ... dependent on corporations.[367]

Look through a list of the largest corporations. You see Big Pharma, Monsanto, Microsoft, the US Postal Service, water companies, energy and transportation companies, and so on. We are now all dependent on the products of the largest corporations if we are to survive. From what I can tell, Americans are typically fooled into believing that consumers control corporations, since

---

[363] Pentagon Creating Student Database: Recruiting tool for military raises privacy concerns," Washington Post, Jonathan Krim, June 23, 2005.

[364] Pentagon Viewing Americans' Bank Records," Associated press, Lolita Baldor, January 14, 2007.

[365] See this news story from an Alex Jones news source: "Big Brother: Watching, Listening, Shouting And Firing X-Rays: Where will the surveillance stop and how do naked pictures of people stop terrorism?" Infowars.net, Steve Watson, January 31, 2007.

[366] One might wonder: What about Enron? Enron problems became public because Enron ran out of "fraud power"—i.e., the fake money ran out of steam.

[367] Hertz 2003, 8.

corporations need consumers to purchase the goods. But at many places in this book, I will show that the real dependency involves the citizenry being dependent on the corporations and corporatists, not the other way around. The resource usurpation by corporations that I discuss in this book *prohibits* real business competition, and if corporations control the resources that any person needs to live, citizens can only be fully dependent on resource-controlling corporatists.

What can anyone do to corporations that have usurped resources in order to create and control the things all Americans need to survive? Can politicians really enforce taxation on them?[368] Can politicians really request an increase in the minimum wage? Can politicians make corporations pay for health care for the corporation's employees? Since the government is comprised of corporatists, why would they impose these sorts of "experiences" on themselves? It would be like taking money out of their own pockets. If a campaigning politician suggests an increase in minimum wage, do you think that the corporatist news media would be safe in fairly reporting on that candidate, or in putting that candidate's advertisements on their media channels? Do you think that the other corporatists that support the corporatist news media via advertising would be happy if that politician is featured in the media? What if CNN reported a story on price gauging of oil companies, who control the very oil that all Americans depend on for their way of life in the civilized world? With such a story, CNN would threaten all their income from oil or related sponsors via advertising. What if CNN reported on the pervasive criminality and fakery involved with Big Pharma companies,[369] which are perhaps the biggest advertisers of all in the corporatist media? Wouldn't all Big Pharma companies question whether or not they should advertise at CNN (i.e., if they should fund CNN). The termination of such support could be so severe to CNN that it could perhaps compromise CNN's existence. So it is easy to see how the corporatist's weapon of total control, even over our media and thus over our own minds, is money.

Lobbyists

A principal way that corporatists control government is to, plain and simple, *buy and pay off the politicians so that they vote and create policy in a way that the highest bidder wishes.* This is specifically how the corporatists' principal weapon—money—functions to control (govern) the world. If think tanks and New World Order organizations are deliverers of *policy* from corporations to government, you can think of lobbyists as deliverers of the pay-off *financing* from corporations and corporate interests to government, needed to purchase the politicians. The primary activity of a politician—whether Republican or

---

[368] See Zepezauer 2004 for a lucid, empirical study of how tax laws are not enforced on the massive monopolizing corporations.
[369] See Angell 2003

Democrat[370]—is, without exaggeration, to merely function as a party-going bribe taker, taking money from corporatist after corporatist, often nightly, in order to be paid to create policy in the interests of the high-paying corporatists. This is hard for some Americans to understand, but that is only because much work is put into keeping this lobbying activity out of sight, and making it look like what politicians do each day is debate issues on the Congressional floor. But when one actually analyzes, and simply researches what it is that lawmakers are doing, and the nature of the lawmaking activity that Congress carries out, for example, and when one studies the lobbyist activities, one can only come to the conclusion that all those debates on the Senate floor are merely a form of lavish, magisterial fakery.

More specifically, a "lobbyist" can be defined as follows.

A **lobbyist** is a money-deliverer, a "stuffed envelope" deliverer, *from* corporations *to* government policymakers, where the money delivered determines how policy is created and implemented in Washington.

Both think tanks and lobbying are what visible government members follow in creating policy. The idea that politicians listen to, or care about, American voters, is an illusion. Both efficiently ban "the people" from having any sort of influence in policymaking, and assure the corporatist vision as fully manifested in Washington. Studying lobbyists offers a productive way to explore the inborn fascism/corporatism of the United States, since it is such an easy way to illustrate how corporatists and only corporatists are behind policy creation.

Silverstein (1998) pretended to be a lobbyist in Washington in the 1990s in order to infiltrate and get a glance into that clandestine world. His book lucidly

---

[370] It is only by *not* taking note of the actual behaviors and activities of policymakers that one can continue to believe there are significant differences between Republicans and Democrats. It seems that today "Democratic" pro-war politicians like Hillary Clinton and Joseph Leiberman use the label "Democrat" in order to get votes via an appeal to the mass of traditionally democratic voters. But it may be the case that the entire idea of a "Democratic Party," where the Democrats (Carter, Clinton, etc.) want to create the appearance that they are for "the people," has always been a sort of mythical and/or propagandisic notion. Consider, for example, what Professor Zinn writes about former President Bush:

> The presidency of Jimmy Carter... seemed an attempt by one part of the Establishment, that represented in the Democratic party, to recapture a disillusioned citizenry. But Carter, despite a few gestures toward black people and the poor, despite talk of "human rights" abroad, remained within the historic political boundaries of the American system, protecting corporate wealth and power, maintaining a huge military machine that drained the national wealth, allying the United States with right–wing tyrannies abroad. (Zinn 2003, 565)

Silverstein gives a quick analysis of the way that the Clinton presidency was dominated by and driven by lobbying, not by "the people." (Silverstein 1998, 4-5)

outlines the roiling world of deception and secrecy going on amid the corporatist system beyond the perception and awareness of Americans. We are led to believe that Congress is working for "the people," but lobbying shows this is completely false, as also discussed above.

Within a day or two of infiltrating the lobbyist world, and just after Silverstein established his fake status as a lobbyist, his name circulated around Washington and he was invited to both Democrat and Republican soirées in order to bring stuffed envelopes so that he could influence (buy) their policymaking. At the parties, the Congressperson would ask him, "what is it that you want," after he delivered the check or implied that he had a check to deliver—and this meant something like: what policy would you like me to attempt to create or vote for as the result of your payment?

At the time Silverstein wrote his book, lobbyists outnumbered Congresspersons in Washington by over 70-to-1.[371] Reading Silverstein (1998) gives the reader the story of politicians as *actors*, in the literal sense, purposely putting on one face to fool the American people, and with the intention of removing it soon after the television cameras are off. And in all seriousness, Silverstein's book also makes Congresspersons, regardless of how they might appear on CSPAN, appear to often resemble drunken fraternity brothers that will do anything for a lavish dinner party and a stuffed envelope. Silverstein's book also makes it appear that Congresspersons are people that, when the cameras are off, have no idea that there really are people "out there" in America. Consider what Caldicott writes on these issues:

> Who runs the Congress all these years? The transnational corporations whose executives wine and dine, woo, bribe, and corrupt the officeholders of the White House and Congress—from the president and vice president to almost all the elected congressional officials. These all-powerful corporations manipulate and control most of the federal legislation, foreign and domestic, that passes through Congress. They do it through a variety of mechanisms: think tanks, corporate mergers, lobbying, and political donations.[372]

Economics of Destruction

On the Rense Radio Show, December 4, 2006, the revolutionary physicists and inventor John Bedini was discussing with Jeff Rense how things like batteries, power plants and most other of the low-tech energy sources used in America are not needed, since there are ways to fuel civilization without them. Rense and Bedini also discussed in this interview that there are other sorts of existent but hidden fuel and energy sources that do not involve having to get an expensive "refill" regularly, and thus are not profitable to the corporatists.

---

[371] Silverstein 1998, 18.
[372] Caldicott 2002, 24.

Batteries have to be replaced, cars need a fill-up, the electricity in your house requires you to pay the bill each month lest your service be cut. With solar energy, wind energy, air or water energy, or with the Bedini-Bearden free-energy generator,[373] things like batteries, fill-ups, electricity bills, and so on are not needed, since energy is free if you merely have a solar generator, a windmill, if you built a Bedini-Bearden free-energy generator, or if you have other sorts of equipment. How about a car that runs on rain water?[374] They have been invented, and have been around for years, but since Americans are not told about them in their mass media or education system, they don't know about them, and thus believe that crude-oil-based fuel is their only option for their vehicles.

The issues just discussed reveal a key issue of the corporatist secret government: profit is made off of destruction (in this case just mentioned, batteries, gasoline, and power-grid energy are destroyed [transformed] in their usage). In business schools, this is called *planned obsolescence*. Few people understand how far-reaching the economics of destruction is. It not only dominates the lives of ordinary Americans in their ordinary way of life, as just explained, but the entire structure of the world—from wars to ecological diseasters to economic hardships—all are based on this philosophy that in order to have profit (by the corporatists) there must be destruction: order out of chaos.

It does not have to be this way, and the corporatists could profit off of people by making them healthy and happy, but this is not in the interest of the occultic corporatists, and they are happy with the lesser profit of having things destroyed (including and especially people and the consciousness of people) so that the citizenry has to keep repurchasing things over and over, and so that the corporatists can revel in the destruction they create.

---

[373] See Bearden and Bedini 2006 for more information on the Bedini-Bearden free-energy generator.

[374] According to Wave-3 News (NBC affiliate) out of Louisville, in an article titled "Car Powered by Water a Reality," by Eric Flack (published Sept. 6, 2009),

> Along Florida's Gulf Coast, water is everywhere. From the bay to the beach to the town of Clearwater, that is where we found Denny Klein. A man driven by water, literally. Klein has invented the world's first water powered car. It runs on what he calls "Aquygen." Aquygen is water or H_2O, broken down and turned into HHO gas, something scientists once thought impossible. "Any PhD or library, they say you can't mix hydrogen and oxygen. And still to this day we get a lot of people who don't believe us because that's what they were taught," Klein said. But people are quickly learning Klein and his car are for real. Klein says his design will retrofit any piston engine. An economic development team from the county and local government TV got a demonstration while we were there. Klein says he initially developed Aquygen to create a safer, less polluting blowtorch. Klein realized Aquygen would clean up car emissions as well. The only thing that would come out of the tailpipe was water. Soon, his vision became a reality.

It is by design that Americans endlessly drain their bank accounts for energy and fuel. The free sources of energy are deliberately kept hidden. Why haven't Americans all heard of, and why don't more of them own, an electric vehicle (the so-called "EV")? (Some readers may believe I am talking about the "fuel cell vehicle," but that is different from the EV.) The technology for electric cars not only exists, but it has been around since *before* the gasoline powered car, and most of the early cars on the street in the very early 1900s were electric vehicles![375] They were removed from commercial sales shortly after the gasoline car was invented, but the EV was starting to explode back onto the consumer market in the early 2000s. But laws were created that forbid their sale, and they were literally forcibly removed from people who had bought them.[376]

Why is this technology, which is obviously far better for Americans, kept out of commercial availability, and even kept somewhat secret? I have met very few people that have heard of the EV—even many who are rather well-read. If one talks about the EV, or if one builds a windmill or a free-energy generator, and tells their neighbor about the EV, the windmill, and the free-energy generator, and if one tells their neighbor: "I don't have to pay for energy, and the fact that you do is because of a covert plan to drain everyone's bank account," the neighbor will most likely reply, *"conspiracy theorist!"*, rather than seeking out the evidence for such claims on their own. But what could be more simple and logical than the idea that corporations are taking covert measures to make greater profits, which is really all this claim to the neighbor involves?

If civilization has such "free energy" technologies as those just listed at their disposal, the citizens of civilization would not have to continue to spend much of their monetary wealth on acquiring energy to finance their daily lives. They would not have to pay monthly energy and heat bills, and so on. In the interview with Bedini mentioned above, Jeff Rense lucidly commented that "we're up against probably the most vicious monolith on the planet, and that is the slave-masters who all want us to keep paying to enjoy our birthright, which is life, liberty, comfort and the pursuit of happiness." This has to do with what I call, "the economics of destruction," and it involves a situation where citizens are forced to buy things that merely get destroyed (gasoline, heating oil, electricity, batteries, etc.) if they are to merely live.

---

[375] See Paine 2006. Also see the BookTV presentation by Edwin Black, author of *Internal Combustion*, about his book that was aired on BookTV on December 16, 2006 (this lecture can be obtained from BookTV.org), and which was of a presentation recorded on October 19, 2006 about the book *Internal Combustion*. Black, who is a top-notch historian, and author of *IBM and the Holocaust* and *Banking on Baghdad*, discusses this history of the electric cars in this lecture. Also see Black's book *Internal Combustion* (2006) for more discussion.

[376] See Paine 2006.

In corporatist America, to live is to pay, and to be forced to pay regularly, lest one starve, grow cold, and die. Life in corporatist America is about not being able to live for free; to be alive means you are forced to come up with payments to do that living, and thus one must have a job, *at a corporation*.

If one gets smart and develops a farm on their land, powers their home via a windmill, and digs a well for water, one still will be forced to pay hefty land taxes to the various governments. In order to live on soil in America, *one must pay*, and to pay, one must go and serve at the corporation in order to get a paycheck that enables you to pay. In America, the only way of life is one where the days and energy of life must be spent acquiring a pittance at the corporation, while others (teachers, daycare "providers," etc.) raise the children of the nation, rather than the parents raising the children of the nation. If one looks closely at this scenario, it is very much like the story described in Orwell's *1984*, which involved a land of forced labor, no families, no love or passion, and fascism everywhere.

Profit off of Destruction

Examples of the economics of destruction go much further than merely energy and fuel. The corporatist government coaxes the citizens to endlessly spend their pittances on things that they do not need, and if the citizens can be coaxed into buying the same things over and over then the corporatists find themselves with greater and greater profits. For example, if you have a car, it will only adequately last for a few years, rather than for decades. If it did last for decades, that would decimate the sales of the corporatist automakers. Instead, the auto must be made to last a very short time—such as about the time it takes to pay-off the five-year loan one typically has to take out in order to acquire the car. At the five year point, the car is made to be far less desirable, since it will likely be in need of expensive repairs (tires, tune-up, wheel job, and various other likely and costly repairs), and not in good condition in other ways (it may have 100,000 miles, and thus be susceptible to expensive repairs), so that the citizen must buy an entirely new car.

In other words, what was initially purchased (the car) is, in essence, *destroyed* (not in or resembling its original or wholly usable state), so that consumer must purchase another one: *she must purchase what she already owns*. This is what I call "the economics of destruction," and in general, it involves the following idea:

> **The Economics of Destruction**: after consumers purchase products, the products must gradually or quickly be destroyed so that consumers must re-purchase them (and this occurs over-and-over). For products that do not get destroyed quickly enough, consumers must be tricked into purchasing/consuming products when the consumer already owns them.

Gulf War syndrome

Part of the difficulty the Defense Department has had in determining any causes of so-called Gulf war illnesses is the wide range of symptoms reported by U.S. troops and the fact no single factor can account for their ailments. Here's a list of the most commonly reported symptoms and some possible causes being investigated.

Symptoms
Fatigue
Joint pain
Headaches
Rashes/skin problems
Memory loss
Insomnia

Possible causes
Physical/psychological stress
Low-level exposure to nerve gas
Low-level exposure to biological weapons
Vaccines given to soldiers
Toxic fumes from burning oil wells
Depleted uranium from munitions
Pesticides

Veterans who served in the Persian Gulf can call toll-free an information helpline at 1-800-749-8387

NBC News / MSNBC

The **economics of destruction** is about destroying things for corporatist profit. One of the principal entities in corporatist culture that is destroyed is a *military soldier*: a war is fabricated by corporatists, through mass media soldiers are tricked into becoming mercenary soldiers for the war, they are destroyed, the culture largely forgets them, and then years later the cycle repeats, wherein new soldiers are purchased and then destroyed. In more recent times, the US government informed the public only about the tiniest fraction of soldiers that are killed by war, and they do not include, for example, casualties of war that occur in hospital beds in the evening after the day's combat activities are finished, or victims that die later in the VA, for example. I document these issues elsewhere in this book.

Babylon

As has been mentioned and discussed at many different places in this book, the same groups of corporatists have controlled the world's resources and citizens as long as human history has been recorded.[377] And throughout that time, they have used the same economical methods, one of which is: *profit via destruction*. A very early example of this is found in one of the earliest known freemasonic events: the fall of the tower of Babylon. Howard lucidly discusses this early secret government false flag event:

> In the Masonic tradition it is said that masons were first organized into a corporate body during the building of the Tower of Babel. The concept of this tower was to reach up to heaven and contact God according to Genesis 11:4-6. The fall of the Tower of Babel destroyed the common language spoken by humanity and ended the second Gold Age which followed the Flood. The architect of the tower was King Nimrod of Babylon who was a mason. He provided his cousin, the king of Nineveh, with sixty masons to assist in the construction of his cities.

---

[377] There are many excellent accounts of this history. One of my favorites is Black 2006. Other excellent accounts are Maxwell 2000; Fomenko 2003; Howard 1989.

The masons were told on their departure to remain steadfastly true to each other, avoid dissensions at any cost, live in harmony and serve their lord as their master on Earth. According to popular belief the Hebrews received their knowledge of masonry from the Babylonians and introduced it to Egypt when they were taken into slavery. In Egypt this knowledge was influenced by the Mysteries and the occult traditions of the pyramid builders who were versed in the techniques of sacred geometry.[378]

It would seem that this is an earlier controlled demolition—an earlier false flag event than WTC1, WTC2, and WTC7 on 9/11. The secret government has a tradition of crumbling impressive structures when it initiates new plans in its movement toward the full implementation of the New World Order.

This passage from Howard illustrates the economics of destruction, the principal feature of corporatist economics: economy must "grow," and it grows by constructing things, destroying them shortly after, and then building up the original thing again, and destroying it again, rebuilding, ad infinitum. The Babel story features that destruction of a tower or city, and this initiates a second expansion: out of destruction and chaos comes construction and increased profit for the corporatists. Destroy and build up, over and over. This is like building a World Trade Center Complex in Manhattan, destroying it, and then building the so-called Freedom Tower that is being constructed at the time this book went to press. The economics of destruction is best illustrated by the military-industrial complex: build things (bombs, etc.) that are used *only* to be destroyed (and to destroy other things), and make incredible profits via warfare in the process, since the more military destruction (the more war) that occurs, the more profit will be gained, due to the fact that the more bombs that ignite means more must be built to replace them.

Clothes, food, cars, electronics, vacations, terminator seeds, electricity, batteries, software, and almost everything humans use in corporatist culture is destroyed and repurchased by consumers. Of course, corporatists don't use the words "destroy" and "repurchase," but use softer, more "friendly" language—for example, "software *upgrade*," in the case of software that needs to be "replaced" (i.e., destroyed, such as when you eliminated the old software from your computer). Even entire cities can be destroyed and rebuilt, for profit, as Chicago was (by fire), New Orleans was (by hurricane, and most likely a HAARP hurricane[379]), Baghdad was (by DU-weaponry), Tokyo was (by nuclear bombs), Babylon was perhaps some sort of planned collapse or demolition, and so on.

---

[378] Howard 1989, 4-5.

[379] See the Chemtrails section of chapter 5 below, where I discuss weather control and legislation S517.

"Economic Growth"

The American economy "grows" when Americans buy items they do not need, and when they buy the same item over and over. This is best done by destroying what consumers already own and repurchasing the very same thing again. But it is interesting to note that "economic growth" is really only growth for the corporatists. During times of what is called "economic growth," does the 7-11 worker or the UPS manager see more money? The UPS worker is salaried, so she/he will not. The 7-11 worker may get a few overtime hours, but her/his pay is so low that the increase in income is so little that it can nearly be disregarded, and all that results for the 7-11 worker is that she/he spends more time at the corporation, rather than at home or elsewhere. So, the question is, Who profits during times of so-called "economic growth?" The answer is of course, only the monopolistic corporatists.

"Economic growth" refers to increased profits due to increased sales, which results in increased accumulation of capital. But as outlined in chapter 3, the only real and genuine capitalists in America are the monopolistic corporatist (and those that are directly aligned with them and those working closely with them), and thus a period of "economic growth" is irrelevant to most of the RP. Times of "economic growth" are greeted with great fanfare in the mass media, and I often see members of the RP expressing happiness over these peaks in the fabricated business cycle. But if those members of the RP merely analyzed their predicament, they would see that little has changed for them in the time of "economic growth," expect perhaps that she/he has to labor more hours at the corporation (which for salaried workers involves no pay increase for the increased hours) in order to keep up with the production and increased profit that goes into the pockets of the corporatists (who likely do not have to work more hours during peaks in the fabricated business cycle).

For these reasons, the concept of "economic growth" appears to be another example of the RP taking in, celebrating, rallying around, and fighting/slaving for, ideas that are harmful to them (harmful due to the aforementioned increase of labor-time they must sacrifice, for example) but which are good for the corporatists. This is similar to the way we saw in previous chapters that corporatists trick the RP into fighting for ideas and lifestyles that are good for the corporatists but which are bad for the RP. For example, the RP will be tricked into giving up knowledge of farming and self-sufficiency in order to acquire all their goods at Wal-Mart, for example. The RP will be tricked into believing that oil prices are cheap (chapter 3), or that private ownership exists in America, or that capitalism exists and is good for America, and so on.

Global Poverty and Slavery:
Free Trade and the New World Order

So far I have discussed wealth, think tanks and New World Order organizations, and the economics of destruction as being principal tools and tactics used by the corporatist secret government to control, engineer, and enslave the world citizens and to generate wealth for themselves. In the next two subsections, I will discuss tw**o** critical tools and tactics used by the secret corporatist government which each fit closely with one another: poverty and ignorance. First I will discuss poverty in this section.

"Free Trade"

Very few people know that there is a plan being carried out to create world government and to bring the entire population of the world into mass poverty and slavery (many anti-globalist activists call this the *global plantation*), so that all wealth, resources, and land can be fully usurped by the corporatists (and by the agencies that serve the corporatists) in a new global feudalism.[380] Although many citizens of the world do not know it, this is, ultimately, what so-called "free trade" is all about, and it is what is secretly behind the mass media fanfare over "free trade." So-called "free trade" is merely a way to let monopolizing corporations move people and resources as they wish to, without rules or regulations, and in a way that maximizes profit at any cost. As Alex Jones, the famous Internet radio scholar, has put it: "free trade is global corporations becoming [y]our government"[381]—and of course, this is *corporatism*.

For these reasons, "free trade" is a rather Orwellian label, since "free trade" sounds like a good thing, but in reality, it is merely a way to eliminate the rules and restrictions for how corporations can more fully monopolize resources, labor, and wealth more than they already do. "Free" = "unregulated." The *freedom* in free trade is really only freedom for corporatists, whereas it is ultimately some degree of slavery for everyone else. This elimination of the rules and regulations for the corporatists in fact creates one *new* rule: the corporatists can do whatever they want, no matter who suffers—even if mass death results (which is very often considered profitable to the corporatists, as will be shown below).

---

[380] For a detailed account of this plan and the process of implementing it, see Brzezinski 1998, McInerney and Vallely 2004, PNAC 2000, Thorn 2003, Chossudovsky 2003, among others. One can also read *Brave New World* by Huxley, or *1984* by Orwell to get ideas on how this corporatistic New World Order is being set up.

[381] Alex Jones Radio Show, www.infowars.com, December 20, 2006.

The New World Order:
Present-Day World Government

The organizations that create personnel and policy for the corporatists, and directly manage the new global free trade networks and rules for the corporatists, are what is often referred to as the corporatistic New World Order. This New World Order consists of the corporatists, and their organizations, such as the World Bank, the CFR, the WTO, the IMF, the WHO, the FDA, the EPA, the CDC, the Rockefeller groups, the UN, the intelligence agencies around the world, the Club of Rome, Bilderberg, administration at various big American Universities, NATO, the Trilateral Commission, various think tanks (such as PNAC and AEI), various secret societies (such as Yale's Skull and Bones), the Red Cross, NASA, and there are others.[382] These are some of the organizations that the corporatists use to set-up and run their world government (New World Order). The world is shaped according to the wishes of the corporatists who work through these organizations. As mentioned in chapter 1, it is standard that corporatists will be members of several different New World Order organizations, but will also be corporatists. For example, R. James Woolsey was the head of the CIA during the first Clinton Administration, he is a principal member of PNAC, he is a regular on CNN and FOX News, he was Chairman of the Executive Committee of the Board of Regents at Stanford University, Vice Chairman of the Advisory Board of Global Options LLC, and he has served in the past as a member of the Boards of Directors of BC International Corporation, Sun HealthCare Group, Inc., USF&G, Yurie Systems, Inc., Martin Marietta; British Aerospace, Inc., Fairchild Industries, Titan Corporation, and DynCorp, and he was a member of the Board of Governors of the Philadelphia Stock Exchange.

The New World Order organizations mentioned in the previous paragraph literally function to not just eliminate rules for corporations, but also to create environments good for labor and work conditions for world citizens to be as slave-like as possible, in order to keep as much wealth as possible out of the workers' hands (and in the corporatists' hands). Wealth is increasing worldwide, but only for the corporatists. This is a globalization of poverty, and it is spreading throughout the world, into Europe and amid the classes of America. In a very powerful passage, Professor Chossudovsky writes:

> G7 governments and global institutions, including the IMF, the World Bank, and the World Trade Organization[383] casually deny the increasing levels of global poverty; social realities are concealed, official statistics

---

[382] There are quite a few others. For example, I did not list many of the overseas organizations that pose as intelligence or regulating agencies for other nations.

[383] These are specifically New World Order institutions that are working to set up the global corporatism, and shaping the world in such a way that corporatists can succeed in setting up the global corporatist labor camp.

are manipulated, and economic concepts are turned upside down. In turn, public opinion is bombarded in the media with glowing images of global growth and prosperity. The world economy is said to be booming under the impetus of "free market" reforms... Without debate or discussion, so-called "sound macro-economic policies" (meaning the gamut of austerity measures, deregulation, downsizing and privatization) are heralded as the key to economic success.[384]

There is a trend currently observable throughout the world: the standard of living for people is lowering and their incomes are remaining the same or decreasing. The trend is also such that more and more people are becoming impoverished, as seen in, for example, America, where "minimum wage" (which is below the poverty line) has remained largely unchanged for over a decade, and before that, the increases were insignificant. (But currently, many of the impoverished in America tend to live lavishly compared to the impoverished worldwide, due to the flux of cheap slave-created goods that flow into the United States.[385])

Americans are directly subjected and victimized by the increasing level of poverty, but they are largely completely oblivious to this phenomenon, and their mass media fools them into believing that there is no such phenomenon as mass poverty that is an existing problem in the United States, and that is currently further creeping in and expanding. Even though poverty can be seen everywhere (such as when one sees many homeless people wandering around in America [but there are so many that it seems that many Americans are used to it, and hardly notice it much these days]) Americans will likely believe the reality presented to them in an episode of *Friends*, or some other show, is real (and they will mimic the behaviors, lifestyles, dress, interests, and attitudes of the people in those shows), rather than the reality they see all around them (which includes the aforementioned homeless people).

The onset of mass poverty is setting in all around Americans, but they do not see it: it is like water to the fish, *invisible*, even though it largely constitutes the environment and make-up of the fish. The salaries of Americans are rising poorly or remaining the same, and many Americans are quickly falling into the poverty category (this actually means wages are *falling*, however, since if wages increase slower than inflation, that amounts to wages *decreasing*, since the money that Americans have will have less and less power: it will be able to purchase fewer and fewer goods). But Americans may be fooled into believing that they are wealthier because they can buy more DVDs at Wal-Mart and because their closets are full of cheap clothing made by slave-labor in Asia or other places other than the United States. But Americans often seem to fail to notice that they cannot afford health care, they can't get out of debt, they can't

---

[384] Chossudovsky 2003, 26.
[385] See Chossudovsky 2003 for more information.

afford (or they struggle to afford) college, they have little or no retirement savings set aside, they often can't get a mortgage, they can't pay off their existing mortgage (if they have one) or loans, and they do not own any capital and wealth-creating items. The standards of living are sharply decreasing for Americans, but rather than understanding what is going on, they appear to prefer to, for example, watch television—which, we will see, is no coincidence.

Education of Ignorance

"The aim of totalitarian education has never been to instill convictions, but to destroy the capacity to form any."
—Hannah Arendt[386]

In a corporatist nation, the primary things that are attacked, captured, enslaved, and ultimately destroyed are *freedom and consciousness*. A human becomes a subhuman, and the spontaneity of the inherently poetical human consciousness is transformed into "television consciousness." There is no place that this is better illustrated than in the hijacking of the education system in America by the corporatists.

What was, at times, the most alive and spirited, energetic and passionate domain of human activity, with American heroes like Emerson, Thoreau, Einstein,[387] Howard Zinn, Helen Keller, and others, who energized and sparked the education system with their minds and writings into being a positive place of transformation and rebirth for students, now is little more than a massive, nationwide "tech school" that is used to brainwash students with an education of non-facts, and which is used to merely train workers for a life of drudgery and obedience in Orwellian corporate America.

In this subsection I will briefly discuss the nature of corporatist controlled education. Education in the United States is largely government-controlled, funded through government use of tax-dollars, where education administrators must serve the interests of their superiors (who are government officials) rather than the interests and needs of the students. As Nathan Tabor carefully outlines in the first chapter of his recent book,[388] the American education is being used to deliberately dumb-down students, rather than to uplift them and give them genuine intellectualism. Government-controlled education has been taken over by the UN[389] and the corporatists in order to become corporatist-controlled education, since it is slavery and obedience, rather than intelligence and skepticism, that needs to permeate education in order to help corporatists create a non-questioning, obedient work-force. Education in America then must be

---

[386] Quoted in Thorn 2003, page 103.

[387] Einstein was not born in America, but worked in Princeton throughout much of his career.

[388] Tabor 2006.

[389] Tabor 2006, chapter 1.

aimed at *harming*, rather than helping, the consciousness of American children and students.

Medicated Nation: All Behavior is "Mental Illness," where the Person is Blamed, Rather than the Corporatized Culture

America is fast becoming a nation where it is believed that the mind of a child does not work right unless it is helped by the billion-dollar-per-year drugs sold by Big Pharma. As Dr. Byron Richards puts it:

> Our children are rapidly being taught that their minds cannot work properly without medication. Under the most feeble disease diagnosis imaginable, known as attention deficit hyperactivity disorder (ADHD),[390] it is now commonly assumed that the brains of millions of American children have a neurological disorder that requires medication. This new disease is based on the subjective observation that a child has difficulty concentrating or starting on a task. If in someone's opinion this results in impairment in academic function, a child is labeled with ADHD, a condition requiring medical treatment.[391]

It is odd that the thousands of doctors and researchers, in addition to the *millions* of parents who stand behind ADD and ADHD for use among the nation's children don't ask themselves a few simple questions:

> Why did American children *not* need medication for ADD and ADHD in the 1950s? Why weren't there any cases of ADD and ADHD at that time; or, if one does believe that there were, how come American children were far more successful in school then as compared to now? At that time, America had the #1 education system in the world (now it is third from the last), so how did children and students change so much and so fast in just 50 years? Is it possible that the changes have had something to do with culture (bad food, bad teachers, too much TV and videogames, fluoridated water, absent and over-worked and distracted parents, neurotoxic vaccines, the style of education from now as compared to the 1950s, and so on), rather than with the brain-structure of the nation's children? Is it possible that culture is the cause of the so-called ADD and ADHD "diseases" and the nation's children are really innocent victims of culture?

Similar sorts of questions could be asked about depression, so-called manic-depressive disorders, obesity, any of the other learning disabilities, and so on.

America is a land where it is believed that if something goes wrong—if one experiences sadness, hardship, or even things like stomach cramps—one needs

---

[390] Many researchers assert that ADHD and ADD actually *do not have a diagnosis*, since the one given is so feeble that it is meaningless and nonsensical.
[391] Richards, 2006, 21.

to get an expensive drug to help correct their "imbalances," "deficiencies," and "problems" to do with *their mind*. If a young student, for example, finds himself or herself restless, having trouble sitting still in a desk for hours and hours each day, the student's restlessness might oddly be considered a *disorder*, and it will not be considered that it is not normal for a young child to sit in a seat listening to boring "information" for hours each day. Genuine childhood education is about getting your hands in dirt and playing with worms; it is about building things, drawing, interacting with friends, talking about nature, learning about letters by drawing and talking about them, and so forth. How can we expect a child to do anything but express irritability when this is taken, and when children are forced to sit in stillness and silence for hours? American government-mandated education for contemporary children is a form of imprisonment, according to what I have just written, and it is a way of stealing consciousness in order to replace it with slave/corporatist mentality.

Similarly, if a worker in the corporatist system becomes depressed because she/he despises her long hours at a job she/he does not like at a corporation that is lifeless, if she or he consults a psychiatrist for help in dealing with this sadness, the doctor will most likely never question the corporation, or American corporatist/Orwellian culture. Rather, the doctor will question the patient, and instead of finding a problem with the culture, she or he will find a problem with the mind of the patient, and the patient will be told that she or he has a "mental imbalance." If you feel sad because you are away from your children all day, working at a job you do not like, you will be described as having a mental problem that must be "fixed" with expensive medications, and you will likely *not* be told that you live in a diseased culture that needs to be fixed.

The mass mis-medicating, with Prozac, Ritalin, and so on, can be summed up and understood with one simple concept:

> Mental illnesses and diseases (depression, learning disabilities, etc.) have one cause: corporatist culture, but corporatism is never cited by doctors as being the cause of mental illness, and instead "brain imbalance" or "chemical imbalances in the brain" are always blamed, and thus, doctors always and only miss the mark in understanding mental illnesses and diseases.

Of course, this is most likely a deliberate "error" on the part of the Big Pharma researchers, since a medicated nation has been the plan all along, as Huxley's Brave New World (which he wrote because he had access to government documents about plans for the future) heralded.

America is now a nation where it seems almost everyone has a counselor or psychiatrist that they visit for "help," and where nearly every other person one meets is on some sort of mind-drug (Ritalin, Prozac, etc.). Culture (corporatist culture) is almost never blamed for the problems people have in America.

Rather, *the individual person is blamed*: it is claimed that the individual person needs to fix mental imbalances, gain more confidence, be more assertive, overcome fears—or in some way or another, people are expected to not let themselves just be who/what they are, everyone is expected to be "fixed," changed, and improved in some way. For example, rather than discussing how aspartame and MSG (which are in most grocery store food) increase appetite,[392] obesity will be blamed on the person's genetics,[393] so it is the individual's fault, and they need expensive medication to "fix" their problem.

Approved behavior and thought are now the primary aspects of the American education system: people are taught to think the right thoughts, say the right things, and believe the right beliefs, and dissent from the accepted thoughts, speech, and beliefs, will be met with serious ridicule, if not rejection. Ridicule and rejection will, nowadays, almost always be met with a non-scientific label: "mentally unstable," "mentally imbalanced," "learning disabled," "manic-depressive," "dysfunctional," and so on. This behavior and labeling is taught through the television shows, in schools, and at the doctors' offices.

Pervasive "medicating" is the heart of the corporatist education system: It makes massive profits off of medicating which (1) robs the person of their passions and their abilities to function, and (2) gets the person in a mode where they will be docile, obedient, and thoughtless, rather than creative, intelligent, and autonomous. The American education system, which is aligned with Big Pharma, is about crushing the minds and spirits of children.

Corporatist Education: "No Child Left Behind"

The Bush family operates a company called Ignite!, Inc. Here is the description of Ignite from the Hoovers.com website, as of February 2007:

> Ignite! creates online, multimedia educational products for middle school students. The company offers courseware for early American history, world cultures and geography, world history, Texas history, and science. The company's Reality, Inc. series of science software programs includes titles for topics such as ecosystems and food webs, Newton's laws of motion and gravity, simple machines, genetics, and tectonic plates. Ignite! was founded by Neil Bush, brother of President George W. Bush.

The curiously named Ignite!, Inc. has become a principal supplier of "education materials" to the American education system (K-12), which has been taken over by the so-called "No Child Left Behind" program—which, in

---

[392] See Blaylock 1997.

[393] This idea of the genetically caused obese person seems to be fueled by the mass media. For example, see, "New Fat Gene Blamed fro Weight Gain," Associated Press, April 13, 2007.

corporatist fashion, has an Orwellian name, since virtually all children are left behind by the UN-based[394] program. This is because "No Child Left Behind," as just mentioned, is actually not firstly a Bush family program, but rather a UN program that has merely been implemented by the Bush Administration, where the UN is *deliberately* destroying American education,[395] in order that corporatists can profit. Ignite, Inc. has transformed (destroyed) the education system in the ways described in the last subsection, and it has given the Bush family tremendous earnings. Ignite! is backed by all sorts of seedy corporatists, it is filled with largely worthless "information" (as most education in America nowadays does), and it literally reduces education to watching television, as the following Business Week article describes:

> Across the country, some teachers complain that President George W. Bush's makeover of public education promotes "teaching to the test." The President's younger brother Neil takes a different tack: He's selling to the test. The No Child Left Behind Act compels schools to prove students' mastery of certain facts by means of standardized exams. Pressure to perform has energized the $1.9 billion-a-year instructional software industry. Now, after five years of development and backing by investors like Saudi Prince Alwaleed Bin Talal and onetime junk-bond king Michael R. Milken, Neil Bush aims to roll his high-tech teacher's helpers into classrooms nationwide. He calls them "curriculum on wheels," or COWs. The $3,800 purple plug-and-play computer/projectors display lively videos and cartoons: the XYZ Affair of the late 1790s as operetta, the 1828 Tariff of Abominations as horror flick. The device plays songs that are supposed to aid the memorization of the 22 rivers of Texas or other facts that might crop up in state tests of "essential knowledge." Bush's Ignite! Inc. has sold 1,700 COWs since 2005, mainly in Texas, where Bush lives and his brother was once governor. In August, Houston's school board authorized expenditures of up to $200,000 for COWs. The company expects 2006 revenue of $5 million. Says Bush about the impact of his name: "I'm not saying it hasn't opened any doors. It may have helped with some sales." ... The stars haven't always aligned for Bush, but at times financial support has. A foundation linked to the controversial Reverend Sun Myung Moon has donated $1 million for a COWs research project in Washington (D.C.)-area schools. In 2004 a Shanghai chip company agreed to give Bush stock then valued at $2 million for showing up at board meetings. (Bush says he received one-fifth of the shares.) In 1988 a Colorado savings and loan failed while he served on its board, making him a prominent symbol of the S&L scandal. Neil calls himself "the most politically damaged of the [Bush] brothers." While hardly the first

---

[394] Tabor 2006.
[395] See Tabor 2006.

brother to embarrass a President—remember Billy Carter's Billy Beer or Roger Clinton's cocaine?—Neil could be the first to seek profit from a hallmark Presidential crusade. And also that of a governor: Jeb makes school standards a centerpiece in Florida, too. Neil says he never talks shop with his brothers. He attributes his interest in education to his struggles with dyslexia. His son, Pierce, also had difficulties in school, he says. "Not one of our investors has ever asked for any kind of special access—a visa, a trip to the Lincoln Bedroom, an autographed picture, or anything."[396]

The next passage shows how the corporatists specifically tailor education to be a form of the aforementioned behavior modification, where that modification is found by ingesting large quantities of pharmaceutical drugs (that give pharmaceutical companies tens of billions in profit each year). This is what is at the heart of the so-called "individualized learning" that is often praised by politicians and media personalities. Consider this passage from an Austin journal about Ignite!, when it was in its early days:

George W. Bush may have left Austin amid much fanfare, but the president's younger brother quietly is heading a local startup that's raising at least $10 million in second-round funding. Neil Bush's Ignite! Inc., which develops educational software, is hoping to raise a second round in the near future, says Pamela Richardson, chief operating and strategic officer for Ignite! The company raised more than $5 million in first-round funding last year, she says. … "We have alternative paths for learning that material -- by exploring music interactively, for example," Richardson says. "Or I may want to read or go through mathematical logical exercises. This is a browser-based hosted application that is high bandwidth-delivered for K-12 schools." Compared with most educational software firms, Ignite! is solely Web-based and tracks individualized learning styles more effectively, says Melinda George, director of the education division of the Software and Information Industry Association in Washington, D.C. Ignite! is a member of the association. Ignite! also targets kids with learning disabilities, ranging from dyslexia to being unable to learn by taking notes, George says. "They really are doing something that's different," George says of Ignite! "They're using the Web and pushing individualized learning. Their individualized learning identifies the learning style of the student. What comes up on my screen will be different from what comes up on another student's screen." [397]

---

[396] From "No Bush Left Behind," BusinessWeek, October 16, 2006, Keith Epstein.
[397] "Neil Bush Ignites Education Software Firm," Austin Business Journal, February 16, 2001, Amanda Bronstad.

The point of education now is to not educate, but to teach behavior—education is social engineering and behavior modification. This is partly verified by the fact that America has a failing education system. Students are not challenged, and teachers are in survival mode, rather than inspiration mode. In college, professors are often scared of students, since often just one complaint by a student—such as a student that merely did not do well on a test—can give the professor a trip in to the Dean's office for questioning. The subjects and books used in the government-mandated education system are not interesting or relevant. Like Alex Jones said on his radio show February 16, 2007: teachers will teach on all sorts of details on the civil war for months, but never will have their students read the US Constitution. American education does not give an accurate picture of reality in any way, and thus contributes to mass brainwashing: American education tricks students into believing in a reality that does not exist. Consequently, the citizenry believes that non-reality is reality, and they often become violently angry when a realist comes along and challenges the dream-state they are caught in by merely pointing them in the direction of reality.

If one watches the interesting films, *The Island*,[398] *1984*,[399] or *Brave New World*,[400] each of these films has brief portrayals of classrooms for the citizens (including adults) of these worlds, and each classroom involves absolutely ignorant and brainwashed students. Also, in the films, the classrooms are merely an extension of, and a reinforcement of, what the citizens are constantly learning outside the classroom, and through the pervasive and constantly-present mass media of each of these worlds. In other words, the citizens of these worlds are subjected to a lifetime of constant televisual stimulation that propagandizes and corporatizes them. Education in these worlds is not a powerful or stimulating part of the lives of the citizens in these worlds, and when a school learning environment is shown in these films, it involves students manually carrying out tasks in an "auto-pilot" mode, and the tasks are far *below* their level.

For example, in *The Island*, the world only consists of adults, and their classrooms consist of adult students reading children's books, such as Dick and Jane books. This is roughly what is found in the United States. For example, if one watches Al Gore's non-scientific, popular film, *An Inconvenient Truth*, that is about the belief in human-caused global warming, and which is supposed to be an educational film, early in the film there is a childish and silly cartoon that, in my opinion, seems completely out of place. (Interestingly, the cartoon contains several classic educational issues, such as a dopey unintelligent child

---

[398] Bay, Michael (director), 2005, *The Island*. Studio: Dreamworks Video. ASIN: B000BO0LH2.

[399] Radford, Michael (director), 1984, *1984*. Studio: Polygram. ASIN: 6304362498.

[400] 1988. Studio: Universal Pictures. ASIN: B00004S32U. This is a "made for TV" film.

being yelled at by an oppressive teacher-like figure, as if this cartoon is trying to show us what we should believe "normal" behavior looks like.) This is supposed to be a film about science, but there is no science in the film,[401] and adult viewers of the film are taught about how global warming supposedly works with a cartoon. In the last section, we saw that the Bush family's "No Child Left Behind" educational "tools" also teach by cartoons. And if one looks at the mass media (television shows, sitcoms, magazines, etc.), one will continually see adults being presented with child-like informational material, and adults in the mass media will be presented as acting like unintelligent buffoons (e.g., you can see this in any episode of *Friends* or *The Brady Bunch*).

In the classic film, Fight Club, directed by David Fincher, we find two anti-heroes who are waking up to the reality of the corporatist culture they live within. Consequently, they each fully drop out of the culture (i.e., they almost fully cease to use money, they turn their backs on the education system, they begin to use the tactics corporations have used on them back on the corporations, and so on). Much of the film was focused on the way that American culture is obsessed with so-called "mental illness," building "self-esteem," self-help groups, and so on. Rather than facts and inspiration, this "feeling good about yourself" philosophy is the backbone of American education.[402]

The Little Child vs. the Massive Corporatocracy

American education is about "the solitary student" *against and encircled* by government, with protective parents and family nowhere in sight, continually attacked and put-down for any little spontaneous gesture or wiggling around in her school desk that an educator might judge to be inappropriate, with a damaged brain from dozens of vaccines and from a lifetime of consuming

---

[401] See Box A.

[402] See Tabor 2006 for more information.

fluoridated water which both inhibit her ability to unwind from the confusion of her life, and in the evening, after a typically long long day at school and the "after-school programs," she will be bombarded with hours of television, rather than with protective companionship from parents. Tabor writes:

> The sad fact is that politically correct thinking has become an outcome valued more highly than individualism, creative independent thought, or academic achievement... [P]arents all too often are viewed as subversive influences in the UN education establishment.[403]

Children are created—via the taxpayer financed public "education" system— to be politically correct thinkers, to stand in line properly, to eat MSG lunch in the school cafeteria, to speak when spoken to, to answer questions in the way instructed to them, to accept facts given to them as ultimate fact, and to not ask too many "tough questions." Quite literally, an American student will graduate from high school and/or college with a knowledge of very little information or education in their minds, even though the majority of her/his life has been spent in the education system up to that point, but the American student will be very clear on one thing: The system is in charge.

Corporatist Education is Military Education

The universities and public schools in the United States are government institutions. When a child is in school, the child is under government control, "care," surveillance and supervision. Given

(i)   what has been written above, and
(ii) the fact that the government has illustrated that it wants to damage virtually all children physically (through vaccinations, water, food, poverty, ignorance and illiteracy, and so on), and
(iii) the fact that the government has proven that it is interested in war for profit as a primary goal of its operation,

from these points we can conclude the following:

> *Government education involves, not learning, but thought-control, where that thought-control has the principal element of teaching students how to be soldiers—soldiers for the corporation and/or for the battlefield. Government education is not about learning how the world works nor how to develop the passion and selfhood one possesses within. Government education involves learning how to forget that one has passion or self, and to learn to believe that passion is only for silly poets and failures. Government education is not about acceptance of the student, but it is about tearing the student down, in military fashion, through punishment, through the so-called "learning disabilities," "mental imbalances" and so on that make a student wrongly believe*

---

[403] Ibid., 3.

that something is wrong with him/her, and the just corporatist state is the healthy organism that one must fit into.

Corporate Terrorism:
Pollution, DU, Population Reduction, Robots, Transhumanism, and Secret Technology

"What exactly are we securing? … We are securing, essentially, ourselves… So what *exactly* are we protecting? … I don't know."

—Capt. Terence Callguire, at Alpha Company debriefing in Iraq before the Battle of Fallujah[404]

The bottom line of the balance sheet defines a business's goal, but not the sum of responsibilities of its leaders. Management should respect workers. A firm should be loyal to the community, mindful of the environment. In America, by far—by far—most businesses fulfill their responsibilities. They do not cut ethical corners, or neglect workers, or disregard community standards. A good business finds opportunities and makes the most of them. And a good business always respects the boundaries of right and wrong. In our country, the law defines many of these responsibilities, from workplace safety to environmental protection. For publicly-held corporations the law goes further, defining standards of disclosure with independent certification by auditing firms.

—President George W. Bush, March 7, 2002, from Washington D.C.

Terrorism is one of the most productive tools that corporatists use. For example, the Nazis had the success they did *only* due to their secret wartime *business partnerships* they had with IBM, Ford, Standard Oil, and other American corporations.[405] There is so much corporate terrorism, it is hard to know where to even begin a discussion on it. What I will do in this section is briefly summarize a number of ways that corporatists use terrorism to torment and deform their workers and the citizenry overall.

For example, depleted uranium (which is in US corporatist-made bombs and bullets) from the wars in Iraq since 1990 is polluting the entire world,[406] and this gas-like chemical acts like a global chemical toxin set on world citizens. More specifically, depleted uranium (DU) is a global terrorist attack against the world's citizens by corporatists. The documents by key operatives,

---

[404] Quoted in Olds and Scott, 2005.

[405] Just to give one example, see Black (2001) for an example of how the Nazi terror really only occurred due to secret business relations American corporations (IBM in the case of Black's book) had with the Nazis, where those corporations awarded top new technologies (in the case of IBM, the first computers), thus enabling them to be an invincible armada.

[406] For more information, see the radio interview with Dr. Leuren Moret, November 14, 2006, and the interview with Dr. Doug Rokke, September 28, 2006, both of which were Rense Radio Shows, www.Rense.com, and can be found at the Rense.com archives.

neoconservatives, corporatist planners, and think tanks (PNAC,[407] *The Grand Chessboard,*[408] *Endgame*[409]) that show us that the DU attack against world citizens endured worldwide since 1990 is just the beginning. DU will spread and intensify dramatically with the upcoming war in Iran, and these terrorist chemical attacks will surely dramatically reduce the population of the world (which is precisely the intention of the Masonic monopolizing corporatists), as has begun in Iraq (the Iraqi population is down 2.5 million since "Desert Storm").

DU has to do with population reduction: reducing the population of the world down to approximately 500 million. Population reduction is a project well under way, as can be witnessed with African AIDS bioweaponry, bird flu and other weaponized bioterrorist weapons, pharmaceutical drugs, the implementation of WHO-created nutricide,[410] and DU. (For verification of population reduction being a deliberate corporatist project, the reader should consult PNAC (2000, see bibliography), for example, or NSSM 200, which is a government report from the early 1970s.)

People are often confused by population reduction since the corporatists need the world citizenry to generate labor, wealth, and taxation for them, and the more people the more labor, wealth, and taxation for the corporatists. So why is there a push by the corporatists to exterminate the vast majority of humans on earth? The answer can be found in listening to what Alex Jones once said: "They [the New World Order corporatists] don't need us!" They don't because the corporatists are developing the technology to power civilization by remote control and without humans: robotic armies, robotic societies, transhumanist and cyborg elites. (This is the subject of the last chapter of this book.) As we will see in the next chapter, the secret government corporatists are also likely transforming the RP into enslaved, hive-mind Morgellonospheric nano-machines.

In the 1800s and to the turn of the century, there were amazing technological advancements by Tesla, Einstein, and Maxwell, all before there were even cars, and while horse-and-buggy were the mode of transportation. Imagine in 1897, when J.J. Thomson discovered the electron, if he rode anything to his lab where he discovered the electron, it was likely a horse and buggy. There is something strange about this picture: society was largely still in the so-called "dark age," but scientists in the labs were so highly advanced that most people in the world have no idea how complex and advanced their scientific research was. This scenario sort of reminds me of the space shuttle, where Americans are told that the shuttle is at the forefront of space technology, whereas in reality it is so

---

[407] See PNAC 2000.
[408] Brzezinski 1998.
[409] McInerney and Vallely, 2004.
[410] See Afrika 2000.

low-tech it is 1970's technology. Do we really believe that no further space exploration research has been made since the 1970s? Do we really believe that the clunky space shuttle is all that NASA could come up with since Tesla, even though they had 70 years of time to progress from the time of Tesla? Given how advanced researchers were in the 1800s, it is a good bet that the technology of the secret government is so far advanced from what most current world citizens know about, that they would probably not even recognize it as being human technology. Remember this fact when we discuss Morgellons disease in the next chapter.

Ray Kurzweil, author of *The Age of Spiritual Machines*,[411] on BookTV in a show that aired in November 2006 (but which was recorded in December 2005) discussed how we are near what he calls "the singularity," where humans become *more than human*, since, like Darth Vader, they will have the technology to gradually replace their body parts with nanobots (cell-, molecule- and atom-sized robots: robo-cells and robo-molecules) that essentially give those lucky enough to have the technology implemented into them *immortality*.[412] As Alex Jones, Jeff Rense, and others have repeatedly pointed out, the monopolistic corporatists, who want population reduction, are preserving that technology only for themselves, and the rest of the population of the world (the RP) is largely in the way, and eventually will need to be either transformed into the most pitiful of slaves, or we will be merely eliminated. (This global slavery is the subject of the last chapter of this book.) This is a likely outcome of our fate, due to the fact that depleted uranium, for example, is deliberately polluting the whole world, and those who are choosing to carry out that mass extermination of the human race are also in reach of immortality technology. Therefore, the corporatists will likely be interested in eventually exterminating all human life, as they transform themselves to robo-humans. As I have said elsewhere in this book: the ordinary American is completely unaware of the level of technology that exists in the world (and has for a long time), in the universities and among the governments across the globe. The average member of the RP does not even know that a remote control army has been developed by various government agencies around the world, even though it has been featured on the Discovery Channel's show, *Futureweapons*.

Pollution Terrorism:
The Largest Chemical Weapons Terrorist Attacks in History

As can be seen from the previous subsection on DU, transhumanism, and the global extermination of humans, if I were to carry out a thorough study of corporation terrorism here, this section would reach thousands and thousands of pages. Therefore, in discussing corporatist terrorism, I am unfortunately forced

---

[411] Viking (Penguin Putnam), 1999.
[412] See Moravec 1999 for more information on the present and future of robotics and transhumanism.

to keep things brief. For that reason, in the rest of this chapter, I will only discuss a few types of corporate terrorism: I will discuss false flag terrorism, PMFs (privatized military forces), CIA and Orwellian terrorists and "terror networks," and in this subsection I will next discuss corporate pollution, which is a form of chemical terrorist attack.

It is nearly unheard-of, these days, to see or hear the national news media cover a story about pollution, about a human death caused by pollution, and so on. In fact, I can't recall ever hearing one such story in all the research I have done for this book—listening, watching, and sensing the channels of the national media during the time that I wrote this book. Petty crime, sex scandals, pedophile Congressmen (i.e., Foley), house fires, forest fires, cruise ships sinking or undergoing food poisoning, shark bites, terrorists, cougars and mudslides in California, kidnapped college students, and all the rest of the petty issues that are put forth in the fabricated news media are ways to cover up the real news, which is about corporatist terrorism: pollution, DU, water and food poisoning, chemtrail activity, mind-control and brainwashing programs, military-industrial complex warfare, controlled "education system," the corporate prison network,[413] pharmaceutical drug poisoning and genocide (e.g., Merck's Vioxx, SSRI genocide, aspartame poisoning, the vaccine holocaust, SV40 and AIDS bioweaponry, etc.), and all the rest. It is well known that the roots of corporate terrorism go way back.

In October 2001 I read in the newspapers and saw on the national news that somebody was deliberately spreading anthrax around the country in order to kill people. This was called "a chemical terrorist attack," by the national media. Now the question is: *How is this different from corporate pollution?* The 2001 anthrax attacks meet all the same criteria as corporatist pollution: they are both deliberate lethal contaminations of people done in full knowledge of the people who are doing the contaminating.

Winslow, in discussing the work of Ralph Estes, shows us how the magnitude of the terrorism of corporate pollution is *much* vaster than the 2001 anthrax attacks, the Vietnam War's Agent Orange attacks, or the British military's smallpox attacks on American Indians hundreds of years ago,[414] or all of the chemical or bioweaponry attacks in history combined:

> Citing several studies on long-term impact of toxic chemicals in the workplace, Estes [showed] that these chemicals cause $274.7 billion dollars worth of economic damage each year and that exposure to carcinogens on the job annually kills about 150,000 Americans. This annual death toll would produce more than 1.5 million deaths in the last

---

[413] See Herival and Wright 2003.
[414] See Cole 1988, 11-12.

ten years, far more than the entire battlefield deaths suffered in every American war since 1860.[415]

Corporate terrorism, in the form of chemical terrorism/pollution, is on the scale of a nuclear holocaust. (If DU is taken into account, which Winslow does not, then corporate chemical terrorism can only be viewed as a real nuclear holocaust, equaling the death of *many* times that of a Hiroshima blast). How am I to consider the 2001 anthrax attacks or corporate pollution as any different from the Agent Orange attacks in Vietnam (Agent Orange that was made by the massive monopolist corporation, Monsanto[416])? It appears that there is no significant difference at all between these two scenarios, since each is merely a deliberate, covert chemical attack leading to the deaths of people in the full knowledge of those spreading the chemicals. Consider the comparison in the following tables, which shows the similarities between the attacks, and which reveals how corporatist attacks are covered up in the national media, but false flag terrorist attacks are not:

Anthrax Attacks	**Corporate pollution attacks**
Killed very few people	Killed (and kills) more people than all major American wars
Described by politicians as the height of evil	Considered just a problem to perhaps be corrected and/or altered (for those politicians that really do consider it a problem)
Covered exhaustingly in the news media	Nowadays virtually ignored in the news media
Described as "terrorist activity"	Described as "business"
Typically kills a person very fast	Typically kills a person over a much longer amount of time.

Agent Orange Attacks	**Corporate Pollution Attacks**
Killed many people, but was only a percentage of the 2-5 million killed in Vietnam	Killed and kills more people than all major wars (see discussion below)
Described by politicians as good, necessary, as aspect of a just war	Considered just a problem to be corrected and/or altered (for those who really do consider it a problem, that is)

---

[415] Winslow 2003, 46.
[416] Achbar and Abbot 2004.

Covered inadequately in the news media at the time of its occurrence, now virtually ignored in the media	Nowadays virtually ignored in the news media
Described as "terrorist activity"	Described as "business"
Typically kills a person somewhat slowly (for example, much slower than anthrax)	Typically kills a person over a much longer amount of time.

Corporatism involves hidden terrorism that far outweighs any horror on the planet. This comes in the form of the terrorization and destruction of the family, Orwellian on-the-job boredom and torment, the destruction of human creativity and consciousness, corporatist pollution, and so on—all of which occur in plain view, but nevertheless out of the sight of the vast majority of Americans. I have never ceased to be amazed about how little my college students in my classes know about corporatism and corporate terrorism that affect them, how badly they are fooled by corporatism, and how eager they are in their ignorance to defend corporatism at all costs. These are college students that are accruing amazing debt that they will have for life due to their college tuition, who are using their valuable college years working at miserable jobs for astonishingly low pay, and who were raised in homes where parents were absent since the parents were working at corporations rather than spending time with their children—but despite all this, they have no idea that corporatism is the reason for these and other problems to do with their lives.

Global Warming, Nature Conservationism, and Hippie Eugenics

In addition to killing citizens, pollution is a key issue used lately by corporatists to also control thought and money. Global warming—or the fabricated thesis that global warming is caused by humans—is a primary tool used in this thought control. The big nature conservation organizations (WWF, Nature Conservancy, etc.) nearly never discuss the unfathomable corporate pollution that is occurring worldwide,[417] instead, they will almost always only discuss some issue that is either intangible to the good of humanity (e.g., the "threatened" polar bear population,[418] etc.), or which is totally irrelevant or

---

[417] For example, among so many other stories, see "Fear for Health of a River: Red Flag Raised Over What Plant Dumps into Water," Delaware News Journal (www.delawareonline.com), by Jeff Montgomery, April 15, 2004.

[418] The mass media will, on the one hand, tell us that polar bear populations are threatened, and polar bears will be near extinction in 40 years (and since this is in the future, it is merely an unverified prediction, See "Polar Bear Population Seen Declining," Associated Press, by John Heilprin, Sept. 8, 2007, an article that was spotlighted in the mass media, which contains no data or evidence of any sort. But then on the other hand, the mass media will also admit the facts, which is that polar bears

unverifiable (e.g., global warming). Whenever the media and the politicians of the visible government push for something, they are surely up to something, and the skeptic must find out what. Few things are being pushed more lately than so-called "human-caused" global warming.[419]

There is a wave of pro-eco talk in the US corporatist mass media, but oddly, the US corporatists are polluting like mad. It seems there is an underlying plot going on, and that plot is the following:

Usuable land and resources give people power, thus, if controlling corporatists want to disempower the masses, they need to take control of land and resources from them.

This is a sort of "hippie genocide:" it is hip and trendy to be eco-friendly, but what it amounts to is helping the corporatists keep world citizens from flourishing and becoming wealthy via the natural elements. Massive rock concerts put all the focus on how being eco-friendly, and being scared of global warming is really cool and stylish, but the science—or lack of it—is rarely discussed. Instead, the mass media will merely tell millions of people that "the majority" of earth scientists believe that CO_2 emissions are heating up the earth, but the mass media will rarely interview more than a few of these thousands and thousands of "the majority," because there is no such majority.[420] Conservation is seemingly always used to limit human farming and resource wealth. For example, consider this critical story about how 20,000 avocado trees had to be cut down in California because they supposedly use too much water (while desalination technologies go unused):

> Before imported water irrigated North County farmlands, the desert here was anything but fertile. Instead of groves of citrus and avocado trees and other crops, rocks and scrub vegetation dominated the landscape. That desert could be returning. Faced with rising water costs and a water shortage, farmers in the breadbasket communities of Valley Center and Fallbrook are cutting back their operations—and cutting down their trees. Dead citrus trees and the white-painted stumps of avocado trees—avocados are one of the county's biggest cash crops—can be found in groves throughout Valley Center, Fallbrook, and other agricultural centers of North County. "I think eventually there'll be no agriculture in Southern California," said Bob Polito, a Valley Center grower with Polito

---

have had their numbers increase five-fold in the past few decades! See "Polar Bears Caught in Heated Eco-debate," USA Today, by Oren Dorell, March 11, 2008, http://www.usatoday.com/weather/climate/globalwarming/2008-03-09-polar-bears_N.htm, which states that, "Polar bears have increased from a population of 5,000 in 1972 to between 20,000 and 25,000 today."

[419] For just one example of this media blitzkrieg, see "Report Blames Global Warming on Humans: Scientists Say Hotter Temperatures to Continue," Associated Press, Seth Borenstein, February 2, 2007, and also see "Warming 'Likely' Man-Made, Unstoppable," Associated Press, Seth Borenstein, February 1, 2007

[420] See Coffman 2007.

Family Farms. "There may be little pockets here and there, using local water, but for the most part agriculture in Southern California is going to disappear." Polito said he's already removed about 1,000 citrus trees from among his roughly 6,000 citrus and avocado trees, cutting them down and turning them into mulch. Stumped avocado trees can regrow, but stumped citrus trees die. Once trees come down, they're usually not going to be replaced, said Gary Arant, general manager of the Valley Center Municipal Water District. Because agriculture is increasingly marginal in Southern California, growers aren't going to make the investment and take the time to plant and water new trees and wait for them to become productive. Citrus trees are the first to go because citrus isn't as profitable a crop as avocados, Arant said. But as water prices inexorably rise, growers say avocado trees will also come down in increasing numbers. About 10 to 15 percent of the 24,000 acres of tree crops in Valley Center have been taken out of production since 2005, Arant said... Growers say they have been able to cope with water prices until recently—in large part owing to a program that provides discounted water from the Metropolitan Water District, the water wholesaler for Southern California. In exchange for a 30 percent discount, growers agree to be first in line to get reductions of up to 30 percent or more if there's a severe enough water shortage. About 80 percent of the agricultural water in Valley Center is purchased under the program, Arant said. Last year, for the first time in the program's two-decade history, that cutback clause was invoked. So growers with thirsty trees have "stumped" some trees to keep the others in production. In Fallbrook, growers are stumping about a third of their avocado trees, said Bob Lucy, partner in the Del Rey Avocado Company Inc. Lucy said his company's growers have between 4,500 and 5,000 acres of avocado trees.[421]

The magnitude of this story simply cannot be underestimated. The US food market is very tight as it is, but this story reveals that tremendous amounts of crops are going to be removed from availability, right when a world food shortage is being orchestrated. Given the fact that desalination technology exists to make salt water fresh, and given the fact that this so obviously will exascerbate the already existent world food crisis that is emerging, it is hard not to come to the conclusion that this is a deliberate eugenics maneuver—it is eco-friendly, "hippie eugenics."

Hippie eugenics reaches its zenith with the global warming hoax—more specifically, the theses that CO_2 is harmful, that it is a significant greenhouse gas, and that human fuel usage is causing global warming. This is is a most clever way of controlling humanity, and it is all done because humans are not properly educated, and thus might believe some of the non-facts in, for example, Al Gore's recent anti-scientific global warming film.

Some readers of this book might find the assertion that Gore's film is not scientific to be confusing, since there might seem to be science in the film, such as with the scientific charts that show up in the film. Gore shows a 650,000

---

[421] "Farmers Struggle with Water Price, Cuts," North Country Times (nctimes.com), by Bradley Fikes, May 3, 2008.

year timeline of temperature and CO_2 levels, and there is, of course, a very rough correlation, as is well-known in geology. But what is important is that Gore does not show a *causal link* between the global warming he is predicting and current escalating CO_2 levels. It is well-known among the scientific community that the solar system is warming, not just the earth.[422] This would indicate that the sun is heating up, in some sort of a sun cycle.[423] Now it is enormously suspicious that Gore *does not* mention this in his film. Solar system warming brings serious question to the "human caused" global warming thesis, and rather, a "solar-cycle caused" global warming suddenly becomes a better candidate. The failure of Gore to bring this critical issue up, not only makes his film non-scientific (since science is about facing the opposing data to one's theory, not ignoring it and/or replacing it with non-verifiable theory), but it also makes it appear that he is covering up this issue. It could be the case that, for example, a warmed earth merely has, for some reason, more CO_2, and there is no significant causal connection between that and the massive warming Gore is fearmongering over. Gore does not explore such issues; he merely shows a rough correlation (and not causation) between CO_2 levels and temperature over 650,000 years, and *quickly* goes on to the long lugubrious morning of the earth throughout the remainder of this film.

Gore's "data" presented also does not support the imminent massive warming for the earth that he wants us to fear. Gore shows how the earth currently has 300 PPM of CO_2, which appears to be human caused. But in the same part of Gore's film, he wants us to believe that temperature and CO_2 levels are strictly correlated. But this is a fatal error for Gore, since 300 PPM is vastly higher than any other CO_2 level for the earth that Gore's graph shows, and thus Gore's data would indicate that the earth should be *far* warmer than it is now. More simply put: *if there is correlation between temperature and CO_2 levels, since the earth now has the greatest CO_2 levels of the past 650,000 years, then it should now have the greatest temperature, but it clearly does not.* This is the fatal flaw in Gore's film: if CO_2 causes warming, then elevated CO_2 should always lead to warming. Yet the highest CO_2 Gore shows in his graph is not associated with the highest temperature, nor any unusually high temperature at all over the 650,000 years Gore shows in his charts. Gore, therefore, can only be incorrect on his global warming theories, and his quick assertion that it is "human caused." Gore does not address the *obvious* issues I am pointing out here. This is not science, since science involves addressing counterpoints and opposing data, not making a quick rough correlation and making a sure conclusion based on a correlation rather than a causal link.

---

[422] there are many stories on this critical, but covered-up issue; here's one example: "Global Warming on Pluto Puzzles Scientists," Space.com, by Robert Roy Britt, October 9, 2002, http://www.space.com/scienceastronomy/pluto_warming_021009.html

[423] I want to thank Alex Jones for alerting me to this issue.

Gore also fails to mention that the "correlations" between temperature and CO_2 over 650,000 years involved temperature, and not CO_2, *increasing first*! The atmosphere warmed hundreds or thousands of years before the CO_2 increased.[424] This has been widely discussed, such as by University of Ottawa paleontologist Ian Clark on the Alex Jones Show, March 9, 2007 (on the 9th, Jones played a clip from a British documentary featuring Clark). This is just the start of the non-science and nonsense in the Gore documentary. Gore fails to mention the fact that many scientists *disagree* with the human-caused warming thesis, and throughout his film, Gore discusses scientists as if there is a coherent mainstream of scientists that have coherent data *proving* the "human caused" theory, which there is not, as of early 2007. Again, a trademark of real science is addressing the opponents of a theory; Gore just ignores them—a key tactic of the mass media. Most interestingly, Gore never mentions the electric vehicle (EV) that I discussed in previous chapters. If Gore was sincere, and really wanted an answer to the "human caused" global warming, he'd just make a film on the EV, since that would solve all his issues. But instead, he just covers that up, and he asks us to blame ourselves and to feel guilty for our American oil-economy (which he says several times is the greatest problem in global warming). Gore does not mention that the oil-economy exists, not because of a careless RP, but because the world citizenry has been imprisoned to it *due to the tactics of the oil corporatists* (This is proven in Paine 2006, Williams 1980, Black 2006, and especially in Clarke 1995). Also of interest is the fact that Gore, like most global warming fearmongers, refers to the active hurricane activity in recent years as being obviously due to global warming (which was proven false in the 2006 hurricane season, which had almost no hurricanes at all), but Gore simply fails to bring up the HAARP technology, which is widely known among weather researchers to be able to create hurricanes (see Begich 1995). With this technology at the US government's fingertips, we *can't* conclude that hurricanes are "acts of God," or acts of global warming, and we must also entertain a better theory: they are government-caused. This is the best theory because it best explains the erratic shift in hurricane activity, from the massive record-breaking season in 2005, to nearly no hurricanes or tropical storms in 2006. This smells like government, not spontaneous nature.[425]

---

[424] See Coffman 2007 for a presentation of the data regarding this issue.

[425] Dr. Michael Coffman (in his DVD lectures, "Prophecy and World Events," and "Final Countdown to UN World Government," also see www.discerningtoday.org) shows that what is *really* behind the global warming media blitz is the initial stages of setting up a one-world religion (what can be called "the religion of the New World Order"), and Alex Jones has pointed out on his radio show (www.infowars.com) in January and February of 2007 that a global fuel tax is being planned, which is another reason for the "human caused" global warming thesis.

Health Care

Heath care is another method of corporatist terrorism, and it is very profitable as well: the more people that are killed, the more a health care company profits, since resisting covering an illness is savings for the health care provider.[426] This is just one example of how corporatist terrorism occurs.

According to Dr. Lorraine Day, Orthopedic surgeon and author of many books, in one 10 year period, more Americans are killed by health care in America (8 million) than have been killed in all the wars that the United States has ever fought in.[427] 7.8 million are killed each decade by doctor-caused death.[428] Untold numbers are killed by Big Pharma's products, and, of course, there is the military-industrial complex.[429]

Industrial Toxic Waste is
Food, Water, and Medicine

If there are waste products (fluoride, benzene, etc.) from toxic industrial processes, it is more profitable for corporations to sell them than to get them disposed somewhere. So what corporations have done is made arrangements for many of these toxic substances to be sold to food and medical industries in order to put them in food and medicine. A few of the many examples are

- Fluoride deliberately placed in drinking water which comes from fertilizer factories and from the industrial production processes of making of atomic bombs being,[430]
- Soy products in the United States, which largely consist of waste products (soy waste products), but which are called "health foods."[431]
- Toxic waste from inside of smoke stacks of oil refineries scraped off and put into fertilizer to be sold to farmers for US farmland and sold at gardening stores for home gardens, which contains lead, mercury, and cadmium. Also, "low-level" radio-active waste has been used as land spread fertilizer.[432]

There is no science or research that shows that these substances (fluoride, soy as it is found in American food, mercury, lead, cadmium, and toxic and nuclear waste) are beneficial to humans, and rather, there is only research that shows

---

[426] See Court and Smith 1999.

[427] Dr. Day discussed this on the Rense Radio Show (www.Rense.com), October 26, 2005. Also see Court and Smith 1999.

[428] Dr. Lorraine Day, Rense Radio Show (www.Rense.com), October 26, 2005.

[429] See Angell 2005.

[430] See Bryson 2004, Introduction.

[431] See Daniels 2005, Introduction.

[432] This information comes from a discussion between Jeff Rense and Geri Guidetti on the Rense Radio Show, www.rense.com, April 21, 2004.

they are catastrophically detrimental to humans (see chapter five for a discussion on how mercury causes autism). Industry just needs a place to put them, and disposal of these substances can be expensive. Also, the corporatists want to make money in the process of disposing the toxic wastes, in order to further their illuminati-based corporatist power and interests. What the corporatists have found is that the best way to dispose of these substances is by the way I have just explained: tell the people that the toxins are harmless (mercury), or that they are healthy and good (soy waste, fluoride), and then put them in food, water, and medicine for human consumption.

Privatized Military Forces (PMFs) and Secret War

When the nightmarish images of Iraqi prisoner abuse at Abu Ghraib began to emerge in May, few investors in Arlington (Va.)-based CACI International ... would have guessed the information-technology services contractor had any kind of involvement. Why would it? After all, CACI's expertise is in organizing and managing data and IT systems for the government. It turned out CACI had 10 employees working at the prison, performing interrogations. At least one of them was named in a military report as a direct culprit of the abuse. And while interrogations account for less than 1% of total revenues, the press reports have cost CACI dearly in stock value and public relations damage, figures Chris Penny, analyst at Friedman, Billings, Ramsey. "[Its] interrogation [business] definitely took investors by surprise," says Penny.
—Business Week[433]

According to Milton Friedman, the "economics god" of the corporatist economic landscape,

> The hidden hand of the market will never work without a hidden fist— McDonalds cannot flourish without McDonnell Douglas, the builder of the F-15. And the hidden fist that keeps the world safe for Silicon Valley's technologies is called the United States Army, Air Force, Navy and Marine Corps.[434]

Privatized military forces (PMFs) are secret armies that are financed and used by corporations to shape the world in the way they desire, and according to their corporatist interests. Of course this is precisely the purpose of the US military also (since most people don't know what the US military does on a day-to-day basis, the US military is best defined as a secret military), which is a corporatist military force that the RP has knowledge of. But in this section, I am not discussing publicly known military forces. Rather, I am discussing private military forces (PMFs), secret warfare, and secret corporatist military forces; and my focus will not be on the public wars (the wars that the American

---

[433] "CACI: Wiping Off Abu Ghraib's Taint," BusinessWeek, August 18, 2004, Amy Tsao.
[434] This is a quote from *The New York Times*, and is quoted in Chang 2005b, xx.

citizenry *knows* are occurring, such as the Iraq Wars), but rather on the secret warfare being conducted all over the world by the armies of corporations: the secret but incredibly powerful military forces that have been created by corporations, which go by the names, CACI, Titan, Blackwater, among others.

Corporate financed militarism and military massacres are not at all new to corporatist American. For example, in 1914, the National Guard in Colorado, financed by one of the most powerful corporatists of all, Rockefeller, was paid to attack and kill miners who were striking his coal mine, and Rockefeller ordered that *especially* women and children be slaughtered. In the history books that include discussion of this terrorist attack, this has been called the Ludlow Massacre.[435]

Military secrecy is nothing new at all to the US taxpayer financed militaries, but often I get the feeling that many of my fellow Americans believe that the wars they see on, and as portrayed by, the mass media are the only wars there are, and that these wars are in fact really occurring just as they are depicted in the mass media: what you see is what you get. I often am called "conspiracy theorist!" if I quote a book about secret warfare conducted by the US government, such as the book, *Safe For Democracy: The Secret Wars of the CIA*, by John Prados,[436] the book *Drugs, Oil, and War,* by Professor Peter Dale Scott,[437] or the book, *Tiger Force*, by Michael Sallah and Mitch Weiss,[438] which is about an ultra-secret US military Vietnam War torture-, slaughter-, and horror-patrol. But regardless of what names I am called, the examples of US military secret warfare are many.

Secret War

One particularly relevant to this book is *Savak*, the secret terrorist army that was actually a CIA operation[439] used to function as and carry out terrorist operations (much like al-Qaeda) in Iran in the mid-part of the twentieth century. Corporatists often need a secret threat, in the form of a terrorist organization, to carry out their war wishes. A "secret threat" was mentioned in the PNAC[440] plan, and in *The Grand Chessboard*,[441] which is obviously al-Qaeda, and has provoked America to fight wars in Afghanistan and Iraq since 9/11. A secret threat can put so much fear in a citizenry that they will be frenzied to do almost anything, such as immediately leave their life of work and family duties, in order to secretly fight in war and secretly massacre ordinary people that they

---

[435] See Zinn 2004 for more discussion.
[436] 2006, Chicago: Iran R. Dee.
[437] 2003, New York: Rowman and Littlefield.
[438] 2006, New York: Little, Brown and Company.
[439] See Jones 2006, and see "The Secret History of the CIA in Iran," New York Times, Apr. 16, June 18, 2000 http:// www.nytimes.com/library/world/mideast/041600irancia
[440] See PNAC 2000.
[441] Brzezinski 1998.

have never met, such as which occurred with the secret mass bombing of civilians in Vietnam (ordered by Kissinger and Nixon),[442] in World War II (civilian massacres in Europe,[443] Japan,[444] and elsewhere), in the Middle Eastern Wars over the past two decades, and with the use of nuclear weapons (DU missiles and bullets) since the early 1990s[445] by the US military in Iraq under Bush Sr., Clinton, and Bush Jr. These are just a few of the plethora of examples where the US military carried out war and massacre in secret. These and other US military operations are all for profit corporatist operations.

These operations all were secretive operations conducted by militaries that Americans were aware of—Americans know of the existence of the Army, Navy, Air Force, and Marines. But PMFs are truly a different brand of military: Americans do not know of the existence of these military forces, and they are true horror forces that are secretly reshaping the world in a way that will set up world government. In his book, *Corporate Warriors*, Singer describes the new "business face of warfare,"[446] and how the economic and social landscape of the entire planet[447] is being transformed to the liking of the corporatists by a force that almost nobody knows about: private corporate armies. These private armies are themselves corporations, who are hired and paid by the largest monopolistic corporations to carry out the professional military action, or outright warfare, or covert-disguised and/or undisguised demented terrorism. These groups are ultra-secretive, they carry out any action requested, just as long as payment is made, and we will see that al-Qaeda appears to be a PMF.[448] Singer lucidly discusses these issues:

> The one aspect that formerly limited the power of multinational corporations was their physical weakness, which kept them dependent on the local state and only able to operate in zones of relative stability. This security was provided by the state, meaning that operations and even survival as a viable business were conditioned on the local state carrying out its responsibilities. Today, this limit no longer necessarily holds true. PMFs possess a capacity for armed force that rivals and even surpasses local state functions. They can transfer this to their multinational corporation clients. Thus, multinational corporations and their allied private military firms now have the capability to engage in

---

[442] This is discussed in Jarecki 2003.

[443] Howard Zinn discussed this in Mueller and Ellis, 2005.

[444] See Morris 2004.

[445] For more information, see the section above about DU, or see Brohy and Ungerman 2001, and Lando 2007. Also see the radio interviews with Leuren Moret, November 14, 2006, and with Dr. Doug Rokke, September 28, 2006, both of which were Rense Radio Show, www.Rense.com, and can be found at the Rense archives

[446] Singer 2003, 18.

[447] Singer 2003, 8-9.

[448] Singer does not appear to notice this, but Gandini and Saleh (2005), who discuss PMFs, do appear to notice this.

what they term "security-led investment," in which the physical weakness of the local state is irrelevant to their business operations. A number of multinational corporations have already created bastions within weak states or situations of internal conflict, protected by their own armed forces hired from military provider sector firms. Unfortunately, the interests of such empowered corporations are often not in line with those of the local society or government. PMFs could thus act as leaders in a new corporate dominance, or as the UN special rapporteur put it, "the multinational neocolonialism of the twenty first century."... At the very least, ... such protected corporate bastions provide security only to rich outsiders and act to deflect threats onto poorer, and thus less protected, portions of local society... Already a number of transnational corporations have been linked to violent conflict, including providing equipment and support to local military forces that do their bidding, in order to expand their own business interests... ...[I]t is important to remember that a number of PMFs possess skills and forces on call that are often greater, or equal to, those of many military forces in weaker states [by "weaker states" Singer means "small countries"]. Many consider the firms to be "powerful enough to dislodge any government in Africa" and thus a real concern for any local authorities that dare to challenge them. [449]

So, let's get this straight. The structure of the planet is being dramatically altered (see Singer's book for all the myriad examples) by militarism which is virtually invisible to the American consumer culture, but fully supported and built up by that consumer culture. PMFs are the face of warfare of the future, and it is all secret.

Rearrangement of the World for the Corporatists

Like UN troops,[450] PMFs are often described as "peacekeepers,"[451] but Rosemann outlines how they have committed atrocities under the financing of the US government in the Iraq War,[452] and where working private security specialists can make up to $1000 per day.[453] And Singer discusses the corporatists' PMF activity in a poignant passage about how the government (not the secret government necessarily, but the visible, phony government) corporatists rearrange the world for corporations:

---

[449] Singer 2003, 188-189.
[450] UN "peacekeeping" troops are some of the most horrific armies on the planet, guilty of some of the greatest atrocities I know of. See Tabor 2006 for excellent discussion of these issues.
[451] Singer 2003, 9.
[452] Rosemann 2005, 77-82.
[453] Rosemann 2005, 83.

Ironically enough, despite being the dominant power on the international scene today, the United States may make the most extensive use of the privatized military industry. Indeed, from 1994 to 2002, the U.S. Defense Department entered into more than 3,000 contracts with U.S.-based firms, estimated at a contract value of more than $300 billion... The areas being outsourced are not just minor ones such as military food services..., but include a variety of areas critical to the U.S. military's core missions... At a time when downsizing [during the Clinton Presidency] and increased deployments have left U.S. forces stretched thin, private firms have provided the United States with an array of services: security, military advice, training, logistics support, policing, technological expertise, and intelligence. In the last few years, the U.S. Department of Defense has outsourced everything from depot and based upkeep to more than 70 percent of army aviation training... such firms operating alongside U.S. forces have become nearly ubiquitous... The result is that while contractors have long accompanied U.S. armed forces, the wholesale outsourcing of U.S. military since the 1990s is unprecedented... Every major American military operation in the post-Cold War era has involved considerable levels of support and activity by private firms offering services that the U.S. military used to perform on its own.[454] (Emphasis added)

Since 9/11, the main military activity of the world has not been in Afghanistan and Iraq, but rather, it is going on all over. "PMF customers... are ranged across the moral spectrum from ruthless dictators, morally depraved rebels and drug cartels" to "legitimate sovereign states, respected multinational corporations and humanitarian NGOs."[455]

False-Flag Terror:
The Principal Tactic of the Corporatists

"He was deceived by a lie, we all were. It appears that the Chancellor [the Emperor] was behind everything, including the war."

—OB1 Kenobe, from *Star Wars, Episode III: Revenge of the Sith*

Terrorism, namely false flag terrorism, is one of the more productive tools that corporatists use, primarily because it has the power to set into motion other corporatist tools, such as brainwashing, population reduction, ignorance, economics of destruction, poverty, military draft, distraction, and so on.

---

[454] Singer 2003, 15-16.
[455] Singer 2003, 9.

Acting dumbfounded, MIT Professor Noam Chomsky has remarked on how utterly amazing the September 11, 2001 attacks were, for the simple reason that in the past several hundred years never has one of the major imperial powers or groups[456] been attacked by a non-imperial power or group.[457] Chomsky is right, but not for his claim that something new happened for the first time on 9/11, but rather he is right for being surprised that such an event could take place. 9/11 *was* an amazing event—so amazing, in fact, that, as we will see, an empirical approach will reveal that it is *too amazing to be true*, and only if magic was real could 9/11 have occurred in the way Americans were told it did on and after September 11, 2001.

Later, in December of 2006, a televised interview was posted on Alex Jones's website, www.infowars.com, of a recent interview with Chomsky, that showed a different commentary by Chomsky, and one that reveals him to be a disguised New World Order agent.

> Did they [the Bush Administration] plan it [9/11] in any way? This seems to me to be extremely unlikely. For one, they would have to be insane to have tried anything like that… There is a huge internet industry from the left… that [purports that] this was all fake, and it was planned by the Bush Administration, and so on. But if you look at the evidence, anybody who knows anything about the sciences, would simply discount that evidence. There is plenty of coincidences,… But the evidence that has been produced is… essentially worthless. And the belief that it could have been done is, … um… has such low credibility… A large part of the left has all kinds of conspiracy theories on this... Even if it were true, which is *extremely* unlikely, *who cares*? … It's just taking energy away from serious issues that matter.[458]

In this section I will discuss an issue that is absolutely critical to any empirical and analytical study of corporatism, namely false flag terrorism, and I will primarily focus on 9/11 (though other false flag events will be discussed). The corporatist has certain tools that, through history, she/he has always tended to use, such as communist labor structure, mass brainwashing, controlling education and information, controlling the food and medical industries, hijacking scientific pursuits, rewriting history, impoverishment of citizens, perpetual war and fear, usurpation of energy and resources, staged elections, and so on, but perhaps the most effective corporatist tool of all is *false flag terrorism*, or what has been called *synthetic terrorism* by Webster Tarpley.

---

[456] Chomsky mentions the United States, a European country, and Japan, perhaps China, Russia, Canada, and more recently Brazil and India could be added to this list.

[457] In Junkerman 2002.

[458] This is from a conference at a location that the video does not disclose, and it appeared December 27, 2006 at http://www.infowars.com/articles/sept11/chomsky_doesnt_matter_if_there_was_conspiracy.htm, and can be viewed there.

The Pentagon on 9/11:
Irrefutable Proof of False Flag Terror

I have mentioned already in this book that empirical evidence from the events of September 11, 2001 show that the story Americans were told about 9/11 is incorrect. This evidence is straightforward and nearly irrefutable. It is so simple to show that it is irrefutable, that it is similar to how simple it is to know that a circle has a different shape than a square. When presented the evidence about 9/11 (which has been so well hidden by the American media channels), understanding that 9/11 is a false-flag operation is as simple as knowing that the sky is blue, or that a triangle is different from a square: there is just nothing complicated at all about the evidence.

Since there is now so much confusion on this issue (for example, the Chomsky disinformation in the quote at the start of this section), I will briefly discuss this evidence. Here are a few points of that evidence (the first point is the only one I will be concerned with in this section after I give this list, and is, in my opinion, the principal piece of evidence that shows that 9/11 was a false flag event):

> There were two stages of Pentagon events on 9/11/2001: a. pre-collapse Pentagon: from the initial explosion, which the world was informed was a 757 shortly afterward; b. the post-collapse Pentagon: about 25 after this initial explosion, the section of the Pentagon which was hit collapsed

Before step a, the roof was undamaged, so when it collapsed, it was an undamaged roof that collapsed. The irrefutable proof that I will refer to in this section comes from step a. Step a is shown in the following picture (you can use the firemen for size scale):

You can verify that step a and step b happened in the way I am describing by watching the original 911 footage, and I will give sources below. You can also verify that the national media is now attempting to *cover up* that step-a in fact occurred. For example, the September 11, 2006 issue of Time Magazine has an issue on "911 Conspiracy Theories," where step-a *is not mentioned*, and only step-b is mentioned, and this is done in a way where it is meant to appear that *only* step-b occurred.

In the first pictures from the Pentagon on 9/11 (during step-a), one must ask:

- Why wasn't there a hole even close to the size of the massive holes caused in the Trade Center Towers by the planes that hit there?
- Why were nearly all the windows in the so-called "damage area" of the pre-collapse Pentagon *unbroken* and *undamaged*?
- How can a 60-ton, 125 foot-wide jetliner, with two 9-foot-tall 9-ton engines, traveling at 450 mph hit a wall without even breaking the windows (see picture above, use the fire truck for scale)?
- Why were there no plane parts found at Pentagon? (First time in aviation history a plane crash had no plane parts found at the site.)[459]

These questions reveal that the Pentagon simply was not a crash site on 9/11, but I will discuss the issue more just so that all the details are hashed out properly.

You can verify all this evidence with the Discovery Channel documentary, "Attack at the Pentagon," where at 1 min and 20 sec. into the documentary, there is footage of the Pentagon collapse that occurred 25 minutes after the initial explosion there on Sept. 11, 2001, and right where step-a changes to step-b. And what you see in that footage is a little-damaged wall (the only real damage seen on the wall is smoke damage) with *unbroken* windows collapsing.

There are further questions. Why were there no marks on Pentagon lawn if the massive plane supposedly skidded on it, as Americans were told it did before hitting the Pentagon wall? Many have maintained that the Pentagon Plane was all sucked through a tiny 15-foot hole in the Pentagon, and that is why the windows were unbroken, wherein the plane turned into a liquid state or evaporated away. But that would require a 4000-11,000 degree F fire, and there was no such evidence of such a catastrophic heat anywhere near the Pentagon on 9/11.

These are just a few of the *uncomplicated* empirical issues which prove that 9/11 was fabricated. The question is this: How is an academic like myself— who is trained to follow empirical evidence at all costs—supposed to interpret these empirical details? Am I supposed to, like Chomsky, just ignore these details? Am I supposed to, like Chomsky, confidently assert that there is just no

---

[459] There were actually two parts found, but see the DVD documentary *Loose Change*, by Dylan Avery to see why these can be disregarded, and why the best statements describing the Pentagon incident on September 11th maintain that *zero* plane parts were found.

evidence? Or is it more in the spirit of intellectual rational inquiry to consider these issues? Also, as an academic, how am I supposed to avoid at least making the hypothesis that there was no plane at the Pentagon? If I am to be an impartial academic, how do I make the rash conclusions that Chomsky did? I certainly cannot, if I am acting as an unbiased, objective researcher. If I am an unbiased researcher, I must consider these facts as strong, powerful, perhaps even haunting pieces of evidence. What I have just written provides a good example (one of many in this book) of academics, like Chomsky, not only are often not unbiased, and do not carry out research in the classical, Enlightenment tradition of rational inquiry, but they also often even appear to be secretly paid off to be government and corporatist agents to spread disinformation.

The Proof: No Pentagon Plane Means there are No Muslim Terrorists out there to be Feared

If there was no plane at the Pentagon on September 11, 2001, then no matter what other convoluted stories about 9/11 that Chomsky, Bill O'Reilly, Sean Hannity, George Bush, or anybody else express to us, one thing is irrefutably true:

> *If there was no plane at the Pentagon on 9/11, but the government corporatists (the visible government corporatists) contrarily said that there was within minutes of the step-a explosion at the Pentagon on 9/11, then 9/11 is a false flag event, and the government corporatists are in some way complicit in 9/11.*

This is the simplest way to prove that 9/11 is a false flag event, and that it was a plot connected to the visible government of the United States. I will discuss this proof in more detail, but for now it can be asserted that there is no way around this proof; I have tried to find one, and I cannot: *no plane means no al-Qaeda terrorist attack*! People like Chomsky and Bill O'Reilly try to confuse the issue, but the simplicity of the Pentagon story clarifies everything for us. People like Chomsky and O'Reilly, or the other people featured on CNN and Fox that are used to make the 9/11 skeptics look foolish, use the same attacks on 9/11 skeptics over and over, and these repetitious attacks basically consist of bringing up the following same irrelevant, distracting, illogical, cloudy issues:

- Did space beams shoot down from US satellites to bring down the towers?
- It is too hard to believe that the Bush Administration, or any elements of the US (visible) government, could have carried out such a savage attack, therefore they did not
- If there was no plane at the Pentagon, then what did the government do with the corpses of the people that were supposedly on the plane that supposedly hit the Pentagon

- It is too big of a secret for 9/11 to have been a secret conspiracy; somebody would have leaked it before it occurred, and when it was in the planning stages; but since nobody did, then it was not a conspiracy, and Osama bin Laden really did it[460]
- Bush did it
- Bush could never get away with this
- If there was evidence that Bush did it, it would be on the front page of the New York Times tomorrow, and since it is not, then there is no evidence
- Saying that 9/11 was an inside job is a desecration to the families of the victims

These are the types of issues that are brought up in the mass media in a attempt to try to confuse the public about the facts of 9/11, but if one merely stays on the issue (step-a Pentagon), one can see that all these issues are distractions that have nothing to do with anything, and that none of these issues matter, then one can see that the issue is perfectly simple: *step-a Pentagon proves there was no plane at the Pentagon, and no Pentagon plane irrefutably proves that 9/11 was not an al-Qaeda terrorist attack, and there is no way around that conclusion.*

Attempts to Explain the Pentagon Plane: Mind-Bogglingly Strong Windows and Wing-Folding. I have seen many attempts to avoid this step-a Pentagon proof. I have heard many assert that, for example, the hole in the step-a Pentagon was so small because the wings broke off the plane in the Pentagon lawn (or the highway along-side the Pentagon) before the jetliner hit the Pentagon wall. But this is impossible, since there were no wings and jets from the wings found on the Pentagon lawn or anywhere outside the Pentagon in the proximity of the crash site on 9/11 (to verify this, all one has to do is view news footage from the 9/11/2001 of the Pentagon after the explosion there). Also, I have heard people assert that the Pentagon windows could be super-strong, and thus could have repelled the plane and remained unbroken. This would mean that the windows at Pentagon must have been stronger than the steel in the trade-centers, since the jetliners went through the trade-center steel about as easily as a bullet goes through a sheet of paper. (Also, the window frames around the windows at the step-a Pentagon were largely unbroken, and the wall of the Pentagon only had smoke damage; so they too would have to be stronger

---

[460] Actually, 9/11 *was* leaked numerous times, and these are very well known—for example, even mainstream news papers were warning about it. See Ruppert 2004, chapter 14 for a very comprehensive account of the forewarning the world and the US government had about 9/11, including reports *before* 9/11 that mainstream press published around the world. This verifies that Chomsky is not just playing dumb in the passage above, but rather, he is deliberately trying to cover up evidence, and he is deliberately trying to brainwash—that is, to get people to believe a false account of reality, and, in Orwellian fashion, to rewrite history in order for tyranny to live uncontested.

than—*far* stronger than—the WTC1 and WTC2 steel in order to repel the 757 allegedly at the Pentagon on 9/11.)

So one would have to find out if this is possible, if windows can be that strong. There is a simple way to do this. Let's pretend that the account I just gave is correct: let's pretend that the step-a Pentagon windows were not broken and were hardly showing any damage due to the fact that they were stronger than trade center steel, and strong enough to repel the massive jetliner. The problem is this: if we look at the visual-photo evidence from 9/11 (such as from the aforementioned Discovery Channel DVD), we should expect to see plane debris, since the 757 alleged to have crashed into the Pentagon on 9/11 weighed 60 tons, and thus there should be tens of tons of some sort of plane debris on the outside of the Pentagon laying at the base of the wall or perhaps sprayed all over the luxurious Pentagon golf-course-like lawn. The problem is that we see absolutely zero such debris.

Another objection I have heard many times is the assertion that the entire jetliner could have all fit through a tiny hole (perhaps 15 feet across), enter the step-a Pentagon, and when inside, melt and literally vanish/vaporize (as if the Pentagon got anywhere near the sort of temperature needed to do this), all while leaving the surrounding parts of the pentagon without even broken windows. There have even been impressive engineers, from my very own university, Purdue University, to give what sound like very impressive reports on this issue, as I will discuss. As for popular press articles on this theory, consider this passage from the very beginning of a now famous Popular Mechanics Magazine article, which is another piece that attempts to make it appear that only step-b at the Pentagon occurred, in a section of an article called "Big Plane, Small Holes:"

> CLAIM: Two holes were visible in the Pentagon immediately after the attack: a 75-ft.-wide entry hole in the building's exterior wall, and a 16-ft.-wide hole in Ring C, the Pentagon's middle ring. Conspiracy theorists claim both holes are far too small to have been made by a Boeing 757. "How does a plane 125 ft. wide and 155 ft. long fit into a hole which is only 16 ft. across?" asks reopen911.org, a Web site "dedicated to discovering the bottom line truth to what really occurred on September 11, 2001."[461]

Do you see what Popular Mechanics (PM) has done here? They have merely denied the existence of the step-a Pentagon, even though the step-a Pentagon is in the aforementioned Discovery Channel DVD, it has been on FOX News numerous times, and I have seen that footage numerous times in numerous media channels in the United States. Luckily for PM, the average American is

---

[461] "9/11: Debunking The Myths. PM examines the evidence and consults the experts to refute the most persistent conspiracy theories of September 11." Published in the March, 2005 issue.

too busy to keep track of, or even to get their mind around, all the details, and thus they will be easily fooled into believing that there is no step-a Pentagon, and thus that the 9/11 skeptics are foolish "kooks" or "conspiracy theorists," as the Big Media puts it.

PM claims there was a 75 foot hole, as if that is all there ever was at the Pentagon, and as if step-a, the pre-collapse Pentagon event, never occurred. PM is owned by the Hearst Corporation, which owns many newspapers and magazines (Teen, Cosmopolitan, Esquire, The Oprah Magazine, Good Housekeeping, just to name a few), partial owners of XM Satellite Radio, Drugstore.com, has shared ownership of ESPN with Disney, just to give a list of a fraction of its assets. The Hearst Corporation has serious questions surrounding it, since, for example, one of its major business partners is Check Point Software,[462] the company that used to be called Data Base Technologies, which helped disrupt over 100,000 black voters in Florida in the 2000 Presidential election,[463] and thus made it a close race that was erroneously given to Bush, even though Gore had majority vote in that state, thus making the US Presidential election in 2000 something like the elections in Iraq. Given the empirical verification in the 9/11 footage of the step-a Pentagon, we have no choice but to reject this first paragraph of this PM article.

Oddly, after this passage I just quoted, this PM article gets nasty and wrathful (but which I have chosen not to cite there, since they are off-topic). This is not a significant issue, but it is interesting to note, since typically if one has clear-as-the-sky-is-blue empirical evidence on their side supporting their position, there is really no need to be perturbed and/or wrathful. The most obvious empirical evidence one can ever have is something on the order of: *the sky is blue.* If somebody is going to try to tell you that the sky is not blue, but is *green*, are you really going to get perturbed over their error? Or are you just going to wonder: What is wrong with her/him? Are you going to try to convince her/him that the sky is blue, or can you just look up and point and say, see, there it is, we can both verify that the sky is blue? So if there is so much evidence that the Pentagon jetliner all nicely fit through a 15-foot hole and then melted, what's the point in being defensive?

Let's consider the next part of this article, which gets into the alleged scientific analysis of the disappearing plane (some of the material below is redundant, but I am merely citing the article as it was written):

> The truth is of even less importance to French author Thierry Meyssan, whose baseless assertions are fodder for even mainstream European and Middle Eastern media. In his book The Big Lie, Meyssan concludes that

---

[462] I learned this from a press release that was posted on the Checkpoint web site: "Check Point Chosen to Secure Hearst Corporation's Global Network," September 2, 2003, http://www.checkpoint.com/press/2003/hearst090203.html.
[463] See Palast 2004.

the Pentagon was struck by a satellite-guided missile—part of an elaborate U.S. military coup. "This attack," he writes, "could only be committed by United States military personnel against other U.S. military personnel."

FACT: When American Airlines Flight 77 hit the Pentagon's exterior wall, Ring E, it created a hole approximately 75 ft. wide, according to the ASCE Pentagon Building Performance Report. The exterior facade collapsed about 20 minutes after impact, but ASCE based its measurements of the original hole on the number of first-floor support columns that were destroyed or damaged. Computer simulations confirmed the findings.

Why wasn't the hole as wide as a 757's 124-ft.-10-in. wingspan? A crashing jet doesn't punch a cartoon-like outline of itself into a reinforced concrete building, says ASCE team member Mete Sozen, a professor of structural engineering at Purdue University. In this case, one wing hit the ground; the other was sheared off by the force of the impact with the Pentagon's load-bearing columns, explains Sozen, who specializes in the behavior of concrete buildings. What was left of the plane flowed into the structure in a state closer to a liquid than a solid mass. "If you expected the entire wing to cut into the building," Sozen tells PM, "it didn't happen."

The tidy hole in Ring C was 12 ft. wide--not 16 ft. ASCE concludes it was made by the jet's landing gear, not by the fuselage.[464]

As for Sozen's comment about a plane punching a cartoon-like outline of itself, the World Trade Centers were made of both steel and concrete (such as concrete floors). Through the walls, and through the layers of flooring, the planes penetrated the Trade Centers like a diver in water (the planes were stopped after clearly they fully entered and disappeared within the buildings), and in the process, they did make cartoon-like cutouts. Therefore, the step-a Pentagon should have at least *some* damage of *some sort*—other than mere smoke damage (and perhaps a small, approximately 15-foot hole, which the pictures also reveal)—to account for the 125-foot wing-span: at least some sort of imprint that the wingspan should make, the nine-foot diameter multi-ton jet engines, given the ease with which Americans saw the 9/11 towers penetrated,[465] but there is no such damage, even the PM article agrees on this.

---

[464] "9/11: Debunking The Myths. PM examines the evidence and consults the experts to refute the most persistent conspiracy theories of September 11." Published in the March, 2005 issue.

[465] My use of the word "ease" here in describing how the World Trade Center Towers were penetrated is not an exaggeration. Going back to the original 9/11 footage, it can be easily observed in some of the more close-up footage of the second plane that hit the Trade Centers, all the way out to its very wing-tips the cutout was made in what appears to be cartoon-like fashion. Therefore, Sozen's claim about no cartoon-like

But it did not, and thus we must consider the theory that the wings folded back and toward the plane fuselage, as the plane entered the tiny hole. But this idea appears to not make any sense. (1) First, there are problems in accounting for how the wings would do this folding action. At over 400 mph—which leads to tremendous forward momentum, rather than inward, fuselage-aimed momentum—there would have had to have been a factor to account for the wings being pulled, or pushed, in towards the fuselage. What factor could account for this? What could go against the massive momentum produced by 60 tons moving forward at over 400 mph that somehow acted so as to make the wings stop that incredibly powerful motion, so that the wings would move in a different direction? Also, (2) there is absolutely no trace of any sort of this sort of "wing-folding" going on with the World Trade Center planes, and we should expect at least some, since we are talking about the same sorts of materials (steel and concrete) from between the Pentagon and the WTCs. How can there be total unexplained wing-folding at the Pentagon, but absolutely none at the WTCs?

I am not an engineer, but I have enough common sense to know that this wing-folding issue is not possible, for the following reasons. The idea that the plane folded up through the very small hole at the Pentagon and then melted and vanished requires that the jetliners engines change direction in the way described above, and that the Pentagon site reach nearly half the temperature of the surface of the sun, which it did not. Consider the 9-foot diameter multi-ton engines. To maintain that they switched direction in the way described above is like saying that these engines that were traveling hundreds of miles per hour, at the moment of impact, *stopped* their momentous forward direction, and without even breaking the windows on the Pentagon surrounding the small approximately 15-foot hole, somehow were transferred sideways and in toward the center where the hole was, and then they somehow propelled forward again with the rest of the plane into the hole and melted. I find this impossible, due to the fact that there is no force possible to act as an inward-pulling mechanism, making the massive wings and jet engines stop moving fully forward, and then instead implode toward the jetliner's center of mass, or move in some direction that is no longer merely a forward motion.

The most logical scenario for this "wing folding" scenario is to consider that, as the name of this theory implies ("wing folding"), the wings folded backward, so that the ends of the wings not only stopped going forward, but they began going approximately *backwards*. Consider the following diagram:

---

imprints into structures of concrete reinforced steel appears to be shattered here by the cartoon-like imprints in the concrete and steel Trade Center Towers.

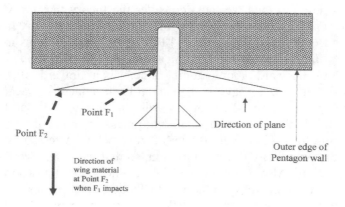

Point F_1

Point F_2

Direction of plane

Outer edge of Pentagon wall

Direction of wing material at Point F_2 when F_1 impacts

The idea is that point F_1 acted like a hinge, for lack of a better word, catapulting the entire left wing backward at the initial point of wing impact, which is where point F_1 is. According to this model, there would have to be a force created at point F_1 that made the entire wing swing back, such as where point F_2 on the wing goes in the opposite direction of the plane's direction, in order for there to be a "folding back" of the wings. There must be something that happens at point F_1 that makes the entire wing change direction from its significant speed of 400 mph, to abruptly stop moving at over 400 mph, and then *reverse* its direction to a speed faster than the original forward speed was (since the wings must fold in *before* they can hit the wall, and thus must reverse direction and go perhaps near 500 mph in reverse). Something at point F_1 would have to impact point F_2 in order to produce a net change in direction of the wing material at point F_2 of approximately 900 mph. Point F_1 would have to cause a twisting force so that the wing swung back with enormous speed.

The questions are: How does the point at F_1 produce this twisting, and why would the impact at point F_1 produce this surplus of velocity at point F_2? It is very easy, however, to show that there is nothing about wing location F_1 that could influence wing location F_2 to make it change directions in any way, and it is thus very easy to show that this "wing folding" theory is entirely incorrect. The issue is this:

> *If the fuselage so successfully penetrated the Pentagon, then why wouldn't the wing material at point F_1 merely penetrate the Pentagon wall also, since the wing material at point F_1 is not less dense material than the fuselage?*

Answer: if the fuselage penetrated the impressively thick Pentagon wall, then wing location F_1 must also penetrate it since it is going at the same velocity as the fuselage, is composed of similar material, and so forth; but the wing folding theory requires that F_1 did not penetrate the Pentagon, and thus the wing folding theory fails:

There is no reason to imagine that the fuselage material would penetrate the Pentagon, but that the F_1 material would not.

Actually, it is more likely that the matter at point F_1 would be *more* heavy-duty than the flimsy fuselage, and thus if we are told by Sozen, for example, that the fuselage successfully penetrated the Pentagon wall, then certainly the matter at point F_1 would also. The problem is that if the matter at point F_1 penetrates the Pentagon, then the Pentagon wall is not providing the needed resistance at point F_1 to create the twisting/folding of the wing needed to swing the wing back, and to make the wing matter at point F_2 change direction at all, let alone by approximately 900 mph. To provide twisting at point F_1, there must be some sort of near total resistance by the wall of the penetration of the matter at point F_1, but if the flimsy fuselage could penetrate the ultra-powerful Pentagon wall, then certainly the durable wing matter at point F_1 would also: no twisting/folding wings, and the wing folding theory fails.

A Melting Jetliner? There is a second problem here: we are told that there actually was a zone of molten metal, so hot that all, or nearly all, of the 60 tons of plane vaporized without a trace. This takes an *incredible* amount of heat, one that would surely be unsafe for humans to be near, and which would take quite a while to cool down. But news footage evidence from within minutes and hours of the 9/11 events at the Pentagon clearly shows there were no such dangers as these.

Direct Empirical Evidence. The simple issue is, as stated previously: there was no flight 77 at the Pentagon, and for reasons give above, and the 9/11 Pentagon was clearly a false flag event. The evidence just given is *direct* empirical evidence, right from the news footage taken from the very day of the attacks of 9/11. Any person can go and verify all this simple evidence *right now*, by watching any of the documentaries that contain the aforementioned wall collapse footage, such as the DVD, *Attack On the Pentagon*, that was made by the Discovery Channel. The simplicity and uncontroversial nature of this direct empirical evidence shows us that, for 9/11 to be covered up, that only can mean that there are *many* people involved in the New World Order, and agents—like Chomsky—appear to be placed all over: throughout media (not must news media, but also educational media, including universities and colleges), throughout the visible government, and throughout corporate America, perhaps at the heads of most or all major institutions, from church to schools to visible government to monopolistic corporations.[466]

---

[466] See Icke 2001, chapter 1, for more information. Also see what is perhaps the best work on this subject, which is Maxwell 2000.

Government Response
and Eyewitness Accounts.

The US government has responded to the extremely active debate of the millions of doubters of the 9/11 story (the so-called "conspiracy theorists"). But to my knowledge, it has not responded to the above points (such as about the step-a Pentagon, which I find is the best piece of evidence of all). It has not perhaps because it *cannot*, since the step-a Pentagon offers *simple* irrefutable evidence of 9/11 being a false flag event. The way that the government has "responded" to the questions regarding 9/11 are, overall, not professional or appropriate. I will give an example. Around the same time that I write these words, the US government put out a web page, on May 17th 2006,[467] which is alleged to be a response to the huge numbers of doubters of the entire 9/11 or war on terror story given out by news media. The explosion at the Pentagon is an important issue, as will be seen above. Every single piece of "evidence" cited on this web page is nothing more than a form of personal testimony from some sort of eyewitness observer, claiming they saw evidence of a plane hitting the Pentagon, along these lines: "Joe said he saw the plane, therefore there was a plane."[468]

Personal testimony is a type of informational knowledge that occurs under the following conditions: person p_1 has information i, and the only way p_1 knows about i is because some other person, p_2, *told* p_1 about i. Personal testimony is a standard type of "evidence" used in the mainstream media, in US

---

[467] http://usinfo.state.gov/media/Archive/2005/Jun/28-581634.html. This documentary, on May 31, 2006, was titled as if it only talks about the Pentagon, but it is rather poorly organized, and parts also randomly bring up insignificant points about the Trade Center Towers also. The only parts of this document that don't involve reliance purely on personal testimony are the issues about the Trade Center Towers, but most of that also is based on personal testimony, the rest is based on pointless issues that nearly no conspiracy theorists are concerned with anyway. Again, this is based on what the report looked like on May 31, 2006; and of course after that it could be changed.

[468] It is amazing how often personal testimony is taken seriously, whether in this ".gov" website, in courts, or on "educational" television (Discovery Channel, National Geographic Channel, etc.), etc. But at the same time, personal testimonies are not admitted into scientific accounts, and the reasons why are simple. A personal testimony basically works like this: Joe says x is true, and just because he did it is. But if that is true, then we can just ignore the obvious rampant lying that people do on a daily basis ("I am not bored in class," "oh, my job is not bad, I like it"), and we sort of have to accept that what people say is in fact true. Therefore, for example, since 3 million Americans (which is approximately 100,000 times greater number than the Pentagon eyewitnesses) claim they have seen a UFO, then that is "proof" that there are UFOs all over. And since there are lots of atheists who have not seen God, this is "proof" there is no God, and there are Christians who say they experience him and thus there is "proof" that, um… there is a God. Clearly giving personal testimonies such credibility is nonsensical.

courts, and among politicians. But in a scientifically oriented pursuit of knowledge—such as the empirical account of the Pentagon I have just given, and such as the very method of inquiry I teach to my philosophy students and which I am attempting to be fully aligned with in this book—mere personal testimony devoid of direct empirical confirmation (or at least the possibility of it if one wanted to seek out such confirmation) is never admitted as evidence. It may work in court, but it will not work in the science classroom and lab.

The History of False Flag Terror

"I can hear you, the rest of the world can hear you, and the people who knocked these buildings down will hear *all* of us soon!"
—George W. Bush (with firefighters and yelling into a bull horn at Ground Zero, acting as if 9/11 was a surprise, a few days after the 9/11 attacks)[469]

Our history books contain numerous accounts of synthetic terror occurring through the eons. It has occurred several times by certain fascist commanders and rulers since America's inception. It has repeatedly been used through history to provoke wars, mass murder, and the rearrangement of populations, where these things were only in the interests of certain fascist rulers of various nations. Some of our most popular American films even involve synthetic terror (such as the second and third films in the *Star Wars* saga, *Attack of the Clones*, and *Revenge of the Sith*, as well as *Wag the Dog*, *Canadian Bacon*, etc.). So do some of our most popular books (*1984*). Most of the major (large) war events that America was involved in during the 20th and 21st centuries were started by staged events: World War II, the Vietnam War, World War I, and the second Iraq War.[470] World War I was started in Sarajevo by a synthetic terror assassination event of Archduke Franz Ferdinand of Austria. World War II was started by a staged attack in 1939 by Germany, making it look like Poland attacked the German Gleiwitz radio station.[471] The Vietnam War was started by the Gulf of Tonkin Incident. This "incident" consisted of the United States military bombing its own ship and blaming it on North Vietnam, and this led US military commanders to initiate an attack. Former Secretary of Defense

---

[469] You can see this event in Jarecki 2005. Bush yelled this to a group of fired-up firefighters who were chanting "USA! USA! USA!", at Ground Zero in New York City shortly after the 9/11 attacks

[470] For an introductory list of synthetic terror events, see Tarpley 2006, 66-70.

[471] There were actually several false flag events involved in World War II. Arguably, the burning of the Reicstagg, which was a false flag event caused by Hitler, was the real impetus of the nightmare of World War II. Also, President Roosevelt knew of the Pearl Harbor for possible attack, and used it to put needed fury into the minds of Americans for upcoming war. There are more recent accounts that show that FDR even helped plan Pearl Harbor. There are many clandestine issues surrounding "the Great War" (World War II), brought up in various places in this book. For more inforamtion on World War II false flag events, see Jones 2006, and Stinnet 2000.

Robert McNamara during the Vietnam War—the best authority and source on the Tonkin event—has indicated that the event did not happen.[472] On Aug. 4, 1964 while admitting to the attack on August 2. In a taped conversation released in 2001, McNamara told President Johnson that he thought that the attack had not even occurred.[473] The Iraq war was started by the September 11 Terror Attacks, due to the fact that the Bush Administration used those attacks to attack Saddam's dictatorship, as is well documented. But the Iraq war was also started by the false story of WMDs in Iraq, and thus that is another staged event.

To conclude, it is worthwhile to consider a few passages from one of the leading experts on synthetic terrorism, Webster Tarpley. He very lucidly sheds light on these issues regarding synthetic terrorism that I am discussing here:

> …what happens when the wars, policies and institutional changes desired by the ruling elite are inimical to the vast majority of citizens and cannot gain their understanding or support? When the oligarchical nature of the system endow it with such inertia that it cannot move in the direction the most powerful oligarchical factions desire? Under these conditions, especially if the political and economic systems are in crisis, state-sponsored terrorism may emerge…
> What we offer here can be thought of as a theory of synthetic terrorism. This terrorism is synthetic because it brings together the efforts of a number of disparate components: patsies, moles, professionals, media, and controllers. It is also synthetic in the sense that it is artificial: it does not grow up spontaneously out of despair and oppression, but is rather the product of an effort of organization and direction in which factions of government play an indispensable role.[474]

Tarpley contrasts this with the *naïve view* of terrorism:

> The naïve view of terrorism is that it grows up directly out of oppression, economic misery, and political despair. Oppressed and exploited people, or those who have been colonized by a foreign power, supposedly come together spontaneously in ones and twos, create an organization, and after a certain time of preparation go over to armed struggle against their oppressors or occupiers…

---

[472] "Cronkite: Gulf of Tonkin's Phantom Attack," by Walter Cronkite, NPR, *All Things Considered,* August 2, 2004, http://www.npr.org/templates/story/story.php?storyId= 3810724. The very best coverage I have seen of the documentation of how the Gulf of Tonkin hoax was staged is Jones 2006.

[473] These conversations can be heard at the NPR website listed in the last endnote.

[474] Tarpley 2006, 59.

This naïve view is blind to the most important institutional actors in the world of terrorism—secret intelligence agencies like CIA, FBI, NSA, KGB, Stasi, MI-6, and the rest.[475]

It should also be clear that state-sponsored terrorism cannot call itself by its own real name. It must necessarily masquerade as an authentic voice of the oppressed—be they Arabs, Muslims, workers, national minorities, or whatever. The terror groups cannot be labeled CIA or KGB—they must call themselves Red Brigades, Red Army faction, ETA, or al Qaeda. The false flag and false ideology allows the terror group to pretend to be something it is not, and to convince billions of naïve viewers of CNN or al Jazeera that the false dumb-show is reality.[476]

9/11 and Brainwashing

The power of a false flag event largely resides in the way that it changes people—in the way that it brainwashes them. Professor Taylor, author of the book *Brainwashing*,[477] discusses how the *timescale* involved in changing the minds of the brainwashed is notable in the process of brainwashing:

> Beliefs and personalities change continually as people grow. My beliefs about the existence of Santa Claus is now diametrically opposed to the belief I had when I was young. Was I brainwashed by the adult world? No. I simply grew up, gradually accepting along the way that there was no such person as Santa Claus. But consider my friend Keith's extremely strong belief in Christianity. If Keith were to vanish for a month and then reappear a fervent atheist I would suspect that someone had been exerting undue influence, whereas if I hadn't seen him for ten years I would be much more likely to attribute the lapse to natural causes. In other words, the shorter the time of transition—between old and new beliefs—the more likely that some form of brainwashing has occurred.[478]

Before 9/11, it may be safe to say that most Americans were not overly concerned about Afghanistan, Osama bin Laden, about various other people they were told about who lived in caves, or preemptive warfare (this is why the American Big Media calls 9/11 "the event that changed everything," or "the event that changed the world forever"). Before 9/11, Americans seemed unable to even muster enough interest to invade Rwanda in order to stop obvious cases of unfathomable genocide. But after 9/11 Americans were eager to invade a country (Iraq) which in no way was a proven threat to them. That is a rather sharp shift in feeling and thought. Since 9/11 was a false flag event, and since

---

[475] Tarpley 2006, 60.
[476] Tarpley 2006, 62.
[477] 2004, Oxford University Press.
[478] Taylor 2004, 11.

there are no terrorist threats, this shift in feeling and thought was based on a reality that did not exist. I am not sure how else to explain this shift in American belief and feeling about non-reality other than as an act of brainwashing that was caused by synthetic terrorism.

Following Professor Taylor's passage just given, it is important to note the timeframe involved in this change. I would guess that at 8 am EST 9-11-2001, the percentage of Americans in favor of going to war in Afghanistan (or Iraq) was so low that it could be disregarded. But I bet you that by the evening of 9-13-2001 (if not before), the percentage was perhaps over 90 percent (this number is based on polls you will see in chapter 6). This miniscule timeframe is important to Taylor's analysis of brainwashing, wherein key parts of the persona are inverted, such as going from pacifistic indifference toward Afghanistan to being riled up and ready to personally kill citizens of that country in only 30 or so short hours. Again, it seems that one of the very best descriptions to put to this phenomenon is to call it outright brainwashing (what other phenomenon in psychology would explain it?) generated by the synthetic terror event—which is of course a standard brainwashing technique for brainwashers. This threat-based synthetic terror is similar to the case explained in Browning's *Ordinary Men*, which is the story of how a few ordinary guys— "middle-aged family men of working- and lower-middle-class background from the city of Hamburg"[479]—were turned into Nazi mass-murderers of over one thousand women and children, including babies.

Another easily identifiable quality of the overall 9/11 experience in America, and also one of brainwashing, is discussed by Taylor:

> People who work with victims of cults, for example, often observe that the new beliefs [that are a product of being brainwashed] are associated with extremely emotional states. Challenging such a belief rationally is difficult if not impossible. The victim not only perceives any such challenge as hostile but refuses to engage in rational debate; the new beliefs are considered 'sacred' and beyond the reach of reason. This is something we all do to some extent, but the hostile resistance of an alleged brainwashing victim can be extreme. The content of the new beliefs can also strike outsiders as bizarre—though, … this is a matter of perspective.[480]

Proof of Foreknowledge of 9/11 by American Corporatists and the Visible Government Corporatists

A comment Defense Secretary Donald Rumsfeld made during a Christmas Eve address to U.S. troops in Baghdad has sparked new conspiracy theories about the terrorist attacks of September 11, 2001. In the speech, Rumsfeld made a passing reference to

---

[479] Page 1.
[480] Taylor 2001, 12.

United Airlines Flight 93, which crashed in Pennsylvania after passengers attempted to stop al Qaeda hijackers. But in his remarks, Rumsfeld referred to "the people who attacked the United States in New York, shot down the plane over Pennsylvania." A Pentagon spokesman insisted that Rumsfeld simply misspoke, but Internet conspiracy theorists seized on the reference to the plane having been shot down.

— Jamie McIntyre, *CNN Washington* [481]

So we know that the 9/11 Pentagon story is a lie. That means that the whole 9/11 story falls into such question, and that the whole 9/11 story is a hoax. This is also the case with the so-called "terrorists," the wars based on 9/11, the surveillance increases, the Patriot Act, and so on—all of it is a hoax, and part of a very sophisticated, elaborate secret government op.

It is rather easy to prove that US "visible government" corporatists, military, and many of the world's most powerful corporatists conspired to secretly plan the 9/11 false flag event. To prove this, only step-a Pentagon news footage is needed. In this section I will prove their foreknowledge, and in the next section I will prove their complicity.

Proof of Foreknowledge. The very first reports Americans heard through the national media from the Pentagon on September 11 were that a jetliner hit it, right from the moments after there was an explosion at the Pentagon on September 11, 2001. Donald Rumsfeld was working at the Pentagon at the time of the September 11th attack,[482] so there is no way he would not have had a better view of the scene—of the unbroken windows on the little-damaged wall—than anybody in the world. But Rumsfeld did not confirm these details; he did not report that there was no evidence of a jetliner, and in fact there was evidence to prove that there was no jetliner at all. Rather, he *confirmed the jetliner story*, even though it was impossible for him to have had any evidence of a jetliner being present, and even though one would think that of the evidence he *did* have could only have looked exactly like a missile blast, in the eyes of such a seasoned and "experienced" military leader. Here is a news report of Rumsfeld's account from the next day, and in the Associated Press:

> Rumsfeld said he "felt the shock of the airplane hitting the building," then went running down to the site where the aircraft hit. "They were bringing bodies out that had been injured, most of which were alive and moving but seriously injured," he said. The defense secretary then went

---

[481] "Pentagon: Rumsfeld Misspoke on Flight 93 Crash: Defense Secretary's Remark to Troops Fuels Conspiracy Theories," December 27, 2004, From Jamie McIntyre, CNN.

[482] This is well-known. See "Analysis/Special Report: Scene at the Pentagon Described," September 11, 2001, Steve Inskeep reporting, NPR. This was also discussed in, "Pentagon Attack Came Minutes after Rumsfeld Predicted: 'There will be another event'," Associated Press, by Robert Burns, September 12, 2001.

to the National Military Command Center in the lower floors of the Pentagon.[483]

The "Pentagon plane" was also confirmed throughout the day on September 11th, 2001 by others who either saw the pre-collapsed Pentagon, or could only have had all the top intelligence on the pre-collapsed Pentagon (via surveillance cameras, etc.). Consider Attorney General John Ashcroft's remarks to the nation on September 11, 2001 at 7:15 PM EST:

> Today America has experienced one of the greatest tragedies ever witnessed on our soil. These heinous acts of violence are an assault on the security of our nation. They are an assault on the security and the freedom of every American citizen. We will not tolerate such acts. We will expend every effort and devote all the necessary resources to bring the people responsible for these acts, these crimes, to justice... The following is a summary of the known facts surrounding today's incidents. American Airlines Flight 11 departed Boston for Los Angeles. Hijacked by suspects armed with knives, this plane crashed into the World Trade Center. United Airlines Flight 175 departed Boston for Los Angeles, was hijacked and crashed into the World Trade Center... American Airlines Flight 77 departed Washington-Dulles for Los Angeles, was hijacked and crashed into the Pentagon. United Airlines Flight 93 departed Newark for San Francisco, was hijacked and crashed in Shanksville, Pennsylvania.[484]

Rumsfeld and Ashcroft would have had better information on what happened at the Pentagon on September 11 than anybody in the world. And, it is impossible that they had any evidence of a plane crash at the Pentagon. There was no plane at the Pentagon, but Rumsfeld and Ashcroft claimed they knew the impossible and told the world that they knew there was one that crashed there. It is unclear what need they had in doing this. Did Rumsfeld and Ashcroft *need* to put forth the false story to the American people? They could have said, "there was no plane at the Pentagon, but rather a missile—apparently the terrorists had a missile that we believe was launched from a missile-launcher that was smuggled into the USA and into the Washington D. C. area." I don't think any conspiracy theory over the Pentagon would have likely arisen if they would have said that—and the Bush Administration *definitely was* concerned with subduing conspiracy theories. Two months after the 9/11 attacks, George W. Bush had the following to say at the UN Headquarters:

> We must speak the truth about terror. Let us never tolerate outrageous conspiracy theories concerning the attacks of September the 11th;

---

[483] "Pentagon Attack Came Minutes After Rumsfeld Predicted: 'There will be another event'," Associated Press, by Robert Burns, September 12, 2001.

[484] As of July 2006, this speech was located at http://www.whitehouse.gov/news/releases/2001/09/20010911-10.html.

malicious lies that attempt to shift the blame away from the terrorists, themselves, away from the guilty. To inflame ethnic hatred is to advance the cause of terror.[485]

And on the same day, in a national radio address from the Oval Office, Bush said this:

> There is no such thing as a good terrorist. Any government that tries to pick and choose its terrorist friends will be regarded by us as a supporter of terrorism. We expect nations to speak the truth about terror. They shouldn't encourage malicious lies and outrageous conspiracy theories concerning the attacks of September the 11th. No government should promote the propaganda of terrorists. We expect nations not to misuse the war against terror as an excuse to persecute ethnic and religious minorities in any country.

Bush makes this statement, as if there is no reason to doubt the government story about a plane at the Pentagon, which, we have seen is impossible—as clear as 1+1=2. We can see in these statements from November 2001 that there is a plan to make it known that anybody who merely points out a problem with the official Pentagon plane story is to be considered a helper of terrorists, and thus her/himself a terrorist—as if somebody who watches a Discovery Channel DVD and thinks to herself, "how can a plane not break windows?" is having terrorist thoughts. This campaign to make questioners identified as terrorists has continued since right after 9/11, and greatly increased in 2006. Here is another example, from November 11, 2005, from Tobyhanna, Pennsylvania, Bush also had similar condemnation for "conspiracy theories:"

> The radicals depend on front operations, such as corrupted charities, which direct money to terrorist activity. They are strengthened by those who aggressively fund the spread of radical, intolerant versions of Islam into unstable parts of the world. The militants are aided as well by elements of the Arab news media that incite hatred and anti-Semitism, that feed conspiracy theories, and speak of a so-called American "war on Islam"—with seldom a word about American action to protect Muslims in Afghanistan and Bosnia and Somalia and Kosovo and Kuwait and Iraq; or our generous assistance to Muslims recovering from natural disasters in places like Indonesia and Pakistan. (Applause.)

Notice that this is almost identical to the UN speech in 2001. Nearly this same paragraph was also uttered on October 28, 2005 from Norfolk, Virginia, and October 25, 2005, from Bolling Air Force Base.

And exhibiting propagandistic name-calling, and very specifically calling al-Qaeda to be "conspiracy theorists" (a term specifically used to describe any questioners of the Pentagon plane and other absurdities about 9/11), Stephen

---

[485] Bush said this on November 10, 2001.

Hadley, the National Security Advisor for the Bush Administration, said on October 31, 2005 from Los Angeles:

> The antidote to this radical vision is democracy, justice, and the freedom agenda. This agenda offers empowerment as an alternative to enslavement. It offers participation in place of exclusion. It offers the marketplace of ideas to counter the dark world of conspiracy theory. It offers individual rights and human dignity instead of violence and murder. Fundamentally, it means people participating in governing themselves, rather than being governed by others whom they never choose, never change, and never influence.[486]

Back to Ashcroft and Rumsfeld, imagine yourself being one of them: being one of the very first officials on the scene at the Pentagon just after the blast, and before step-b: before part of the Pentagon "collapsed." Imagine yourself on the scene, you are at the Pentagon site and you see smoke and fire coming out of a few windows at the Pentagon. If you are imagining yourself as Rumsfeld, you are (supposedly) in total shock at what is going on at the Pentagon, and you have almost surely seen two jetliners hit towers in New York and thus you might spontaneously suspect a jetliner had hit the Pentagon while you are running around in bewilderment and confusion on the Pentagon lawn. But being more precise, part of you really would have no idea what is going on at the Pentagon as you first went outside on the lawn, *if* this was indeed a surprise attack for you. So, you arrive at the lawn, and you see the outer wall in place, and windows in place, you see no substantial plane debris, you see fires *inside* the building, and you see firefighters right up near the building (so the building can't have been too hot). If you are in total shock and surprise, with no real idea what is going on, and if there have been no government officials and media personalities that have told you that a 60-ton jetliner traveling at 400 miles per hour, inches above the ground, did this damage, why would you think it was a plane? Why would Rumsfeld tell the world shortly after that there was a plane that caused the Pentagon damage? Answer: there is no reason to, and we can verify that his doing so only reveals a cover-up.

But imagine the impossible: imagine that somehow you just thought that the mess at the Pentagon was caused by a plane, even though there was no evidence of one. You saw the New York planes, and due to the shock of that, you mistakenly thought there was another plane at the Pentagon. This seems impossible given the description of the Pentagon wall before its collapse, and I am not sure how anybody would ever imagine the wall to have been hit by a jetliner, but just imagine it for the sake of discussion.

As the day (September 11) unfolds, and you sort through the mess at the Pentagon, looking at media coverage and other photos, reviewing the

---

[486] As of July 2006, this speech this was located at http://www.whitehouse.gov/news/releases/2005/10/20051031-4.html.

surveillance cameras at the Pentagon, inspecting the crash scene, you would probably start to second guess your initial hysterical and irrational belief that a plane was responsible. Quite likely, if you were Rumsfeld, you would know by the time of Ashcroft's statements at 7:15, to tell Ashcroft that you don't have any evidence there was a plane at the Pentagon, and he should tell the American people as much. Or certainly by the next day or in the next week you would come to that conclusion, if you were Rumsfeld. *Certainly* by the time that President Bush made his tribute to the Pentagon mid-day on October 11, 2001, where he again confirmed the Pentagon jetliner story while also discussing the children killed in the attack, you would have come to your senses and realized there was no plane. Here are those confirming words:

> We have come here to pay our respects to 125 men and women who died in the service of America. We also remember 64 passengers on a hijacked plane; those men and women, boys and girls who fell into the hands of evildoers, and also died here exactly one month ago.

If 9/11 was a truly surprise attack, and if there was nothing to cover up, then if you were Rumsfeld, *why wouldn't you* come to understand that there was no plane at the Pentagon, and why wouldn't you just tell Americans that? Why not merely revise your position? Instead of demanding the plane theory, if you are Rumsfeld, you (and Bush, Ashcroft, etc.) could say, "we first thought it was a plane, but it was not, it was a missile, not a plane, we now know, and we don't know what happened to the hijacked plane." If anybody knew and saw the empirical data of the crash scene, it would be the people just mentioned. So there is absolutely no reason why they would keep it concealed. If they were as surprised and unaware of the attacks as anybody else, and since there would be no reason to *withhold* that information.

It is impossible that Rumsfeld and others that I will mention shortly, did not have foreknowledge of 9/11. When you first get on the scene at the Pentagon, the only conceivable reason to imagine that you should suddenly have "jetliner" flash through your mind as you are there on the Pentagon lawn, as stated above, would be because you likely just saw two planes hit WTCs 1 and 2 in New York on television. But if you think about this assumption a bit deeper, you will see that it is an impossible state of affairs. What, precisely, did you just see on television in New York City? What you saw were jetliners, but you saw them make massive 100+ foot holes in the trade centers, with *major* damage all around the boundaries of the hole. But at the Pentagon you have the *inverse* of that situation in New York City: very small hole, only smoke discoloration around it (not even damaged windows). Who in their right mind would think that these situations, which are the inverse of the other, are the same situation? That is like saying that a square is a circle, which makes as much sense as maintaining that a 15 foot hole is identical to a 120 foot hole. These scenarios are not possible, and if one is truly in shock over the attacks, they could not have come to the conclusion that a wall with little more smoke discoloration and a 15-20 foot hole just got hit by a 400 mile per hour 60-ton 125 foot wide jet liner in anything resembling the WTCs. Being in total shock in the surprise attack when you are on the scene at the Pentagon, you could not see a 15-20 foot hole and have it flash through your mind: "ah ha! That could only be caused by a 125 foot jetliner! I must tell the American people this news in a press conference in one hour!"

There is no reason that the persons on the crime scene would not have changed their story unless they were concealing it. As we will next see, this is a proof that those purporting the story from 9/11 were intentionally putting forth a false story, and thus can only be considered complicit for that reason. This is because they would have had no reason to hide the real story, and thus that lack of reasoning verifies their preparedness for a cover-up. With no plane for evidence, no significantly damaged Pentagon wall (before it collapsed), such simple and irrefutable empirical evidence could have only been known to government officials (Ashcroft, Bush, Rumsfeld, and any other government official carefully inspecting the details and data regarding the Pentagon damage and/or video footage). If they were in a state of shock over this attack, why did they all create a different story? The simple evidence that they would have had, compared to their behavior and actions in spreading a false story, only leads to one simple result: they were trying to prevent Americans from knowing what happened.

As of early July 2006, there is huge controversy swirling in America over the inconsistencies of the 9/11 attacks. This movement has been growing incredibly fast. The Bush Administration is clearly interested in not having conspiracy theories spread, as the above quotes mention, and as some of the documents I mentioned elsewhere in this book show (such as the website discussed in a chapter above that involves all the personal testimonies of eyewitnesses of the Pentagon crash).[487] Also, never have the above people merely said, "yeah, it's

---

[487] As of July 13, 2006, that page was still online at this location: http://usinfo.state.gov/media/Archive/2005/Jun/28-581634.html. Here is an excerpt (notice how explicitly the article is trying to focus specifically at the "obvious flaws" of the so-called conspiracy theories).
Did a Plane Hit the Pentagon?
French Conspiracy Theorist Claims It Did Not
In 2002, French conspiracy theorist Thierry Meyssan wrote a book suggesting that a cruise missile instead of a plane hit the Pentagon on September 11, and the planes that hit the World Trade Center towers had not been hijacked but were piloted by remote control. Mr. Meyssan believes both attacks were masterminded not by al Qaeda, but "from inside the American state apparatus." (*9/11: The Big Lie*, p. 139.)
Mr. Meyssan's claims suffer from numerous obvious flaws.
With regard to the Pentagon attacks, Mr. Meyssan ignores or dismisses the facts that:
• many eyewitnesses saw a plane crash into the Pentagon

impossible that there was a plane at the Pentagon; it's as clear as day, the terrorists used a missile ." But that never happened, and as we just saw, there was a deliberate cover-up.

Osama Bin Laden is a Corporatist, and the "Terror Economy" is a Trillion Dollar Corporatist Economy.

Loretta Napoleoni, in her incredible book, *Terror Incorporated: Tracing the Dollars Behind the Terror Networks*,[488] has traced the way that Islamic terrorism is funded, and she has found that it is a trillion dollar industry (with a bigger GDP than Great Britain), which is funded by Saudi, American, and other corporatists, and has become an interfused but invisible part of the visible American and world corporatist economy. Even Osama bin Laden is a corporatist, where his company's products are imported to the United States, and where ordinary Americans have contributed to filling him with riches. (So I guess he is not hiding in the mountains between Afghanistan and Pakistan.[489]) Al-Qaeda is partnered with the United States corporatists. It is this funding, via American, Saudi, and other bankers and corporatists, that gave rise to al-Qaeda.

- the passenger and crew remains from American Airlines flight 77 were recovered at the Pentagon crash site
- eyewitness reports and photographs show plane debris at the Pentagon crash site
- passengers on American Airlines flight 77 made phone calls, reporting their aircraft had been hijacked
- senior Al Qaeda leaders have admitted they conducted the September 11 attacks…

Numerous Eyewitness Accounts

Mr. Meyssan suggests that a cruise missile with a depleted uranium warhead, not a plane, struck the Pentagon on September 11. But he never traveled to the United States to conduct research or interviewed any of the many eyewitnesses to the attack on the Pentagon. He ignores or dismisses the many eyewitness accounts -- some of which specifically identified the plane as having American Airlines markings, as a Boeing 757, and as a plane with passengers onboard, visible through windows. On May 16, 2006, the Pentagon released videotape footage showing the plane hitting the Pentagon. Excerpts from some of the eyewitness accounts are included at the end of this document.

Of course, the video they refer to did not show a plane, and all this is personal testimony. This document goes on to explain how remains of two passengers were found, which is a humorous part of the "official view:" the plane vaporized at a liquid state due to the impact, but there were remains of two passengers found.

[488] 2005, New York: Seven Stories Press.

[489] I give this comment in humor, but it is related to an important point about this supposed hiding. If Americans were more informed, they would know that this sort of hiding in the mountains is impossible, because the HAARP technology of the United States military can allow American physicists to see through mountains, and thus would have been able to catch anybody hiding in the mountains. But of course this was all a ruse, and thus no such HAARP was sought out.

Summary. Now consider a summary of what has been said so far, and in order to see how this proof works:

i.   Al-Qaeda and world corporatism are interlinked to such a degree that they are indistinguishable.

ii.   There is irrefutable proof that there was no plane at the Pentagon

iii.   The "Pentagon plane" theory and hoax was started and perpetrated by the highest Pentagon and US government officials,

iv.   The "Pentagon plane" theory was actually a cover-up.

v.   As of early 2007, there is a raging controversy in America over whether or not the US government is secretly responsible for 9/11

vi.   The controversy described in point iv is primarily aimed at maintaining that the government (Bush, military) is behind 9/11.

vii.   Bush and others want to clearly discredit so-called conspiracy theories

viii.   Bush and others *absolutely will not* discuss point-i above (no plane at Pentagon) in order to quite simply clear their name; they will not show pictures of the Pentagon plane, and they will not tell us how step-a and step-b of the Pentagon could have been caused by Flight 77 hitting the Pentagon

Now ask yourself: If these people listed above (Bush, Ashcroft, etc.) were *uninvolved* in 9/11, and *unaware* of the 9/11 attacks before they happened, and they were just as shocked as everyone else, why would point vii exist? If they are truly innocent, they would merely take the steps needed to show this, and to discredit the "conspiracy theorists" with counter evidence. *Why wouldn't they simply empathize with the 9/11 skeptics and call for an investigation over the obvious anomalies of the Pentagon plane story.* Instead, they remain absolutely silent on the issues regarding the Pentagon on 9/11. Why wouldn't they merely acknowledge the anomalies? If there is nothing to hide, why not discuss it with the people who are legitimately concerned? Instead: *silence.* Why not release some of the copious amounts of Pentagon surveillance footage. Without a doubt, this would put an end to the issue. As the narrator in the DVD documentary *Loose Change* (second edition) asks: "If the government is innocent, why not just release a few tapes?"

I assert that it is *impossible* for an absolutely innocent and blameless group of people that are in power to take blame for the crime of the century and just remain absolutely silent on the issue, instead calling the accusers terrorists, when they could merely show the world a simple videotape and prove their innocence—*if* there really was a Pentagon plane, and *if* they really are in fact innocent.

Imagine the CEO of an ultra-massive corporation, called the Innocent Corporation. Now imagine that at Innocent Corporation, a stunning postal-style shooting and attack of some sort occurs, but one which is with the "shock and awe" of a 9/11, perhaps on a miniature scale, and such that it truly shocks the employees to their bones for years, putting fear and horror in their hearts. Now imagine that the CEO of Innocent Corporation truly has nothing to do with this, had no prior knowledge, and was just as shaken and horrified as anybody else at the Innocent Corporation. Now imagine that through the years the employees of Innocent Corporation talk and think about the incredible atrocity, but interestingly, a few years after it happened, about 30-40 percent of the workforce started very aggressively bringing forth what they said was irrefutable evidence that there were some serious anomalies to do with the story about the shooting, and which showed what everyone thought happened on that day did not, and it was not a spontaneous event, but one pre-planned and orchestrated by the CEO of Innocent Corporation. Imagine that the CEO has the ability to very simply show and prove his/her innocence with videotape evidence. Why wouldn't she/he? Imagine that 30-40 percent quite vocally, confidently, and convincingly begin accusing the CEO of ultimately being behind the the attack. Would the accused get nervous, and begin defensively saying, "don't listen to the rumors, the people spreading them are evil," when the CEO can dispel them instantly by presenting the proof of innocence?

My claim is that this is an impossible state of affairs. Of course, in this example, the CEO is a member of the government who has the best information on the circumstances of what happened on 9/11 at the Pentagon (Bush, Rumsfeld, Wolfowitz, Cheney, Mueller, Ashcroft, many members of the CIA, NSA, military, and Pentagon, among others), the vocal 30-40 percent are the so-called "conspiracy theorists," the postal shooting was 9/11, including the Pentagon attack, and proof of the innocence of Innocent Corporations CEOs is something like one of the surveillance cameras at the Pentagon that filmed the explosion at the Pentagon on 9/11. *This is an impossible state of affairs because it is not in the realm of possible human behavior for a truly innocent person, who can prove her/his innocence with the simplest of simplicity, to take misplaced blame for the most demented horrific crime her/his workforce can imagine and not say a word in response, and instead merely bad-mouth the vocal 30-40 percent when he/she gets the chance to others.* As is described elsewhere in this book, humans have predictable behavior. But what has just been described is not in the domain of the predictable; it is not real. This account proves that the government was ready to cover-up 9/11, and thus they knew about it beforehand, they allowed it to happen since they made no effort to stop it, and thus are complicit in their allowance of the attack.

What I have described in this section proves that the government members I have mentioned here were aware that there was not a Pentagon plane right from the moment that the 9/11 attacks happened, but lied to the American public right from that moment also. This proof is simple, and it shows that anybody who was an originator of the story about the Pentagon on 9/11 who is also a person that could only have the highest level of knowledge of the state of affairs at the Pentagon, *can be proven to have known about the 9/11 attacks before they occurred*, and can be proven to have had a synchronized cover-up plan in place.

Who are the Perpetrators of 9/11? So who are these people? They would be any of the people in the government administration where

- They had top knowledge and intelligence information of all the specific events that occurred at the Pentagon on 9/11
- They had the political position where *they* were the folks on television telling the world what happened (e.g., plane hit the Pentagon), setting the false agenda for the world,
- They were on television telling a false story about a plane at the Pentagon. Such people can be proven to be involved in the cover-up: aware beforehand, and voracious in readiness to carry out a cover-up with a false agenda.

An example of such a person is, of course, Robert Mueller, head of the FBI:

I want to start by saying that the men and women of the FBI join the nation in expressing our deep sympathies for the victims of these horrific tragedies and their families. And we—all of us in the FBI— pledge to those directly affected by these attacks that we will leave no stone unturned in our quest to help find those responsible and to bring those individuals to justice. Now let me turn, if I could, for a moment to the effort that we have undertaken at the FBI to investigate these tragedies. Early after the planes started to fall yesterday, as soon as we heard that there was a particular city that was either a city of origin for a flight or a city, such as New York, where a flight went in, we established command posts. We have at those command posts, and at a number of offices around the country where there are leads, more than 4,000 special agents who are assigned to assist this investigation; 4,000 special agents and 3,000 support personnel. We have over 400 of our laboratory personnel deployed at the crime scenes in New York City, south of Johnstown in Pennsylvania, and at the Pentagon.[490]

And here's a press conference with Colin Powell on September 12, 2001 discussing the "Pentagon plane:"

Sec. POWELL: With who? Oh, yeah. I've already had some conversations with Saudis and I'll be doing more this afternoon. We're still changing time zones as I catch up on my phone calls. Thank you.
ALAN: Thank you.
Unidentified Reporter #10: Secretary Powell, ABC News is reporting...
CONAN: Secretary of State Powell halfway off the stage before being called back by this question. Now he's listening to another one.

---

[490] Associated Press, September 11, 2001

Unidentified Reporter #10: ...the target was not the Pentagon, but, in fact, the White House and that Air Force One was also a target.

Sec. POWELL: Ari said that?

Unidentified Reporter #10: Yes. Have you heard that?

Sec. POWELL: Yes.

Unidentified Reporter #10: Could you give us more detail about that, what you've heard...

Sec. POWELL: No.

Unidentified Reporter #10: ...about the intended target ... (unintelligible)?

Sec. POWELL: No. I don't have anything to go beyond what Ari said, and I really need to yield that part of it to intelligence and law enforcement agencies. Thank you.[491]

Proof of Complicity in 9/11
by American Corporatists

The "war on terrorism" is a fabrication.

—Professor Michel Chossudovsky, University of Ottawa

In politics, nothing happens by accident. If it happens, you can bet it was planned that way.

—Franklin D. Roosevelt

Imagine a world where people fear that their opinions cannot be expressed freely, leaders are not held accountable for their deceptions, and perpetual war is waged against an unseen enemy; a world where Ignorance is Strength, Freedom is Slavery, War is Peace, and Big Brother is watching you. George Orwell created this world more than half a century ago in his novel *1984*, but his text continues to raise provocative questions in today's society.

—Theater poster for a performance of George Orwell's *1984*[492]

"These terrorist organizations burrow in with the population, ... They burrow and hide."

—Condoleeza Rice[493]

In the last section, I proved that top elements of the US government contributed to a cover-up of 9/11. In this section, I will prove that they secretly carried it out.

Everyone is Watching "The Orwell Channel." In Michael Redford's film, *1984*, based on George Orwell's book, we find the citizens are barraged by a constant stream of media information about a war and enemy that is nearby but is never directly seen, and their existence can never be truly verified. There are

---

[491] NPR, September 12, 2001.

[492] Directed by Tim Robbins, Friday & Saturday, November 3 & 4, 2006, at the Loeb Theater, on the campus of Purdue University, West Lafayette, Indiana.

[493] August 1, 2006, 11:04 pm EST, on the Fox News Channel's "The Factor."

endless media stories about the enemy, and we hear bombs going off at many points in the film, but we never *see* "the enemy," and thus we never have any direct verification other than from the testimony of the state-sponsored media information that the enemy really exists. I see no reason why this is any different from the stories of the cave-dwelling, mountain-dwelling al-Qaeda Network that Americans have heard since 9/11: the terrorists are an invisible group that Americans literally never see with their own eyes. The only verification that Americans have that there are any terrorists is through the corporate-owned, war-minded media (many media corporations also own much of the U.S. military) and through the paid-off politicians and psychopathological military commanders.[494]

The CIA Employee Named *Osama bin Laden*. Americans are fooled into believing they should perpetually be afraid of "the terrorists," but according to Alex Jones,[495] more Americans are killed by swimming pools and lightning every year than terrorists. It is easy to verify that Osama bin Laden, the head terrorist of the world (as the US visible government has told us he is), is actually an employee of the CIA, and a leader of a corporatist PMF. It is not even controversial that US military forces had interaction with bin Laden during the Russian war with Afghanistan a few decades ago, and news papers widely reported that bin Laden was a CIA employee throughout the 1980s and 1990s.[496] But much more importantly, in the Bush Sr. CIA in 1976 and 1977, a

---

[494] For example, the head of the most secretive military agencies in the United States, Lieutenant-General William G. Boykin, head of United States Intelligence, preaching in his uniform at a large church, explained that "it's not Osama bin Laden, it's not what you can see. It's the enemy in the spiritual realm." (You can see Boykin say this in Karel 2004) "Spiritual war," "spiritual warriors," and "spiritual terrorists" are one step "more invisible" than clandestine and invisible cave-dwelling terrorists. The New York Times has published an opinion on the ministry of the head of US Intelligence.

> The first reports sounded like an over-the-top satire of the Bush Pentagon: the deputy secretary of defense for intelligence - the ranking general charged with the hunt for Osama bin Laden - was parading in uniform to Christian pulpits, preaching that God had put George Bush in the White House and that Islamic terrorists will only be defeated "if we come at them in the name of Jesus." But now a Pentagon inquiry has concluded that Lt. Gen. William Boykin did indeed preach his grossly offensive gospel at 23 churches, pronouncing Satan the mastermind of the terrorists because "he wants to destroy us as a Christian army." ("Holding the Pentagon Accountable: For Religious Bigotry," August 26, 2004, New York Times.)

[495] From the Alex Jones Show, January 5, 2007.

[496] For example, consider this MSNBC article.

> As his unclassified CIA biography states, bin Laden left Saudi Arabia to fight the Soviet army in Afghanistan after Moscow's invasion in 1979. By 1984, he was running a front organization known as Maktab al-Khidamar—the MAK—which funneled money, arms and fighters from the outside world into the Afghan war. What the CIA bio conveniently fails to specify (in its unclassified form, at least) is that the MAK was nurtured by Pakistan's state security services, the Inter-Services

plan emerged to usurp Middle Eastern oil—where the aforementioned fabricated scarcity of the monopolized oil would be used to initiate wars and boost profits: to carry out business. Some say that the plan was first called "The Carter Plan," but by the late 1980s it was called "The Wolfowitz Plan," and by 2000, it was called "Rebuilding America's Defenses."[497] The "Wolfowitz Doctrine," and its later version, PNAC's "Rebuilding America's Defenses," was the "policy bible for George W. Bush,"[498] and was principally about imperialism and controlling the artificially scarce oil.[499]

What is notable about PNAC (2000) is that it is maintained that on page 51 it says that a new Pearl Harbor type of event is needed to rally the nation for the PNAC war-goals (invade various several Middle Eastern countries, starting with Afghanistan and Iraq), much like FDR permitted, if not help to plan, Pearl Harbor. Here is the passage:

> Further, the process of transformation, even if it brings revolutionary change, is likely to be a long one, absent some catastrophic and catalyzing event—like a new Pearl Harbor.

Immediately after 9/11, 9/11 was called by the Big Media "the new Pearl Harbor." Tarpley discusses this use of the "Pearl Harbor" statement:

> An even more explicit call for US world domination came from the Project for a New American Century, a neocon movement that provided most of the top officials for the Bush 43 administration. After discussing their imperialist plans, the PNAC authors, led by chickenhawk William Kristol, focused on the way of duping the American people into supporting the raft of new foreign adventures: "…the process of transformation is likely to be a long one, absent some catastrophic and catalyzing event—like a new Pearl Harbor." (PNAC, September 2000) It is in this restless mood, desirous of a new global conflict to pre-empt the emergence of challenges to a new Anglo-American world order, viewing the democratic system as unresponsive to their elitist

---

Intelligence agency, or ISI, the CIA's primary conduit for conducting the covert war against Moscow's occupation… So bin Laden, along with a small group of Islamic militants from Egypt, Pakistan, Lebanon, Syria and Palestinian refugee camps all over the Middle East, became the "reliable" partners of the CIA in its war against Moscow. ("Bin Laden Comes Home to Roost: His CIA Ties are Only the Beginning of a Woeful Story," by Michael Moran, August 24, 1998, MSNBC.)

There are too many other examples to list, such as, "CIA-Made Terrorists Source of Saudi Bombings?," by Nicholas Goldberg, July 10, 1996, The Seattle Times, page A3.

[497] See PNAC 2000 in the bibliography.

[498] Felton 2005, 272.

[499] Felton (2005, chapter 13, esp. p. 272) confirms that the PNAC "Rebuilding America's Defenses" document was principally about oil (in addition to wild imperialism). This is a critically important issue given what will be said in another bulleted point about the end of Saudi oil.

warmongering, and eager for the assistance that a spectacular external attack would bring, that the roots of 9/11 are to be sought.[500]

Now consider that Bush Sr. is well-known to excel in, and relish in, fabricating intricately and lavishly staged events and "wars" in locked secrecy, such as the "war on drugs" which was created by the CIA during the time Bush headed the CIA,[501] to give just one example. Through its history before 1982, one of the primary functions of the CIA had been to set up terrorist groups all over the world that are to appear to be autonomous and which created havoc around the world for corporatistic US interests.[502] A relevant example is SAVAK and the Shah in Iran from 1953-1979.[503] The CIA was well-known to work with certain peoples of the Middle East to create Middle Eastern terrorist groups that operated from the 1950s to the 1970s (e.g., SAVAK in Iran) and had the function of doing little more than create staged terrorist attacks. SAVAK was installed during the same era as the US-installed puppet government was installed in Iran, with the Shah of Iran (Mohammad Reza Pahlavi), in the early 1950s. SAVAK and the Shah of Iran were set up by the CIA in Iran in the 1950s as a result of long planning beforehand. Iranians worked for the CIA and specifically pretended to be communists to harass Iranian religious leaders and commit bombings. *So the CIA's task was specifically to set up a terror group that looked like something it was not.*[504] Zbigniew Brzezinski wrote *The Grand Chessboard*[505] in 1997. He was National Security Advisor to Jimmy Carter, CFR member, trustee and founder of the trilateral commission (a principal New World Order organization), worked under Reagan conducting intelligence work, and co-chairman of the Bush National Security Task Force. His book spelled out a plan similar to PNAC (2000), where he wrote on page 211 that there needs to be a widely perceived

---

[500] Tarpley 2006, 135.

[501] See Professor Peter Dale Scott's detailed account of this in his 2003 book. Tarpley 1992 also gives an excellent account of the Bush Sr. shenanigans. Felton 2005 also involves useful information in various places on much of the staged wars and conflicts. Fabricating wars and enemies of any sort is one of the principal ways that wars can exist. And creating enemies and wars is the principal task of the military industrial complex.

[502] This is widely documented, and even has a CIA name—*Operation Gladio*—referring to all the operations as a whole. A good summary of this found in Jones (2006).

[503] For a good summary of this operation, see the *New York Times* story on this on the web (this story includes book references that can be sought): http://www.nytimes.com/library/world/mideast/041600iran-cia-index.html

[504] Relevant to this claim, it is interesting to note that Leuren Moret, who is an expert researcher on various contemporary warfare issues (especially DU), said on the Rense Radio Show (www.rense.com) on November 14, 2006 that the CIA's principal job is to get the American people to hate certain peoples in the world so much that they will limitlessly spend their money and wealth on war.

[505] Brzezinski 1998.

direct external threat needed to carry out these goals and motions towards world government.

So the plan is pretty clear: the CIA is carrying out business as usual with Osama bin Laden and bin Laden's al-Qaeda network. In the 1970s and 1980s, in seeking a fabricated/staged threat in the form of the latest CIA terror group, Bush Sr. sought a leader for this group, and he chose his close friend's son, Osama bin Laden, who years later would pose as a terrorist that would give the United States supposed reason to invade more than one country, and to set up "the threat of terrorism." The group of imperialists in control of the US government and US corporatism have always sought to rule by persuasion rather than by force,[506] so they would have needed a persuading factor to rile up Americans to support their imperialism. al-Qaeda served this purpose, and if you combine this last point about the rule by persuasion with all I have just written about Osama bin Laden, it is apparently proven that Osama bin Laden is a CIA employee, and the entire global war on terrorism is a fabrication, to put it in the way that Professor Chossudovsky does.

It is important to note that PNAC is one of the most powerful think tanks in the world if not the most powerful one of all. It consists of many government corporatists (Cheney, Jeb Bush, Rumsfeld, Steve Forbes, etc.) and their top agents, such as former CIA heads. PNAC exists because of corporatist funding, and it is dictated by corporatist interests, and thus it is a corporatist instrument. Out of this corporatist instrument emerges the plan to implement world government via fabricated global terror networks, and it can be verified that PNAC is behind 9/11 also (since PNAC's members consist of those people that were proven to be behind 9/11 in the previous section), then the corporatists are also behind 9/11. This is just the beginning of the abysmal agony of what the horror corporatist state is capable of, as we will see.

Invisible Cave-Dwelling Warriors

In the remaining two subsections of this section on false flag terrorism, I will discuss two critical issues in how this operation is carried out: anonymity and invisibility of the synthetic terrorists.

---

[506] In an indirect tyranny (a tyranny of persuasion), the corporatists/government does not want the citizens to know their horrific nature and will disguise themselves as "good guys," and shape the world so that citizens are forced to choose to do what the corporatists want (e.g., if the corporatists want to invade Afghanistan, they will create a false flag event that riles up the American people to do so). In a direct tyranny (a tyranny of force and intimidation), they reveal their real nature and their real horrific motives, and the populace is horrified, and the corporatists/government rules by force—by the gun.

According to George W. Bush,[507] "We're at war with these folks, but they don't wear uniforms." After 9/11, it is safe to say that the main news story that has persisted for the half-decade since is the story of the terrorists that lurk in the shadows, that nobody ever sees, but which could be living next door to you, and they are out there, ready to strike. They are always out there, planning to kill or torture us, but we never see them, because they are remarkably secret, and we are expected to believe that they are, so secret that we can't even catch some guys (Osama and friends) walking around in the mountains, even though they are apparently communicating wirelessly on laptops, which is trackable. Consider these passages from George W. Bush from the Capital on September 20, 2001, about "the terrorists," and when he was first setting the propaganda about Osama bin Laden into the minds of a scared American citizenry:

> The terrorists practice a fringe form of Islamic extremism that has been rejected by Muslim scholars and the vast majority of Muslim clerics—a fringe movement that perverts the peaceful teachings of Islam. The terrorists' directive commands them to kill Christians and Jews, to kill all Americans, and make no distinction among military and civilians, including women and children. This group and its leader—a person named Osama bin Laden—are linked to many other organizations in different countries, including the Egyptian Islamic Jihad and the Islamic Movement of Uzbekistan. There are thousands of these terrorists in more than 60 countries. They are recruited from their own nations and neighborhoods and brought to camps in places like Afghanistan, where they are trained in the tactics of terror. They are sent back to their homes or sent to hide in countries around the world to plot evil and destruction... These terrorists kill not merely to end lives, but to disrupt and end a way of life. With every atrocity, they hope that America grows fearful, retreating from the world and forsaking our friends. They stand against us, because we stand in their way.

---

[507] July 6, 2006, speaking on *CNN's* "Larry King Live."

There is little, if any, searching for "Osama bin Laden," now, years after 9/11. Homeland Security is fully focused on monitoring ordinary Americans, instead of "Osama." "Osama bin Laden" allegedly lives in the mountains, and uses a laptop.

And consider this passage from George W. Bush's 2006 State of the Union Address, on January 31, 2006:

> No one can deny the success of freedom, but some men rage and fight against it. And one of the main sources of reaction and opposition is radical Islam—the perversion by a few of a noble faith into an ideology of terror and death. Terrorists like bin Laden are serious about mass murder—and all of us must take their declared intentions seriously. They seek to impose a heartless system of totalitarian control throughout the Middle East, and arm themselves with weapons of mass murder. Their aim is to seize power in Iraq, and use it as a safe haven to launch attacks against America and the world. Lacking the military strength to challenge us directly, the terrorists have chosen the weapon of fear. When they murder children at a school in Beslan, or blow up commuters in London, or behead a bound captive, the terrorists hope these horrors will break our will, allowing the violent to inherit the Earth. But they have miscalculated: We love our freedom, and we will fight to keep it. (Applause.)

The similarity between the Orwellian war in *1984* and the "war on terror" appear to be considerable. The passages from Bush describe al-Qaeda as having many Orwellian properties: they are invisible (cannot be seen except on television), they want to kill children, they are like animals, and they are all around and could strike at any moment. Both are created in, and exist in, the

American media. There are no enemies that we can see with our eyes, just endless stories every day in the media about the terrorists: about the animal-like cave-people[508] that want to slaughter Americans.

As with the United States, through media, in the Orwellian world, citizens are made to hate or fear people they have never met, due to being constantly told how much these people want to rip them to pieces. 9/11 was the start of a new era of news media in the USA, as if the entire news media became a fabricated Orwellian information service: what could be called, "The Orwell Channel."

Nothing Can Be Verified in the Terror War

Above I have written that the Orwellian warriors (al-Qaeda) are never directly visible, and we cannot verify their existence. But this is true for virtually all issues in the fabricated global war on terrorism. The terror networks, the war on terrorism, Osama, al-Qaeda, and the rest, only exist in the televisual media, and if suddenly for some reason Americans en masse stopped watching television and avoided all corporatist-controlled news media (which is all media except for parts of the internet), they would soon forget that there is this spooky-invisible Orwellian-style enemy "out there", somewhere.

What I have just written can be summed up and better understood by considering the following diagram, which shows the direction of information in for "The Orwell Channel," and how the sequence of events are reported to and reach the American person's mind. The diagram shows that all terrorist events (step-A in the diagram) are *not verifiable*: they are beyond the sight and senses of Americans or really anybody at all:

---

[508] What I mean by "cave-people" is the somewhat Orwellian personification of Al-Qaeda as living like animals. Consider this statement from Ontario, California by Bush shortly after 9/11 on January 5, 2002:

> We're now in a dangerous phase of the first front in the war against terror. Because of the terrain in Afghanistan and because there's still hostile elements, we're pursuing our objective cave by cave. You see, the people that tend to send young, innocent boys to their death in the name of Allah want to save their own skins by hiding in caves. And I've told the world, just like I've told our military, we will do whatever it takes to bring them to justice. (Applause.)

A

Threatening ultra-secretive terrorists or terror groups/cells carry out threats, attacks, etc.

(It is standard that this information in step-A is full of conflicts and contradictions and absurdities.)

B

Detector of, reporter of, and source of information about, A.

(This will often be small FBI, CIA, or other military groups, an embedded reporter, or something like this. Usually this step-B person is *anonymous*)

C

Government press conferences or announcements, or media performances, announcing B's information that was given to C

D

The rest of the news media picks up on C and reports it

E

Information from D, about A, enters the minds of virtually all Americans

This is the way that Americans typically are led to believe that news information regarding terrorism is conveyed and revealed. Nearly all of the details about step A, or even about the existence of A, is only known to B, and that A even happened can only be verified by B. For example, we are told that on 9/11, hijackers took over planes, but that information is given to Americans at step-D, and it involves step-A information that is only given at step B, and thus the only evidence for it is the testimony of the step-B persons (in this case, Rumsfeld, Cheney, Bush, etc.). In other words, step-A information is such that not a person on the planet knows about A except the ultra-secretive, clandestine and often even anonymous As and Bs. Americans receive the information (which is box E in the diagram) due to C or D, and never have awareness of or evidence of information from B level. The A and B events are literally invisible to Americans, or when they are not, they are shrouded in lies and mystery (e.g., Americans see damage at the Pentagon, but the reasons that are given for the damage are not the real reasons). Americans only see the testimonies and reports given at the D and C levels. Step-A news is not a secret.

Consider the words of attorney general Gonzales from a well-known speech he gave in August 2006 shortly after the fanfare of the August 10, 2006 staged terror bust:

> In a few weeks, we will mark the five-year anniversary of those attacks. During this period, our way of life has changed so much. Our children and grandchildren will grow up in a world much different than ours. With advances in technology, such as the Internet, change is natural, of course, among successive generations. But the most dramatic change is the nature of the enemy our country today faces—*a stateless enemy sometimes hidden and nurtured here in our neighborhoods,* taking advantage of the very laws they mock with their killing and destruction, as a shield from detection and prosecution.[509] (Emphasis added)

In a quote where he is discussing his P-R-S thesis that I quoted a passage about above, David Icke also touches on this issue where the information humans believe about their world is routinely not verifiable:

> The media play their part to perfection in [the] "P-R-S" scenarios. At ownership level, people like Conrad Black at the Hollinger Group know what is going on and use their news papers to pursue the Illuminati agenda. The key editors they appoint might know something of it and also certain columnists. But most of the journalists will have no idea. The editor is always there to block anything they write that is against the interests of the Illuminati and if they insist on pursuing an unwelcome story they find themselves looking for another job. And, anyway, most of what journalists write comes from official (Illuminati) sources. In the immediate aftermath of a major event such as Oklahoma, where are the

---

[509] "Text of Attorney General's Speech," *Pittsburgh Post-Gazette*, August 16, 2006

reporters getting their information? From official sources. We are told that White House sources say this and FBI sources say that. This is how the Illuminati transmit through the media the version of these events that they wish the public to believe. These reports are blazed across the front page of newspapers and the top of radio and television news bulletins throughout the world and what they say becomes the "norm".[510]

The corporatist news media admits that their coverage is of a step-A step nature. Just to give one example, in response to the alleged 8/10/2006 UK jetliner bomb bust, at 2.34 am,[511] it was admitted on the *Fox News Channel,* on the show *NewsWatch,* August 14, 2006, that with these terror stories, our only information is from the government, and the terror stories only have to do with what the government knows. John Flannary, a judicial worker in the USA, said at 2:54 pm on August 19, 2005 on *The Fox News Channel* that there is no evidence that has been presented as to the guilt of the people who had been by that time held for many days for their alleged plot to blow up around a dozen planes.

Planned, Fabricated War: The Military-Industrial Complex and Globalization

Everything that has transpired has done so according to my design.
—The Emperor, *Star Wars: Return of the Jedi*

"If you study history, what you learn is that wars are always accompanied by lies. Wars are always accompanied deceptions."
—Howard Zinn[512]

"[T]his is a war [in Iraq] that is benefiting major companies with billions of dollars."
—Osama bin Laden, April 2004, referring to Halliburton

The last corporatist instrument I will discuss is *war.* Along with false flag terror, war is a key corporatist tool. By this point in this chapter, we can see that the corporatist secretly plans wars, terrorism, poverty, and various other forms of horror in order to control people, and in order to torture and/or kill countless people, but while doing so, making a lot of money. There are many ways this is done: creating addictions and illnesses that the citizenry will dump their money into, creating disasters or wars that the public must be forced into pouring their souls, children, and money into, and so on. With warfare, the world (resources, people, ideologies, states of consciousness, etc.) can be rearranged precisely in the way that the corporatist wishes.

---

[510] Icke 2001, 8.

[511] This was a rerun of the afternoon show on *Fox* from August 13, 2006.

[512] From Mueller and Ellis, 2005

Private Contractors

As Klein (2007) thoroughly discussed, the world is becoming a privatized world: all military, industry, research and development, war, education, farming, and so forth, are falling out of the hands of the voters, and falling into the hands of corporatists who want to profit off of them.

Wars do not happen spontaneously, accidentally. They are planned, and they are business ventures. FDR said: "In politics, nothing happens by accident. If it happens, you can bet it was planned that way." In Greenwald (2006), it was pointed out how virtually every aspect of the war in Iraq was controlled by private for-profit contractors. If a plane needed to be fixed, a corporation was there to do the job at a high price. The high price was a price that American taxpayers had to cover, due to the fact that the decisions about war in the United States occur in Congress and by the President, and they are not voted on. Also, Americans have not had the opportunity to vote President Bush out of office due to the fact that the Presidential elections in the United States are not genuine, and they are staged.[513] Also, if Americans do not pay their taxes, their wages will be frozen, and/or their land seized by the IRS. Therefore, the American citizen has no choice but to finance a war that pours money into the hands of the military-industrial complex (which is merely the set of companies that make the war supplies—tanks, planes, military bases, trucks, boats, food, and so on—at a huge profit, all on the taxpayer's bill: 40 cents of every $1[514]), and which kills American and Iraqi children every day. Amazingly, with the power of the mass media, this corporatist war enterprising can be sold to the average American in a way where she/he will support this sort of war activity, because she/he does not know all the facts of war.

Mental Disorder

There are few better tools for tyrants to use than the concept of "normality:" the idea that there is a proper set of behaviors that citizens can express, and to express behaviors not in the acceptable set is *a problem*—it is "bad." For example, watching hours and hours of television is permitted behavior (the average citizen will not think it is odd), but veganism, antivaccinationism, or polymathy is not, and likely will be rebuked to some degree by the average citizen.

In America, non-normalcy is often considered criminality, or mental illness. It is essential to have this sort of paradigm in the minds of the citizenry if they are to be tricked into taking SSRIs and any other sorts of behavior drugs. And

---

[513] See Miller 2005.
[514] Greenwald 2006.

the tactic is working: in the United States, children use five times the amount of Ritalin than the entire rest of the world uses altogether![515]

Americans are trained, nearly from birth, to blame themselves for things. If one does not have enough money, they are likely to think to themselves: "I wish I studied engineering in college," rather than saying, "I am underpaid, and my suffering is not due to me, but rather due to the unfairness of the corporatists."

Reason seeks control. The quest for, and belief in, understanding, indicates that a human is interested in control of nature. That which is not able to be brought into control receives special labels, like "pathology," "dangerous," "abnormal," etc.

Best and Kellner write:

> He argues that various human experiences, such as madness or sexuality, become the objects of intense analysis and scrutiny. They are discursively (re)constructed within rationalist and scientific frames of reference, within the discourses of modern knowledge, and thereby made accessible for administration and control. Since the eighteenth century, there has been a discursive explosion whereby all human behavior has come under the 'imperialism' of modern discourse and regimes of power/knowledge. The task of the Enlightenment, Foucault argues, was to multiply 'reason's political power'... and disseminate it throughout the social field, eventually saturating the spaces of everyday life.[516]

In simplest terms: what is not good for the corporation and the corporate attitude (the attitude desired by corporate tyrants) is called disorder, abnormal, a problem that can be fixed. The very best example we know of—but which is only one of many—is the ADD/ADHD phenomenon, which I think it is somewhat safe to say has swept the nation. This is a perfect example of the attempt of the corporateness of the United States to control literally everything about it: to change the human Vitalism and replace its every interest, thought, and behavior we spontaneously can have in any given instant. Here is an "expert's" account of what ADD/ADHD is all about, from the very first lines of the wildly popular book, *Driven to Distraction*:

> Once you catch on to what this syndrome is all about, you'll see it everywhere... You may even recognize some of the symptoms in your own behavior. Many of the symptoms of ADD are so common to us all that the terms ADD to have specific meaning, rather than be just a

---

[515] This is according to Dr. Ross Pelton, on the Rense Radio Show, www.rense.com, July 21, 2004.
[516] Best and Kellner 1991, 38.

scientific-sounding label for the complex lives we lead, we need to define the syndrome carefully.[517]

ADD is a neurological syndrome whose classic defining triad of symptoms include impulsivity, distractibility, and hyperactivity or excess energy.[518]

Doesn't that just sound like a frustrated parent who is trying to get their child to learn their math, their George Washington, their American history of the 1800s (found in the government created/mandated textbooks[519]), their spelling words?

…one bases the diagnosis of ADD not on the mere presence of these symptoms, but on their severity and duration, and the extent to which they interfere with everyday life.[520]

This could be merely subjective and non-measurable.

I often feel it is surprising that I have to remind people that this is just the description of natural, pure-and-good *human-ness*. Let me explain what I mean more thoroughly.

Think back to when you were in grade school or high school, where you were instructed (forced?) to read some bit of reading material on, perhaps, American history of the 1800s (found in the government created/mandated textbooks) for your history assignment, or geometry for your math class, or whatnot. And remember during these times that you found yourself in the familiar position that we have all found ourselves in where we read through a paragraph and we can't remember really much of what we've just read. Then we read it again, and by the time we are on the second sentence, we may be reading, but we are not comprehending anything, and we have to go back and read the paragraph again and again, and it just does not work. The official view is that there is a problem with the person in this situation, as the passage above shows. So we are supposed to find ways, such as drugs (specifically, Ritalin), in order to change our minds to fit better with what has been assigned to us. Professor David B. Stein, who has explained why ADD and ADHD are "nonexistent,"[521] claims that ADD/ADHD children are indeed "different" in

---

[517] Hallowell and Ratey, 1995, 3.

[518] Hallowell and Ratey, 1995, 6.

[519] See Hoffman 1991 for a truly excellent, incredibly well-researched account of what this history really involved, and why the history taught to children in elementary schools and colleges is on the border of being a complete fabrication.

[520] Hallowell and Ratey, 1995, 6.

[521] Stein 2001, xi. In this book, Stein explains how the wildly popular drug Ritalin is now often being theorized to be largely a ploy by big drug companies to sell a blockbuster drug to the *two million* (2001, p. x) children who allegedly have this "disease." (See Stein 2001, chapter 3)

some ways but also are entirely "normal"[522]—and I interpreted him to mean that ADD and ADHD are personality traits, and thus the whole ADD/ADHD frenzy is that some parents and perhaps their child psychologists label the kids as "diseased" because their behavior does not fit in to the local tyranny. He explains how "the primary characteristics of ADD/ADHD children are that they don't pay attention and they misbehave a lot."[523] But in chapter 4, Stein makes the argument that social conditions in the USA are ripe for such behavior among children:[524] divorced, busy, distracted, unfocused parents, poor communication skills among families, overreaction in the media and among schools or families to misbehaving (which was probably caused by the things just listed anyway), and so on. In sum: it is the corporate dictatorship's stress on the family, and robbing of the intellectual mind that causes this.

But what of this changing our minds to fit the system better? What is really going on with that? I take that as not expressing a great respect for our innermost subjective selves, since we are quick to try to change it rather than to respect it and see what it is telling us. Perhaps if we listened, we'd know that it was telling us an astonishingly simple message, with respect to the above scenario about the inability to comprehend the paragraph: That message is that if the material is not interesting to us, our mind cannot stay focused! So is there really a problem with us? It sounds more like the teacher did not assign compelling material, which could perhaps make the class reading easy to comprehend. Think of a time when you have read something that you utterly loved, and interested you to the maximum degree. Did you have trouble comprehending it? I doubt it. You probably read through it effortlessly, almost perfectly comprehending every bit of it. Now imagine reading something a bit less interesting. You probably can still comprehend it well, but not as well. Now think of the paragraph mentioned above, the one you could not comprehend. You probably did not comprehend it because it was not interesting to you. So would it be more sensible to think there is a problem with you, or that the situation is perfectly normal, and you just did not find the passage interesting?

This illustrates how in a tyrannical corporate state, there is a quest to change the person to fit the tyrannical interests, and respect for the person is not there. Indeed, the idea that people are diverse and highly varied might often be mocked (and I am not referring at all to skin color—levels of skin pigment—here).

---

522 Stein 2001, 30-31.
523 Stein 2001, 58.
524 Stein 2001, 61-83.

Conclusion

The national corporatist mass media will push, glamorize, and sell various corporatist-endorsed programs and ideas (such as globalization, the anti-unionization, low pay, "free trade," the "North American Union," war, hatred of the terrorists, vaccines, junky food, and so on) to the citizenry, as if they are things that will benefit everyone everywhere, and as if they will help everyone become wealthier worldwide. All one needs to do is look around the United States to see that the corporatist plan is not beneficial to anyone but the corporatists. Homelessness, slums, and poverty pervade the United States. Wages and minimum wage have been largely frozen for a decade. Fatality rates from pollution caused by industry are up (as outlined above). The percentage of Americans with no health care is increasing. Disease and illness are increasing.[525] Fuel costs are soaring. The rich man's media has become the only media (except the internet, but that will be changed soon[526]). Industrial pollution is increasing at a nightmarish pace. A new age of synthetic (false flag) terror and corporate-based war has emerged, where we invade sovereign countries (like Iraq) and then quickly move in American "contractors" (i.e., corporate activity) to "rebuild" the country, while the citizens of the country battle in their destitution and poverty. 9/11, Iraq, depleted uranium, the concentration camp buildup, North American Union set-up, a looming draft (probably shortly after war with Iran begins),[527] and so on. In light of all this, most Americans I meet become irritated with me if I start citing this sort of evidence, and if I discuss the monopolization of resources and consciousness by corporatists, and if I discuss the mass oppression and the mass slavery that exists worldwide.

---

[525] There are currently all sorts of new epidemics: pancreatic cancer, diabetes, prostate cancer, respiratory illnesses, Alzheimers, irritable bowel syndrome, thyroid disorders, child leukemia, brain cancer, asthma, allergies, autism, eczema, Morgellons disease, brain tumors, lupus, speech delay (children not saying many words until they are 2, 3, or 4 years old), depression, all sorts of auto-immune disorders, obesity, and so on.

[526] See the interesting discussion in Pappas 2003 on this issue.

[527] "See Charles Rangle Thinks He Owns You," Chicago Sun Times, November 6, 2006, Gina Cobb.

5 The Global Contamination of Humanity: The Primary New World Order Tactic

Introduction

In this chapter I discuss three more corporatist tactics: vaccines, chemtrails, and Morgellons disease. I devote a separate chapter to these three items because (i) each of these items are closely related to each other as corporatist tactics, and (ii) each has to do with one specific issue: for centuries, the corporatists have concocted various substances and they have found ways to implant and/or inject them into humans in order to deform, torture, poison, and genetically and structurally alter humans. This is done most effectively through vaccines, food, medicine, chemtrails, and Morgellons disease (where Morgellons appears to be spread via chemtrails, as I will discuss). Since I have already discussed medicine and food contamination at length, I will now proceed to discuss chemtrail and vaccine contamination.

The subject-matter of this chapter is similar to the discussion in previous chapters about fluoride, GMO food, chemotherapy and radiation treatment, the drugs of Big Pharma, and pollution—which are all also acts of corporate terrorism that deform the RP. But the subjects of this chapter—vaccines, chemtrails, and Morgellons—are similar to fluoride, GMO food, and pollution, but vaccines, chemtrails, and Morgellons are a different breed of contaminant: they are all aimed at transforming and severely injuring and dejecting *the entirety* of humanity. This is on a different order than, for example, fluoride contamination in drinking water, which is debilitating, but a person is not damaged so much that their mind might be literally destroyed, as is the case with vaccines and chemtrail contaminants. For example, as stated elsewhere in this book, and as will be proven in this chapter, mercury in vaccines is solely responsible for the autism epidemic that is raging in the United States,[528] and the result is that, without exaggeration, *all children in America are severely damaged* in one way or another by infant vaccines, and the symptoms can be observed in all children, as I will discuss below. This is the nature of vaccines, chemtrails, and Morgellons: they are meant to severely transform all humans of

---

[528] At the time of the writing of this book, 1 in 166 children have autism (Kirby 2005, xiv). Alex Jones reported, in late 2006, on his radio show at www.infowars.com, that he had reports that indicated that the level was up to 1 in 80. There could be some cases where aspartame causes autism, since it is a brain damaging excitotoxin (similarly but less severely to the way that mercury is when aspartame is in the brain), but my evidence in this chapter will show that mercury is much greater of a cause.

planet earth in a global cosmogenesis that will, it appears, lead to an entirely new species of human, in what is often called "our transhuman future."

Vaccines

There has never been a vaccine that has eliminated any disease, or that has decreased the frequency of any disease, ever at any time in history.

During and before I was writing this book, I never stopped being surprised at how little the public knows about vaccines. But at the same time, nearly anybody I would talk to about vaccines would thoughtlessly tell me something like this: "we [Americans] are so lucky to have vaccinations that keep our children safe." Also, I would be told, out of the blue, by all sorts of people, things like this: "don't forget to get your flu shot, Jeff!" No matter who I talked to, such as a pediatrician, a biologist, a person from the American Medical Association, the garbage collector, or almost anybody else, I was always astounded at how little was known about these vaccinations, even though these same people urged me to run and get my vaccinations as soon as possible.

For example, I never met a single person who knew that the level of mercury in the flu shot for infants contained over *50 times* the "safe level" of mercury recommended as the adult "safe limit!"[529] This is one example of perhaps dozens of examples I could give in this book of how little is known about vaccines, and about how badly misled the public is on the issue. Most interestingly, it seemed that the lack of knowledge and the breadth of misunderstanding were certainly not confined to the public. The same ignorance over the vaccination issue was observed regardless if I was talking to a pediatrician, a biologist, a nursing student, an anthropologist, a bioethicist, a nutritionist, and, as mentioned, a person employed by the American Medical Association.

Doctors

The average doctor does not spend her/his days doing research, digging for knowledge, verifying the information she/he had been told in medical school, and so forth. They spend their days earning money seeing patients, and talking to "drug reps" (i.e., salespersons for Big Pharma).[530] This means that the bulk of their information was acquired through their four-year rush through medical school, but after that, not much at all is learned, and for that reason, the average doctor's knowledge only comes from medical school (and the medical schools

---

[529] Kirby 2005, xii. On that page, Kirby writes that mercury levels are "in amounts that exceed federal safety exposure levels for *adults* by up to fifty times per shot…"
[530] See Angell 2005 for more information on this issue.

are controlled by Big Pharma[531]). It is hard to believe that four years of rushed study through sleep deprivation can give a person enough background to understand illnesses, the incredible complexity of the human body, medications, nutrition, the pharmaceutical industry, and the health care industry, just to name a few things. But nevertheless, doctors are not afraid to quickly and confidently tell us that our infant children need dozens of shots, even though they have done no real research on the issue. "It's all safe and effective, and that is well-established in the scientific literature," they will tell you.

What has just been written may indicate that doctors act like non-scientists most of the time. It also may indicate that they are not trustworthy sources of information—how can they be if they are not steeped in research, if they are hardly ever seen doing research, and if their "education" comes primarily from Big Pharma. It appears to be the case that doctors are mostly unknowingly being used as agents of the secret corporatist government to carry out Nazi tactics (I will discuss this much more in a section below), where Americans—*especially American babies*—are being transformed into subhumans, like the creatures on Moreau's Island. Americans are perhaps the sickest, fattest, least intelligent people in the world. And it is not the fault of biomedical experts and doctors, nor the people who are sick, fat, and dumbed-down. They have all been tricked into poisoning themselves. It's all part of the deliberate plan of the secret government: it's all *a trick*, and it all happens covertly, like putting mercury in a vaccine and telling people it's not in the vaccine, and then blaming the parents, or genetics, when a child gets brain damage or autism.

A Note About the State of Scientific Research

Science is supposed to be unbiased. Therefore, vaccine research is supposed to be unbiased. Yet in vaccine research, as Dr. David Ayoub has pointed out exhaustively,[532] there are all sorts of cases of misleading articles in prestigious scientific journals. They will have titles like "No Evidence of Harm for Children Vaccinated with Thimerosal Preserved Vaccines," but when one reads through the article, the research is, without exaggeration, *a joke*. So the title of the article makes it look like the article proves that vaccines are safe and effective, and many might not read the article since, well, who *would ever guess* that the prestigious medical researchers and their journals would conduct themselves in this way.

For these reasons, doctors, corporatists, and government researchers in the United States can boast that vaccines are safe and help to eradicate disease, and they can inform the public that it is "well established in the scientific literature." And few people will go through and thoroughly read these articles,

---

[531] Angell 2005; Richards 2006.
[532] Ayoub 2005, 2006.

in order to take in all the data to see that it is bogus—to show that it is *non-data*, as Ayoub has shown with a number of examples.[533]

So why does this happen? The simple reason is: when journal editors, scientists, and researchers are offered incredible amounts of money, they will do almost anything for it (including publish non-scientific articles that lead to false information about vaccines), even if it damages tens of millions of children. Consider what Dr. Marcia Angell writes about the issue of shoddy and suspicious articles being published in "prestigious" academic journals:

> I witnessed firsthand the influence of the industry on medical research during my two decades at *The New England Journal of Medicine*. The staple of the journal is research about causes of and treatments for disease. Increasingly, this work is sponsored by drug companies. I saw companies begin to exercise a level of control over the way research is done that was unheard of when I first came to the journal, and the aim was clearly to load the dice to make sure their drugs looked good.[534]

The secret government—through the mask of "benevolent" Big Pharma—has infiltrated and polluted scientific research. As Angell implies, university and other medical researchers have, sadly, proven to us that we can no longer trust what goes on inside of, and what comes out of, their labs, hospitals, clinics, and academic departments. I will document a case below where vaccine makers paid university researchers to publish a report on vaccines, and you will see that the report is sloppy, to put it mildly. Jordan Maxwell has pointed out that a politician from long ago once said that

you cannot be free and ignorant at the same time.[535]

America is a culture without a scientific base, and the sciences themselves have been corrupted. Without a scientific base, a nation is ignorant, lost, and suffering. In such a climate, without exaggeration, people do not know anything, as this book proves. They are told x by politicians, media personalities, teachers, and ministers, and they unquestioningly believe it, and will fight to the death for it. But x will be unverified, and almost always, *unverifiable*; while not-x will be most likely a simple empirical issue. (Jim Marrs once said: "I don't believe anything is true, until the government denies it."[536]) Nevertheless, they will ridicule and attack questioners and skeptics. But through this fog of ignorance, I intend to get to the bottom of the vaccine issue, as I will begin now.

---

[533] Ayoub 2005, 2006. Tenpenny 2005 also contains information on these issues.
[534] Angell 2005, xxvi.
[535] This was pointed out in Maxwell's DVD lecture, *Astrotheology*, which can be found at sovereignearth.org.
[536] Rense Radio Show, www.rense.com, March 14, 2007.

Why No Vaccine has Ever Eradicated or Reduced
the Frequency of Any Disease

Vaccines are not about medicine or medical technology. They are about profit, destruction, and control. They are also about creating and manufacturing as much illness in people as possible (since medical industries profit off of increased illness: the more sick a population is, the more money the medical industries take in). Vaccines are also about social engineering. Vaccines do not work: they do not eliminate disease, they cause it—that's what the data shows, as you will see. This includes diseases, like polio and smallpox, which Americans (including American medical students) are told were eradicated *by vaccines* (and it is very easy to show that this is untrue). Although it is hard for people to believe it, the standard data that is presented to people via the mass media and medical schools is fabricated and/or slanted (I will prove this by example below). The accurate and full historical data on vaccinations and disease, which can be obtained from governments, and which is found in books such as Neil Z. Miller's Vaccines,[537] shows that vaccinations have had nothing to do with the eradication of vaccinations and disease (see Miller 1999, pages 18-23). Hiding or altering data is a common practice in corporatistic profit-seeking medical industry, and it is specifically meant to cover up the verifiable finding that the medical industry (especially Big Pharma) is about killing people, as victims of Vioxx, Prozac, Zyprexa, vaccines, chemotherapy, and radiation treatment know. Readers of this book should consult Richards 2006 and Angell 2005, and the various books I cite in this chapter regarding vaccines, for more information on my claims here. Here's a sample of what you will find when you seek the empirical data on what the medical industry, especially Big Pharma, is unfortunately all about:

> Eli Lilly's best-selling drug is called Zyprexa, which generated $4.2 billion in 2005 sales, or twenty-eight percent of Lilly's total drug sales. It was the third consecutive year that Zyprexa topped $4 billion in sales. This one drug generates as much revenue as the entire National Football League. Seventy percent of Zyprexa sales occur through taxpayer-funded Medicare and Medicaid programs. Zyprexa is a powerful antipsychotic medication approved for serious mental-health illness. The FDA approved its use based on a 1996 clinical trial for the treatment of adult schizophrenics. Two-thirds of the 2,500 participants had so many adverse side effects that they dropped out of the clinical trial. Of those remaining, twenty-two percent suffered serious adverse health effects... FDA reviewers found an average weight gain of almost one pound a week for subjects during the six-week trial, and a twenty-six-pound increase for Zyprexa patients who remained in the trial for a year. Eli

---

[537] 1999, Santa Fe: New Atlantean Press. Dr. S. Tenpenny has commented on how trustworthy a source of information Miller's thesis is, in Tenpenny 2005.

Lilly and the FDA covered up twenty deaths and twelve suicides among individuals taking Zyprexa, never reporting them to medical doctors or the American public. Instead, they turned this drug loose on unsuspecting American children with mild mental health issues... On June 15, 2005, Eli Lilly settled an estimated 8,100 lawsuits pending in the United States. These concerned the company's alleged failure to warn of the known risk that Zyprexa could cause diabetes. The company agreed to pay $690 million but denied any wrongdoing... As of March 2006, the settlement had not been paid.[538]

To echo something Dr. Angell said in her recent book,[539] if you seek to understand the actual nature of the medical industry, you will see that it is not a pretty picture.

Vaccines are created by Big Pharma. In fact, the company just mentioned in Richards's passage, Eli Lilly, is the chief company responsible for manufacturing the mercury that goes into children's vaccines—including all 12-hour-old-babies born in the United States who are given the Hepatitis B shot. Vaccines have never been needed. The healthy immune system—which is built out of a strong vegan diet—is miraculous in how it can fight disease. Even breastfed babies are very well protected (assuming the mother has the sort of diet just mentioned). But most Americans have no idea that this is the case, since from birth they are told that the immune system does not do its job (which, in America, is because the average diet is hugely mineral and vitamin deficient, and in fact consists of poisonous food), and that they need to supplement it with vaccinations.

We can see that vaccinations are a hoax with one simple graph, which I have drawn here below, which shows US Death Rates over a 63 year period for five diseases (but only three of which are vaccinated against as part of the routine American childhood vaccinations):

---

[538] Richards 2006, 14-15.
[539] Angell 2005.

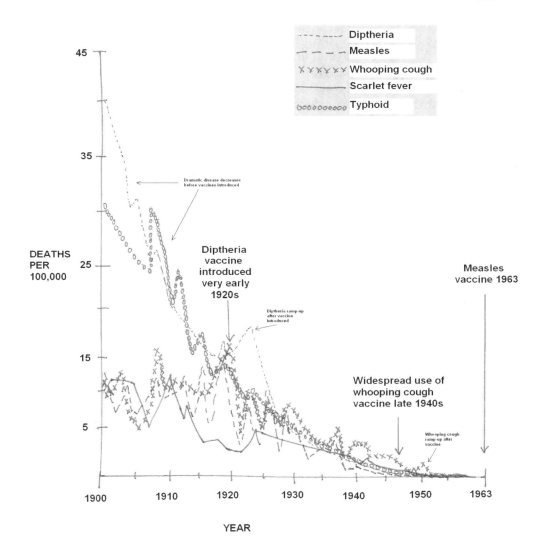

This chart contains the replication of the data that is found in Eisenstein (2002), Golden (1998), Horowitz (1999, 2001), Miller (1999), Scheibner (1993), Tenpenny (2005), among other books, and which shows that vaccinations were *not* responsible for ending the three vaccinated-against diseases in the chart (pertussis, measles, diphtheria—scarlet fever was never vaccinated against, and the typhoid vaccine has hardly ever been used). All the diseases vaccinated against were on their way to being eradicated naturally, most likely because of improved sanitation in cities throughout the 1900s.

Golden points out in the Australian DVD lecture, *Vaccinations: The Hidden Truth* (which contains interviews with Golden, Scheibner, and others), that researchers have had to go to the health officials of governments of nations to get the information and data to build the curves of these charts. I was puzzled when I first heard Golden mention that was the case in the DVD lecture. I wondered: Why did he have to go to *that* source (government), rather than to academic or medical sources, for example. (At the time, I did not know that big government, big medicine, and big academia were all largely indistinguishable.) But later I found out that it was because the information in the above graph is ubiquitously *hidden by academics* (in medical schools, in bioethics courses, in research, and so on). Most people do not believe this when it is told to them, and it took me a long time to figure this out. But to verify it, all one has to do is peruse the academic textbooks used in medical schools, biology departments, nursing programs, and the textbooks about disease and immunology—*you won't see the above graph in those textbooks*. I will give an example shortly.

It is notable that *only some of the diseases charted in the above figure were vaccinated against*. For example, scarlet fever was never vaccinated against, but it decreased in just the same way as diseases that were vaccinated against. This is the first bit of evidence from the data that shows that vaccines were not responsible for eliminating the diseases in the above graphs.

Ramp ups after vaccination. Not only were diseases being eradicated naturally, apparently by better hygiene and/or some other unknown factors,[540] but also, diseases often underwent a *ramp-up* after vaccination campaigns, as is shown in the graph with respect to whooping cough and diphtheria. (Measles was so rare by the time the vaccine was introduced that the graph is not fine-grained enough to indicate any data.) This is more evidence—if not conclusive proof—showing that vaccines were not responsible for eliminating diseases. The very diseases that involved vaccination in the above diagram in fact *increased in frequency after vaccination*—and this is no small issue, since *it reveals that the vaccines were not working*: they were not working because, simply put, they were not decreasing disease! If a vaccine works, then in a culture that is vaccinated over the so-called "herd immunity" level, there should be absolutely no increase in disease frequency whatsoever, and the disease should drop-off in frequency completely. This has never occurred with diseases that are vaccinated against, and in fact no disease data shows any sort of drop-off phenomenon at all (rather, there are only ramp-ups and epidemics that occur). At this point, the reader of this book might be inclined to ask: Are there any doctors at all out there who are reading the scientific literature that contains facts such as these?

There may be many reasons why there was such a ramp-up (including deliberate spraying of the populace with diseases such as whooping cough, as

---

[540] Often it is assumed that better nutrition contributed to the decrease in the disease rates. This is however not possible, since nutrition quality *decreased* in the 1900s. (See Pawlick 2006; Simontacchi 2000 [Introduction and Chapter 1].)

will be pointed out in the chemtrail section below), but what is clear is this: the vaccines did not immediately decrease the diseases, and thus *one cannot claim that the vaccines helped contribute to a downturn in the diseases vaccinated against that was already in progress throughout the 1900s before vaccination occurred.* There is one conclusion to be drawn from this information: if there is a ramp-up in a disease within a few days, months, or years after a vaccine is introduced, then that vaccine does not work, since it did not contribute to a downturn in disease.

Often I find people objecting to me on the above conclusions about vaccines with the following rejoinder:

> **Objection**: vaccines helped decrease disease after they were introduced, even though diseases were already being reduced naturally, and were already nearly eliminated.

We can see, however, that this objection fails, due to the fact that there were significant *ramp-ups* in occurrences of the diseases *after* the vaccines were implemented into society, as already stated.

An Example of How Big Pharma Pays-Off Vaccine Researchers to Conduct Favorable "Research"

This ramp-up in disease after vaccination is a very revealing issue, and it is astonishing how often this fact is missed, due to the poignant information it reveals regarding the failure of vaccines. And it is no secret that vaccination does not work. Consider this recent news article on whooping cough:

> State laws that make it easy for children to skip school-required vaccinations may be contributing to whooping cough outbreaks around the country, a study suggests. All states allow children to be exempted from school immunization requirements for medical reasons—because they might have a bad reaction, for example, or have weak immune systems—and 48 states allow exemptions for personal or religious beliefs. To get non-medical exemptions, some states require documentation, notarized paperwork and even visits to a local health department. In other states, parents merely have to sign an exemption letter. Compared with stricter states, those with easy exemption policies had about 50 percent more whooping cough cases, according to the study. Also, about 50 percent more people got whooping cough in states that allowed personal-belief exemptions, compared with those allowing only religious exemptions, the study found. States increasingly are being pressured to relax their exemption requirements, often by *parents with unfounded fears* about the risks of childhood vaccines, said University of Florida researcher Daniel Salmon, a co-author of the study. But loosening these policies would be a public health threat, he said. The study appears in Wednesday's Journal of the American Medical Association. It was partly funded by the federal Centers for Disease

Control and Prevention. Researchers from Johns Hopkins University's Bloomberg School of Public Health contributed to the study, including two who reported financial ties to vaccine makers. Salmon said he has no financial connection to vaccine makers. Whooping cough, also called pertussis, is a bacterial infection that causes severe coughing spells. It is highly contagious and can be deadly in infants. *The first whooping cough vaccine was licensed for U.S. use in 1948 and led to dramatic declines in disease.* But reported cases have increased more recently, from 1,020 nationwide in 1976 to 25,827 in 2004.[541] Public health officials *believe* the numbers are up because the vaccine's protection wears off. Booster shots are recommended for teens and adults. Salmon said liberal exemption policies may have contributed to the increase. The highest average annual number of whooping cough cases from 1986 to 2004 was about 13 per 100,000 people in Vermont, a state with relatively loose exemption policies, the study found. The rate was well under one per 100,000 in Mississippi and several other states with stricter policies. Dr. Samuel Katz, a Duke University vaccine specialist who has consulted for vaccine makers, said he is not convinced loose state exemption policies are linked with whooping cough prevalence. He said not all states with liberal policies have high disease rates. But Dr. William Schaffner, an infectious-disease specialist at Vanderbilt University who has worked with vaccine manufacturers, said the connection is plausible. Schaffner said non-medical exemptions should be allowed, but only if parents get educational information about vaccines. They should also be required to renew their exemption status each year, as some states now mandate, Schaffner said.[542]

This article contains simple non-information: "The first whooping cough vaccine was licensed for U.S. use in 1948 and led to dramatic declines in disease." The data given in the chart in the previous section shows that there is no evidence that whooping cough decreased because of a vaccine (and the data indicates that it did not, since the disease was decreasing on its own already, thus giving no reason to conclude that vaccines were suddenly responsible for decreases of disease frequency). And furthermore, whooping cough *increased* (ramped-up) after the vaccine was introduced, as the chart in the previous section shows, and as I have already stated several times. This misinformation in the AP article gives a good lesson of what the real motives are in the profit-seeking mass media (in this case, those motives would be to publish pro-Big-

---

[541] These are most likely the "reported cases," which indicates that whooping cough was far more widespread in 2004, with perhaps over 100,000 cases, ore more. This will be significant below, where I discuss how this sort of epidemic should not occur in a vaccinated population, if the vaccine works.

[542] "Whooping Cough Outbreaks Tied to Lax Laws, Study Says," Associated Press, October 11, 2006, Lindsey Tanner.

Pharma information since Big Pharma gives billions of dollars each year to the mass media via advertising).

Notice that the article is quick to only blame "lax laws" for this "outbreak." But the obvious questions are never brought up in the article, which are these:

> *If the vast majority of American children (infants) are repeatedly vaccinated with the pertussis vaccines (as has been the case for many decades before and up to the time of this AP article), then how can there be an outbreak? More succinctly put: How can there be an outbreak in a heavily vaccinated culture (vaccinated near or over the so-called herd immunity level)?*

Answer: there can't, unless the vaccine does not work.

It is well-known that children in America are being vaccinated at or near the so-called "herd-immunity" rate, which is at most 92-94 percent for any given disease that children have routine vaccinations against in infancy and toddlerhood.[543] If there is no external cause (no cause other than whooping cough carriers passing the disease to one another via normal transmission), and if sanitation levels of a community remain relatively constant, then if there are increased cases of whooping cough, it proves that the vaccine is not protecting people from the disease.

This AP story was, for example, the top story on AOL news and Google news for over a day in October 2006, but apparently nobody put it together that this AP article reveals that it is not the laws (specifically, the so-called "lax laws") that are the problem, but rather that the problem is that the whooping cough vaccine does not work. It would appear to be the case that such a glaring error was made because this is a story from the mass media, and the mass media is funded to a huge degree by Big Pharma,[544] and Big Pharma profits unimaginably with vaccines.

And indeed this is apparently the case with the whooping cough study discussed in the AP article. Consider this information form the Johns Hopkins University Gazette, which discusses this whooping cough study:

> Daniel Salmon, senior author of the study and an associate professor of epidemiology in the University of Florida's College of Medicine, said, "Our results add a new piece of information in our effort to control

---

[543] According to "Lower Vaccination Rates Put Children at Risk," *Science Daily*, April 29, 2005 (University of Alberta source), 8.9 percent of children were not properly vaccinated against. The National Vaccine Information Center's page titled "Whooping Cough, the DPT Vaccine, and Reducing Vaccine Reactions" (located at http://www.909shot.com/Diseases/whooping.htm), informs us that "the U.S. has a 95% vaccination rate with pertussis vaccine," which is well over the herd immunity rate for pertussis.

[544] See Angell 2005.

pertussis. A reduction in the number of U.S. children receiving school immunizations hinders one of our most effective methods in preventing outbreaks of vaccine-preventable diseases," added Salmon, who is also an adjunct associate professor in the Bloomberg School's Department of International Health...

In a May 2005 article published in the *Archives of Pediatrics and Adolescent Medicine,* Salmon and colleagues reported that parents who requested immunization exemptions perceived vaccines to be unsafe and ineffective, despite strong scientific evidence to the contrary. They also believed their children were less susceptible to vaccine-preventable diseases and that the diseases were less severe. Parents of exempt children also had low levels of trust for the government.

The study, partially funded by a grant from the Centers for Disease Control and Prevention, was co-authored by Omer, William K. Y. Pan, Neal A. Halsey, Shannon Stokley, Lawrence H. Moulton, Ann Marie Navar, Mathew Pierce and Salmon. *The co-authors have received payment for consultant work or testimony unrelated to the current study on behalf of Sanofi Pasteur, GlaxoSmithKline, Merck, Chiron and the U.S. Department of Justice.*[545] (Emphasis added.)

There are many interesting issues revealed in this Johns Hopkins University Gazette article. The last part of the article (which I have italicized) plainly admits that the ultra-rich vaccine manufacturers[546] have paid the researchers for this study. This is analogous to if the ultra-rich meat industry paid the farmers to create news reports on how their meat is safe, clean, and free of mad cow disease. It is very interesting to note that the AP article does not contain this information, and instead only informs the reader that the group was paid off by government organizations (CDC, etc.).[547] Instead, the AP article only vaguely indicates that two of the researchers involved had "ties to vaccine makers." The AP article informs us that the head of the research team, Daniel Salmon, of the University of Florida, does not have financial ties to the vaccine makers. But the AP article does not clarify on what this means. It does not tell us if Salmon has other "non-financial" ties to vaccine makers – were prestige, career advancement or other benefits given to Salmon? This is relevant, since it is common to find covert non-financial ties between researchers and industry. Also, the AP article does not tell us if Salmon was given money from other

---

[545] From, "High Rates of Whooping Cough Associated With Easy Exemptions," Johns Hopkins University Gazette, Kenna Lowe, October 23, 2006.

[546] Angell (2005), Kirby (2005), and Richards (2006) discuss how stratospherically wealthy and powerful the Big Pharma corporatists really are (which is not well-known among the public).

[547] In Richards 2006, it is shown that "regulating agencies" like the CDC, FDA, AMA, ACS, and so on, are not regulating agencies: they do not regulate Big Pharma. Instead, Richards points out how these agencies are actually for profit corporations that are controlled and managed by Big Pharma.

sources to do the research (such as the University of Florida, the CDC, the FDA, etc.). The AP article does indicate that the study was funded by the CDC, which is controlled by Big Pharma, so Salmon could have (and likely was) paid by the CDC, and thus was indirectly paid by Big Pharma, wherein the AP article could then misleadingly say that Salmon had no financial ties to the vaccine makers. It is very hard to believe that Salmon worked "for free" on this project, since, as Angell points out,[548] university researchers are now typically paid in various ways for research, and the "pure researcher," doing research for its own sake, and for the glory of discovery, has been lost from scientific realms of academia.

Given Big Pharma's record for corruption, and for simply paying for fabricated data,[549] it appears that our best conclusion would be to conclude this study also involves the same sorts of corruption, and that Big Pharma has merely paid off the researchers involved in order to get results that reveal pro-vaccine findings. This is a safe inductive conclusion, and the sloppiness of the information in the study indicates that this is likely a true conclusion.

The study has an overt emphasis on *attacking* parents. The AP article mocks parents for their "unfounded fears," and the Johns Hopkins University Gazette article contains this odd sentence, which appears abruptly and out-of-the-blue:

"Parents of exempt children also had low levels of trust for the government."

It is very puzzling that this sentence appears in the Johns Hopkins University Gazette article. What is it there for? It has nothing to do with the AP article, or with the information in the Johns Hopkins University Gazette article.

I don't see any way to avoid the conclusion that the sentence is there for the following reasons: to attack parents, to provoke animosity and scorn toward questioning parents, to deter freedom of thought, to deter parental autonomy, and to provoke fear in those who question corporatists and the visible government. It is as if the article states the following:

If you question the government, you are a criminal.

(In this case, the criminality involved would be the idea that the parents are anti-government, or that they are negligent in not "protecting" their children with vaccines.)

What is *very* interesting, in my opinion, is that if you read *both* the AP and the Johns Hopkins University Gazette articles carefully, you will see that they each involve the same somewhat hidden message: the articles are not ultimately blaming laws, doctors, politicians, vaccines or vaccine-makers, schools, poor health, obesity, increased poverty in America, or the unhealthy food supply in

---

[548] Angell 2005, chapter 1.
[549] There are a plethora of examples of this given in Angell 2005 and Richards 2006.

America for the whooping cough outbreak. Rather, the articles both clearly blame whooping cough outbreaks *on parents*, as if to say:

Whooping cough outbreaks are caused by anti-government parents!

The AP article indicates that "Public health officials *believe* the numbers are up because the vaccine's protection wears off." (Itals added.) Notice the italicized word "believe." *This is an admission that the AP article is non-scientific*, and thus can be discarded, since belief is not scientific. It is also interesting to note that this sentence indicates that apparently everything about this AP article is based on belief, not science. Also, this sentence pushes on the reader that the outbreak is caused by the fact that people are not getting enough boosters (hence, again, the parents are to blame). *This is an admission that the vaccine does not work.* It is as if the article is saying this: the existing vaccine has not been shown to protect populations, therefore, we don't conclude that the vaccine does not work, we instead conclude that the solution is to get more vaccine (boosters). (This is like saying: putting honey on the floor does not keep the cockroaches away, so the best way to get rid of them is to dump more honey on the floor.) But no evidence is presented for any of these ideas, and it is only an unargued-for assumption that lack of booster shots is the reason there have been recent whooping cough outbreaks. In summary:

The admitted need for more boosters = admission that the vaccine does not work.

It is also interesting that no other possible causes for the outbreaks are stated in either article: in addition to defective vaccines, outbreaks could be caused by the increased poverty in America (which has to do with the implementation of the North American Union), or the abysmally poor nutrition and very high obesity rates in America. It just seems that parents are to blame (for having so much irresponsibility in face of the (lax laws"), according to the articles.

Also, the article from the Johns Hopkins University Gazette shows that the researchers demand that there is "strong evidence" that the whooping cough vaccine works (i.e., it prevents disease). But didn't we just see (above) that this is not the case? It is interesting that the articles do not clearly inform us of what this evidence is, or, for example, show us a clear breakdown of the data that shows this "clear evidence." Instead, the articles just tell us the following:

There is a pertussis epidemic, and the pertussis vaccine is a successful vaccine!

According to Orwell's 1984, this is called doublespeak: x is not-x.

It is also interesting to note how aligned the articles are in their information (disinformation). This is a good example of how the mass media does not exhibit diversity of information or viewpoint. For example, your cable television might have several cable news channels, but all of them will report the same information, and none of them will report on how, for example, the number of honeybees in America is declining dramatically, how the US dollar is declining dramatically (as of April 2007), and so on. Rather, the mainstream news media is all about Michael Jackson, Duke Lacrosse, Janet Jackson, Hillary Clinton, Martha Stewart, Anna Nichole Smith, Monica and Bill, and other tabloid characters.

Furthermore, the vaccine data from the 1900s given in the chart above shows that the whooping cough vaccine

(i) is unneeded,
(ii) is followed by ramp-ups in whooping cough (as if to possibly cause whooping cough, rather than prevent it), and
(iii) has never been shown to contribute to eliminating or decreasing whooping cough.

Now what is interesting is that the researchers who were funded by the vaccine makers to create this study that was discussed in the AP (and in the Johns Hopkins University Gazette) are plainly ignoring points (i) – (iii), and thus it can only be concluded that they are covering up simple scientific data which falsifies their "study." Is this cover-up and unscientific untruthfulness further evidence that the researchers (headed by D. Salmon) were merely paid off by Big Pharma to construct their study? Is this dishonesty further effect of the fact that the researchers were driven to merely fabricate research in order to arrive at the desired pro-Big-Pharma conclusions (which is: whooping cough is caused by parents) by covering up real data, as I indicated above?

The AP article does not tell us how there is a connection between the states with so-called "lax laws" and increased whooping cough. It does not tell us how many more cases there were in the "unstrict" states, nor how it is so much more difficult in some states to get an exemption, as the article implies is the case. The articles do not tell us if there were other factors other than "lax laws" (which, as stated, really means "bad, anti-government parents") involved (nutrition, chemtrails,[550] etc.), and which were responsible for the outbreaks. Instead the article reasons sort of like this:

There was more whooping cough in state X than state Y, so therefore it is the fault of the anti-government parents.

If you strip away the veneer, that is what these articles both conclude, which is precisely what one would expect from corporatist media: pro-corporatist disinformation. These and other omissions (the revelation that the vaccine does not work) show that this article is not only non-scientific, but clearly is leaving out information that would discredit and negate this article. This is, of course, a key component of how the mass media conducts its information and reporting: only report some of the details, in such a way that it changes the story in favor of the corporatists.

---

[550] This is a critical omission, which will be discussed later in this chapter, and it is an issue that clarifies on what is really behind the vaccines.

Also note that the AP article informs the reader that parents have "unfounded fears" about vaccines. But not only will I disprove this with scientific evidence below, since the whooping cough vaccine has been shown in dozens of medical journal articles to be the cause of SIDS, brain damage, and auto-immune diseases, but furthermore, *the AP article indicates in the second sentence that there are problems with the pertussis vaccines*, such as when a child "might have a bad reaction, for example." So this article involves a simple contradiction in "reasoning:" there is nothing to fear from vaccines, but you might get a bad reaction from them (and thus there is something to fear). Thus, the AP article tells us that x is not-x. Again, this is called doublespeak, as Orwell pointed out in his book, *1984*.

Media and Education Blackout
of Empirical Data on Vaccines

The widely used immunology and immune system textbooks used by nursing students and medical students in America do not include charts like the one given above! For example, the widely used textbook, *The Immune System*, by Stanford professor, Peter Parham (New York: Garland Publishing), does not include any of the above information in this chapter, such as the chart given above. Instead, Parham only includes charts for smallpox, polio, diphtheria, and measles (but not for any of the other diseases!), but what is most important is that he alters the charts, and he does not start the charts at 1900, as the chart above does. This hides the fact that diseases were hugely decreasing before vaccinations were introduced, and instead makes it appear that the diseases began decreasing at the time of national vaccination implementation.

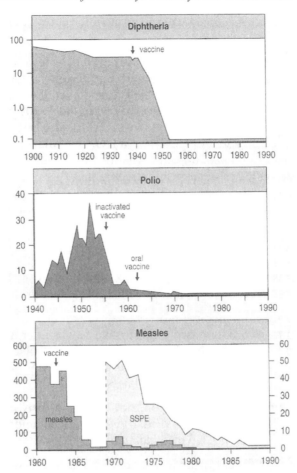

Reported Cases per 100,000 population

"Successful Vaccination Campaigns. Diphtheria, Polio-myelitis and measles have been virtually eliminated in the USA, as shown by these three graphs. The arrows indicate when the vaccination campaigns began. Subacute sclerosing panencephalitis (SSPE) is a brain disease that is a late consequence of measles infection for a minority of patients. Reduction of measles was paralleled by a reduction in SSPE 15 years later. Because these diseases have not been eradicated worldwide and the volume of international travel is so high, immunization must be maintained in much of the population to prevent disease recurrence."
From page 27 of Parham's *The Immune System*

　　Notice that by starting the measles graph at 1960s, it makes it appear that the vaccine *caused* the downturn (even though the graph indicates a nearly 100-case increase right after the vaccine, which should not have happened if the vaccine worked). Showing data from the smaller time-frame from 1960 onward, as these graphs do, rather than from 1900 onward, hides the *huge* decrease in disease before that, and shows that vaccines were not responsible for anything other than the aforementioned ramp-ups of the diseases right after vaccination. This gives a nice example of the utter deceit and fabrication that is now standard in academia.

As for the other graphs in Parham's diagram, I have absolutely no idea where the diphtheria chart he provides comes from. There is nothing factual about it. Parham indicates that the chart is for the US, and even the WHO website agrees that US vaccinations against diphtheria started in the 1920s, not 1940. And this drop-off of diphtheria Parham's book shows is simply not the drop-off of diphtheria that other sources (such as WHO, and the books I cited above) reveal. The page shown above from Parham's book indicates that it is the USA that is being discussed, so one would assume that this is a US chart, since the page does not indicate otherwise. But again, that just means that the chart is, well,… a fabrication, it seems. (I will discuss why the polio chart is deceitful below.)

Correlation and Causation

What Doctors Say about Children Who are Very Sick After Vaccinations: It's Just a Coincidence that Vaccine and Illness Happened at the Same Time

What are doctors and medical professionals taught to say when parents report that, for example, two hours, two days, or two weeks after a vaccination, their child is damaged with violent illness and/or disease? Doctors always seem to say the same thing: "just because the child gets sick right after a vaccine does not mean that the vaccine caused the sickness."

This is to claim there is correlation, not causation, between the two events (between vaccination and sickness): the two events coincide in time, but in a way where they each do not have connection.

Correlation is different from causation. Correlation is when two events happen at the same time, but no connection can be drawn between them, and causation is when the two events are shown to have a connection. A correlation is, for example, like jumping in a rainstorm: both happen at the same time, but apparently the events do not cause one another (for example, the frog might have been jumping if it was windy, sunny, or foggy too). Causation is, for example, like a tornado and a damaged house: both happen in the same time and the same location, and the only way we can account for the damaged house is by the only known item that could have been powerful enough to damage the house (namely the tornado). What is critical about the difference between correlations and causation is that the frog could jump regardless of whether or not it was raining (and thus the rain is not the cause of the frog's jumping), but the house could only have been damaged if the tornado was present (and thus the tornado is the cause of the damaged house). Now in the case of a vaccine, if a toddler comes up with autistic symptoms not long after a vaccine (e.g., the toddler had been talking well, but then stops talking days after a vaccine), and exhibits autistic symptoms (which you will see in a section below are identical to mercury poisoning symptoms), then the only thing that can account for the autism/mercury-poisoning symptoms is massive amounts of mercury entering the body, and that mercury inundation *could only occur with* the vaccine. As with the case of the tornado, that's causation, not mere correlation.

Causation can be defined as follows:

Causation: y occurs only if x first occurs, and removal of x leads to y not occurring. For example, autism (y) only occurs if there is mercury poisoning (x).

Now I will discuss this further, through an example.

Frequency of Occurrence

If a pattern is repeated through time, where two things often or only correlate with one another, it will start to *look like* causation, not correlation. For example, if the frog jumps every time it rains, and one sees this occur dozens of times, it might start to look like the rain is causing the frog to jump. But until a causal connection is drawn between the frog and the rain, it can only be considered to be correlation.

Now consider another example. If I get flu-like sickness (call this S) from going to a specific restaurant once or twice where I eat the same meal (call this event RM: going to a specific *R*estaurant eating a specific *M*eal), I do not know that the restaurant caused the sickness; I only know that the two things occurred simultaneously. But if I go to the restaurant 50,000 times with long breaks (say one month) between visits to the restaurant, and 25,000 times I get the sickness, but never get it elsewhere, that indicates that there might be causation going on (rather than correlation), since there is so much correlation: in this case, there is a *repeated event that is accompanied by the same circumstances 50 percent of the time in a huge sample*. But strictly speaking, this is not proof of causation, this is just a good indication that there might be causation—in this case, 50 percent of the time the restaurant is shown to cause the illness.

When It's *Correlation* and When It's *Causation*

In the example above, S only occurred if RM occurred first. The simple questions are these: Is this really only correlation between S and RM, or is there causation, where RM causes S? How can we tell about this? The answer is simple: if S *only* occurs with RM preceding it, and where there is always a similar amount of time between S and RM when S occurs, then that is causation, not correlation. The reason it is correlation is simple: S only can exist if RM occurs, and without RM, there is no S.

The summary of this is as follows: I can only get S if I do RM, but if I don't do RM, I won't get S. This is how philosophers define causation: S occurs if and only if RM exists first. This is just like the case of the tornado and the mercury in the shot.

It could be that there are factors in place that merely cause me to endure two events: going to restaurant R and then acquiring sickness S, but where RM is not a cause of S. But if I go to another restaurant *several times* and eat the very same dish or meal each time (call this occurrence RM_2), but S does not ever follow, then I know that RM_2 is not causing S, and I need to implement RM to initiate S. Now I can prove that RM causes S if I go to numerous (for example, 100) restaurants (call this RM_{2-101}), but S never occurs, then I know that it is only the case that RM causes S, and unless I do RM, S won't follow. This is called causation, not correlation.

Doctors often claim that what appears to be vaccine damage to a child is *a correlation event*, but parents will often claim that it is *a causation event*. To settle the issue, it would need to be shown that the damage to the child only exists because of the presence of the vaccine's toxic ingredients (e.g., point out how mercury poisoning [which will be proven below is merely autism] only occurs with the presence of mercury injection). As we will next see, there are many cases where this has been proven, and specifically, where it has been proven that vaccines cause autism, brain damage, auto-immune diseases, SIDS, death, and mental disturbance, to name a few—and without vaccines, these sicknesses would not exist.

Vaccination vs. Immunization

Now I will go through specific information about vaccines, which is important to know so that we can understand how they are a corporatist tool. First:

Vaccination: giving a shot (giving a toxoid, an immunobiologic)
Immunization: the process of inducing artificial immunity by administering a vaccine

These are different. Administering a toxoid does not automatically lead to development of adequate immunity, as we have seen above. It must be proven that vaccination *causes* immunization, or else there is no science involved in vaccination and immunization studies. We will see that, in fact, there is no connection between vaccination and immunization, and thus the process is not scientific—it is, rather, a corporatist tool, which means it is genocidal and meant to instill mass misery.

Effectiveness of Study

Dr. Lorraine Day gives the following two categorizations:[551]

Research Effectiveness: the theory and practice that if you inject a person with vaccine, you can prove that they develop antibodies against the virus/disease given to the individual

Clinical Effectiveness: the empirical study and checking of whether or not research effectiveness occurs: you show that those antibodies that a person has in fact protects them from a disease. (You check to see if the disease was reduced, or if it vanished.)

Clinical effectiveness is *never* studied with any vaccine.[552] The vaccine is said to be effective based only on research effectiveness. Research effectiveness does occur (antibodies are created, they show up), *but that is all that is known*, and if the antibodies protect against disease is not known. Data shows that clinical effectiveness in fact does not occur.

So, in reality, it is *not known or verified* with science if any vaccine works (as Viera Scheibner shows in the Australian DVD lecture, *Vaccination: The Hidden Truth*[553]). Due to this fact, I am forced to assert that vaccination and clinical effectiveness is devoid of science: there is no science in vaccine research.

Data on Smallpox

Next I will briefly show why all cases of mass vaccination do not involve science, but rather involve all sorts of outlandish things, thus showing that vaccinations are not what they are advertised to be in the immunology textbooks and television commercials for Big Pharma. First I discuss smallpox.

Illness:[554]

- 1980: claimed to be eradicated from USA by WHO
- In India, amid 88% vaccinated populations, huge smallpox outbreaks have recently occurred[555]
- It has been widely reported that Bayer's smallpox vaccine was infected with AIDS[556]
- Smallpox vaccine has not been shown to work[557]

---

[551] She outlined the following information on the Rense Radio Show, www.rense.com, November 11, 2005.

[552] Ibid.

[553] This lecture was created in DVD format by the Vaccine Information Service, of PO Box 4, Turramurra NSW 2074 Australia (www.vaccination.inoz.com).

[554] Much of this information comes from Tenpenny 2005.

[555] Tenpenny 2005.

[556] "Bayer Sold HIV-Risky Meds," Frankfurt, Germany," CBS/AP, May 22, 2003. (Also located at http://www.cbsnews.com/stories/2003/05/22/health/main555154.shtml.)

Consider the following charts:

England & Wales: Mean Annual Death Rate Due to Smallpox

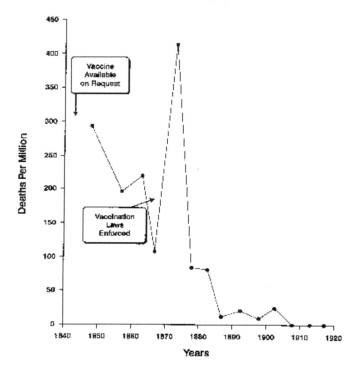

[557] Tenpenny 2005.

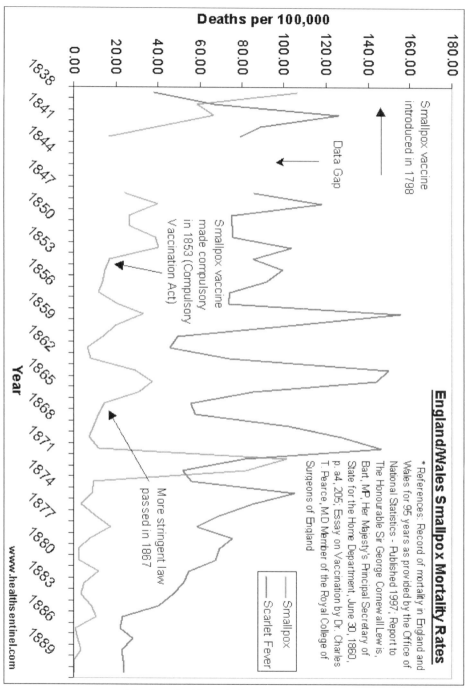

England/Wales Smallpox Mortality Rates

Deaths per 100,000

Year

Smallpox vaccine introduced in 1798

Data Gap

Smallpox vaccine made compulsory in 1853 (Compulsory Vaccination Act)

More stringent law passed in 1867

* References: Record of mortality in England and Wales for 95 years as provided by the Office of National Statistics - Published 1997; Report to The Honourable Sir George Cornewall Lewis, Bart, MP, Her Majesty's Principal Secretary of State for the Home Department, June 30, 1860, p. a4, 205, Essay on Vaccination by Dr. Charles T. Pearce, MD Member of the Royal College of Surgeons of England

Smallpox
Scarlet Fever

www.healthsentinel.com

Thanks to healthsentinel.com for this chart.

(The top line is Scarlet Fever, and the bottom line Smallpox.)

The charts above show that fully vaccinated societies regularly experienced epidemics of smallpox. This reveals that smallpox vaccines did not lead to obliteration of smallpox and in many cases did not lead to a decrease in the frequency of smallpox.

> 1900: just over 21,000 cases of smallpox were recorded by countries, and 894 died: 4.2 percent death rate

This shows that there is a problem with the commonly purported *30 percent* death rate of smallpox that researchers typically discuss.[558]

Furthermore, it does not make sense that smallpox would kill a lot of people, since it is just a skin disease.[559] Therefore, virtually all claims of the dramatic drop-off in smallpox rates (purportedly due to the vaccine) are inaccurate. How could a mere skin disease that kills at only 4.2 percent undergo such a huge decline in frequency? Dr. Tom Mack of the University of Southern California said at a CDC meeting June 6, 2002 that "death rates of smallpox are not as advertised."[560] Dr. Mack also said that "[e]ven with mass vaccination, smallpox would have died out anyway. It was already on its way out. It just would have taken longer."[561] This is, of course, what we would expect, given the data above regarding diseases decreasing in the 1900s before vaccines were implemented.

Lastly, Tenpenny (2005) has shown that, amazingly, nobody knows why people die from smallpox, and nobody knows what causes death from smallpox, in the rare cases where it kills its victims.

In summary, the information and data and smallpox and the smallpox vaccine is rather stunning. None of it makes any sense, and all of it is shockingly sloppy, amateurish, and devoid of any science or coherence. This all *does* make sense, however, when we consider what was discussed in chapter 1 about the secret corporatist government. Then we find that the smallpox vaccine merely fits into their agenda.

Data on Polio

- 90 percent of people exposed to the polio virus just get a headache or a cold[562]
- 54 percent of people exposed to the polio virus get abortive poliomyelitis (an idiosyncratic illness that is not serious, such as a strange sore throat)[563]

---

[558] See Tenpenny 2005 for more information on these issues.
[559] Tenpenny 2005.
[560] Tenpenny 2005.
[561] Mack said this at the meeting of Advisory committee of Immunization Practiced (ACID) that occurred June 19 and 20, 2002. Thanks to Tenpenny (2005) for this quote.
[562] Tenpenny 2005.
[563] Tenpenny 2005.

- 3 percent of people exposed to the polio virus get non-paralytic poliomyelitis (semi-serious illness, such as severe headache), no lasting effects, manifests in ways that appear like a viral meningitis[564]
- 2 percent of people exposed to the polio virus get *paralytic polio* (which is what most Americans appear to believe is the only symptom-set that arises when one a person is exposed to the polio virus). 50 percent of people who get *paralytic polio* recover fully. Only 2 percent of the 2 percent that get *paralytic polio* (which is *under* a tenth of 1 percent of all people exposed to the polio virus— which is a very tiny fraction of all people that get exposed to polio)[565]
- Polio is not equal to paralysis
- 1955 mass vaccination started. Change in definition of polio accompanied it, where instead of *polio* being defined as "two trips to the doctor within a few days where there is some paralysis in each case," it was instead the case that the two reports had to be 60 days or so apart, so naturally, most cases of polio are missed (since polio is usually so inconsequential that it merely goes away in a few days), and the data misleadingly shows that polio decreased. Also, at the same time (1955), the definition of an epidemic was changed from 6 per 100,000 to 35 per 100,000, where you then have to have more people with paralysis to call it an epidemic.[566] So, polio actually *increased* from 1955 into the few years after, but doctors reported that it *decreased.*[567]

There has been no polio in the United States since 1991, and it appears that polio was never a great threat in the first place. But American children are given *five* vaccine doses for it from zero to five, and these doses are now well known to contain dozens of cancer viruses (such as the SV40 cancer virus).[568]

---

[564] Tenpenny 2005.

[565] Tenpenny 2005.

[566] *American Journal of Public Health*, v. 45, sup 1-63, 1955 (thanks to Tenpenny 2005 for this citation). Also see Tenpenny 2005.

[567] This is discussed in Miller 1999, and in the aforementioned Australian DVD lecture, *Vaccinations: The Hidden Truth*.

[568] See Bookchin and Schumacher 2005. This is also discussed at length by Horowitz in his book (see bib.) and Russell Blaylock has discussed this on the Nutrimedical Report Radio Show (www.nutrimedical.com) and the Rense Radio Show (www.rense.com).

Data on Hepatitis B

Illness:[569]

- Caused by a virus
- Sick for 4-8 weeks
- Very bad flu with jaundice
- Acquired from blood to blood contact, sex, or mother to baby
- By far most prevalent among extreme drug abusers, prostitutes, and homosexuals (*extremely* rare among pregnant women)
- 50 percent who get it are unaffected
- 30 percent get a flu
- 20 percent get Hep. B symptoms (nausea, vomiting, jaundice) and go to the doctor (95 percent of this group make a full recovery)
- Of the 5 percent who *do not* make a full recovery:
  - 75 percent have asymptomatic infection (infection without symptoms), so it does not matter that they have not made a full recovery (this is 3.75 percent of the total of those who are exposed to Hep. B)
  - 25 percent of that 5 percent develop liver disease or liver cancer *decades after the infection* (if later developing liver problems are, in fact, indeed caused by Hep. B). (This is 1.25 percent of the total of those who are exposed to Hep. B.)

As Tenpenny says (my paraphrase): we vaccinate millions of children in order to allegedly prevent a few hundred or thousand cases of chronic liver disease in the aforementioned high-risk groups thirty years later, if, that is, the liver problems were not caused by other factors (alcoholism, etc.).[570]

Vaccine:

- Called "Recombvax" (Merck)
- given to day-old infants, never been studied if it is safe for infants[571]
- Contains mercury[572] and aluminum
- Genetically engineered vaccine[573] (so it implants extraterrestrial DNA into day-old babies)
- Made of 1 percent yeast[574] (grown in GMO yeast)
- Very unstable, easily deconstructs over short amount of time[575]

---

[569] Much of this information comes from Tenpenny 2005.
[570] Tenpenny 2005.
[571] Tenpenny 2005.
[572] Tenpenny 2005.
[573] Tenpenny 2005.
[574] Tenpenny 2005.
[575] Tenpenny 2005.

I would like to add a theory that I have about the Hep. B vaccine (notice I used the word "theory," so this is speculation, not fact). The Hep. B vaccine is widely known (among vaccine researchers) to cause significant long-term irritability[576] in people that get the shot - such as 1- to 2-day old babies. I suggest that the reason this needless vaccine is forced upon the children of unsuspecting parents at such a young age is because the parents have not known their infant long, and when the infant becomes irritable after the vaccine is given, they will not notice the marked difference between their baby from before to after, becoming more irritable.

Side-effects:

- "There is no doubt that the new recombinant[577] hepatitis B virus vaccine has the ability to trigger autoimmunity." (*Journal of Autoimmunity*, "Vaccine-Induced Autoimmunity", 1996, 9(6))[578]
- This vaccine results in molecular mimicry. In children, the vaccine leads to Juvenile rheumatory arthritis, type I diabetes, Kawasaki disease, and in adults, vasculitis.[579]
- 30-50 percent of all vaccinated persons lose all anti-bodies in 7 years; 60 percent lose all in 12 years.[580]
- Since the vaccine contains mercury, it contributes to causing autism (see section on autism below)

Data on DTaP Vaccine

The DTaP vaccine is three vaccines in one (which is a very dangerous process of vaccination, since it piles up vaccine ingredients [e.g., aluminum,

---

[576] See "Hepatitis B Vaccination of Premature Infants: A Reassessment of Current Recommendations for Delayed Immunization," *Pediatrics*, vol. 103, no. 2, 1999. In the "Vaccination" section of that article, it is reported that three days after the Merck's Recombvax vaccine had been administered there was irritability in infants, but curiously, it did not say to what level, nor what percentage of infants had it. No data is presented beyond that. But according to the VAERS data (which has even been noted by the Dept. of Health and Human Services regarding irritability and the Hep. B vaccine, at http://www.hhs.gov/asl/testify/t990518a.html), irritability and prolonged crying was much more marked than the three days of data than *Pediatrics* noted. It is interesting to note that so many articles report that the irritability is "transient" (such as "Comparison of Two Hepatitis B Vaccines (GeneVac-B and Engerix-B) in Healthy Infants in India," Clin. Vaccine Immunol. 2006 June; 13(6): 661–664), which is a very vague word, and which could mean almost anything, and none of these articles cite data that shows just *when* after the three days that the irritability ceases.
[577] Recombinant DNA is DNA that has been created artificially. DNA from two or more sources is incorporated into a single recombinant molecule.
[578] Thanks to Tenpenny 2005 for this quotation.
[579] All this information comes from Tenpenny 2005.
[580] Thanks to Tenpenny 2005 for this quotation.

mercury, etc.] in the baby's body), covering three diseases that are vaccinated against: diphtheria, tetanus, and pertussis.

Here's a chart from the entire USA, and Orange County California, from the website, http://www.ochealthinfo.com/newsletters/phbulletin/2005/2005-sf.htm, that shows how the vaccine does nothing to halt the rise of whooping cough:

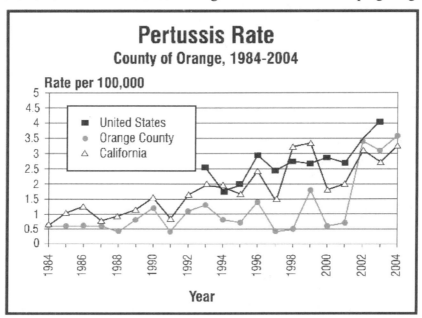

This chart shows epidemic behavior in a fully vaccinated society, as I already discussed above when I discussed the whooping cough epidemic. Now I will discuss all elements of the DTaP vaccine.

1. Diphtheria
Illness:[581]

- Diphtheria is a bacteria
- Diphtheria as a bacteria is not around any more (nobody ever gets it), but still vaccinated against
- It is like a super-flu
- 10 percent of those exposed die, but only if there is no medical care around (such as penicillin).

Vaccine:

- Disease was nearly extinct when vaccines were introduced in the 1950s
- Currently there are only 1-3 cases of diphtheria per year in the United States, but kids still get 5 vaccinations against it[582] (one might wonder why this is the case)

---

[581] All this information comes from Tenpenny 2005.

- Toxoid, developed around 1921, widely used in 1930s
- In the 1940s, diphtheria toxoid was combined with pertussis vaccine and tetanus toxoid to make the combination DTP vaccine
- In 2005, two new tetanus toxoid, reduced diphtheria and acellular pertussis Vaccines were licensed. These vaccines are the first licensed acellular pertussis-containing vaccines that can be given to persons older than 7 years
- Very little research on safety (including long-term safety) issues regarding either of the vaccines exists[583]
- Diphtheria vaccines are purported by "experts" to have few side effects[584]

2. Tetanus
Illness:[585]
- Tetanus is a spore bacteria
- Tetanus causes muscles to never relax, spasms, lock-jaw, very serious
- Tetanus grows in soil, it can't survive in oxygen
- Recovery takes several months
- Recovery for 89 percent who get it (medical schools tell students there is zero recovery, and that it is uniformly fatal)

Vaccine:[586]
- Americans have been vaccinated against tetanus since the 1940s
- 14 days after exposure bacteria multiplies (spore germinates), and a person can get a shot any time before that without risk
- It is very common to have tetanus erupt in fully vaccinated individuals
- Vaccine is grown in beef, detoxified with (and contains) formaldehyde and thimerosal

Side-effects:
- Vaccine known to produce Gullian-Barre syndrome (a significant autoimmune disease), encephalopathy (brain disease), vomit, pain in joints, and many other problems[587]

3. Pertussis
Illness:[588]
- Toxins and neurotoxins emitted from a bacteria
- Might cough until you throw up

---

[582] Tenpenny 2005.

[583] Tenpenny 2005.

[584] Tenpenny 2005.

[585] Tenpenny 2005.

[586] All information comes from Tenpenny 2005.

[587] Tenpenny 2005.

[588] All information, except the last bullet, comes from Tenpenny 2005.

- There are sensationalized and legendary cases of people breaking ribs and getting brain damage from so violently coughing while sick from whooping cough, but it might be that the virus causes the brain damage
- 16 percent of those exposed to the bacteria get pneumonia
- 3 percent of those exposed to the bacteria get encephalopathy
- 0.02 percent of those exposed to the bacteria die
- This is one of the diseases we know that humans are sprayed with (see the chemtrails section)

Whooping cough is widespread in the United States right now, but the mass media will not report that, since that reveals that the vaccine does not work. This is a primary fearmongering disease. But only 92 deaths occurred from 1980-1995 (6 per year).[589] Many more children die yearly from swimming pool accidents.

Vaccine:

- Whole-cell (pre-2001): cheaper to make, has formaldehyde (extremely dangerous)
- Encephalopathy: 1 in 60,000 get general (not low level) brain damage. Many more get high-percentage conditions: low-level brain damage, speech delay,[590] lowered IQ test scores, and so on[591]
- In 2001 a new vaccine was developed. It took 64 years to get this new, safer vaccine to be used (since it was developed in the 1930s). Not much is known about this vaccine, except that it still has formaldehyde.

DTaP Vaccine Side-effects:

- Known to stimulate CNS disorder: SIDS, infantile spasms, seizures, epilepsy. (CDC, Epidemiology and Prevention, the Pink Book, 6 Ed., ch. 6, Pertussis, p. 80.)[592]
- Contains copious mercury and aluminum

Data on Pneumococcal Disease and Prevnar

Illness:

- Used to prevent pneumococcal disease, which is very low risk for kids that are of normal health.[593]

Vaccine:

---

[589] Tenpenny 2005.

[590] This may be associated with autism, as if it is a low- or early-stage autism.

[591] Tenpenny 2005. Tenpenny cites medical journal articles to verify this point. Also see Scheibner 1993, Miller 1999.

[592] Thanks to Tenpenny for this citation. Also see Scheibner 1993, Miller 1999. There are many other academic accounts of the side-effects.

[593] Tenpenny 2005

- Prevnar is produced from seven genetically engineered strains of streptococcus pneumonia bacteria, so it's like getting seven vaccines
- Vaccine contains 0.125 mg of aluminum, a *major* neurotoxin[594]
- Aluminum said to be used to stimulate the immune system to get high antibody levels
- Aluminum in vaccines has been in use since the 1940s (the same time that the Nazi "doctors" were also experimenting with phony medicine and vaccines)
- Never has there been developed any test that shows what the aluminum really does to humans.[595]

Side-effects:[596]

- One percent of babies have itchy nodules at the shot entry *for four years*, and this is very likely because of aluminum
- Kids often get multiple aluminum shots in one doctor visit, so that the aluminum toxicity in the child is staggering (aluminum removal in the body is done through the kidneys, but a baby's kidneys do not have productive functioning of any sort until one or two years of age; babies have very low kidney function until that time)
- One percent of adults tested with the vaccine had to be rushed to the ER
- Doctors say that symptoms of Prevnar are apnea and *breath holding in babies*! (Have you ever seen a baby hold its breath?) But often they attempt not to blame the vaccine for this.

Data on Haemophilus Influenza type B (HIB)

Illness[597]

- Named Haemophilus influenza type B
- Flu-like illness, causing various infections around the body (lungs, etc.) including possible meningitis
- 12,000 cases annually, with five percent death rate
- Neurological complications in 25-35 percent survivors (e.g., hearing loss).

Vaccine and side effects:

- Injection of a piece of a bacteria (not the full bacteria), and an antibody for the full bacteria is consequently developed
- Contains sucrose[598]
- Contains formalin (formaldehyde)[599]

---

[594] *Pediatrics*, vol. 97, no. 3, 1996, 413-416. Thanks to Tenpenny for this citation.

[595] All this information comes from Tenpenny 2005.

[596] All this information comes from Tenpenny 2005.

[597] All this information comes from Tenpenny 2005.

[598] Connought Labs vaccine.

[599] Connought Labs vaccine.

- Contains yeast, and thimerosal[600]
- It is verified that many (4-5) doses cause type 1 diabetes.[601]

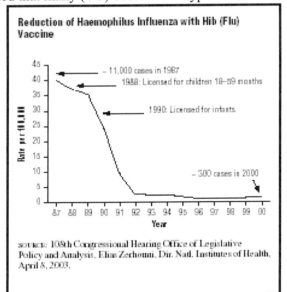

Reduction of Haemophilus Influenza with Hib (Flu) Vaccine

SOURCE: 108th Congressional Hearing Office of Legislative Policy and Analysis, Elias Zerhouni, Dir. Natl. Institutes of Health, April 8, 2003.

When introduced, there were sudden decreases in the type B of H flu. This made it appear that Haemophilus influenza was decreasing. But the vaccine still was not successful in eliminating or decreasing Haemophilus influenza, because other strains of H. flu increased at the same time, so the HIB vaccine did not help H. flu victims overall, and HIB is just another example of a failed vaccine.[602]

The vaccine's antibodies do kill the Haemophilus influenza type B, but then they attack the pancreas, creating an autoimmune disorder of the pancreas (and this pancreatic debilitation has a string of other problems). A vaccine is, in turn, needed to kill those HIB anti-bodies.[603] This resembles the usual Big Pharma scenario: give people poisons in food, water, medicine, and so on that makes them sick, and then push medications on them to fix those sicknesses, but where the medications just cause more problems that need more medications, and so on

Data on the MMR Vaccine

1. Mumps

---

[600] Wyeth-Ayerst vaccine.

[601] *Autoimmunology*, 35, 247-53, 2002. Thanks to Tenpenny for this citation.

[602] This is according to Meryl Dorey, author of *Vaccination Roulette*, Australian Vaccination Network (AVN), 1998. She said this on the Rense radio show, www.rense.com, January 7, 2004.

[603] All this information comes from Tenpenny 2005.

Illness:

- Feverish
- Harmless
- Full recovery is standard
- *Very* rarely causes sterility problems in males,
- No evidence of any sterility in females[604]

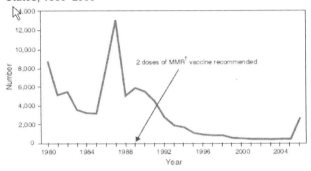

FIGURE 4. Number of reported mumps cases, by year — United States, 1980–2006*

* Data for 2005 and 2006 are provisional.
† Measles, mumps, and rubella.

(From blog.vcu.edu/cbuttery/epidemiology/, the site of Dr. C.M.G. Buttery, a professor at Virginia Commonwealth U.)

This chart is interesting, since it seems to correlate with a decrease in mumps cases at the time that the vaccine was put on the recommended list. But this could be merely a correlation, and it likely is, since the disease was already decreasing as charts I have given above, and as this chart from Dr. Buttery shows, and since it was at far lower rates at times before the vaccine was given. A connection between the decrease in mumps and the vaccine would have to be found.

But it seems there is reason to assert that the vaccine is not the cause of the downturn, due to the fact that there have been recent mumps outbreaks all over the United States (such as Iowa,[605] among other places) in a fully vaccinated

---

[604] Tenpenny 2005

[605] This has been widely reported on, and even made a national slot in the mass media for a while (probably to scare people into getting more vaccines). But the epidemic occurred in fully vaccinated populations, as usual. Consider the following MedPage Today report:

DES MOINES, Iowa, April 4 - The tally of mumps cases has climbed to 300 in an outbreak that started in Iowa and has spread to all bordering states, with the exception of South Dakota. Meghan Harris M.P.H., of the Iowa Department of Public Health said that the latest state affected by mumps is Missouri, which has reported a single case.

culture, as this chart shows (at the end of chart there is a ramp-up, which should not occur if the MMR vaccine was working).

Here is a chart from Britain, showing epidemic characteristics of Measles and Mumps in a fully MMR-vaccinated culture, from http://www.statistics. gov.uk/cci/nugget.asp?id=1361:

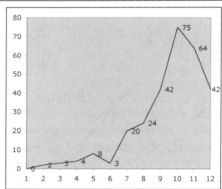

The tally, which was released today here, increased by 55 cases since Friday. Harris said she expects the numbers to be higher when the next scheduled update is issued Thursday. *Follow-up reports have been completed on 154 cases. Of those 68% occurred in people who had received the recommended two doses of the measles-mumps-rubella (MMR) vaccine.* Iowa, according to Harris, is a state with a high vaccination rate, and she anticipates the majority of mumps infections will occur in people who are considered safe on the basis of their immunization records. *"But we know the vaccine doesn't work in everyone," she said.* Harris said published data suggest that the vaccine failure rate for mumps is about 5%. "So by my estimate there are about 200,000 people in Iowa who have received the recommended vaccinations but who have no immunity to mumps." ... The 300 confirmed, probable, or suspected cases of mumps represent the nation's largest mumps outbreak in 17 years... (Emphasis added.)

This is from "Iowa Mumps Outbreak Linked to Primary Vaccine Failure," MedPage Today, Peggy Peck, Senior Editor, MedPage Today, April 4, 2006, http://www.medpagetoday.com/PublicHealthPolicy/PublicHealth/tb/2987.

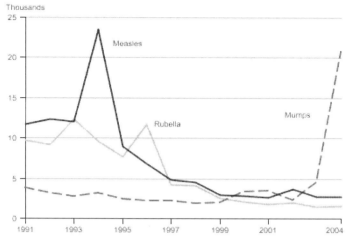

This chart is significant since it shows an epidemic forming in 2004 in a fully vaccinated culture, and which involves the same strain of mumps as found in the United States.[606]

Vaccine:

- The mumps vaccine is made from a live attenuated (weakened) virus. It is unclear what the side effects are, since the vaccine is mixed with the "M" and the "R" parts of the MMR, and it is difficult to tell which parts cause which side effects.

2. Rubella

Illness:[607]

- Tiny rash
- Lasts for approximately three days
- 50 percent of people don't even know that they have it
- Worst case scenario: insignificant runny nose, small fever. Again, most kids don't even know they are sick.

Vaccine:

- Live virus
- Contains fetal bovine serum
- Contains human serum albumin (originating from human aborted fetal tissue)—this means there are dead pieces of aborted fetus in Rubella vaccines
- sucrose (table sugar)

---

[606] They are described as being the same in "Iowa Mumps Outbreak Linked to Primary Vaccine Failure," MedPage Today, Peggy Peck, Senior Editor, MedPage Today, April 4, 2006,
http://www.medpagetoday.com/PublicHealthPolicy/PublicHealth/tb/2987.
[607] This information comes from Tenpenny 2005.

- sorbitol (sweetener, artificial sugar)[608]

Side-effects:

- Clear link from vaccine to acute arthritis (fifteen percent of adult women)[609]
- The vaccine goes into joint fluid, causes infection in various places in the body[610]

3. Measles

Illness:

- German measles
- Cough, rash, lasts a week
- Low mortality rate
- No complications
- Vitamin A reduces symptoms
- Vaccine started in 1963, but disease was basically already gone in the late 1950s
- In 2001, there was one case per one million children (fifth year in a row that this occurred), and over seventy percent of them were from outside the USA.[611]

MMR Vaccine:

- Contains thimerosal
- Live virus
- Grown in chick embryo (and thus contaminants from chick are likely in the vaccine)

Why is Mercury Bad for the Nervous System

There are few more heated issues in the vaccine debates than mercury in the vaccines. Health officials, government officials, and academics nationwide typically say there is no risk, and that the mercury in the vaccines does not cause any damage to children (or adults). Is this really true? Dr. David Ayoub, of the Southern Illinois University Medical School, tells us that mercury is toxic to any bit of human tissue it touches.[612] Is he right? How could he be right, and the numerous other professors and medical officials be wrong? Why do we have this situation, where one side says one thing, and the other side says another, which clearly reveals that one of the sides is lying? Is this a case where Big Pharma and the genocide of the secret government are in play, again? Alas,

---

[608] All this information comes from Tenpenny 2005.

[609] Tenpenny 2005.

[610] IOM Academic Press, 1991, pages 194-95. Thanks to Tenpenny 2005 for this citation.

[611] All this information comes from Tenpenny 2005.

[612] Ayoub 2006. Ayoub backs this up with appropriate scientific documentation.

I will show that this is the case, and as you will see, it is astonishingly easy to show that (i) mercury is detrimental to any person who has any amount injected into them, and that (ii) mercury is the sole cause of the autism epidemic that is currently out of control in the United States.

But how, specifically, can it be shown that mercury is bad for the nervous system, wherein causing autism, speech delay, vision problems, digestive problems, brain injury, and many other issues? That is the subject of this section. I have found that the American citizenry appears to be rather suspicious of vaccines, but the public is completely in the dark on nearly all of the issues surrounding mercury in vaccines. For example, I often hear people tell me that, "oh, I thought mercury was removed from all the vaccines."[613] This is the error that arises from misleading mass media reports, from erroneous medical school information, among other sources. Ayoub,[614] Kirby,[615] and Tenpenny[616] each discuss the levels of mercury in vaccines, and how the erroneous idea that they have been removed has been spread throughout culture. In fact, the truth is, the restrictions on the amounts of mercury that can be put into vaccines is lowering, and in many ways, there are *no restrictions*: vaccine makers can put as much mercury in as they want. According to the California Healthline: California Healthcare Foundation, October 25, 2006, in an article titled, "FDA Rejects Thimerosal Petition," which is about an article that appeared in the Associated Press[617] shortly before,

---

[613] For a news story discussing the lack of knowledge that Americans have on this issue, see, for example, "Americans Surprised, Concerned that 90% of Flu Shots Contain Mercury," PR Newswire, November 13, 2006. As an interesting note, I once even had a Purdue University immunologist utter this statement to me!

[614] 2005, 2006.

[615] 2005.

[616] 2005.

[617] That article is, "Government Rejects Petition that Sought New Limits on Mercury Preservative in Vaccines," Associated Press, October 24, 2006, Andrew Bridges. And here's what that AP article said:

> WASHINGTON (AP) -- Federal health officials won't put new restrictions on the use of a mercury-based preservative in vaccines and other medicines, denying a petition that sought the limits because of health concerns. A group called the Coalition for Mercury-free Drugs petitioned the Food and Drug Administration in 2004 seeking the restrictions on thimerosal, citing concerns that the preservative is linked to autism. ... Thimerosal, about 50 percent mercury by weight, has been used since the 1930s to kill microbes in vaccines. There have been suspicions that thimerosal causes autism. However, studies that tracked thousands of children consistently have found no association between the brain disorder and the mercury-based preservative. Critics contend the studies are flawed. ... Most doses of the flu vaccine still contain thimerosal...

FDA has rejected a petition that sought new restrictions on the use of the preservative thimerosal in vaccines and medications, the agency said in a reply dated Sept. 26 that was made public on Tuesday, the *AP/Seattle Post-Intelligencer* reports. The Coalition for Mercury-free Drugs filed the petition in 2004 over its concerns that thimerosal is linked to autism. The coalition and some other groups maintain that thimerosal, which is about 50% mercury by weight, causes the condition. All vaccines given to children aged six and younger since 2001 have been thimerosal-free or contained only trace amounts of the preservative.[618] Some adult vaccines, eye ointments, nasal sprays and nasal solutions still contain thimerosal. Jeffrey Shuren, assistant commissioner for policy at FDA, wrote in the denial of the petition, "Only a small number of licensed and approved products still contain thimerosal, and the available evidence supports FDA's conclusion that all currently licensed vaccines and other pharmaceutical drug products containing thimerosal are safe."

What Does Mercury Do to the Nervous System?

According to Dr. Russell Blaylock of the University of Mississippi Medical School, author of the book *Excitotoxins*,[619] the tiniest level of mercury in the brain triggers excitation (via the excitotoxins), secreting large amounts of glutamate (which is an excitotoxin), where this extra glutamate destroys the connections between brain cells (but does not destroy the brain cells themselves).[620] If this is true, then we should expect to see widespread, catastrophic mercury damage (such as an autism epidemic) to children in any parts of the world that involve cultures that inject repeated doses of mercury into infants and toddlers.

I will focus only on autism, since if I can prove that one affliction alone is caused by the mercury in vaccines, that will be sufficient to settle the debate over whether or not mercury in vaccines is safe.

How to Prove
Mercury in Vaccines Causes Autism

Consider the following data points, all of which add up to a proof that mercury causes autism:

---

[618] Ayoub (2005, 2006) discusses what is meant by "trace amounts," and he has found that in fact the amounts of mercury in vaccines are huge, and thus the term "trace amounts" is simply misleading and inaccurate.

[619] 1997, Santa Fe: Health Press.

[620] This is from an interview with Blaylock from the Rense Radio Show, www.rense.com, July 24, 2006.

- According to Dr. Ayoub,[621] it can be shown that *mercury poisoning symptoms = autism symptoms;* the approximately 15 symptoms of mercury poisoning are identical to the symptoms of autism[622]
- According to Kirby, amounts of mercury that are placed in vaccines will perfectly correlate to the resultant percentages of autistic kids that show up in a culture; in other words, the correlations are *predictable*[623]
- Kirby[624] and Olmsted[625] both have shown that unvaccinated populations do not have autism[626]
- According to Dr. Ayoub,[627] it can be shown that autistic children have far less mercury expulsion from the body (as measured in hair samples), indicating that autistics do not release the mercury from their bodies, and instead, it gets caught up in tissue, such as the brain[628]
- Congress has passed laws that protect big pharmaceutical corporations from suit by anybody suing the corporation for vaccine injury.[629] Why would Congress (which is largely controlled by Big Pharma [e.g., Bill Frist]) pass such laws if vaccines are safe?

---

[621] 2005, 2006.

[622] This is an astounding bit of evidence that Ayoub has shown, and it indicates a hard-science proof that mercury causes autism.

[623] Kirby discusses this early in his 2004 book, *Evidence of Harm*. He discusses how if there is a certain level of mercury put into a vaccine, and the vaccine is given to the infants of a society, then you can predict the percentage of children that will show up with autism. Lower the mercury, and autism decreases in a predictable statistical fashion. Raise mercury, and it rises in a predictable statistical fashion. For example, if x amount of mercury is put into the sum total of shots for the children in England and the United States, then in each nation there will be the same percentage, call it p, of children with autism, and p will not show up in cultures that do not have x.

[624] 2005.

[625] 2005 (see bibliography).

[626] For example, in Olmsted's article about the unvaccinated Amish, he shows that of tens of thousands of children, there were only three cases of Autism, and each of those were children that were adopted into the culture, and they came from toxic environments (e.g., a coal-mining town [coal smoke can lead to mercury poisoning since there is mercury in the smoke]). Olmsted also discusses how the FDA mocked people who claimed that this issue about the unvaccinated Amish should be looked into. The FDA said it was not the sort of serious research that research money should be spent on.

[627] 2005, 2006.

[628] For more information, see "Reduced Levels of Mercury in First Baby Haircuts of Autistic Children." Amy S. Holmes, Mark F. Blaxill, and Boyd E. Haley. *International Journal of Toxicology*. 2003. 22: 277-285.

[629] This is thoroughly discussed in Kirby 2005.

- According to Dr. Ayoub,[630] it can be shown that animals develop autistic-like symptoms when randomly injected with mercury
- Golden, Scheibner, Lorraine Day, and Leonard Horowitz (see bibliography), all show, and exclaim, that *there is no science involved in vaccination studies*

If you add up each of these points, it leads to a simple proof that mercury in vaccines is solely responsible for the autism epidemic.

So far in this chapter I have established that vaccines are not scientifically created medical tools. They bear all the marks of the secret corporatist government, including genocide, mass misery, targeting children more than any other age group, and they involve a poisoning of the citizenry that is "hidden in plain view." Vaccines leave humanity deformed and dumbed-down, just like fluoride, pesticides, chemical sweeteners, GMO food, and television do, but to a far more severe level. It can be concluded that virtually all children injected with mercury vaccines have some level of brain damage (which will manifest in speech delays, and other symptoms), and thus, virtually all children in America are savagely damaged by vaccines.

Nazification of Medicine

Since I have discussed vaccines, food, water, and other contaminated items that are ubiquitously used by Americans, and which are produced by the biomedical and food industries, I feel that what I wish to discuss next—the *Nazification of medicine*—has had a proper introduction. The Nazification of medicine is also a good foreword to the remaining subjects in this chapter: chemtrail contamination of humanity, and Morgellons disease. Thorough and pervasive contamination is part of the corporatist dream-state. This dream-state is exemplified in this section by the summary of the medical industry, which I give next.

The contemporary American biomedical industry is not only tied to the Nazi empire via its historical roots and origins,[631] it is actually carrying out tactics that mimic it to a precise and remarkable degree, as this book shows. Dr. Bill Deagle, of the Nutrimedical Report radio show (www.nutrimedical.com), has discussed what he calls "the Nazification of medicine." I have been interested in this project of his, since it appears to empirically describe how the American biomedical industry is very similar to Nazi concentration camp mechanics. In this section, I will list a number of points that show this correlation. Some of the points listed were formulated by Dr. Deagle, and some by myself.

1. Victims of concentration camps are treated very similar to hospital and doctor's office patients: injections, forced nudity, torture, poisoning,

---

[630] 2005, 2006.
[631] See Horowitz, 1999; 2001.

killing, and other general horror (via chemo, radiation, experimental drugs, forced drugging of children, forced vaccination of children and adults with biotoxins and neurotoxins, pushing Big Pharma products, recommending a bad diet [the animal-food-based diet], etc.)

2. Doctors damage *all* children and adults, nationwide, with irreparable injuries. This is done via vaccines, chemo, radiation, mercury, promotion of a diet not appropriate to humans [promote food pyramid rather than veganism], etc.

3. Doctors do not promote cures, but rather "treatment," but where the treatment is in accord with points 1 and 2 just given.

4. Medicine is not distinguishable from torture (shots, chemo, radiation, pain medication restrictions, experimental drugs, etc.).

5. The patient is not a paying customer, but rather is a person who is supposed to feel honored to be medicalized.

6. Medicine is about letting people die, and making a lot of money in the meantime.

7. "Legitimate" medicine is determined by law enforcement and by centralized big government (which is structured and supported by corporatists).

8. Physician-patient relationship is often to some degree a belittling, non-informative, disempowering, tyrannical, mocking, vassal-lord relationship. Even in the case of "the nice doctor," the mood of the doctor's office will be that the doctor knows best (even though this book shows that doctors only know what Big Pharma wants them to know).

9. The public is secretly poisoned (through food, water, air, vaccines, television, education, and chemtrails), and consequently gets sick, and thus must seek medicalization (since they will, in general, not know what else to do other than seek medicalization), where medications and treatments they are then given are so expensive that they make people go broke, and where treatment is in accord with points 1 - 8 above.

10. Doctors actually do not generally do medicine.

11. Doctors do whatever the state says (e.g., vaccine laws, cancer treatment laws, CPS-doctor partnerships, etc.).[632]

---

[632] *CPS* stands for "Child Protective Services." Many have noted for years that CPS is little more than a government kidnapping ring, where, in many cases, the government steals children without due process, without law, without evidence of abuse, and via militarized swat-team force. This has been hard for many to believe, but the April 2006 CPS roundup of over 400 children at a polygamous ranch in Texas brought the issue out for all to see. It occurred with no criminal evidence presented, was later declared illegal, and was later said to be instigated merely by an anonymous "tipster" call that was later thought to be a hoax. See "Texas Seizure of Polygamist-sect Kids Thrown Out" (Associated Press, May 22, by Michelle Roberts), which told us that

> In a ruling that could torpedo the case against the West Texas polygamist sect, a state appeals court Thursday said authorities had no right to seize more than 440 children in a

12. Doctors do not do research (this was discussed above).

13. Doctors act like police ("the law says you need to get your foot prick for the baby, so you can't leave the hospital until you do").

12. Doctors do unnecessary procedures (all the shots, useless but profitable checkups and visits, etc.).

15. Cancer treatments (chemo, radiation, tumor-reversal) are tortures, directly analogous to concentration camp eye and pain "experiments," for example.

16. Vaccines are like gas in the concentration camp showers: come get your shower/vaccines, it will help you, it is our gift to you. But the showers released poison gas, and the vaccines are poisons. Vaccination injuries are like a holocaust, as Dr. Leonard Horowitz has stated.

17. American medicine specializes in various sorts of Orwellian torture and subversion, such as the lobotomy ("chemical lobotomy "via vaccines), where the frontal lobe of the brain is virtually shut down (this is done through vaccines, SSRIs, Ritalin, food, television, etc.), where people can't think straight, can't put things together, can't keep details straight or gather them up efficiently, can't take care of children or develop motivation or prioritize the things of their lives.

Chemtrails
Introduction

One of the best ways to understand how the biomedical industry works is by studying chemtrails. Chemtrails are used to spray the citizenry with things that make them sick, and the public—not knowing what else to do—turns to Big Pharma for help, draining the citizenry of their independent, money, and health. In general, the pattern works like in the following diagram.

And this is how we get to chemtrails. They are perhaps at the same time both the most covert, but also the most obvious and visible chemical contamination of the citizenry.

Let me introduce you to the study of chemtrails with a passage from a Professor from Rutgers. Writing in 1988, Professor Leonard Cole wrote that

---

raid on the splinter group's compound last month. The Third Court of Appeals in Austin said the state failed to show the youngsters were in any immediate danger, the only grounds in Texas law for taking children from their parents without court action. It was not clear when the children - now scattered in foster homes across the state - might be returned to their parents. The ruling gave a lower-court judge 10 days to release the youngsters from custody, but the state could appeal to the Texas Supreme Court and block that... Every child at the Yearning For Zion Ranch in Eldorado was taken into custody more than six weeks ago after someone called a hot line claiming to be a pregnant, abused teenage wife. The girl has not been found and authorities are investigating whether the calls were a hoax.

During the 1970s, Americans learned that for decades they had been serving as experimental animals for agencies of their government. The Central Intelligence Agency had secretly been dropping mind-altering drugs into the drinks of citizens to watch their reactions. The U.S. Public Health Service fooled syphilitic blacks into thinking they were undergoing treatment when in fact they were being observed as their disease worsened. In battlefield tests, soldiers were marched to nuclear explosion sites, where they were exposed to dangerous levels of radiation. For these experiments thousands of Americans served as unsuspecting guinea pigs, and many suffered illness and death as a consequence. But the scope of these projects was dwarfed by an army program to assess the country's vulnerability to biological weapons. For at least two decades, the army secretly exposed millions of Americans to huge clouds of bacteria and chemical particles. The organisms and particles were sprayed over populated areas to observe their paths, in preparation for an attack by the Soviets with more lethal germs. But while the army was measuring air currents and survivability of the bacteria, no precautions were taken to protect the health and welfare of millions of people exposed. Like the other experiments that government agencies had been conducting, the public found out about the germ warfare tests through newspaper accounts in the 1970s. Like the other experiments, these tests were no longer taking place at the time of public disclosure. But unlike the other experiments, germ warfare testing is not merely a matter of history. The possibility of spraying the public congressional hearings that the army might resume testing when it finds an "area of vulnerability that takes additional tests." … Such an area evidently has been found. A 1986 army report reveals that open air testing is taking place again, at least on a limited basis.[633]

---

[633] Cole 1988, 3.

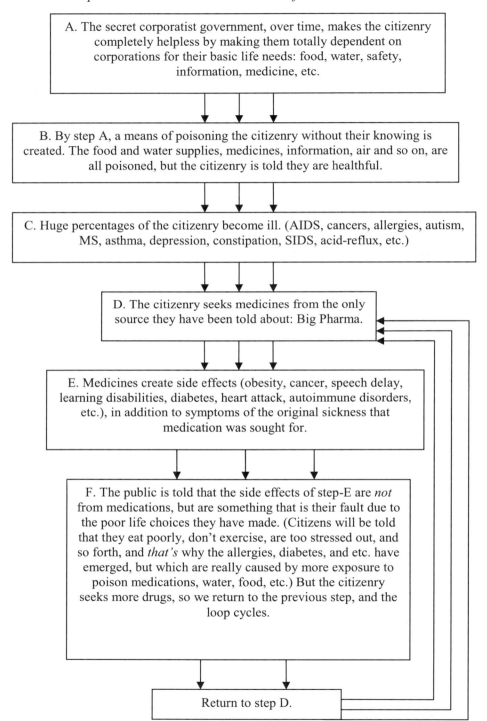

Given the fact that the cold war between the US and the Soviets was a sort of false flag event—a staged event to set up an empire threat in order to provoke the cold war[634]—the story that the spraying was due to war studies regarding the Soviets cannot be correct, and must be fully disregarded. Further, this means that the government was deliberately covering up their motives. So, this leaves the question: What is the purpose of the spraying?

This chemical spraying is not really a secret, it's just the case that the public does not know about it, as is the case with most other secret government issues addressed in this book. The military confidently boasts that it is legal for them to spray Americans with toxins (and you will see below that it is in the US code), Cole writes: "Alexander M. Capron, who served as executive director of the President's Commission on Bioethics, said that under existing rules, the army could be spraying over heavily populated areas, and the public would not know."[635]

The bottom line is this: Americans are continually being sprayed with mysterious chemicals via aircraft far above their heads, and anybody can verify this by merely looking up, but very few do.

On many sunny days, Americans who are paying attention, by looking up, will see very out-of-the-ordinary aircraft contrails in the sky. They will sit up in the sky for hours, *without dissipating at all* (that is the key characteristic of a chemtrail, as opposed to a contrail, which does dissipate), and they will form patterns that one would not expect from ordinary passenger jetliners. There is a massive spraying program that has been in effect for over a decade, and it could be the most significant human contamination of all, so much so that it may even be a contamination of the entire biosphere, even leading to some sort of a 2012 cosmogenesis, as I will discuss below. But first, how do we really know that this is going on?

How do we Really Know we are being Sprayed?

The US Code of Law

First of all, it has been made legal to spray Americans via chemtrails, as I will prove below. In fact, not only is that the case, but it has even been made legal to *kill* Americans via chemical spraying against them. The law is written in the US Code of Law, US code title 50 chapter 32 subsection 1520a paragraph b.[636] One can access the code since it is available online at this URL: *http://uscode.house.gov.* Here is a copy of the law from the US Code website:

Office of the Law Revision Counsel, U.S. House of Representatives

---

[634] See Thorn 2003, Section Six.
[635] Cole 1988, 4.
[636] Thanks to Alex Jones for alerting me to this part of the US Code.

-CITE--
   50 USC Sec. 1520a
01/19/04
-EXPCITE-
   TITLE 50 - WAR AND NATIONAL DEFENSE

   CHAPTER 32 - CHEMICAL AND BIOLOGICAL WARFARE
PROGRAM
-HEAD-
   Sec. 1520a. Restrictions on use of human
   subjects for testing of chemical or biological
   agents

-STATUTE-

   (a) Prohibited activities

   The Secretary of Defense may not conduct
(directly or by contract) -

      (1) any test or experiment involving the use
          of a chemical agent or biological agent
          on a civilian population; or

      (2) any other testing of a chemical agent or
          biological agent on human subjects.

   (b) Exceptions

   Subject to subsections (c), (d), and (e) of
   this section, the prohibition in subsection
   (a) of this section does not apply to a test
   or experiment carried out for any of the
   following purposes:

      (1) Any peaceful purpose that is related to
          a medical, therapeutic, pharmaceutical,
          agricultural, industrial, or research
          activity.

      (2) Any purpose that is directly related to
          protection against toxic chemicals or
          biological weapons and agents.

      (3) Any law enforcement purpose, including
          any purpose related to riot control.

   (c) Informed consent required

   The Secretary of Defense may conduct a test or
   experiment described in subsection (b) of this

section only if informed consent to the
testing was obtained from each human subject
in advance of the testing on that subject.

(d) Prior notice to Congress

Not later than 30 days after the date of final
approval within the Department of Defense of
plans for any experiment or study to be
conducted by the Department of Defense
(whether directly or under contract) involving
the use of human subjects for the testing of a
chemical agent or a biological agent, the
Secretary of Defense shall submit to the
Committee on Armed Services of the Senate and
the Committee on Armed Services of the House
of Representatives a report setting forth a
full accounting of those plans, and the
experiment or study may then be conducted only
after the end of the 30-day period beginning
on the date such report is received by those
committees.

(e) "Biological agent" defined

In this section, the term "biological agent"
means any micro-organism (including bacteria,
viruses, fungi, rickettsiac, or protozoa),
pathogen, or infectious substance, and any
naturally occurring, bioengineered, or
synthesized component of any such micro-
organism, pathogen, or infectious substance,
whatever its origin or method of production,
that is capable of causing -

   (1) death, disease, or other biological
       malfunction in a human, an animal, a
       plant, or another living organism;

   (2) deterioration of food, water, equipment,
       supplies, or materials of any kind; or

   (3) deleterious alteration of the
       environment.

The code begins by discussing how it is illegal to chemically spray Americans, then it however retracts that in paragraph b, where it says something to the effect that if the government wants to spray Americans, it is legal, if it is for peaceful purposes. But we have to remember that politicians don't usually use the word "peace" in the way that the rest of the citizenry does. For example, George Bush Jr. told us we needed to invade Iraq in order to establish peace in the Middle East. This is like saying that we have to start war to have peace. So, peace might not have a lot of meaning here in the Code, and instead, it might just be the case that paragraph b indicates that they can carry out whatever spraying they wish to.

2

107TH CONGRESS
1ST SESSION

H. R. 2977

To preserve the cooperative, peaceful uses of space for the benefit of all humankind by permanently prohibiting the basing of weapons in space by the United States, and to require the President to take action to adopt and implement a world treaty banning space-based weapons.

IN THE HOUSE OF REPRESENTATIVES

OCTOBER 2, 2001

Mr. KUCINICH introduced the following bill; which was referred to the Committee on Science, and in addition to the Committees on Armed Services, and International Relations, for a period to be subsequently determined by the Speaker, in each case for consideration of such provisions as fall within the jurisdiction of the committee concerned

---

A BILL

To preserve the cooperative, peaceful uses of space for the benefit of all humankind by permanently prohibiting the basing of weapons in space by the United States, and to require the President to take action to adopt and implement a world treaty banning space-based weapons.

1 *Be it enacted by the Senate and House of Representa-*
2 *tives of the United States of America in Congress assembled,*
3 SECTION 1. SHORT TITLE.
4   This Act may be cited as the "Space Preservation Act
5 of 2001".

1 SEC. 2. REAFFIRMATION OF POLICY ON THE PRESERVA-
2   TION OF PEACE IN SPACE.
3   Congress reaffirms the policy expressed in section
4 102(a) of the National Aeronautics and Space Act of 1958
5 (42 U.S.C. 2451(a)), stating that it "is the policy of the
6 United States that activities in space should be devoted
7 to peaceful purposes for the benefit of all mankind.".
8 SEC. 3. PERMANENT BAN ON BASING OF WEAPONS IN
9   SPACE.
10   The President shall—
11   (1) implement a permanent ban on space-based
12   weapons of the United States and remove from
13   space any existing space-based weapons of the
14   United States; and
15   (2) immediately order the permanent termi-
16   nation of research and development, testing, manu-
17   facturing, production, and deployment of all space-
18   based weapons of the United States and their com-
19   ponents.
20 SEC. 4. WORLD AGREEMENT BANNING SPACE-BASED WEAP-
21   ONS.
22   The President shall direct the United States rep-
23 resentatives to the United Nations and other international
24 organizations to immediately work toward negotiating,
25 adopting, and implementing a world agreement banning
26 space-based weapons.

Space Preservation Act: H.R. 2977 of the 107th

In addition to the US code, the bills of Congress have open statements about chemtrail activity. For example, Representative Kucinich (D, OH), established legislation that was meant to ban chemtrails, it was however not passed by Congress. The question is: If there are no chemtrail sprayings going on, then why was this legislation introduced? The answer appears to only be because chemtrail spraying is going on, has been going on, and has contaminated all Americans, as will be seen in the next section.

Kucinich's legislation is what is called the "Space Preservation Act." The reference to chemtrails is in 2 (B) (ii) of the legislation. I have put the entire bill into this book in order to show the reader how incredibly out of touch the average American is with the real weapons technology that the US military and

3		4	
1	SEC. 5. REPORT.	1	(2)(A) The terms "weapon" and "weapons sys-
2	The President shall submit to Congress not later than	2	tem" mean a device capable of any of the following:
3	90 days after the date of the enactment of this Act, and	3	(i) Damaging or destroying an object
4	every 90 days thereafter, a report on—	4	(whether in outer space, in the atmosphere, or
5	(1) the implementation of the permanent ban	5	on earth) by—
6	on space-based weapons required by section 3; and	6	(I) firing one or more projectiles to
7	(2) progress toward negotiating, adopting, and	7	collide with that object;
8	implementing the agreement described in section 4.	8	(II) detonating one or more explosive
9	SEC. 6. NON SPACE-BASED WEAPONS ACTIVITIES.	9	devices in close proximity to that object;
10	Nothing in this Act may be construed as prohibiting	10	(III) directing a source of energy (in-
11	the use of funds for—	11	cluding molecular or atomic energy, sub-
12	(1) space exploration;	12	atomic particle beams, electromagnetic ra-
13	(2) space research and development;	13	diation, plasma, or extremely low frequency
14	(3) testing, manufacturing, or production that	14	(ELF) or ultra low frequency (ULF) en-
15	is not related to space-based weapons or systems; or	15	ergy radiation) against that object; or
16	(4) civil, commercial, or defense activities (in-	16	(IV) any other unacknowledged or as
17	cluding communications, navigation, surveillance, re-	17	yet undeveloped means.
18	connaissance, early warning, or remote sensing) that	18	(ii) Inflicting death or injury on, or dam-
19	are not related to space-based weapons or systems.	19	aging or destroying, a person (or the biological
20	SEC. 7. DEFINITIONS.	20	life, bodily health, mental health, or physical
21	In this Act:	21	and economic well-being of a person)—
22	(1) The term "space" means all space extend-	22	(I) through the use of any of the
23	ing upward from an altitude greater than 60 kilo-	23	means described in clause (i) or subpara-
24	meters above the surface of the earth and any celes-	24	graph (B);
25	tial body in such space.		

corporatist government have at their disposal (having a grasp of how dramatically out-of-touch Americans are on this issue will be helpful when we discuss Morgellons disease below).

There is a lot of information to be gathered from this bill. [637] Firstly, as stated, if the chemtrail issue is a hoax, then why do we need a state representative to create a bill that prohibits their usage? It was reported on the Rense Radio Show (www.rense.com) on May 7, 2007 (chemtrail expert Mike Castle, PhD, was on the show as a guest that evening) that there are good reasons to conclude that Kucinich "stared death in the face" due to death threats and harassment by the military-industrial complex for putting the word "chemtrails" in a piece of legislation.

What is more interesting about this bill is that it refers to a plethora of weapons that most Americans have no idea exist. For example, there is reference to ELF weaponry, which has to do with the HAARP technology in Alaska, and other similar devices around the world. This technology can fully control weather worldwide, including creating or stopping hurricanes. This

---

[637] Thanks to Leonard Horowitz for alerting me to this legislation.

issue also was the subject of a recent bill, S 517 in the 107th Congress. Here are the first few pages of that bill, too.

These sorts of disclosures about weather control bring events like Hurricane Katrina[638] and the current nationwide famine[639] as being "natural events" into question, since they may be corporatist weather control operations and projects that are being used to rearrange the world (resources, people, and consciousness) since the corporatists have control over the weather.[640] Referring to the world controllers while in a discussion with Dr. Bill Deagle about weather control and Hurricane Gonu that hit Oman and Iran oil reserves in early June 2006, Alan Watt[641] said, "[a]nd watch the oil prices go through the roof. It's interesting how Mother Nature always cooperates with them at the right time."[642] Watt also said that he has old school books from Canadian school systems where it shows pictures of oil wells in Canada all capped off in the 1920s, not used and the existence of kept secret—all in order to hide the supply in order to fabricate shortages needed for price fixing.

The text of HR 2977 can be viewed at http://www.carnicom.com/hr2977.htm. The proposed law would have banned the US from using space-based weapons, including missiles, energy weapons, including molecular or atomic energy, subatomic particle beams, electromagnetic radiation, plasma, or extremely low frequency (ELF) or ultra low frequency (ULF) energy radiation), radiation, electromagnetic, psychotronic, sonic, laser, or other energies, information war, mood management, or mind control, chemical or biological agents, electronic, psychotronic, or information weapons; chemtrails; high altitude ultra low frequency weapons systems; plasma, electromagnetic, sonic, or ultrasonic weapons; laser weapons systems; strategic, theater, tactical, or extraterrestrial weapons; and chemical, biological, environmental, climate, or tectonic weapons; 'exotic weapons systems' including weapons designed to damage space or natural ecosystems (such as the ionosphere and upper atmosphere) or climate, weather, and tectonic systems with the purpose of inducing damage or destruction upon a target population or region on earth or in space.

---

[638] Also see my discussion about Hurricane Katrina in chapter 4 in the 'Economics of Destruction' section.

[639] See "A Drought for the Ages Spreads Across U.S." Patrick O'Driscoll, USA Today, June 8, 2007.

[640] The first time former TV news weatherman Scott Stevens (www.weatherwars.info) appeared on the Rense Radio Show, he suggested that the government weather control program was to massive, that basically *all* weather—down to the creation of the lowliest cloud—is now under government control. For more information on weather control and weather weaponry, the reader is strongly encouraged to consult Weather Warfare: *The Military's Plan To Draft Mother Nature*, by Jerry E. Smith, Adventures Unlimited Press, 2006.

[641] Alan is the auther of *Cutting Through the Matrix*, which can be found at www.cuttingthroughthematrix.com.

[642] Nutrimedical Report Radio Show, www.nutrimedical.com, June 5, 2007

5

(II) through the use of land-based, sea-based, or space-based systems using radiation, electromagnetic, psychotronic, sonic, laser, or other energies directed at individual persons or targeted populations for the purpose of information war, mood management, or mind control of such persons or populations; or

(III) by expelling chemical or biological agents in the vicinity of a person.

(B) Such terms include exotic weapons systems such as—

(i) electronic, psychotronic, or information weapons;

(ii) chemtrails;

(iii) high altitude ultra low frequency weapons systems;

(iv) plasma, electromagnetic, sonic, or ultrasonic weapons;

(v) laser weapons systems;

(vi) strategic, theater, tactical, or extraterrestrial weapons; and

(vii) chemical, biological, environmental, climate, or tectonic weapons.

6

(C) The term "exotic weapons systems" includes weapons designed to damage space or natural ecosystems (such as the ionosphere and upper atmosphere) or climate, weather, and tectonic systems with the purpose of inducing damage or destruction upon a target population or region on earth or in space.

109TH CONGRESS
1ST SESSION

S. 517

To establish the Weather Modification Operations and Research Board, and for other purposes

IN THE SENATE OF THE UNITED STATES

MARCH 3, 2005

Mrs. HUTCHISON introduced the following bill; which was read twice and referred to the Committee on Commerce, Science, and Transportation

A BILL

To establish the Weather Modification Operations and Research Board, and for other purposes.

Be it enacted by the Senate and House of Representatives of the United States of America in Congress assembled,

SECTION 1. SHORT TITLE.

This Act may be cited as the "Weather Modification Research and Technology Transfer Authorization Act of 2005".

SEC. 2. PURPOSE.

It is the purpose of this Act to develop and implement a comprehensive and coordinated national weather modification policy and a national cooperative Federal and

2

State program of weather modification research and development.

SEC. 3. DEFINITIONS.

In this Act:

(1) BOARD.—The term "Board" means the Weather Modification Advisory and Research Board.

(2) EXECUTIVE DIRECTOR.—The term "Executive Director" means the Executive Director of the Weather Modification Advisory and Research Board.

(3) RESEARCH AND DEVELOPMENT.—The term "research and development" means theoretical analysis, exploration, experimentation, and the extension of investigative findings and theories of scientific or technical nature into practical application for experimental and demonstration purposes, including the experimental production and testing of models, devices, equipment, materials, and processes.

(4) WEATHER MODIFICATION.—The term "weather modification" means changing or controlling, or attempting to change or control, by artificial methods the natural development of atmospheric cloud forms or precipitation forms which occur in the troposphere.

Admission of Spraying by the US Government

So far we have seen that the US government has legalized chemical spraying of Americans, and at least one representative of Congress has attempted to make it illegal. Now consider more evidence: the US military *admits* that, not only are they carrying out spraying of citizens, but they have been since at least the World War II era, and the spraying has been so extensive that it can be concluded that *all* US citizens have been thoroughly sprayed multiple times. According to Professor Cole:

> Hearings held by the Senate Subcommittee on Health and Scientific Research of the Committee on Human Resources in 1977 revealed the awesome scope of earlier germ-warfare testing program. Army spokesmen acknowledge that 239 populated areas from coast to coast had been blanketed with bacteria between 1949 and 1969. Tests involved covering areas of Alaska and Hawaii and the cities of San Francisco, Washington D.C., Key West, and Panama City in Florida. Some tests were more focused, such as those in which bacteria were sprayed onto the Pennsylvania Turnpike or into the New York City subway system.[643]

In chapters 1 and 2 of Cole's book, he describes how these sprayings by the army occurred "over San Francisco in 1950," and there were accounts of fatalities.[644] He also points out that Merck Pharmaceutical Company was one of the corporations driving this pervasive military spraying program, and where the operations, development, and carrying out of the spraying program was conducted in the "strictest secrecy."[645] Cole also discusses how the US military claimed that they were conducting benign operations in order to learn about chemical weapons threats, such as the (staged) threat from Russia, as if the spraying was ultimately for the "safety" of Americans. But it is also pointed out by Cole that military personnel behind the operations admit that nothing was learned from these experiments,[646] that it was not ever proven that the tests and the substances sprayed on humans were safe, and that the testing must resume at greater intensity.[647] Cole writes:

> During the 1960s, as other documents revealed, the army released various gases and hallucinogenic drugs in open-air tests in Maryland and Utah. Thousands of soldiers were exposed. Shortly after reports about the tests were uncovered in 1979, the army announced that it would try to contact the victims to see if there were long-term effects…. Nothing has been heard from the army about the matter. These tests involved biological, chemical,

---

[643] Cole 1988, 5-6.
[644] Cole 1988, 5-6.
[645] Cole 1988, 15.
[646] 16.
[647] 17.

and radioactive agents known to be virulent and toxic. *Many more people, perhaps tens of millions, were exposed to bacterial and chemical agents* that the army alleged, and continues to allege, were harmless. These so-called simulants of pathogenic bacteria have been sprayed in every region of the United States, from coast to coast, over cities, in buildings, on roads, and in tunnels. The medical literature at the time of the tests… raised questions about the safety of each of the simulants used. Nevertheless, the United States government continues to dispute evidence that its stimulant agents ever caused disease. Indeed, some of the same agents are being used in the army's current open air tests.[648] (Emphasis added)

Visual Evidence: Contrails Vs. Chemtrails

We have all seen jetliner contrails in the sky: trails left by jetliners traveling to who knows where. Contrails are different from chemtrails. Here's the simplest way to consider the difference:

> A **chemtrail** is: a trail of steam and exhaust that forms behind a jetliner that *does not disappear and dissipate*.
> A **contrail** is: a trail of steam and exhaust that forms behind a plane and then gradually *disappears and dissipates*.

This is the central and critical difference between contrails and chemtrails: chemtrails do not evaporate, but contrails do. As you will see below, this proves that there is more to the exhaust of the chemtrail than should be there: something else is coming out of the plane's exhaust other than what would be expected from ordinary jetliner engine activity. You will see below that this is because something is being sprayed on the American citizenry out of jetliners, via both commercial and non-commercial (e.g., military).[649]

Contrails can only form if the air is *very cold*,[650] since steam forms from a warm watery substance when that substance is in a very cold body of air. This is why contrails do not form behind planes, for example, when they are just taking off, landing, or flying low, in warmer air (although on some cold days you will see contrails form after the plane right after takeoff, for example). We have all seen this phenomenon occur when we see our breath when it gets very cold.

---

[648] Cole 1988, 18-19.
[649] Commercial jetliners appear to have something added to their fuel, since that is the only way to account for how ordinary jetliners can create chemtrails.
[650] Thomas 2004, 9-10.

Here is picture of steam emerging from a stack in Calumet, Indiana, at the campus of Purdue University-Calumet. This steam does not appear when it is warm at this plant, and it was 17 degrees F when this picture was taken (which was 9 am, January 20, 2007).

Also, clouds and contrails cannot form in very dry air, below around 50 or 60 percent humidity.[651] Ed Hopkins, Professor at the University of Wisconsin, has put on his website:

> The condensation trail left behind jet aircraft are called contrails. Contrails form when hot humid air from jet exhaust mixes with environmental air of low vapor pressure and low temperature. The mixing is a result of turbulence generated by the engine exhaust. *Cloud formation by a mixing process is similar to the cloud you see when you exhale and "see your breath"*.[652]

So just like when your breath evaporates, so should the contrails. Hopkins continues:

> If you are attentive to contrail formation and duration, you will notice that they can rapidly dissipate or spread horizontally into an extensive thin cirrus layer. How long a contrail remains intact, depends on the humidity structure and winds of the upper troposphere. If the atmosphere is near saturation, the contrail may exist for sometime. On the other hand, if the atmosphere is dry then as the contrail mixes with the environment it dissipates.[653]

Hopkins does not tell us what he means by "the contrail may exist for sometime." But I presume that he does not mean, *it does not dissipate*, as is the

---

[651] Thomas 2004, 10-11.

[652] As of January 9, 2007, Hopkins had this up on a web page at this address: http://cimss.ssec.wisc.edu/wxwise/class/contrail.html.

[653] Ibid.

case with chemtrails. I also assume that he does not mean that they can spread out and cover wider-and-wider areas, without dissipating. Therefore, if such activity is spotted, where contrails do not dissipate, the most rational thing to do is to presume that it is not contrail activity.

But this means that a simple conclusion must be drawn: if contrails do not dissipate, then they are not made of merely moist plane exhaust, and thus are made of something in addition. What, exactly, it is that is being sprayed, and proof that there is something being sprayed, will be discussed below, after I discuss what NASA says about contrails.

NASA Says Contrails Do Not Dissipate

In disagreement with everything just written in the previous section, NASA claims that some contrails do not dissipate:

> Sometimes contrails will actually take on the characteristics of a natural cirrus cloud and no longer look like contrails after only a half hour or so. Persistent contrails can exist long after the airplane that made them has left the area. They can last for a few minutes or longer than a day [i.e., they do not dissipate]. However, because they form at high altitudes where the winds are usually very strong, they will often move away from the area where they were born. When we look up into the sky, we may see old persistent contrails that formed somewhere else but moved overhead because of the wind... Persistent contrails are those most likely to affect climate.[654]

Given what Hopkins wrote, and given what was covered in the last section, it must be the case that NASA is referring to the contrails that have something else in the exhaust (and thus which are chemtrails, not contrails), which I discussed at the very end of the last section. It would appear from this passage from NASA's web site that NASA is attempting to change the definition of contrails so that they include non-dissipating contrails [i.e., chemtrails]. It appears that NASA—which is widely known to be a secretive and corrupt part of the secret corporatist government[655]—wants us to believe that steam *does not dissipate*, even though we all have seen it do so with our very own eyes countless times on cold days? Why would NASA put out information that is contrary to what, for example, Hopkins states, and which is so contrary to our everyday experience about what steam's properties are? Also, why would NASA put out information on contrails that plainly avoids discussion of the properties of humidity, temperature, and so forth, in the more technical way that Hopkins does?

---

[654] http://asd-www.larc.nasa.gov/SCOOL/contrails.html.
[655] See *Dark Moon*, 2001, by Mary Bennett and David Percy, Adventures Unlimited Press.

We will find out that the answer to these questions have one answer: because NASA is in on, and taking part in, the chemtrail spraying (you can verify that they are taking part in weather study and/or weather control through this University of Washington website: http://cargsun2.atmos.washington.edu), and apparently they want to hide this fact, and the http://asd-www.larc.nasa.gov/SCOOL/contrails.html web site I quoted above appears to be part of a cover-up. How else do we explain the amateurishness of the quote from NASA above from the http://asd-www.larc.nasa.gov/SCOOL/contrails.html web site? NASA is, of course, no stranger to cover-ups of the highest order.[656]

Chemtrails Characteristics

The following is a list of the characteristics of chemtrails. If you see any of these characteristics among jetliner contrails, you will be able to determine that they are in fact *chemtrails*, rather than contrails:

1. Chemtrails occur all at once. You will see the sky as clear blue all morning, and then all of a sudden, at noon exactly, for example, there will be non-dissipating trails all over the sky, extending far across the sky. Then again at 3 or 5 pm, for example, there will be none (and the sky will likely be hazy then, rather than blue, until the haze passes by).
2. Chemtrails tend to be non-random: they come in specific patterns, such as tic tac toe sorts of grid patterns, parallel or roughly parallel line patterns, asterisk stars, or Xs, as the following pictures illustrate.
3. Non-dissipating trails (chemtrails) are formed in such a way where they are not controlled by humidity levels, as is supposed to be the case for ordinary contrails. This would show that the contrails are not contrails, but are *chem*trails. One would expect, in more humid conditions, to see the atmosphere being more conducive for cloud or contrail formation, since increased humidity would lead to increases for each. But this is not what occurs for the non-dissipating contrails (i.e., chemtrails). There may be observed at times the expected scientific correlation between humidity conditions and cloud or contrails formation, such as when a jetliner travels through a cloud and its contrail becomes more pronounced when it does, only to become less pronounced when it leaves the cloud. This is expected since the increased humidity would lead to increased (more pronounced) contrail formation while the plane was traveling through the cloud. But chemtrails are such that they are not generally correlated with cloud activity and humidity levels in these sorts of ways. Chemtrails can be formed regardless of what the humidity levels are.

---

[656] Ibid.

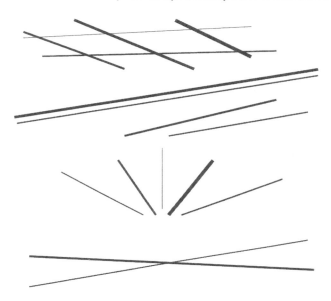

Here are a few examples of how humidity level and cloud activity do not correlate when the non-dissipating contrails (chemtrails) are present in the sky, and where this non-correlation does not make sense if we are to believe that the non-dissipating contrails are merely ordinary contrails, rather than chemtrails:

a. It is observed that there are jetliners flying right near one another where one will form a non-dissipating trail (a chemtrail), and the other will form a very quickly dissipating trail (an ordinary contrail). This would not be expected if humidity is presumably similar for each jetliner.

b. It is observed that there is trail formation in 20% or 50% humidity, for example, which is far too low for the formation of clouds or any sort of ordinary contrails. Clifford Carnicom (www.carnicom.com) noted this sort of chemtrail phenomenon in New Mexico, where he carried out much of his now-famous chemtrail research. He witnessed and documented many low humidity days that had so much chemtrail activity that they would lead to conditions that were overcast or hazy, in very low humidity.

c. It is observed that there is trail formation that does not dissipate, as would *not* be expected if trail formation were just a humidity issue, as seen with the way that clouds are controlled by humidity and continually form and dissipate.

d. As noted above, the sky may be clear all day (showing that the atmosphere is not in a state that is conducive for clouds or ordinary contrails to form), but then *suddenly*—often in a matter of minutes—the sky will be filled with non-dissipating trails (but *no clouds have formed*), even though the sky would not have radically changed in humidity level in that short amount of time, and even though jetliner activity will not have been heavy enough to account for all those "contrails."

4. Chemtrails have *endpoints*, or *endcaps*, as if the trail (the spraying) just abruptly starts and/or stops. This is a very important characteristic. The endcaps may look like this:

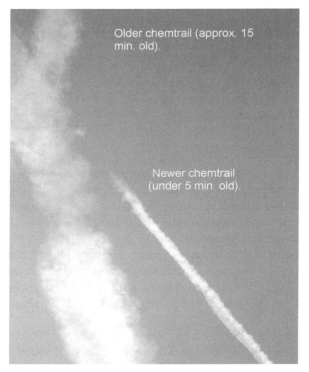

A newer contrail next to an older contrail. The newer contrail is more spread, and *neither has dissipated at all*. The newer, thinner "contrail" has an abrupt endcap. This is a picture I took from West Lafayette, Indiana, December 5, 2006, which shows how chemtrails are abrupt with the endpoints they exhibit.

If these were just "normal contrails," then it seems that they would not have endpoints (starts and stops to their contrails), but rather the trails would be continuous (not broken, as is the case with the trails with endcaps/endpoints) or they would fade away (dissipate) gradually, resembling the way steam fades away, rather than all-at-once. In other words, it seems that they would exist without choppy "starts and stops," and would gradually fade out, rather than abruptly start or stop. The picture above, of the plant from Purdue University - Calumet shows a thick bit of steam that *gradually* fades away over the next few dozen feet.

There can only be choppy and absolute "starts and stops" if the engines of the jetliners are being *shut off and restarted* as the jetliner flies. This certainly appears an impossibility for a jetliner, since if it shut off its engines mid-flight, it would begin a free-fall, and soon after, a nose-dive. Any of us who have flown in commercial jetliners, and who have heard the soft continuous and unbroken hum of the engines throughout the flight, know that commercial jetliners, of course, do not involve such starting and stopping of the engines midflight.

Furthermore, since the chemtrails occur in a pattern, then that implies that the "natural contrails," if they were such, occur in a pattern as the jetliners "stop and start" their engines in the same place in the sky over and over. These seem to be impossibilities, and thus it seems that the endcap trails can only be *chemtrails*—trails of chemicals that are not just water and fuel from the jet engines—that are being released from the jetliner. Contrails cannot have the aforementioned endcaps/endpoints. These endcaps/endpoints can only be the result of the abrupt starting and/or ceasing of something other than ordinary jetliner exhaust commencing and/or ceasing in the plane exhaust.

Many people, including myself, have watched chemtrail spraying events, and have seen planes with ordinary contrails that are fading away as one would expect, suddenly exhibit a chemtrail, as if they *started* spraying while being observed.

5. Chemtrails often will only cover *half of* the sky: one half of the sky is clear blue, the other is filled with lines, even though jetliners are flying over both areas. I would often see this from my house in West Lafayette, Indiana, where if I looked south, toward where the sky over Indianapolis is, I would see a huge amount of chemtrail (non-dissipating) lines, but where the sky was clear blue over my head—even though there was also significant jetliner activity over my house in West Lafayette. Were conditions such that trails could not form over my house, but where 40 miles south conditions were so right that a *massive* set of non-dissipating trails could form *all day* and hang in the sky all day? It does not seem that this makes much sense, unless the lines over Indianapolis were chemtrails.

6. The last chemtrail characteristic is the one I have already addressed: as stated above, unlike contrails, chemtrails *do not dissipate*, and they hang in the sky all day.

So What's Getting Sprayed on Americans?

In this chapter, it has been proven that the US corporatists are spraying Americans regularly. But with what?

Professor Cole points out that none of the materials sprayed on Americans were known to be harmless during the sprayings up to 1988: they were either harmful, or they were not known to be safe.[657] Cole writes about how spraying killed large mammals in the Caribbean,[658] and thus it is clear that humans would have been killed also.

In Chapter one of his book, *Clouds of Secrecy*, Cole describes how the US military reported during the decades before and up to 1988, that their tests were safe and harmless, but where in reality they were deliberate poisonings. Also Cole reports how Americans were repeatedly told that the tests were conducted for the safety of Americans, and in order to try to understand the Russians, but then we are told that after decades of tests, oddly, the military learned *nothing* from them, and thus had to conduct more tests (which they were resuming at the time of the publication of Professor Cole's book).[659]

If there are no epidemic-creating conditions present (municipal filth, immigrating infected people, newly created mosquito-passing diseases, etc.), but an epidemic or pandemic arises quickly (such as in the way the flu does each fall), then another cause must be sought out. Chemtrails are a very good alternative causal source, due to the fact that we know chemtrails have often been a source of epidemics and pandemics in the past. Furthermore, it is documented in this book that the corporatists behind chemtrails have a long history of poisoning the citizens of the world (through the vaccines they make, the food and water they monopolize worldwide, and through the medicines they make), and chemtrails would merely be another extension of this contamination of the world citizenry. If a person understands vaccine contamination, then chemtrail contamination can merely be seen as another facet of the deliberate and pervasive contamination and poisoning of the RP;[660] it is not much more complicated than that.

Morgellons Fibers and red blood cells. Clifford Carnicom (www.carnicom.com) has presented research that has been studied all over the world, inside and outside of universities. He has reportedly found that red blood cell types of matter, and some sort of unknown fibers, have been found to be associated with the chemtrail spraying. Apparently people had found these materials floating in the air and on the ground as chemtrails floated overhead.

Pertussis Spraying. Professor Cole reports that there was spraying of whooping cough bacteria on Americans in the 1950s, wherein the whooping cough rate increased dramatically shortly after in some locations.[661] Due to the findings of this book, where it is found that corporatists pervasively contaminate humanity in a plethora of ways, we can inductively conclude that

---

[657] Cole 1988, 17-18.
[658] Cole 1988, 18.
[659] Cole 1988, 16-17.
[660] Contamination of the RP is not the only function of chemtrails; weather control is another, as will be very briefly discussed below.
[661] Cole 1988, 18.

this is not an isolated incident, and we can predict that humanity is constantly being sprayed with bacteria, viruses, and other agents that will make them sick. This is a crucial issue, since it shows how the citizenry will be deliberately contaminated in order to make them sick so that Big Pharma can come in and profit off of a "solution" to the sickness that results due to the contamination (in this case, the solution is the expensive whooping cough vaccine).

Cole's source for this is a newspaper (International Herald Tribune[662]). Is that a problem? A news story is covered up if it is not reported on. For example, when it was discovered that George W. Bush's grandfather was a top Nazi financier,[663] it was reported on initially in a few newspapers, but then the story—which is certainly a blockbuster—did not appear in any more papers. This does not indicate that the story is *not* a good money-maker for the newspapers (since it surely is), but rather that the story is being covered up, and profits are being sacrificed to keep the cover-up going. This appears to be analogous to what occurred with the report on whooping cough bacteria being sprayed on Americans, which is certainly another massive news story (that would lead to huge news paper sales). If a news story is a blockbuster story, but is only reported on by one or a few news papers, and ignored or ridiculed by all the rest of the mass media (e.g., Fox News, New York Times, CNN, etc.), that is an indication that the story is true, since it's an indication of cover-up, as revealed by the lack of reporting. Instead, the news will be littered with insignificant tabloid-like stories, as Americans had to listen to for months in 2007 when the tabloid story of Anna Nichole Smith broke, or when it was reported on in the mass media that Brittany Spears shaved her head. Stories that are widely reported on tend to have some degree of untruth or distortion of reality—at least to the extent that they misleadingly pose as news, thus keeping the real news covered up. For this reason, Cole's citation of a news paper is a strong informational source, in this case. The government deliberately infecting the citizenry with whooping cough should have been the biggest news story of the decade, but only one news paper reported on it.

Conclusion of Chemtrails Discussion

Since the secret corporatist government has been proven to have torment and horror in store for humanity, we might conclude that chemtrail spraying is part of this project, and perhaps that it is connected to the rash of outbreaks that have occurred around the world with diseases, such as Morgellons disease. There have been reports that chemtrails can put humans to sleep, change the atmosphere into a plasmic sort of entity that will be conducive for various sorts of mind-control devices, and so forth. I will next discuss one of the horror stories of chemtrails.

---

[662] It should be noted that the report from IHT is before IHT was in sole control of the New York Times and the Washington Post (which occurred in 1991).
[663] I discuss this elsewhere in this book.

Morgellons Disease

Introduction. To understand Morgellons disease, one has to go outside the box, and one has to understand that the government has secret technologies that are so advanced that they are literally beyond most people's imagination.[664] Morgellons disease is the infestation of humans, insects, and animals by an ultra-high-tech nanomachine or hive-like fibrous nano-intelligence. Since Morgellons is a major global pandemic currently being studied by top university researchers, but is blacked-out of the mass media, and mocked by the FDA and CDC, this seems to indicate that the corporatists are behind it, since they are merely using their corporatist media to cover it up, as they have done with so many other things.

> The name "Morgellons Disease" is based on the description of a similar fiber producing condition, found in children by Sir Thomas Browne in 1674. Microscopic drawings, dating from 1682 by Dr. Michel Etmuller appear to be similar to the fibers from present-day sufferers.[665]

> To my knowledge, the first person to identify that Morgellons disease is a largely silicon-based extraterrestrial-like nano-machine that, it seems, is thousands of years ahead of any known technology, was Dr. Bill Deagle of the Nutrimedical Report (www.nutrimedical.com).

> The Morgellons Research Foundation began registering people with symptoms of the disease in 2002. [But] [t]here are patients who have claimed to have had the symptoms for as long as two decades. Most were diagnosed with Delusional Parasitosis.[666]

---

[664] A good example of this is the "invisible soldier suit." The military has a suit that turns one *invisible* when one puts it on. Most people, upon hearing this, completely reject the idea as impossible. But that's only because they have no idea how it works, and how simple it is. The suit consists of tiny cameras and hi-tech tiny video recorders. What the suit does is records what is, for example, behind the soldier who is wearing the suit, and then projects that image of what's behind her/him on the front of the soldier's suit with tiny cameras that are on the front of the solider's suit. All that is seen when looking at the "invisible soldier" is the image behind the soldier. See "Widespread Military Applications Seen for Invisibility Technology," The Scotsman, James Reynolds, March 1, 2005. Also see the DVD lecture, *Weapons of Mass Control*, by Bob Fletcher, 1997, available from World News Insight, P.O. Box 216, Bayview Idaho, 83803.

[665] This is from the Oklahoma State University Center for Health Sciences website, http://healthsciences.okstate.edu/ morgellons, from March 2007.

[666] This is from the Oklahoma State University Center for Health Sciences website, http://healthsciences.okstate.edu/ morgellons, from March 2007.

In 2006, it was reported that at least 5000 households have it—this is just the group of households that have registered at morgellons.org, and it could represent 1 or more people per registry, depending on how many in a household are infected.[667] But after word started to get out about the disease through the popular Rense Radio Show, on April 3, 2007 it was reported that 60,000 people had registered as victims suffering from Morgellons,[668] and thus at that time it rivaled the number of cases of polio during the height of the 1950s polio vaccination craze.

> Most cases in the United States are from California, Texas and Florida, though all 50 states have had reported cases. There are clusters of the disease in specific geographic regions of California and Texas. It has been reported throughout Europe, South Africa, Japan, Philippines, Indonesia and Australia.[669]

What is Morgellons? The general public has a hard time believing that Morgellons disease is real. This is primarily because it is a completely new sort of incomprehensible, surreal "life"-form, and it appears to be machine-like—meaning that somebody created it in a lab. Since Americans are totally unfamiliar with this sort of an advanced technology, they will often laugh it off, perhaps out of fear that they are being fooled to believe in the next superstitious hoax, for example. But regardless of what ordinary Americans think about Morgellons, the fact is that there are real samples of the disease that are being studied in the most prestigious American universities, and thus the evidence is there.

There seem to be three options for what Morgellons is:

a). A secret government experimental infestation, or
b). A disease of extraterrestrial origin,
c). A combination of (a) and (b).[670]

There is evidence for (a), through patents that have been acquired for technology very similar to the Morgellons nano-fibers.[671] And Dr. Bill Deagle,

---

[667] Rense Radio Show, www.rense.com, July 17, 2006.
[668] Nutrimedical Report Radio Show, www.nutrimedical.com, April 3, 2007.
[669] This is from the Oklahoma State University Center for Health Sciences website, http://healthsciences.okstate.edu/
morgellons, from March 2007. Some of these issues were also discussed on the Rense Radio Show, www.rense.com, June 22, 2006.
[670] Dr. Bill Deagle has endorsed this position, in addition to the position that Morgellons is a silicon nano-"life"-form.
[671] This is according to Dr. Hildegarde Staniger, author of the international environmental bestseller, *Comprehensive Handbook of Hazardous Material: Regulations, Monitoring, Handling & Safety*, Lewis Publishing/ CRC Press, from an interview on the Nutrimedical Report Radio Show, www.nutrimedical.com, April 3, 2007.

who has connections to people in government, maintains that there is evidence for (b).[672] I will not discuss these issues further, I will, rather, merely assume (a) is true given the patent information that Dr. Staniger has reported, and which is available at the Rense.com website, as of April 2007. (a) is particularly important to this book, since it would verify that Morgellons is a corporatist project, as I will discuss shortly.

Morgellons Defined. On April 5, 2007, on the Rense.com web site, a page was put on that site that listed the definition of Morgellons is as follows:

A communicable nanotechnology invasion of human tissues in the form of self-assembling, self-replicating nanotubes, nanowires, nanoarrays with sensors, and other nano configurations, some carrying genetically-altered and spliced DNA/RNA. These nano machines thrive in alkaline ph conditions and use the body's bio-electric energy and other (unidentified) elements for power. There is some evidence these tiny machines possess their own internal batteries. They are also believed to be able to receive specific tuned microwave, EMF and ELF signals and information. To what end is not known. The symptoms vary from open skin lesions from which colored or plain fibers emerge, which do not scab normally, heal extremely slowly and never become bacterially-infected -- to brain fog, fatigue and depression, etc. It is also established that Morgellons nano machines are commonly found in all body fluids, orifices and often even hair follicles, and are believed to routinely achieve total body systemic penetration. It is reported by nearly all afflicted that Morgellons nano machines seem to have some kind of hive or 'group intelligence.' Communicability appears to be possible/ probable through shedding of the fibers by the infected and through all normal bacterial or viral vectors. Some fibers have been shown to withstand temperatures in excess of 1400 F, routine sterilization for Morgellons nano machines in all reusable medical/ dental medical equipment and instruments is moot. There is also strong evidence linking Chemtrail aerosol fibers to Morgellons fibers although proof of transmission through aerial spraying remains anecdotal.

The Basics. It is unclear whether Morgellons is passed by food,[673] insect bites, vaccines, water supply, air, or by direct transmission from human-to-human or animal-to-human; but as discussed above, there is some evidence that Morgellons is being dropped via chemtrails.[674] One thing that appears to be the

---

[672] Nutrimedical Report Radio Show, www.nutrimedical.com, April 3, 2007.

[673] It has been reported to have been found in food. Rense Radio Show, www.rense.com, August 16, 2006.

[674] See "Morgellons: First Observations," Clifford E Carnicom, Aug 12 2006, Edited Aug 16 2006, Copyright 2006 by Clifford E Carnicom and Jan Smith, http://www.carnicom.com/morgobs1.htm. Clifford Carnicom has been a regular guest

case is that only certain people can be infected with Morgellons, as Dr. Bill Deagle has discussed, and it may be the case that Morgellons is passed to the citizenry in a selective manner, but in general is beginning to cover the entire earth.[675]

Morgellons consists of tiny motile and intelligent fibers that work together in hive-like fashion to infest the entire body of a biological host, gradually taking over and replacing parts of the host's body. It is like the worst nano-bug infestation imaginable.

Morgellons is aggressive. The more one attacks it, the more it appears and attacks its victims. Jeff Rense said that this suggests that the Morgellons fibers have *intelligence*,[676] as if the fibers are part of a hive-like pseudo-organism. This hive-like behavior could be perhaps loosely compared to the way an ant colony functions like a single problem-solving organism, but the difference is that ants communicate by directly contacting one another (they touch heads in order to pass chemicals in a chemical communication system), and Morgellons fibers appear to communicate across a distance, without directly touching, and thus by some sort of unseen communicative intermediary between the fibers. Perhaps this is some sort of unseen sound or ELF communication. It is widely reported that Morgellons victims emanate an intense electric field that non-infected people do not have, and thus, that e-field could have something to do with the communicative mechanism.

Morgellons manifests visibly as a severe skin rash, and fibers are found in the open sores. But victims can feel the fibers moving on and *inside* of their bodies. The fibers can be seen to withdraw back into the body when a victim tries to pull them out of the open sores.[677] In response to this, Jeff Rense said, "they are smart, and they know how... to get out of harm's way."[678] This further suggests some sort of hive-like, ant-colony-like behavior. Victims report that they sense, or intuit, that the remnants of the hive-like quasi-organismic "entity" that is infecting them is only the surface, or externality, of what is a much more complex and/or larger "organism" that is inside of them, pervading all parts of their body. Cliff Mickelson, who has Morgellons, said that we do not have the language or concepts to describe this affliction. He said this is from the "deepest well anyone has ever plumbed... It affects everything about you; you are "never alone" with this [disease]."[679]

---

on the Rense.com Radio Show, and as mentioned above, his research has been studied at a few universities around the world (but it has been ignored by the FDA).

[675] Rense Radio Show, www.rense.com, August 16, 2006.

[676] He uttered this on the Rense Radio Show, www.rense.com, June 22, 2006.

[677] Rense Radio Show, www.rense.com, November 9, 2006.

[678] Rense Radio Show, www.rense.com, November 9, 2006.

[679] He uttered this on the Rense Radio Show, www.rense.com, June 22, 2006.

Claims of Psychological/Neurotic Cause. Modern medicine largely does not know what to do about Morgellons, it offers no theories, no research, and thus they have mostly banished it to being a "psychological problem."[680] Therefore, Morgellons is merely one of countless ailments that are called "psychological problems" by the "dart-board diagnosis" practices that are so often carried out in the modern medical establishment, as will be discussed below regarding anti-depressants and sleep disorders.

There are also reports that hospitals turn away patients since the symptoms do not fit any known ailment, and since it will be claimed that the conditions are caused by psychological illness or sadomasochistic behavior.[681] It is claimed that victims are DoP: having delusions of parapsytosis.[682] But Morgellons is being studied in top university laboratories (such as MIT[683]), and by top university professors (Yale, Oklahoma State, etc.), and it has measurable observable symptoms that these top scientists are studying, who are using real clinical samples (according to Dr. Wymore, "samples… come directly from patients in a clinical setting."[684]); so it seems very difficult to account for how this is merely a mind-creation.

This claim of delusion should be investigated, but given what has just been written, it seems more to be the case that the "delusion diagnosis" is something analogous to the often sloppy nature of where doctors will reject real data and real research and merely make something up. For example, doctors have been known to do things like claim that Prozac is a cure for sleep disorders.[685] Perhaps it is for these sorts of reasons that professors like Randy S. Wymore, Ph.D. (assistant professor of pharmacology and physiology, Oklahoma State University) say things like "Preliminary evidence suggests that Morgellons Disease is not DoP (delusions of parasites)."[686]

Many victims take antipsychotics for Morgellons, as prescribed by a doctor, and for a while they appear to work, and thus it might appear that they are crazy after all, and that's the reason for the onset of the Morgellons. But the

---

[680] Rense Radio Show, www.rense.com, June 22, 2006.

[681] Rense Radio Show, www.rense.com, June 28, 2006.

[682] For discussion of this issue, see "The Mystery of Morgellons Disease: Infection or Delusion?" 2006. *American Journal of Clinical Dermatology.* Virginia R. Savely, Mary M. Leitao, and Raphael Stricker. Vol. 7. No. 1. Pages 1-5.

[683] Dr. Hildegard Stanninger, Rense Radio Show, www.rense. com, March 29, 2007.

[684] This comes from the website of Professor Randal Wymore of Oklahoma State University, http://www.healthsciences. okstate.edu/morgellons/research.cfm.

[685] For a discussion of this, see Richards 2006, 12-13.

[686] This comes from the website of Professor Randal Wymore of Oklahoma State University, http://www.healthsciences. okstate.edu/morgellons/research.cfm.

antipsychotics all have thorazine, and this contains certain chemicals used in pigs that are not for mental conditions, and thus may be responsible for the change in Morgellons.[687] Also, Morgellons reacts to, and fights, against a person based on their stress level, and since SSRIs and anti-psychotics make a person more zombic, thus decreasing their inner tension, it could be the case that SSRIs and anti-psychotics may temporarily help because they may reduce a person's stress level.

Basic Characteristics.

- Often fibrous
- Commonly have geometric structure (pyramidal, etc.)
- Living (exhibit lifelike motion, have central nucleus)
- They grow very quickly.[688]
- The fibers glow in the dark and are fluorescent[689]
- Immune system will leave it completely alone.[690] The white blood cell count of the afflicted is typically more-or-less normal, and this indicates that the immune system is not responding to it[691]
- Fibers are roughly like a fungal emanation, but far larger[692]
- Not a virus, not a bacteria.[693] This is simply not a known life-form. This is because of the temperature issues, and their withstanding of heat, and the lack of internal structure the fibers exhibit
- Swim in 91% alcohol, don't die[694]
- Do not burn[695] except at well over 1000 ° F[696,697]
- Can burn with butane, and it will not affect them[698]

Jeff Rense has suggested that the fibers observed throughout the body are an emanation of an "organism" or life form, or a nanobacteria that is submicroscopic.[699]

The gel is not a scab, but a part of the organism tenting over the open wound. Victims assert that activity is carried out underneath the "patch," with fibers around the edge, and where its scab can expand slowly. Victims report that

---

[687] Rense Radio Show, www.rense.com, November 9, 2006.
[688] Rense Radio Show, www.rense.com, June 22, 2006.
[689] Rense Radio Show, www.rense.com, June 22, 2006.
[690] Rense Radio Show, www.rense.com, June 28, 2006.
[691] Rense Radio Show, www.rense.com, June 28, 2006.
[692] Rense Radio Show, www.rense.com, June 28, 2006.
[693] Rense Radio Show, www.rense.com, October 24, 2006.
[694] Rense Radio Show, www.rense.com, June 22, 2006.
[695] Rense Radio Show, www.rense.com, June 22, 2006.
[696] Rense Radio Show, www.rense.com, October 24, 2006.
[697] Rense Radio Show, www.rense.com, June 28, 2006.
[698] Rense Radio Show, www.rense.com, June 28, 2006.
[699] Rense Radio Show, www.rense.com, June 28, 2006.

under the patches, parts of their bodies are replaced, with masses of entangled fibers, which is not even really a tissue, but a new sort of "tissue", or "photissue," as Jeff Rense has put it. Also, the fibers are often clear (transparent),[700] and they have various other colors—red, blue, black—where each colored fiber has specific behaviors and functions. The fibers form colors in a way that one would not expect a carbon-based creature would be able to manufacture, since a tiny carbon-based creature does not have constituents needed to do this.[701]

If one attempts to pluck the fiber (in the case of the larger fibers that are clearly visible and that can be grasped), often the fiber will eject a goo out upon being attacked.[702]

Chimera. The hive-like Morgellons material has the ability to, and it seems always prepared to, take over any earthly life-form it infests: insect, reptile, mammalian, and so forth. According to Jeff Rense, it "is a gel-mass, ... a template waiting for something to impress upon it a genetic signature or code which that gel-mass would apparently grow to become."[703] Rense went on to say, it is waiting to become something, and it becomes what it is nearby or inside of.

This is where most people have a difficult time in accepting that Morgellons is real, due to the fact that it is so vastly different and more sophisticated than any sort of technology that has ever been comprehended by most humans. For most Americans, they view the space shuttle as high-tech, due to the fact that they have no idea of the real developments of technology that have occurred. For example, most Americans do not even know that their US military has developed a robot army (discussed in chapter 6). Also, Americans have learned to ridicule one another whenever a person brings up a new, daring, or unfamiliar idea,[704] and thus, Americans will tend to not accept that there could be something new under the sun.

---

[700] Rense Radio Show, www.rense.com, Nov. 9, 2006.

[701] Rense Radio Show, www.rense.com, June 28, 2006.

[702] Rense Radio Show, www.rense.com, July 17, 2006.

[703] This is a quote from Jeff Rense of the Rense Radio Show, www.rense.com, Nov. 9, 2006.

[704] If you doubt this, then go up to a group of friends and tell them that you believe that there was no jetliner that hit the Pentagon on 9/11, that NASA has been developing a "space plane" (since the 1980s), that elephants communicate with one another across miles using ultra-low frequencies that humans usually cannot hear (see *Animal Talk*, by Eugene S Morton and Jake Page, 1992, New York: Random House), or that UFOs exist. None of these ideas are absurd, and all are about real observations that people and scientists have researched, but that will not prevent your friends from likely giggling and laughing, as they have been trained to do through the insecurity and nervousness that the government-mandated education system has imprinted in their minds indefinitely.

Life, but not Biological. Professor John Janovy, Jr., of the University of Nebraska in Lincoln, and the Secretary/Treasurer of the American Society of Parasitologists, and author of one of the landmark books of parasitology, made the comment that the Morgellons symptoms are *not cellular* (eukaryotic): do not resemble any life form of any sort whatsoever; do not appear to be under genetic control.[705] Prokaryotic cells have DNA material in the cell membrane. Morgellons fibers have no cell membrane, and no nuclear membrane. It is not a cell, it is more like an asbestos fiber, like a nanomaterial. There are no organelles, DNA, floating DNA, and so on.[706] There is nothing resembling anything animal, vegetable, bacterial, and so on. They have no substructure and no cell structure.

Illness Symptoms: Mental and Physical. "Screaming pain." In general, fibers infest the entire body, giving rise to stunning joint pain, horrible bowel movements, where the body is totally riddled with the fibers. There is a full takeover for some victims, but for others, fibers only pop out now and then.[707] Victims also report that it feels "itchy, crawly" under the skin.[708] It is as if you can feel an organism crawling not just on your skin, but, for example, *inside* your foot.

Other symptoms reported are: short term memory problems, concentration problems, and inability to think.[709] It can be seen in victims of Morgellons that their spark of humanness, or personality, decreases (and this usually is exhibited before fibers are discovered, and often when the disease is at a minimal symptomatic level),[710] and that they often can't think clearly, can't multi-task, can't use language clearly, and can't make a thought into words.[711] Victims have reported that the thoughts they hear in their head during thinking and the process of making language won't match up to what is said verbally through intercommunication with others.[712] As Jeff Rense said to a victim: "[s]o you were not able to manifest the spoken words you would think you were saying?" The victim that Rense was speaking to confirmed, and said that she did not know that this was happening (apparently others had to tell her).[713]

Victims report a continual increase of losing interest in doing the practical issues of life, such as losing interest in chewing food.[714] Further, victims would often notice this *before* the skin symptoms show up, which implies that there is an "organism" working inside the body before the disease appears on the skin,

---

[705] Rense Radio Show, www.rense.com, Nov. 9, 2006.
[706] Dr. Hildegard Stanninger, Rense Radio Show, www.rense.com, March 29, 2007.
[707] Rense Radio Show, www.rense.com, Nov. 9, 2006.
[708] Rense Radio Show, www.rense.com, Nov. 9, 2006.
[709] Rense Radio Show, www.rense.com, June 28, 2006.
[710] Rense Radio Show, www.rense.com, May 10, 2007.
[711] Morgellons #4.
[712] Rense Radio Show, www.rense.com, May 10, 2007.
[713] Rense Radio Show, www.rense.com, May 10, 2007.
[714] Rense Radio Show, www.rense.com, July 17, 2006.

and working in the brain[715] (and brain scans reveal that there are lesions in the white matter of the brain of Morgellons victims[716]), doing manipulation of the brain in some way, which opens up the idea that the "entity" is taking over the mental capacities of the host. Victims have reported that the "entity" gets hardwired into their personality, and seems to provoke and increase the negative traits of the person that existed before they were inflicted. For example, if you struggled to get yourself to balance the checkbook before Morgellons, then after it is literally impossible.[717]

Morgellons is reported to make one lose motivation to, for example, clean the house. It has been claimed by afflicted persons, that if you are active, it will "knock you down," but if you go inside and rest on the couch, it will leave you alone. The more you work, sweat, and get physical, the more it will flare up. "It does not want you to get physical."[718]Victims develop ticks, twitches, bell's palsy (which attacks a cranial nerve).[719]

Aggressive if Attacked. "It" becomes instantly *very* aggressive if the host attacks it (such as by plucking the fibers).[720] This is widely reported in the victims, who have also reported that if you apply topicals meant to kill the "entity" it becomes aggressive, as if to go into a "hyperbreeding" mode, causing the visible skin legions to worsen, and which would make black, red and white fibers come out, victims report.[721] If one attacks it, in the way suggested in the last sentence, at, for example, one location on the body (for example, the wrist), then an appendage/mass on your angle, for example, will start to attack you with fury—as if there is a network of communication or interconnection between fibers and/or between parts of the "organism." Victims tell us that the fibers are micro-integrated, with some level of communication and life. It is as if the life form is learning to assimilate with the host, not meaning to torture it, but incidentally doing so as it learns to work with and take over the host.[722] This issue of take-over will be important in later discussions.

"Another Presence." Along these same lines, 24 hours per day, we are told by the victims, that there is a feeling that there is "another presence," "a monkey on your back," that is "with" the afflicted, as if in symbiotic partnership, and where the "entity" conflicts or perhaps stridently partners with the host.

---

[715] Morgellons #4.
[716] Rense Radio Show, www.rense.com, May 10, 2007.
[717] Morgellons #4.
[718] Rense Radio Show, www.rense.com, June 28, 2006.
[719] Morgellons #4.
[720] Rense Radio Show, www.rense.com, June 28, 2006.
[721] Rense Radio Show, www.rense.com, Nov. 9, 2006.
[722] Rense Radio Show, www.rense.com, June 28, 2006.

It is as if there is another intelligence in the body that has a kind of awareness, with a direction, an agenda, a program.[723] You know it senses you, like you know a person you are talking to senses you.[724] The afflicted are "colonized"—not in the way a bacteria colonizes the body, but an "imperialistic colonization;" it "feels" like the afflicted is fighting against another intelligence, which is learning, is *feeling* its way as it goes.[725]

The Fibers. If you remove fibers from a victim, put them in *pure* bleach, and come back six hours later, you will see that the fibers have *climbed up* the jar to the top,[726] which again indicates some sort insect-mimicking behavior. Ammonia does not impede it.[727] But again, and in accord to what I have written above, it does not act like a known life-form, as the bleach example shows, and because, for example, ammonia mixed with bleach (which produces a gas deadly to humans), does not harm the hive-forming fibers.[728] Morgellons is not biological.[729]

Hive Characteristics. If fibers are removed from a victim, and put in a bucket of water (such as if the victim washes hands in it), the fibers start to "attract" and swirl (always clockwise, and this was reported in the northern hemisphere) around to form a bundle.[730] One victim reported that this could be like a sort of organism that can be destroyed and reassembled, so it is the mix between unicellular life and multicellular life.[731]

There appear to be some fibers that are more motile than others, and then fluorescent ones that come up through the skin and stick out through it.[732]

Skin Symptoms. The most visible symptom is a major skin rash, with fierce and *constant* itching involved. Victims report non-healing sores all over the skin, with sensations of biting around them. And they report to having very weak skin that easily breaks open. Initially Morgellons looks like a terrible case of poison ivy that begins with a fury, lasts for six weeks, then disappears, only to return a year later (sometimes *to the day*), and this cycle can continue and escalate. There was reportedly an eczema outbreak among children in Britain, but which, when looked at through a microscope, the fibers where observed, and thus there could be latent varieties of Morgellons.[733] It has been suggested that more minor varieties of Morgellons are misdiagnosed as many of the new

[723] Rense Radio Show, www.rense.com, June 28, 2006.
[724] Rense Radio Show, www.rense.com, June 28, 2006.
[725] Rense Radio Show, www.rense.com, June 28, 2006.
[726] Rense Radio Show, www.rense.com, June 22, 2006.
[727] Rense Radio Show, www.rense.com, June 22, 2006.
[728] Rense Radio Show, www.rense.com, June 22, 2006.
[729] Rense Radio Show, www.rense.com, June 22, 2006.
[730] Rense Radio Show, www.rense.com, Nov. 9, 2006.
[731] Rense Radio Show, www.rense.com, Nov. 9, 2006.
[732] Jan Smith, Rense Radio Show, www.rense.com, March 29, 2007. This may strike some as astonishing that the fibers are luminous, but luminescent life forms are common in nature, such as deep in the ocean.
[733] Rense Radio Show, www.rense.com, July 17, 2006.

ailments that have shown up worldwide over the past decade or two: arthritis, chronic fatigue, etc.[734]

Over time, wounds stop healing, lesions are kept open, but do not get infected,[735] fibers start flooding the body (under fingernails, when you blow your nose, etc.). Victims report profusely shedding the fiber matter all around the house, to the extent that it is impossible to keep the house clean.[736]

Entangled wades of fiber look like multi-colored dyed cotton. Fibers are usually very tiny, but can be up to an inch or two—they will grow, and the longer you let them grow in time, the longer their length will get. They congregate along the edges of a lesion. A Morgellons sufferer will spit them up, wherein there will be thousands of them, indicating that they are running rampant throughout the body. A Morgellons sufferer will feel them moving in their lungs, nasal passages, hair follicles, etc. Constant pain is reported, but which is instantly relieved when they are pulled. When pulled, they can be seen to move when outside the body (the white and clear fibers are the ones that move).

It migrates around the body, if the open wounds that the "organism" "breathes" through are blocked, the organism will move to sinus cavities, for example, and then to the lungs.[737]

Replacement of the Human Body with the "Morgellonobody." Morgellons fibers can kill hair follicles and grow in their place, as "Morgellons hair."[738] This is one way that Morgellons starts to replace portions of its victims.[739] Potentially every hair follicle can be replaced, covering the entire body, sticking out of the body from head to foot, but always particularly near the legions.[740]

Small hairs grow out of wounds, where pulling them instantly makes them feel better, but they grow back in a few hours. Different hairs grow in different open wound tissues.[741] When pulled from the skin, fibers quickly change their structure and become hard.[742] This resembles somewhat what Thomas has reported about fibers that reportedly fell from chemtrail aircraft: "After cobweb-like filaments fell in Santa Cruz, one resident collected some, only to see the strange strands disentangle in a jar."[743] There are many reports of

---

[734] Rense Radio Show, www.rense.com, March 29, 2007.

[735] Rense Radio Show, www.rense.com, October 24, 2006.

[736] Rense Radio Show, www.rense.com, July 17, 2006.

[737] Rense Radio Show, www.rense.com, June 22, 2006.

[738] Rense Radio Show, www.rense.com, June 22, 2006.

[739] Rense Radio Show, www.rense.com, June 22, 2006.

[740] Rense Radio Show, www.rense.com, June 22, 2006.

[741] Rense Radio Show, www.rense.com, June 22, 2006.

[742] Rense Radio Show, www.rense.com, June 22, 2006.

[743] Thomas 2004, 24.

Morgellons being associated with encounters with these "cobwebs from the sky."

There are reports of ovaries growing to abdominal walls, cartilage in joints completely removed (even though the subject can walk),[744] and it appears to be that the joint gets replaced. Morgellons is believed by the victims to be through-and-through their bodies, and they can see the fibers working deep in the body. Surgeries reveal massive fiber activity deep inside the body. Many of the fibers have to really be looked for with urgency, because they are so small.[745]

No Secondary Infections. Amazingly, despite the massive damage and open wounds to the human, literally never do the Morgellons carriers get a secondary infection. One victim said that he has "done major surgery on himself," numerous times, and never has he (or the others who have also done such self-surgery) gotten a secondary infection—and these are people that have had the ailment for almost a decade.[746] Further, normal bacteria that are typically found in the skin and in parts of the body are found missing in Morgellons sufferers. Combining this with the lack of secondary infection could imply that the invading Morgellons "life-form" is eating the bacteria of the body to survive, and perhaps as a way of keeping the host alive.[747]

Victims of the disease report that after they carry out the aforementioned self-surgery, they will heal *remarkably* quickly.

Choosiness of Infection

According to a researcher at Oklahoma State University, "There is no conclusion yet as to whether it is contagious. Some families have only one member who is affected, even after long exposure, while other families report multiple sufferers."[748] But entire families are reported to have it, which makes it appear that it could be contagious,[749] at least in some circumstances. But on the other hand, there are cases where mothers have it but their babies (whom they will even breast feed) do not.[750] Then there are cases where the mother does not have it, but the baby does.[751]

I believe that this strongly supports the aforementioned claim of Dr. Bill Deagle that Morgellons only afflicts *specific* people, as if the disease is "choosy"—attacking one person, but then leaving the next alone. And it has

---

[744] Rense Radio Show, www.rense.com, June 22, 2006.
[745] Jan Smith, Rense Radio Show, www.rense.com, March 29, 2007.
[746] Rense Radio Show, www.rense.com, June 28, 2006.
[747] Rense Radio Show, www.rense.com, June 28, 2006.
[748] This is from the Oklahoma State University Center for Health Sciences website, http://healthsciences.okstate.edu/morgellons, from March 2007.
[749] Rense Radio Show, www.rense.com, June 22, 2006.
[750] Rense Radio Show, www.rense.com, June 28, 2006.
[751] Rense Radio Show, www.rense.com, June 28, 2006.

been stated that there is evidence that the Morgellons affliction is targeting, and can target, specific people, as if to be very specific in whom it can afflict.[752] Perhaps this is similar to the sorts of "race-specific" weapons that the ultrapowerful think tank, PNAC (2000, see bibliography), asserted they were supporting the development of.

Non-Human Animal Affliction. Morgellons kills plants very efficiently and spreads through all sorts of creatures: insects, reptiles, humans.[753] The disease does not appear to kill humans, but it does kill insects and reptiles.[754] It is also reported to have afflicted dogs,[755] cats, and horses.[756] In general, it is spreading through the entire animal kingdom, and may be passed by an insect (which could, I suppose, explain the selectivity of those who have it).[757] Infestation of Morgellons appears to be an infestation of the entire biosphere: in house flies, dogs, cats, livestock, and animals in the wild.[758]

Transformation of the Biosphere Into the "Morgellonosphere." As discussed, Morgellons "life"-forms continue to evolve into new bio-life-forms, and they can transform into all sorts of different ones.[759] This implies that it is possible that Morgellons is turning significant portions of the biosphere into Morgellons material-"organisms." This leads to the question: will this escalate, and if so, will the entire biosphere turn into Morgellons "life"—that is, into a *Morgellonosphere*?

Dr. Bill Deagle of the Nutrimedical Report has implied that is possibly the case, and that Morgellons may be a first wave of infestation that will be followed by more intensive waves, which, if correct, would imply such a transformation into a Morgellonosphere. Morgellons hive-"organisms" replicate themselves into the form of the living thing they inhabit, in the space the living thing is,[760] so there should be great concern over the prospect just discussed, especially since now 60,000 people are claiming to have the disease.

One victim reported that in samples taken from his body there was a fly larva in it (from his leg).[761] It has been suggested that this is because either a fly landed on the host, found, for some reason, the drive to lay an egg, and the Morgellons victim provided reasonable environment for the egg to live. Or, it has also been suggested that the Morgellons matter has the ability to turn into other life-forms, as discussed above, where this occurs *within* the Morgellons

---

752 Nutrimedical Report Radio Show, www.nutrimedical.com, April 6, 2007.
753 Rense Radio Show, www.rense.com, July 17, 2006.
754 Rense Radio Show, www.rense.com, June 22, 2006.
755 Rense Radio Show, www.rense.com, June 28, 2006, July 17, 2006.
756 Rense Radio Show, www.rense.com, July 17, 2006.
757 Rense Radio Show, www.rense.com, August 16, 2006.
758 Dr. Hildegard Staninger, Rense Radio Show, www.rense.com, March 29, 2007.
759 Rense Radio Show, www.rense.com, March 29, 2007.
760 Rense Radio Show, www.rense.com, March 29, 2007
761 Rense Radio Show, www.rense.com, November 9, 2006.

victim. If the latter is the case, then the Morgellons "entity" reads a genetic blueprint and becomes it, as Jeff Rense has put it.[762]

Possession

Now add to what has just been written the idea that Morgellons fibers are able to take over and possess consciousness. This is hinted at by the fact that Morgellons victims can always sense and feel the fibers within them, where the victim will not be free of the Morgellons "organism" for even a moment. They feel the presence of "foreigners" in the body, in the words of Jeff Rense.[763]

Doctor Bill Deagle has described Morgellons as something that possesses the person, taking over their spirit.[764] People have reported that their minds are being lost, overtaken, as if they feel something is trying to usurp their selfhood from their body-container that they reside in. Dr. Staniger has said that Morgellons victims report the following: "I feel that my soul has been shattered, and is leaving me."[765]

Morgellons does not kill its victims, but it does convince its victims that their body is no longer possessed by them, and it convinces them to commit suicide.[766] It's about causing strain on the person, giving them hell, but not about killing them.[767]

Replacing the Body, and the Nanobot Experimentation Theory. Ray Kurzweil, author of the famous book, *The Age of Spiritual Machines*,[768] on BookTV in November 2006 (in a show that aired in December 2005) discussed how we are near what he calls "the singularity:" where humans become *more than human*, since like Darth Vader, they will have the technology to gradually replace their body parts with super nanobots (atom-sized robots) that essentially give those lucky enough to have the technology implemented into them *immortality*—transforming themselves to super-humans.

This brings the real-ness of the Morgellons situation to light. Kurzweil is part of Bush's technology council, and he is one of the most famous inventors in the world—yet there he was on BookTV (CSPAN) discussing the basic aspects of Morgellons technology, as if it was as expected and "everyday" as CNN or McDonalds.

Given that Americans are experimental victims of government programs, as discussed in the chemtrails section above, and given that Kurzweil said that this

---

[762] Rense Radio Show, www.rense.com, November 9, 2006.

[763] He uttered this on the Rense Radio Show, www.rense.com, June 22, 2006.

[764] Nutrimedical Report Radio Show, www.nutrimedical.com, April 3, 2007.

[765] Dr. Hildegarde Stanninger, Nutrimedical Report Radio Show, nutrimedical.com, April 3, 2007.

[766] Rense Radio Show, www.rense.com, June 22, 2006.

[767] Rense Radio Show, www.rense.com, June 22, 2006.

[768] Viking 1999.

technology is in the developmental phase, it is likely that experimentation is needed. This leads to the theory that Morgellons is part of an experimental contamination phase of a larger or perhaps total (Morgellonospherical) contamination of the earth.

Why do, specifically, the fibers replace body parts in a specific way, where, for example, it is very common that hairs, knee parts, and so on, are replaced by the new Morgellons "life matter"?[769] This certainly sounds like an operation where there is a part-replacement of the body, one segment at a time, as if, for example, when a dying person might want to have new body parts replace their old dying parts.

As for the fast healing reported above, Morgellons victims report that it is as if a patch-like cover develops over the open Morgellons wounds that are created by the disease, but where it is as if the "cover" is not a part of the human body's creation, but rather is a byproduct of the other, Morgellons, "life-form," rather than part of the natural healing processes of the body. [770] Advanced healing technology, including advanced healing abilities, are being developed out at various corporations, such as Cryolife Corporation, which has such a product called Bioglue.[771] Interestingly, Cryolife's product is a covering, a patch, called ProPatch, somewhat mimicking what has just been described above. But I do not know if there is a direct connection that has been drawn between these technologies and Morgellons. It has been suggested by some victims that the fibers observed throughout the body are being assembled in this patch when it is in its gel form initially,[772] perhaps to create new Morgellons-"life-matter."

"The Body Has Been Chipped." The title of this section is a quote from Jeff Rense: "The body has been chipped."[773] Jeff Rense and a victim named Cliff, have discussed how many of the pictures of Morgellons structures look like antennae, and how Morgellons plexuses appears to be waiting to receive a signal.[774]

It is now well-known that the secret government wants to chip all humans on the planet. This would be a final stage of total control of humanity. Since it is hard to believe that humans will ever voluntarily all be chipped, then an infestation would be the next best for the secret corporatists to chip the human population.

---

[769] Rense Radio Show, www.rense.com, June 28, 2006.

[770] Rense Radio Show, www.rense.com, June 28, 2006.

[771] See "CryoLife Receives FDA 510(k) Clearance for ProPatch(TM) Soft Tissue Repair Matrix," *Genetic Engineering News*, Dec 11 2006.

[772] Rense Radio Show, www.rense.com, June 28, 2006.

[773] Rense Radio Show, www.rense.com, March 29, 2007.

[774] The reader should go to http://www.rense.com/Datapages/ morgdat.htm to view several photos.

I assert that there are three leading theories for what Morgellons really is, and why it is infesting humans:

    a. It will function as a very productive, all-encompassing super-chipping.
    b. It will transform humanity into a next phase of existence, which I theorize is what the 2012 Mayan cosmogenesis is all about (discussed below).
    c. A mixture of a and b.

According to Dr. Staninger, Morgellons fibers are nanotechnology: a life-form and mini-robotic machine, created atom-by-atom.[775] Dr. Staninger says that the following picture of a Morgellons fiber from her datafile[776] resembles a nanotube, as do so many of the pictures:

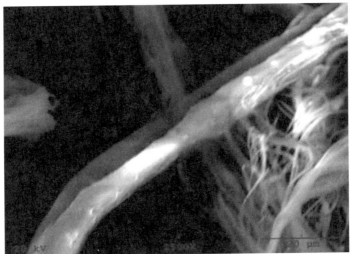

She tells us that this tube has high concentrations of calcium and iron. And she tells us that zinc, aluminum, iron, and sulfur are present in other patients' Morgellons fibers.[777]

It is theorized that since the human body is a bioelectric organism, and since the infected person feels a massive loss of energy, that the Morgellons structure is using the some of the human body's bioelectricity to power itself.[778] If Morgellons is a nanoweapon, it will likely function like nanomaterials do, with two parts: (1) an assembler, which creates other parts, and which needs a power

---

[775] Dr. Hildegard Stanninger, Rense Radio Show, www.rense.com, March 29, 2007.
[776] Datafile located at http://www.rense.com/morgphase/ phase2_1.htm
[777] Dr. Hildegard Staninger, Rense Radio Show, www.rense.com, March 29, 2007.
[778] Rense Radio Show, www.rense.com, March 29, 2007.

source, and (2) functional units: created nanobots with a specific task to carry out.[779]

Additionally, the Morgellons fiber-network in the body appears to create its own electric field, since the skin of the Morgellons victim is measured to be extremely conducive, usually about seven times more than the uninfected non-Morgellons patient.[780] A network of agents sending signals to each other, as Morgellons fibers may be doing, will create their own field.[781] And it has been reported that Morgellons victims can turn on computers and trip lights or humidifiers,[782] as if their own electrical field overtly interacts with other electrical entities. Dr. Bill Deagle, and Jeff Rense, have queried as to whether or not the Morgellons "organisms" have ELF frequency, and if they can receive external signals and/or are electromagnetically connected to other Morgellons masses in other hosts. If this is the case, it would further support the chip theory discussed in the last subsection.

ESP and Transhumanism. Further aspects of the secret government's planned mass chipping program involve transforming humans into a hive mind. When Morgellons victims get near each other, say a few feet, they can feel each other across that distance.[783] Jeff Rense has commented that this is like "the hive reaching out to the other hive."[784] This may have transhumanist applications, since DARPA wants a chipped humanity to have a interconnected hive mind in the transhumanist future.

The 2012 Mayan Cosmogenesis and the Morgellonosphere. The ancient Maya of the Yucatan Peninsula in Mexico, were an amazingly advanced culture, who in many ways far exceeded contemporary America. One thing that is extremely notable is their account of time and their calendar system. The Mayan calendar ends at a specific date in 2012. The "Mayan Cosmogenesis" is a term that involves the idea that this abrupt end in the calendar indicates that something major is going to happen in 2012, perhaps the end of the world.

Many researchers, such as Michael Tsarion,[785] have suggested that the Mayan Cosmogenesis is not about the end of the world, but rather is about a *transformation* of the world—perhaps a transformation of consciousness—and an irreversible and approaching change in humanity. These changes happen frequently in history. The last one noted was around 500 to 300 B.C.E., where

---

[779] This information comes from Dr. Hildegard Staninger, Rense Radio Show, www.rense.com, March 29, 2007.

[780] Dr. Hildegard Staninger, Rense Radio Show, www.rense. com, March 29, 2007.

[781] Dr. Hildegard Stanninger, Rense Radio Show, www.rense. com, March 29, 2007.

[782] Jan Smith, Rense Radio Show, www.rense.com, March 29, 2007.

[783] Dr. Hildegard Stanninger, Rense Radio Show, www.rense.com, March 29, 2007.

[784] Rense Radio Show, www.rense.com, March 29, 2007.

[785] Tsarion is a writing on human history. His website is http://www.taroscopes.com/.

humanity worldwide experienced a radical change, as evidenced in culture (writing, architecture, religion and philosophy, and so on).

There are so many utter disasters for humanity discussed in this book that are looming on the horizon, and that will surely wipe out most of the world's human population throughout the next one or two decades, that it almost appears that there is going to be something behind this predicted Mayan Cosmogenisis which is scheduled to commence shortly, if the Mayans were right. Following Tsarion and others that suggest that 2012 represents the next major shift in human life and consciousness, I would like to add that transhumanism likely represents this next shift, and Morgellons, in addition to the various robotics technologies that I will discuss in the last chapter, account for an imminent shift in humanity. It may be a coincidence that all these disasters, including Morgellons, are approximately coinciding with the time-frame of the theory of the Mayan Cosmogenesis, but the point is that they do, and that this shift is coming. I maintain that, for all the reasons given in this book, this shift will involve an ultramassive reduction in the human population of the world, as many have pointed out before me, and then the remaining people will experience and undergo the Cosmogenic shift into Morgellono- or Morgellono-like infestation and consequent take-over of life and consciousness.[786]

As Morgellons information shows, and as the robotics technology I will discuss in the last chapter reveals, the age of being human as we know humans to be, *is coming to an end*, and the age of transhumanism (superhuman telepathic machine/slave-humans) is commencing. For many readers, Morgellons may seem too odd and surreal to be believable, since it is so unlike anything humans have encountered up to this time, even in Hollywood films. But the fact is that there are real samples of Morgellons matter that are being studied by top researchers in prestigious universities who are confirming what I have written in this chapter on Morgellons. Therefore, it would surely appear to be real, and the reader must be absolutely awestruck at the advanced technology that Morgellons involves—clearly technology that is far beyond anything that ordinary humans are aware of, or that has been knowingly invented by the US government. The real catch is that the mass media will not cover Morgellons in significant detail, even though the numbers of victims are staggering, going far beyond other epidemics that receive huge press-time. This indicates that the media is covering up Morgellons. If you combine all that I have written in this paragraph, and in this section and the one before it, a theory comes out of all that information: the theory that Morgellons is a movement from the ordinary human body to the chipped Morgellons body, where consciousness will be hive-like, and thus the biosphere and humanity will undergo Tsarion's aforementioned 2012 shift in consciousness, from the biosphere to the Morgellonosphere.

---

[786] One of the best accounts of this upcoming shift is found in Moravec 1999.

Conclusion.

In this chapter I have discussed the deliberate and pervasive contamination of humanity by the corporatist secret government. The information of this chapter shows that the contamination is total (mind, soul, and body), and that what is behind it is torture, domination, and more severe enslavement. Most of these contaminations humans willingly take part in (e.g., going to the grocery store to buy aspartame-containing foods.) Even before the most severe contamination occurs (which should begin in 2009 after Codex Alimentarius is implemented), the result of this contamination is that humanity is a deformed species. Much like the creatures on Moreau's island, who had no idea that they were diseased, deformed, and foolish, Americans are also fooled into loving their Brave New World rather than waking up to what is hidden in plain view. As with the other corporatist tactics, contamination primarily about mind-boggling sadistic torment, such as is the case with the autism epidemic that torments so many families all over the world. Perhaps at this late point in this book it should be noted that there is something strange about the corporatists: they do not act like the ordinary people that I know and have grown up with, they hold entirely different belief structures and actions. Even the most cruel people I have known throughout my life were, I believe, not eager to damage and torment virtually all babies (and their families) world-wide, as is done with vaccines. It is almost as if the corporatists are so vicious and rapacious, secretive and well-planned-out, that they are, without exaggeration, *not human*.

6 The Corporatist Dream-State: A World of Death Camps

Winston was dreaming about his mother. He must, he thought, have been ten or eleven years old when his mother disappeared... His father he remembered more vaguely as dark and thin, dressed always in neat dark clothes... and wearing spectacles. The two of them must evidently have been swallowed up in one of the first great purges of the Fifties.

—*1984*, p. 29, Signet Classics Edition

You are either with us, or you are with the terrorists.

—George W. Bush, shortly after 9/11

I want to run, I want to hide, I want to tear down the walls that hold me inside. I want to reach out and touch the flame, where the streets have no name. I want to feel, sunlight on my face, see the dust cloud disappear without a trace, I want to take shelter from the poison rain, where the streets have no name... The cities a flood, and our love turns to rust, we're beaten and blown by the wind, trampled in dust, I'll show you a place high in the desert plain, where the streets have no name.

—U2[787]

In this chapter I will show that

1. The US has a massive "camp" system located all over its territory that is not being utilized (i.e., these camps are fully functional, huge concentration camps that are empty, as if waiting to be used/filled).
2. The "camp" system is designated to hold ordinary Americans in the future.

You will see in this chapter that US military leaders are preparing for "another 9/11" that will "make Americans question the US Constitution," as Tommy Franks (top military leader, responsible for the "Shock and Awe" invasion planning). With this sort of terrorism (which, of course, will be a false flag attack), US military leaders will transform the United States into a fully

---

[787] These are lyrics from "Where the Streets have no Name," from U2's Joshua Tree CD. This appears to be a song about the Orwellian, death-camp/concentration-camp city. U2 has somehow been imagined to be a political activist band, but it is quite clear that they are New World Order agents. This was fully revealed when Bono was made a candidate, along with Wolfowitz, for the job as the head of the World Bank. (See, "Bono, World Bank chief? A Los Angeles Times editorial proposes a new gig for the U2 frontman." Reuters, February 26, 2005; "Bono Eyed for World Bank Chief?," CBS News / Associated Press, March 6, 2005). Also, Bono is widely known to be perhaps the worlds' most famous pro-vaccine advocate, and he is the number one advocate for vaccines in Africa, where clearly the vaccines there are contaminated with AIDS, and are the real source for the massive Subsaharan epidemic there. (See Horowitz 1999) And the story, "Bono Avoids Taxes, Joins Forbes" (Newsmax, August 8 2006), shows that Bono and U2 are strongly partnered and aligned with Steve Forbes, who is a principal PNAC member.

military fascist police state, and they will fill the aforementioned concentration camps with anybody who is judged to be an "enemy combatant" (whatever that means) by a secret committee that determines such, and which is specified in recent bills, such as the 2006 "Military Commissions Act" which I have discussed in previous chapters. FEMA will be the primary group to round people up when this second 9/11 occurs. What is most interesting, and most relevant to this book, is that FEMA, the military, and any other government entity that will be in charge during these times of chaos (because, as I will discuss, politicians and police will not be in charge) will follow orders *from the corporatists*: corporatists are, and will be, behind the society planning and reorganization, during the aftermath of this second 9/11.[788]

Guantanamo Bay should serve as a good case study for any readers of this book who have a hard time believing that the corporatist government would ever have the will to build massive "detention camps" (death camps) where they plan to hold countless untried, unconvicted Americans.

Few people know that one of the main Fox News Channel newscasters, Michelle Malkin, has written a book where she attempts to justify racial profiling and the mass enslavement of millions of Americans in concentration camps.[789] If Guantanamo, the first of the publicly known "terrorist camps,"[790] is our guide for what the future will hold, the roundup of innocent people will occur all in the name of the phony "war on terrorism," and it will involve years and years of torture of many "prisoners" (known torture techniques used at Guantanamo are, for example, extreme sleep deprivation for years and years, where, for example, "prisoners" are made to sit naked or with nearly no clothes, in uncomfortable positions, without changing positions, in cold temperatures, with a fan blowing on them while being blind-folded and having loud and horrible static noise blared into their ears via headphones[791]—and, as stated, this is done over and over *for years*, or decades, for simply no reason other than the "joy" of torture (since the war on terror is a fabrication). Since there is no "war on terrorism," and since the Guantanamo "prisoners" were imprisoned due to a *staged* event (9/11), then the only reason Guantanamo could exist is because the government corporatists desire the existence of a torture camp where they can torture people, apparently just for the sake of torture. That is

---

[788] For copious information on this issue, the reader should consult the lecture given by Professor Daneen Peterson on the Rense Radio Show, www.rense.com, from June 27, 2007.

[789] Malkin, Michelle. 2004. *In Defense of Internment: The Case for 'Racial Profiling' in World War II and the War on Terror*. Regnery Publishing.

[790] See Erik and Tarik (2005) and Carter (2005) for information. Of course, Guantanamo-style concentrations camps or torture camps are nothing new, and Guantanamo was just the first one made widely known to the public. See Paglen, Trevor, and Thompson (2006) for information on other secret CIA concentration/torture camp programs.

[791] See Carter 2005 for more information.

why I used the word "joy" above, and that is why a nation of concentration camps is the corporatists' dream state: a state of nationwide or worldwide abysmal mass-misery, where eventually all citizens (except the corporatists) are enslaved, brainwashed, and tortured, and where only corporatist "law" exists, in order that the corporatists tactics and tools discussed in previous chapters can be fully implemented.

The existence of the concentration/death camp nation is critical for the corporatist, since, as I pointed out by example in chapters above, the corporatist is obsessed with hating his slaves, and with the lust to see them feel perpetual agony, horror, and various forms of direct or indirect, deliberate, high- or low-level torture. The corporatist only loves his slaves to the degree that he/she can torture them. Torture is deeply sacred to the corporatists, as was illustrated with the torture of Winston in Orwell's *1984* (and as Guantanamo, the US prison system, secret CIA prisons, and the US public education also illustrate). And to put significant portions of the world population into a global plantation/death-camp would be maximal pleasure for the torture-loving corporatists.[792]

"But *really*! How preposterous!" you say? Would they really carry out such a plan? In the mania of a false flag event, well… who is really worried about a humanitarian existence? And with all the fear they spread around, who is really in the mood for civil liberties? In the chaos after 9/11, when people's psyches were changed by the trauma of that event, but wherein all that had happened was just an Orwellian ruse, in *The National Review*, Sept. 13, 2001, Ann Coulter—who is one of the chief voices of the mass media (especially Fox News) —wrote:

> This is no time to be precious about locating the exact individuals directly involved in this particular terrorist attack… We don't need long investigations of the forensic evidence to determine which scientific accuracy the person or persons who ordered this specific attack… The nation has been invaded by a fanatical, murderous cult. We should invade their countries, kill their leaders and convert them to Christianity. We weren't punctilious about locating and punishing only Hitler and his top officers. We carpet-bombed German cities, we killed civilians. That's war. And this is war.[793]

This is a request, if not a demand, from a top media personality—similar to the stature of Rush Limbaugh—to abandon any process of law, to carry-out reckless war to kill at will and without aiming our guns carefully (while knowing that children are in the line of the gun), to engage in killing civilians, to imprison and/or slaughter entire nations—all before we even think about

---

[792] There is no exaggeration here. The corporatists utterly relish torture. For an interesting account of how integral and sacred torture is to the overall corporatist world government, see Klein 2007.

[793] Thanks to Greg Felton for this quote.

asking the government to explain how the step-a Pentagon could occur. Coulter's call for anti-civilized war-madness reflects the dark-age-mentality exemplified by Ashcroft, who was known also to earnestly say, for example, if you disagree with my policies, and if you are not with our Administration, you will be considered a terrorist.[794] This reflects Bush's comment at the start of this chapter: "you are either with us or you are with the terrorists." This indicates that disagreement with the current Administration's policies means perhaps you are a terrorist, and thus belong in a death camp. The Bill, HR 6166, passed in fall of 2007 by the 109th Congress (it was passed as S3930 in September 2006 as the Military Commissions Act), made these actions "lawful."

The Machine World

...[L]et us postulate that the computer scientists succeed in developing intelligent machines that can do all things better than human beings can do them. In that case presumably all work will be done by vast, highly organized systems of machines and no human effort will be necessary. Either of two cases might occur. The machines might be permitted to make all of their own decisions without human oversight, or else human control over the machines might be retained. If the machines are permitted to make all their own decisions, we can't make any conjectures as to the results, because it is impossible to guess how such machines might behave. We only point out that the fate of the human race would be at the mercy of the machines... On the other hand it is possible that human control over the machines may be retained. In that case the average man may have control over certain private machines of his own, such as his car or his personal computer, but control over large systems of machines will be in the hands of a tiny elite - just as it is today, but with two differences. Due to improved techniques the elite will have greater control over the masses; and because human work will no longer be necessary the masses will be superfluous, a useless burden on the system. If the elite is ruthless they may simply decide to exterminate the mass of humanity.

—Bill Joy, Cofounder and Chief Scientist of Sun Microsystems[795]

In the chapters above, I discussed how the corporatists are planning both global extermination for approximately 9 of every 10 people on planet earth, and those that remain will be forced into labor camps and death camps that are part of planned global slave plantation of the future. It is difficult to tell exactly how this will be carried out, and/or why they are doing it. All that is truly known is what can be verified with certainty, which is that the corporatists are vigorously building death camps, and that they are building a massive slave-state, police-state infrastructure system, as I write this book.

Also what can be verified with certainty is the fact that this horror state will be run by very few people, and the corporatist controllers will not need to utilize large amounts of stormtroopers and police to the degree that, for

---

[794] This was shown in Marshall 2003.

[795] This is from, "Why the Future Doesn't Need Us," by Bill Joy, *Wired Magazine*, August 4, 2000.

example, the Nazis needed to. This is because the corporatists have technologies available to them that are little known to the RP (even though they were funded by the RP), and a large portion of which is to, for example, consist of robots[796] that will comprise horror-armies. The corporatist controllers themselves will also likely be transformed into transhumans,[797] where technologies will be (if they are not already) implanted into their bodies in order to give them super-human qualities: absence of aging, absence of disease, superpleasures, etc.[798] The American public is, for the most part, completely oblivious to the technology being developed[799] for use against them and against the people of the world—an unstoppable force that protests and maybe, eventually, even boycotts of corporatists' enterprises, will be powerless against.

Many people may have a hard time believing that this is true. But that is only because they do not know that books being written by Moravec, Kurzweil, and other inventors who are connected to top universities and to the government (e.g., Kurzweil is on President Bush's technology panel), confirm these details in their books, interviews, and lectures. Writing in 2000, Bill Joy, *cofounder and Chief Scientist of Sun Microsystems*, wrote:

> From the moment I became involved in the creation of new technologies, their ethical dimensions have concerned me, but it was only in the autumn of 1998 that I became anxiously aware of how great are the dangers facing us in the 21st century. I can date the onset of my unease to the day I met Ray Kurzweil, the deservedly famous inventor of the first reading machine for the blind and many other amazing things.... ...I had always felt sentient robots were in the realm of science fiction. But now, from someone I respected, I was hearing a strong argument that they were a near-term possibility. I was taken aback, especially given Ray's proven ability to imagine and create the future. I already knew that new technologies like genetic engineering

---

[796] See Kurzweil 1999 and Moravec 1999 for more information on the reality of robotics technology.

[797] See Kurzweil 1999 and Moravec 1999 for more information on this technology.

[798] See Kurzweil 1999 and Moravec 1999 also discuss issues to do with transhumanism.

[799] For a good survey of this and similar technology, see the DVD lecture, *Weapons of Mass Control*, by Bob Fletcher, 1997, available from World News Insight, P.O. Box 216, Bayview Idaho, 83803. Also see the episodes of *Futureweapons* that has aired on the Discovery Channel and the Military Channel (the show really should be called *Futurewar*, since it profiles mostly existing technology for warfare of the future, even though much of the technology featured on the show has been already deployed in Lebanon, Iraq, etc.) to see all sorts of examples (for example, on April 5, 2007, the Discovery Channel aired an episode that featured many of the technologies that allow war to be remote control and robotic, much like a video game player can control war from a distance, and much in the way that the *Star Wars* films illustrate a droid army). Also, see *MIT Technology Review* magazine for further information, and see the many of the military magazines.

and nanotechnology were giving us the power to remake the world, but a realistic and imminent scenario for intelligent robots surprised me.[800]

As discussed in chapters above, this technology is real, and *it is ready for deployment*. The corporatists' robots are killers the size of hornets,[801] they are high-tech enough to resemble the film Terminator 2,[802] and the robo-killers are controlled by AI master computers, as in Terminator 3, where the AI masters can write music, learn, and can create swarming behavior in the robots it controls against enemies.[803] These robots are specifically for a state of war and control—they are all-powerful armies unperturbed by any weather, and they come with, of course, all sorts of super-human abilities.[804] Like Alex Jones said, "this stuff is exponentially growing; it's doubling every year,"[805] meaning that more and more of this technology is being developed and created. I have had students who were in the know at Purdue University Calumet tell me that they have seen a huge shift in focus in the engineering programs at that and other Purdue University campuses toward just this sort technology, all because they have seen government funding dictate that military robotics technology is being made top research priority at those campuses.

---

[800] This is from, "Why the Future Doesn't Need Us," by Bill Joy, Wired Magazine, August 4, 2000.

[801] "Israel Developing Anti-militant 'Bionic Hornet'," Reuters, November 17, 2006.

[802] "Future Police State Use of ASIMO The Robot?", Infowars.com, December 17, 2004.

[803] "Experimental AI Powers Robot Army," Wired, David Hambling, September 14, 2006.

[804] "Israel Unveils Portable Hunter-Killer Robot," Reuters, March 8, 2007; "TALON Small Mobile Robot," GlobalSecurity.org, January 24, 2005; "US Plans Carlyle Group's 'Robot Troops' for Iraq," BBC, February 17, 2005.

[805] Alex Jones Show, www.infowars.com, March 8, 2007.

Here is a picture of "TALON ... a powerful, lightweight, versatile robot designed for missions ranging from reconnaissance to weapons delivery. Its large, quick-release cargo bay accommodates a variety of sensor payloads, making TALON a one-robot solution to a variety of mission requirements. Built with all-weather, day/night and amphibious capabilities standard, TALON can operate under the most adverse conditions to overcome almost any terrain. The suitcase-portable robot is controlled through a two-way RF or F/O line from a portable or wearable Operator Control Unit (OCU) that provides continuous data and video feedback for precise vehicle positioning... TALON's payload and sensor options include: multiple cameras (color, black and white, infrared, thermal, zero light), a two-stage arm, gripper manipulators, pan/tilt, two-way communications, NBC (nuclear/ biological/ chemical) sensors, radiation sensors, UXO/ countermine detection sensors, grenade and smoke placing modules, breaching tools, communications equipment, distracters and disrupters."[806]

This chapter outlines the upcoming global concentration-, slave-, and death-camp system. In general, this system follows from population reduction: the aforementioned population reduction programs (world war, epidemics, nutricide, DU) will spread mass chaos that will force the governments of the world (the secret corporatist New World Order) to step in and act like they are saving humanity by cracking down on the chaos with severe martial law, vaccination programs, war, and so on, but which in reality are only the initiation of plans to set up a global death-camp.

One can see the start of this in the United States, with the onset of the North American Union[807] and with the mass exodus of industry from the United States.[808] The plan of the North American Union is being used to largely supplant the American population with a Mexican population, for the purpose of helping corporations sidestep labor laws (such as minimum wage) for American citizens. With the supplanting and removal of American citizens, they will have to either be exterminated or enslaved. And since robot armies are being developed by the corporatists, given what I have disclosed in chapters above, we must assume they will be used, and that the massive prison system being built by the corporatists will also be used.

How Will the Transformation into Global Death-Camp Occur?

The way that every totalitarian country takes control and controls the population ... [is with] the control of food. [This is t]he means of eradicating by eliminating portions—huge portions—of the population (Stalin, Hitler, in Cuba, in China...)... They don't waste the bullets, they don't have the manpower... They starve the people.

---

[806] From "TALON Small Mobile Robot," GlobalSecurity.org, January 24, 2005.

[807] "North American Union leader Says Merger Just Crisis Away," WorldNetDaily, Jerome R. Corsi, December 15, 2006.

[808] For just one example, see "Ford Had Its Worst Loss Ever In 2006: Carmaker Struggles To Correct Mistakes," Washington Post, Sholnn Freeman, January 26, 2007. On February 15, 2007, Alex Jones said on his radio show that corporations were being paid to leave the country by the US government.

—Steve Shanks[809]

It is not a secret that the secret corporatist government is planning for the full takeover of the people in order to set up the Orwellian neofeudal state. Consider the following critically important news article from the Washington Post, which announces that with the next 9/11, the "shadow government" will be in command:

> President Bush issued a formal national security directive yesterday ordering agencies to prepare contingency plans for a surprise, "decapitating" attack on the federal government, and assigned responsibility for coordinating such plans to the White House. The prospect of a nuclear bomb being detonated in Washington without warning, whether smuggled in by terrorists or a foreign government, has been cited by many security analysts as a rising concern since the Sept. 11, 2001, attacks... After the 2001 attacks, Bush assigned about 100 senior civilian managers to rotate *secretly* to locations outside of Washington for weeks or months at a time to ensure the nation's survival, *a shadow government that evolved based on long-standing "continuity of operations plans." Since then, other agencies including the Pentagon, the Office of the Director of National Intelligence and the CIA have taken steps to relocate facilities or key functions outside of Washington for their own reasons, citing factors such as economics or the importance of avoiding Beltway "group-think."* Norman J. Ornstein, a scholar at the American Enterprise Institute and an adviser to an independent Continuity of Government Commission, said the order "is a more explicit embrace of what has been since 9/11 an implicit but fairly clear set of assumptions." He added, "My frustration is that those assumptions have not gripped the Congress in the same way." Other former Bush administration officials said the directive formalizes a shift of authority away from the Department of Homeland Security to the White House. Under an executive order dating to the Reagan administration, responsibility for coordinating, implementing and exercising such plans was originally charged to the Federal Emergency Management Agency and later DHS, the Congressional Research Service noted in a 2005 report on a pending DHS reorganization. The new directive gives the job of coordinating policy to the president's assistant for homeland security and counterterrorism—Frances Fragos Townsend, who will assume the title of national continuity coordinator—in consultation with Bush's national security adviser, Stephen J. Hadley, with the support of the White House's Homeland Security Council staff. Townsend is to produce an implementation plan within 90 days. Homeland Security Secretary

---

[809] From the Nutrimedical Report Radio Show, www.nutrimedical.com, March 5, 2007.

Michael Chertoff will continue to coordinate operations and activities, the directive said.[810] (Emphasis added.)

This story consists of an admission that the real power of military and government is not in the hands of Congress, but rather in "the shadow government," in order to prepare for the next 9/11, which will be a nuclear attack.

As discussed in chapter 3, it is in the downturns of "the business cycle" that the tragedies happen—that is when the corporatists plan them to occur—and therefore, we can conclude that most likely during the upcoming American depression, the great purges will begin and we will have the movement to global slavery.

What will likely occur from 2008-2020 is as follows.[811] First, there will be a massive "burst of the debt-bubble," to put it as the economist George Whitehurst does.[812] This will lead to a global depression. This will appear to be a time of chaos, even though it is carefully planned by the corporatistic secret government.

Second, there will be a false flag event in order to orient the US population to support a massive invasion and war (presumably Iran).

Third, in this time of chaos, all hell will break loose in the form of war, plague, and mass-death, just as with what happened in the events surrounding World War II.

---

[810] "Bush Changes Continuity Plan: Administration, Not DHS, Would Run Shadow Government," Washington Post, By Spencer S. Hsu, May 10, 2007; page A12.

[811] Strictly speaking, the movement to the global death-camp has already started. But the "formal" initiation point will be, I estimate, 2009, for several reasons. That is the time that much of the destruction from worldwide DU contamination will be manifesting itself, and that is also when the Codex Alimentarius is to be implemented and enforced by the WTO worldwide (see Afrika 2000, and Laibow and Stubblebine 2006). Also, there are reasons to believe that will be a huge dip in the economy, as indicated by the planned massive 3M stock buyback scheduled for 2009 (see "3M Declares $7B Buyback Program," Associated Press, February 12, 2007). (Companies plan to buyback stock in the low points of the fabricated "business cycle," not the high points.) There are other reasons (e.g., implementation of the National ID) in addition to this; but this provides a good introductory list. And when you combine these pieces of information with the pattern I discussed in chapter 3 for how economic activity is always carried out (by the following pattern: economic crash➔false flag terror event➔war and disease), these pieces of information imply that 2009 will be a low point in the economic dip, and thus the point at which this pattern will be carried out.

[812] To understand the real nature of economics, and what is meant by the "debt bubble collapse," see the lectures by George Whitehurst in the archives of the Rense Radio Show (www.rense.com) from 2005 and 2006.

If one looks back through history, these sorts of events (economic collapse➔false flag event➔massive warfare➔global disease) almost always all occur in the same order, as pointed out in chapter 3. All sorts of hokey "explanations" are invented by academics to explain why this pattern occurs (for example, as for the Great Depression, we are told by academics that the Great Depression was caused by problems with farmers, or that World War II did not start because of oil or IBM or the Rockefellers, but rather, because of Hitler's ability to build up Germany). But they nearly never hit upon the best theory as to why they do: the secret government engineers a repeat of what has happened so many times in history. But the public will remain oblivious to this, and the disease, chaos, population reduction, and so forth, will be called by them "spontaneous events," like the weather: "acts of God."

The mass disease will be blamed on viruses spreading from person to person, or on unplanned starvation, but in reality they will be the planned result of nutricide,[813] DU, deliberate vaccine contamination, and planned plagues.[814] This mass death will complete the goal of the corporatist secret government to reduce the population of the world down to around 500,000 people, which is widely known by those who study the secret government to be the ultimate secret government project at the moment.

The Pre-Planning and Execution
of a Society of Death Camps

As I have mentioned above, in 2005 and 2006, the world learned how the US government was spying on virtually all information (banking, emails, etc.) of the American public because they said they were looking for terrorists. Now add to this idea that there are no terrorists, also as I have shown: there are no threatening terrorists to find amid the United States population. Now here is a question: *Why the need for comprehensive information gathering on virtually all Americans?* If not for terrorists, then why? We will see that it can be proven that it's for Americans. Now let's get into the details.

The ability to detain *millions* is quite a real possibility:

FEMA, the federal agency charged with disaster preparedness, is engaged in a crash effort to prepare for multiple mass destruction attacks on U.S. cities - including the creation of sprawling temporary cities to handle millions of displaced persons, NewsMax has learned. FEMA is readying for nuclear, biological and chemical attacks against U.S. cities, including the possibility of multiple attacks with mass destruction weapons. The agency has already notified vendors, contractors and consultants that it needs to be prepared to handle the

---

[813] See Afrika 2000

[814] See Horowitz 1999, 2001 for an excellent discussion of what these plagues might look like.

logistics of aiding millions of displaced Americans who will flee from urban areas that may be attacked. The agency plans to create emergency, makeshift cities that could house hundreds of thousands, if not millions, of Americans who may have to flee their urban homes if their cities are attacked. Ominously, FEMA has been given a deadline of having the cities ready to go by January 2003 – in about six months. A source familiar with the deadline believes the effort is related to making the U.S. prepared for counterattacks if the U.S. invades Iraq sometime next year. FEMA is currently seeking bids from major real estate management firms, and plans to name three firms in the near future to handle the logistics and planning for these temporary cities. FEMA officials have told these firms they already have tents and trailers ordered. The tents and trailers would provide shelter for displaced populations. The real estate firms are expected to provide engineers and architects to lay the plans for emergency infrastructure needs, such as sewage and electricity.[815]

It might just seem like a coincidence that the corporatists have built the apparatus for death camps, but it might be just too hard to believe that they would do so. But that doubt can be squelched when you remember Guantanamo Bay and other camps utilized right after the staged 9/11 event, and if you familiarize yourself with the past history of the Bush family and the Cheney, Ashcroft, and friends preference for eugenics and population reduction.[816] I will not discuss these at length here, since others have done that adequately, and since this chapter is only about the corporatist tool of death camp slave labor.

KBR/Halliburton "Detention Camps"

George Bush's grandfather, the late US senator Prescott Bush, was a director and shareholder of companies that profited from their involvement with the financial backers of Nazi Germany. *The Guardian* has obtained confirmation from newly discovered files in the US National Archives that a firm of which Prescott Bush was a director was involved with the financial architects of Nazism.

—*The Guardian* (major British news paper), September 25, 2004[817]

---

[815] "FEMA Preparing for Mass Destruction Attacks on Cities," John O. Edwards," July 15, 2002, NewsMax.com.

[816] See Tarpley and Chaitkin 2004.

[817] For the most detailed account of this Bush-Hitler connection, see Tarpley 1992. This story is also discussed by experts in Karel 2004. Also see "Of skulls and bones: More secrets of the tomb," by Noam Rudnick,, October 24, 2003, The Yale Herald, Vol. XXXVI, No. 8; "Skull and Bones," June 13, 2004, CBS News. The corporatist media tried to assert when this story came out in 2004 that Prescott Bush severed his ties to Hitler back in the 1930s, but the Nazi holocaust archive data does not at all match up to this, and neither do the press stories from the 1940s. See "Thyssen Funds Found in US," July 31, 1941, The Zanesville Signal (Zanesville, Oh).

How much camp space is there? Here's a story, this one from Businesswire that details more information about the detention camp construction going on.

> KBR announced today that the Department of Homeland Security's (DHS) U.S. Immigration and Customs Enforcement (ICE) component has awarded KBR an Indefinite Delivery/Indefinite Quantity (IDIQ) contingency contract to support ICE facilities in the event of an emergency. KBR is the engineering and construction subsidiary of Halliburton (NYSE:HAL). With a maximum total value of $385 million over a five-year term, consisting of a one-year based period and four one-year options, the competitively awarded contract will be executed by the U.S. Army Corps of Engineers, Fort Worth District. KBR held the previous ICE contract from 2000 through 2005. "... The contract, which is effective immediately, provides for establishing temporary detention and processing capabilities to augment existing ICE Detention and Removal Operations (DRO) Program facilities in the event of an emergency influx of immigrants into the U.S., or to support the rapid development of new programs. The contingency support contract provides for planning and, if required, initiation of specific engineering, construction and logistics support tasks to establish, operate and maintain one or more expansion facilities. The contract may also provide migrant detention support to other U.S. Government organizations in the event of an immigration emergency, as well as the development of a plan to react to a national emergency, such as a natural disaster. In the event of a natural disaster, the contractor could be tasked with providing housing for ICE personnel performing law enforcement functions in support of relief efforts.[818]

It is interesting to note that there is no denial here by politicians of a massive camp building program. It is admitted, and all that needs to be investigated is the claims over what the camp system is really to be used for.

This next article, from the New York Times, claims that the camps will be used for "new programs that require additional detention space:"

> The Army Corps of Engineers has awarded a contract worth up to $385 million for building temporary immigration detention centers to Kellogg Brown & Root, the Halliburton subsidiary that has been criticized for overcharging the Pentagon for its work in Iraq. KBR would build the centers for the Homeland Security Department for an unexpected influx of immigrants, to house people in the event of a natural disaster *or for new programs that require additional detention space*, company executives said. KBR, which announced the contract last month, *had a similar contract with immigration agencies from 2000 to last year...* A

---

[818] "KBR Awarded U.S. Department of Homeland Security Contingency Support Project for Emergency Support Services," January 24, 2006, Businesswire.

spokeswoman for Immigration and Customs Enforcement, Jamie Zuieback, said KBR would build the centers only in an emergency like the one when thousands of Cubans floated on rafts to the United States. She emphasized that the centers might never be built if such an emergency did not arise… A spokesman for the corps, Clayton Church, said that the centers could be at unused military sites or temporary structures and that each one would hold up to 5,000 people. "When there's a large influx of people into the United States, how are we going to feed, house and protect them?" Mr. Church asked. "That's why these kinds of contracts are there." Mr. Church said that KBR did not end up creating immigration centers under its previous contract, but that it did build temporary shelters for Hurricane Katrina evacuees… In recent months, the Homeland Security Department has promised to increase bed space in its detention centers to hold thousands of illegal immigrants awaiting deportation. In the first quarter of the 2006 fiscal year, nearly 60 percent of the illegal immigrants apprehended from countries other than Mexico were released on their own recognizance… Advocates for immigrants said they feared that the new contract was another indication that the government planned to expand the detention of illegal immigrants, including those seeking asylum. *"It's pretty obvious that the intent of the government is to detain more and more people and to expedite their removal,"* said Cheryl Little, executive director of the Florida Immigrant Advocacy Center in Miami."[819] (Emphasis added.)

This article shows that the story Americans are being given about these massive camps does not make sense. KBR has been building these concentration camps since the year 2000, but they were not used for Hurricane Katrina victims.

How many detention centers exist if they have been built over the course of the last six years? There must be huge amount of them. Bush, Cheney and other involved corporatists have proven that they are uninterested in using the camps for natural disaster victims (since Hurricane Katrina victims were not put in them) and "illegal immigrants" (since the "illegals" are not being put in the camps), so the idea that Bush-Cheney and other involved corporatists want to build detention centers for disaster victims, as told to the New York Times by members of the Bush Administration, is simply untrue information (i.e., a lie). The statement, "new programs that require additional detention space," is so vague that it can only be this vague *deliberately*, as is standard for the government corporatists (e.g., Guantanamo is "in line with the Geneva Convention," as Rumsfeld has said). It seems unlikely that immigrants will come into the country in the way being suggested in the articles, and even if

---

[819] "Halliburton Subsidiary Gets Contract to Add Temporary Immigration Detention Centers," February 4, 2006, By Rachel L Swarns, New York Times.

they did, why do we need to "detain" them? America has used camps for the detention of "criminals" in the past and in the present (Japanese citizens during World War II, American Indians, African slaves, citizens of present-day Iraq, the contemporary American prison system, Guantanamo Bay, secret CIA prisons, etc.), but they have not been for mass immigration or natural disasters. So what are they *really* for?

The New York Times article says that these centers are needed for situations like when thousands of Cubans arrived at times in the past. But "thousands" means perhaps 2000, or 12,000, presumably, and not 100,000, for example, since if "thousands" denoted 100,000, then the wording of the article would be "tens of thousands," or "one hundred thousand." Each KBR detention center holds *5000* people, and there must be a lot of them if they have been vigorously built since 2000. So it would appear that the space in camps that KBR has built contains a whole lot more room than is needed for "thousands" of immigrants.

It is possible that the current planned immigrant invasion of America (especially from Mexico) to set up the North American Union is being planned only to have the "illegals" put in the camps, but this too is very unlikely. Consider Hurricane Katrina, a disaster that the world had over a week of notice for, and which involved a sudden mass of instantly homeless people which, in essence, functions like an immediate influx of immigrants. But, as mentioned, detention camps were not used in Katrina, and there was no real government rescue effort. Given this fact, what choice do we have but to firmly conclude that the camps are not for disasters. Furthermore, the KBR camps are just the tip of the iceberg. The Rex 84 camp system is another system started in the 1980s, which has far more camp space all around the nation than the KBR camps. Also, FEMA is well known to have FEMA camps all over the nation, as 1999 Seattle IMF-UN protesters, and some of the Hurricane Katrina victims discovered. And many American schools, national parks, Wal-Mart stores, military bases, and other corporatist institutions have been set up in such a way where they could be used as concentration camps.

Beech Grove, Indiana, is a small town south of Indianapolis which has a very large gated Amtrak station that is supposedly mostly shut down and is now mainly a tourist attraction. This Amtrak station is the large patch that is shaped like an inverted broken pyramid (an inverted all-seeing eye pyramid) in the left half of the picture. But looking closely at this "Amtrak station" (such as by visiting it by car) reveals that it is some sort of an empty military prison fortress, equipped with sophisticated fencing and other prison features, and thus is speculated by many to be a concentration camp "hidden in plain view," and ready for use when the final corporatist phase discussed above and in chapter 1 is meant to commence. There are other suspicious issues also, such as the fact that as of March 2007, if one were to go to the Beech Grove city website (http://www. beechgrove.com), one cannot find any mention of the Amtrak station being a tourist attraction. Since Beech Grove is a tiny town, one would assume that they would spotlight their big train station as a tourist attraction, wouldn't they?

In summary, the information on these camps does not make any sense, at least in the way the politicians and the national media are describing them for us. We must abandon all the reasoning listed above, and we must go further and find the real reason for the existence of the camps: the corporatist dream-nation of mass labor/death camps, as if to regress and return to the days of the African slave trade but on a far larger, even global, scale.

Why the Camps Are For Ordinary Americans

"The Shroud of the Dark Side has fallen."

—Yoda

Consider what we know so far, given what has been written up to this point in this book:

1. There is no war on terrorism, no terrorists, and 9/11 was a false flag event.
2. Given 1, the US government, in spying on Americans, is not looking for terrorists, as they say they are, but can only be making databases about information on Americans for other reasons.
3. Guantanamo, the US prison system, the secret CIA prisons, and other American death-camp systems show camp systems and torture facilities are a huge priority for the American corporatists.
4. There is enough camp space to house nearly half of all Americans (150 million people) in camps (if one sums up all the different projected camp space mentioned in the last section).
5. There are not *nearly* enough immigrants, terrorists, invaders, disaster victims to fill the massive camp space that the corporatists have waiting to be filled.

6. The illegal immigrants coming into the United States, via the new North American Union, are doing so with the help of the US corporatist secret government. The immigrants are good cheap labor (slave labor). Thus, they have more value to corporatists than American citizens.

7. The corporatists are building the New World Order, and this New World Order requires the destruction of America (in other words, in a world government, there cannot be a superpower, and thus America, which is a tremendous superpower, must be radically de-powered).[820]

8. Are the government corporatists building the camps for *no reason*, or *for a reason*? Obviously the latter.

9. The reasons the corporatists have given us for building the camps are to be rejected.

These nine points, when put all together, appear to verify that the massive matrix of empty camps set-up around America are intended for ordinary Americans. Let me explain.

If America is to be destroyed by the corporatists, recent history shows us that the corporatists have carefully mapped-out the manner in which they engineer the downfalls of cities, nations, or races. For example, the following disasters were specifically planned disasters with similar characteristics: the Iraq War, Hurricane Katrina,[821] AIDS in Africa, the profitable and interconnected drug and prison industries, the Vietnam War, US military operations in Central America in the 1980s, among others. These all have a similar set of qualities:

> A disaster occurs, the US visible government says they will intervene and help out where they will save the population, but they in fact take measures to provoke as much chaos as possible and do nothing to help at all, leaving people without food or housing or water and with nowhere to go, and thus they need to seek the government's help and they are therein merely put into concentration camps,[822] where they are unknowingly poisoned and mistreated (by being given poisoned water, etc.), and the disasters lead to huge financial profits for the corporatists.

These events have a very specific pattern, and they are done to a group of people that the US government corporatists *want to remove from a land mass* (in the cases above: oil-rich Iraq, "prime" real estate in New Orleans, Africa, and American neighborhoods).

---

[820] As I cited above, there are many excellent accounts of this, such as Perloff 1988, Chossudovsky 2003, and others.

[821] To understand how Hurricane Katrina could be a planned event, see Manning and Begich, 1995.

[822] In the case of AIDS, the "concentrations camps" would be the orphanages. In the case of Hurricane Katrina, this would be the FEMA camps, many of which the secret government-controlled mass media did not report on.

This is a critical point, since it ties in to the North American Union, which is largely a project that involves removing American citizens from US soil in order that non-citizens can invade, and thus set-up a new nation that is not governed by citizens, and thus not by the US Constitutional system. Therefore, as was verified in above chapters, the American corporatists want the American citizens seriously dejected (and therefore, removed), and thus history shows us that they will do so by the past techniques.

In order to deject, remove, and/or exterminate such a large portion of the world's people, a huge amount of death-camp space is needed to do so. There are many scenarios that could be imagined to be carried out there—perhaps something like Iraqi tent concentration camps amid the DU-zones,[823] or the prison labor carried out for the massive corporations inside the American prison system,[824] or, less recently, perhaps something like the African slave trade, or perhaps a Nazi-style camp set-up. But what is assured, is that the camp set-up, implementation, and operation will be specifically set-up to give massive financial profits to the corporatists in the process, and unimaginable misery to the slaves, if, that is, history is our guide (history of the 1800s, 1900s, and so far in the 2000s). In these situations, a crisis is created deliberately, the people—who are dependent on the resources (food, money, water, etc.) that the corporatists bind them to—are suddenly without basic life resources, and thus are stuck stranded in the street, pathetically helpless, but typically still trusting the corporatist government, as observed when they go to the pre-planned corporatist concentration camp system.

It is interesting to note how often this sort of pattern is found in the dark Masonic-corporatist society. For example, as documented above, Americans are perpetually toxified and deformed, with worthless, harmful and poisonous and addicting "food," chemicals (e.g., aspartame, etc.), poisoned water (e.g., fluoride, etc.), poisoned vaccines, air that is poisoned with chemical weaponry against Americans, chemtrails poisoning us further, diseases like pertussis being sprayed on citizens, diseases like AIDS, Ebola, and others created in the laboratory and sprayed on humans, in order to keep people sick and weak, in order that people remain addicted to Big Pharma's products—which is also a trap full of poisons. The formula is: covertly take measures to make humans weak and helpless, and then present them with a "solution," which, in reality, is merely another poison and the cycle begins all over again.

---

[823] See the film, *Caught in the Crossfire: The Untold Story of Falluja,* for documentation and film footage of these concentration/tent camps or cities. This film is mostly banned in the United States (for example, it cannot be purchased on Amazon.com), and it is available through www.conceptmedia.net.

[824] See Herival and Wright 2003.

Martial Law

It is unclear if a roundup is to happen all-at-once, or gradually through time. If the round-up is fast, a system of martial law would be needed. There has already been perfumed talk of the martial law state of the future in America, as this report from MSNBC's "Countdown" show, which is about the now somewhat famous remarks of Tommy Franks (US military, recently retired):

> OLBERMANN: The commander who led U.S. military operations in Afghanistan and Iraq has revealed that he fears that the fabric of our Constitution could "unravel" in the event of an attack on this nation with weapons of mass destruction… Our third story on the COUNTDOWN tonight, General Tommy Franks, retired for not even four months from the leadership of CENTCOM, saying he foresees a scenario in which our population would move to "militarize our country." His comments appear in an unlikely venue. Franks, who rarely accepts interview requests, has conducted one with an upscale men's magazine called *Cigar Aficionado*. It is in here that he defends the actions in Iraq, even if no weapons of mass destruction are ever found, by asking and answering the rhetorical question, what is the worst thing that can happen in our country? Franks telling the magazine that the worst thing comes in two steps. "The first step would be a nexus between weapons of mass destruction and terrorism. That goes to step number two," Franks continues, "which is that the Western World, the free world, loses what it cherishes most, and that is freedom and liberty we've seen for a couple of hundred years in this grand experiment we call democracy." The general goes on. He fears a "massive casualty-producing event somewhere in the Western world—it may be in the United States of America -- that causes our population to question our own Constitution, and to begin to militarize our country in order to avoid a repeat of another mass casualty-producing event." General Franks concludes, "Which in fact, then begins to potentially unravel the fabric of our Constitution." We asked Tommy Franks to join us on this program or to give us some kind of statement clarifying his remarks, which from any perspective are disturbing. General Franks declined.[825]

Now consider another story that shows how prominently on the minds of some politicians martial law is. The following is a story circulated through the New Jersey news papers just before the Iraq War.

> TRENTON - If the nation escalates to "red alert," indicating an imminent attack, you will be assumed by authorities to be the enemy if you so much as venture outside your home, the state's anti-terror czar says. "This state is on top of it," said Sid Caspersen, New Jersey's director of the office of counterterrorism. Caspersen, a former FBI agent, was briefing reporters

---

[825] "Countdown," MSNBC, November 21, 2003

alongside Gov. McGreevey Thursday when, for the first time, he disclosed the realities of how a red alert would shut the state down. Red would also tear away virtually all personal freedoms to move about and associate. "Red means all noncritical functions cease," Caspersen said. "Noncritical would be almost all businesses, except health-related." A red alert means there is a severe risk of terrorist attack, according to federal guidelines from the Department of Homeland Security. "The state will restrict transportation and access to critical locations," says the state's new brochure on dealing with terrorism. "You must adhere to the restrictions announced by authorities and prepare to evacuate, if instructed. Stay alert for emergency messages." Caspersen went further than the brochure. "The government agencies would run at a very low threshold," he said. "The State Police and the emergency management people would take control over the highways. "You literally are staying home, is what happens, unless you are required to be out. No different than if you had a state of emergency with a snowstorm. "The reason being is, what we're saying is: 'Everybody sit down!' "If you are left standing, you are probably a terrorist. And if you are not law enforcement or emergency response - that's how we're going to catch you. "You're not going to have a seat to go to. That is the basic premise of it," he said.[826]

John Judge, political activist from Washington D. C.,   founder of the Coalition on Political Assassinations,[827] has researched and discussed how after a 9/11 level event, the entire structure of the government in many way changes, where only a few people have to make decisions without consulting the "elected" representatives.[828] Instead, it is the DoD, FEMA, and the NSA who makes the decisions on what occurs with law and the activities of policymakers. (The budgets of these agencies are massive. FEMA is over $6 billion per year![829] But, interestingly, much of what FEMA needs for this budget is "classified," or *secret.*) These are unelected groups that are appointed by the Presidential Branch—which is, of course, the very group proven above to have been the masterminding force for 9/11.

This alteration in government has largely happened without the public knowing, since the corporatist media has been dominated on other issues since 9/11 (Martha Stewart's criminal investigation, Anna Nicole Smith, Michael Jackson's child sex scandal, the Duke University lacrosse team sex scandal, the Coby Bryant sex scandal, the weapons of mass destruction said to be in Iraq, Brittany Spears, the terror networks, and so on).

---

[826] "'Red alert' translated: Stay home," Asbury Park Press (Neptune, NJ), March 16, 2003, Tom Baldwin/Gannett State Bureau Staff
[827] Judge was featured in Marshall 2003.
[828] This is documented in Marshall 2003.
[829] http://water.usgs.gov/osw/pubs/FEMA.htm. (This page was up as of July 2006)

The Rounding-Up of *Millions*

Judge points out how there is a step-by-step process of government removal of freedom up to martial law where the government can, at will, place people in detention camps, by rounding up people from certain neighborhoods, where, presumably, somehow entire neighborhoods could be considered "terrorist threats." (This idea that an entire neighborhood, which presumably includes the children and whomsoever, could be considered "terrorist threats" is somewhat akin to the way that I have discussed in this book the current government and corporatist media in place in the USA labels entire nations—such as Iran—as "terrorist".) According to Judge, we are in step two of a three step phase where step three is martial law. 9/11 was step two, and one might assume that another, greater, false flag terrorist strike on the USA in the future would initiate step three.

It is with "emergency situations" that the government is suddenly able to do things, such as plan for detention camp round-ups, and move all control of mass media, email, telecommunications, mail, and anything else under the full control of the Offices of Emergency Preparedness (FEMA, etc.) and under military control. All that is needed is "an emergency," and once there is one, "elected" government has no control, and all control goes to this "shadow government," as it is often called (FEMA, NSA, CIA, etc.) which most Americans know virtually nothing about.

WORKS CITED

A

Alterman, Eric. 2003. *What Liberal Media?*. New York: Basic Books.

Achbar, Mark, and Abbon Jennifer (Directors). 2004. *The Corporation*. DVD lecture. ASIN: B0007DBJM8.

Anderson, Mike. 2004-2006. *The Rave Diet and Lifestyle*. Self-published by Mike Anderson. ISBN: 0-9726590-48.

Anderson, Jeffrey J. 1992. *The Territorial Imperative: Pluralism, Corporatism, and Economic Crisis*. New York: Cambridge University Press.

Angell, Marcia, MD. 2005. *The Truth about Drug Companies*. New York: Random House.

Afrika, Llaila. 2000 (1993). *Nutricide: The Nutritional Destruction of the Black Race*. New York: A & B Publishing Group.

Ayoub, David, MD. 2006. "Thimerosal in Vaccines and Autism." DVD lecture. Foundation for Autism Information and Research (FAIR). http://www.autismmedia.org/index.html.

Ayoub, David, MD. 2005. "Mercury, Autism and the Global Vaccine Agenda." Radio Liberty Conference (www.radioliberty.com), November 19. Aptos, CA. USA. Viewable on Google.com Video: http://video.google.com/videoplay?docid=6890106663412840646&q=ayoub&hl=en

B

Bagdikian, Ben H. 2004. *The New Media Monopoly*. Boston: Beacon Press.

Bales, Kevin. 2004 (1999). *Disposable People: New Slavery in the Global Economy*. Berkeley, Los Angeles: University of California Press.

Bearden, T.E., and Bedini, John. 2006. Free Energy Generation: Circuits and Schematics. Cheniere Press.

Begich, Nicholas J. 2005. *Mind Control*. DVD lecture. Anchorage: Earthpulse Press. ISBN: 1-890693-50-2.

Begich, Nicholas J. 1995. *Angels Don't Play this Haarp*. Anchorage: Earthpulse Press.

Berman, Morris. 2006. *Dark Ages America: The Final Phase of Empire*. New York: W. W. Norton.

Berne, Eric. 1992 (1964). *Games People Play: The Handbook of Transactional Analysis*. New York: Ballantine Books.

Best, Steven, and Kellner, Douglas. 1991. *Postmodern Theory*. New York: The Guilford Press.

Black, Edwin, 2006. *Internal Combustion: How Corporations and Governments Addicted the World to Oil and Derailed the Alternatives*. New York: St. Martin's Press.

Black, Edwin. 2001. *IBM and the Holocaust: The Strategic Alliance between Nazi Germany and America's Most Powerful Corporation*, New York: Crown Publishers.

Blaylock, Russell. 1997. *Excitotoxins: The Taste that Kills*. Santa Fe: Health Press.

Bookchin, Debbie, and Schumacher, Jim. 2005. *The Virus and the Vaccine: Contaminated Vaccine, Deadly Cancers, and Government Neglect*. New York: St. Martin's Press.

Brzezinski, Zbigniew. 1998. The Grand Chessboard: American Primacy and Its Geostrategic Imperatives. New York: Basic Books.

Bright, Stephen E. 2003. "The Accused Get What the System Doesn't Pay For." In Herival, Tara, and Wright, Paul. *Prison Nation*. New York: Routledge. Pages 6-22.

Brohy, Audrey, and Ungerman, Gerard (directors). 2000. *Hidden Wars of Desert Storm*. DVD lecture. Studio: Arab Film Distribution. ASIN: B00008OOTA.

Browning, Christopher R. 1993. *Ordinary Men*. New York: Harper Collins.

Bryson, Christopher. 2004. *The Fluoride Deception*. New York: Seven Stories Press.

C

Caldicott, Helen, 2004, "Introduction to the 2004 Edition," in Caldicott, Helen, 2002, *The New Nuclear Danger: George W. Bush's Military-Industrial Complex, with a New Introduction on the Situation in Iraq*. New York: The New Press. Pages XXI - L.

Caldicott, Helen, 2002, The New Nuclear Danger: George W. Bush's Military-Industrial Complex, with a New Introduction on the Situation in Iraq. New York: The New Press.

Carter, Tim (director). 2005. *Torture: The Guantanamo Cookbook*. Film documentary. (This documentary aired on British television in London on Channel 4,[830] and on the Sundance Channel in the USA.)

Cervi, Carmine (director). 2003. *Axis of Evil*. DVD lecture. Studio: Qualiatica. ASIN: B0006H31K8.

Chang, Matthias. 2005a. *Future FastFoward* (2nd Edition), Malaysia : Thinker's Library.

Chang, Matthias. 2005b. *Brainwashed for War Programmed to Kill*. Malaysia: Thinker's Library.

Chossudovsky, Michel. 2003. *The Globalization of Poverty and the New World Order*. Second Edition. Pincourt (Quebec): Global Research.

Clarke, Anthony (director). 1995. *Hemp Revolution*. DVD lecture. Studio: Vanguard Films. ASIN: B00005LO4T.

Cockburn, Alexander, and St. Clair, Jeffrey. 1998. *Whiteout: The CIA, Drugs, and the Press*. New York: Verso.

Coffman, Michael S. 2007. *Global Warming or Global Governance?* DVD lecture. Bangore, Maine: Sovereignty International, Inc. 207-945-9878.

Cole, Leonard A. 1988. *Clouds of Secrecy: The Army's Germ Warfare Tests Over Populated Areas*. New York: Rowman & Littlefield.

Court, Jamie, and Smith, Francis. 1999. *Making a Killing: HMOs and the Threat to Your Health*. Monroe ME: Common Courage Press.

---

[830] "C4 lines up Guantánamo-style torture show," Dominic Timms, February 8, 2005, London Guardian. I could not find Studio information on this documentary.

D

Daniel, Kaayla. 2005. *The Whole Soy Story*. Washington, DC: New Trends Publishing.

Davies, Paul, and Gribbin, John, 1992, *The Matter Myth*, Touchstone: New York.

Deffeys, Kenneth. 2003. *Hubbert's Peak: The World's Impending Oil Shortage*. Princeton: Princeton University Press.

de la Peña, Nonny (director). 2004. *Unconstitutional*. DVD lecture. Studio: The Disinformation Company.

DiLorenzo, Thomas, J. 1993. "Economic Fascism." *Truth Seeker*. V. 121. No. 3. < http://www.banned-books.com/truth-seeker/1994archive/121_3/ts213l.html >

E

Earp, Jeremy, and Jhally, Sut (directors). 2004. *Hijacking Catastrophe: 9/11, Fear & the Selling of American Empire*. DVD documentary. MEF (Media Education Foundation). ISBN: 1-893521-97-4.

Eisenstein, Mayer. 2002. *Don't Vaccinate Before You Educate*. Ann Arbor: CMI Press.

Elster, Jon. 1986. *An Introduction to Karl Marx*. New York: Cambridge University Press.

Epperson, Ralph. 1985. *The Unseen Hand: An Introduction to the Conspiratorial View of History*. Tucson: Publius Press.

Estes, Ralph. 1996. *The Tyranny of the Bottom Line*. San Francisco: Berret-Koehler Publishes.

F

Fagin, Dan, and Lavelle, Marianne. 1999. *Toxic Deception: How the Chemical Industry Manipulates Science, Bends the Law and Endangers Your Health*. Monroe Maine: Common Courage Press.

Felton, Greg. 2005. *Enemies by Design: Inventing the War on Terrorism*. Joshua Tree: Banned Books/Progressive Press.[831]

Fitrakis, Bob, Rosenfeld, Steve, and Wasserman, Harvey. 2006. *What Happened in Ohio?* New York: The New Press.

Fomenko, Anatoly T. 2003. *History: Fiction or Science*. Chronology 1. Douglas (UK): Delamere Resources.

Fukayama, Francis. 2002. *Our Posthuman Future*. New York: Farrar, Straus and Giroux.

G

Gandini, Erik, and Saleh, Tarik (directors). 2005. *Gitmo: The New Rules of War*. DVD documentary. Red Envelope Entertainment (A Netflix Company)

Garcia, Deborah Koons (director). 2005. *The Future of Food*. DVD lecture. Studio: Cinema Libre Distrib. ASIN: B000BQ5IXM.

---

[831] This book is an historical, scholarly, empirical study. It can be purchased at Progressive Press. Professor Mazin Qumsiyeh of Yale University writes that Felton's book is "a lucid and timely compilation of information and questions that should be the fodder of discussions in America and beyond."

Geyman, John. 2006. Shredding the Social Contract. Monroe, Maine: Common Courage Press.

Gitlin, Todd. 2002. Media Unlimited: How the Torrent of Images and Sounds Overwhelms Our Lives. New York: Henry Holt and Company.

Gleason, Abbot, Goldsmith, Jack, and Nussbaum, Martha. 2005. "Introduction." In Gleason, Abbot, Goldsmith, Jack, and Nussbaum, Martha, (Ed.s). 2005. *On Nineteen Eighty-Four: Orwell and Our Future*. Princeton: Princeton University Press.

Goldberg, Michelle. 2006. *Kingdom Coming*. New York: W.W. Norton.

Golden, Isaac. 1998. *Vaccination? A Review of the Risks and Alternatives* (5th Edition). Canberra, Australia: National Library. ISBN: 0-7316-8099-5.

Gowan, John Curtis. 1975. *Trance, Art, and Creativity*. Buffalo: The Creative Education Foundation.

Greene, Gregory (director). 2004. *The End of Suburbia*. DVD lecture. Studio: Electric Wallpaper. ASIN: 097369470X.

Greenwald, Robert (director). 2006. *Iraq For Sale: The War Profiteers*. DVD lecture. Studio: The Disinformation Company. ASIN: B000HWXOT0.

Greenwald, Robert (director). 2004. *Uncovered: The War On Iraq*. DVD documentary. Studio: Cinema Libre. ASIN: B0002ZDWGC.

Griffin, Edward G. 1997. *World Without Cancer: The Story of Vitamin B17*. Westlake Village, CA: American Media.

Gross, Martin L. 1999. *The Conspiracy of Ignorance: The Failure of American Public Schools*. New York: Harper Collins.

Grossman, Gene M. 2000. "Special Interest Groups and Economic Policy." *National Bureau of Economic Research*. < http://www.nber.org/reporter/ >.

Grupp, Jeffrey. 2006. "Mereological Nihilism: Quantum Atomism and the Impossibility of Material Constitution." *Axiomathes*. Vol. 16. No. 3. Pages 245-386.

Grupp, Jeffrey. 2005. "The R-Theory of Time, or Replacement Presentism: The Buddhist Philosophy of Time." *Indian International Journal of Buddhist Studies*. 2005. No. 6. 51-122.

H

Hachmeister, Lutz (director). 2004. *The Goebbels Experiment*. DVD lecture. Studio: First Run Features. ASIN: B000EULK1O.

Halberstam, Michael. 1999. *Totalitarianism and the Modern Conception of Politics*. New Haven: Yale University Press.

Halter, Ed. 2006. *From Sun Tzu to Xbox*. Berkeley: Thunder's Mouth Press.

Hansen, Eric. 2000. *Stranger in the Forest: On Foot Across Borneo*. New York: Vintage.

Harris, Sam. 1997. *The End of Faith: Religion, Terror, and the Future of Reason*. New York: W. W. Norton & Company.

Harvey, Peter. 2000. *An Introduction to Buddhist Ethics*. New York: Cambridge University Press.

Herival, Tara, and Wright, Paul. 2003. *Prison Nation*. New York: Routledge.

Hertz, Noreena. 2003. *The Silent Takeover: Global Capitalism and the Death of Democracy*. New York: Harper Business (Division of Harper Collins).

Hoffman, Michael A. 1991, *They Were White and They Were Slaves*. Coeur d'Alene, ID: The Independent History and Research Company.

Hollowell, Edward, and Ratey, John. 1995. *Driven To Distraction*. New York: Touchstone (Reprint Edition).

Horgan, John, 2003, *Rational Mysticism*, Houghton Mifflin, New York.

Horowitz, David. 2006. *The Professors: The 101 Most Dangerous Academics in America*. New York: Regnery Publishing, Inc.

Horowitz, Leonard G. 2001. *Death in the Air: Globalism, Terrorism and Toxic Warfare*. Sand Point, Idaho: Tetrahedron Publishing Group.

Horowitz, Leonard G. 1999 (1996). *Emerging Viruses: AIDS and Ebola*. Sand Point, Idaho: Tetrahedron Publishing Group.

Howard, Michael. 1989. *The Occult Conspiracy: Secret Societies—Their Influence and Power in World History*. Rochester VT: Destiny Books.

Hufschmid, Eric (director). 2003. *Painful Deceptions*. DVD lecture. Studio: Hufschmid. ASIN: B000BHNNO2.

Hudson, Michael (Editor). 1996. *Merchants of Misery: How Corporate American Profits from Misery*. Monroe, Maine: Common Courage Press.

Hustin, Aletha, Donnerstein, Edward, Fairchild, Halford, Fashbach, Norma, Katz, Phyllis, Murray, John, Rubinstein, Eli, Wilcox, Brian, and Zuckerman, Diana. 1992. *Big World, Small Screen: The Role of Television in American Society*. Lincoln: University of Nebraska Press.

I

Icke, David. 2005. *Infinite Love is the Only Truth; Everything Else is Just Illusion. Exposing the Dreamworld We Believe to be 'Real'*. Wildwood, USA: Bridge of Love Publications USA.

Icke, David. 2001. *Children of the Matrix: How an Interdimensional Race has Controlled the World for Thousands of Years—and Still Does*. Valencia, CA: Bridge of Love Publications USA.

J

James, William, "On A Certain Blindness in Human Beings," in Myers, Gerald E. (ed.). 1992. *William James: Writings: 1878-1899*. New York: The Library of America. Pages 841-860.

Jarecki, Eugene (director). 2005. *Why We Fight*. DVD lecture. Studio: Sony Pictures. ASIN: B000FBH3W2.

Jarecki, Eugene (director). 2003. *The Trials of Henry Kissinger*. DVD lecture. Studio: First Run Features. ASIN: B00009V7S0.

Jones, Alex (director). 2006. *Terrorstorm*. DVD lecture. Studio: Alex Jones Productions / Infowars.com.

Jones, Alex (director). 2005. *Dark Secrets / The Order of Death*. DVD documentary. Studio: Alex Jones Productions / Infowars.com.

Jones, Alex (director). 2001. *Comprehensive Annual Financial Reports Exposed!* VHS documentary. Studio: Alex Jones Productions / Infowars.com.

Junkerman, John (director). 2002. *Power and Terror – Noam Chomsky in Our Times*. First Run Features. ASIN: B00008XS1C.

K

Karel, William. 2004. *The World According to Bush*. DVD lecture. Studio: Flach Film. ASIN: B00067WSV6.

Kawin, Bruce F., 1978, *Mindscreen: Bergman, Godard, and First-Person Film*, Princeton University Press: Princeton.

Keith, Jim. 2004 (1999). Saucers of the Illuminati. Kempton, Illnios: Adventures Unlimited Press.

Kirby, David. 2005 Evidence of Harm: Mercury in Vaccines and the Autism Epidemic: A Medical Controversy. New York: St. Martin's Press.

Klain, Naomi. 2007. *The Shock Docrtime: The Rise of Disaster Capitalism*. Metropolitan Books.

Korten, David C. 2001. *When Corporations Rule the World,* Second Edition. San Francisco: Kumarian Press.

Krebs, J.R., and Davies, N.B. 1993 (1981). *An Introduction to Behavioral Ecology. Third Edition*. Oxford: Blackwell Publishers.

Kurzweil, Ray. 1999. *The Age of Spiritual Machines*. New York: Viking.

L

Labow, Rima MD, and Stubblebine, Albert Maj Gen. 2006. *Codex and Nutricide.* DVD lecture of Keynote Address at Bauman College, for the Annual Meeting of the National Association of Nutritional Professionals (www.nanp.org). San Rafael, CA. October 28-30, 2005. Available from www.healthfreedomUSA.org.

Lamb, Sharon, and Brown, Mikel. 2006. *Packaging Girlhood: Rescuing our Daughters from Marketers' Schemes*. New York: St. Martin's Press.

Lando, Barry. 2007. *Web of Deceit: The History of Western Complicity in Iraq, from Churchill to Kennedy to George W. Bush*. New York: Other Press.

Langdon, Sean (director). 2003. *Mission Accomplished*. DVD lecture. Studio: Doc Workers. ASIN: B0007ZOO9K. (I believe this film is also associated with, or was produced by, the BBC, since that is advertised at the end of the film.)

Lardner, James, and Smith, David (ed.s). 2006. *Inequality Matters*. New York :New Press.

Leeb, Stephen. 2006. *The Coming Economic Collapse: How You Can Thrive When Oil Costs $200 a Barrel*. New York: Warner Business Books.

Lewis, Avi (director). 2004. *The Take*. DVD lecture. Studio: First Run Features. ASIN: B000CCD1X4.

Lewis, Justin. 2001. *Constructing Public Opinion*. New York: Columbia University Press.

Lifton, Robert. 1989. *Thought Reform and the Psychology of Totalism: A Study of "Brainwashing" in China*. Chapel Hill: University of North Carolina Press.

Luce, J. V., 1992, *An Introduction to Greek Philosophy*, Thames and Hudson: London.

Luderman, Gerd. 1996. *The Unholy in Holy Scripture*. Louisville: Westminster John Knox Press.

M

Maddock, Kenneth, 1972, *The Australian Aborigines*, The Penguin Press, London.

Maher, John, and Groves, Judy. 1997. *Introducing Chomsky*. New York: Totem Books.

Mankiw, Gregory N. 1998. *Principles of Economics*. New York: the Dryden Press.

Manning, Jeane, and Begich, Nick. 1995. *Angels Don't Play This Haarp: Advances In Tesla Technology*. Anchorage: Earthpulse Press.

Marshall, Steven (director). 2003. *Aftermath: Unanswered Questions from 9/11*. DVD lecture. Studio: Disinformation (in collaboration with the Guerrilla News Network [GNN]).

Matsumoto, Gary. 2004. *Vaccine A: The Covert Government Experiment That's Killing our Soldiers and Why GI's Are Only the First Victims*. New York: Basic Books.

Maxwell, Jordan. 2000. *Matrix of Power: Secrets of World Control*. San Diego: The Book Tree.

McElroy, Ann, and Townsend, Patricia K. 1989 (1979). *Medical Anthropology in Ecological Perspective*. Boulder: Westview Press.

McInerney, Lt. General Thomas, and Vallely, Maj. General Paul. 2004. *Endgame: The Blueprint for the Victory in the War on Terror*. New York: Regnery Publishing, Inc.

Milgram, Stanley. 2004. *Obedience and Authority: An Experimental View*. New York: Perennial Classics.

Miller, Judith, Engleberg, Stephen, and Broad, William. 2001. *Germs: Biological Weapons and America's Secret War*. New York: Simon and Schuster.

Miller, Marc Crispin. 2005. *Fooled Again*. New York: Basic Books

Miller, Marc Crispin. 2004. *Cruel and Unusual*. New York: W.W. Norton.

Miller, Marc Crispin. 1989. *Boxed In: The Culture of TV*. 3rd Edition. Evanston: Northwestern University Press.

Miller, Neil Z. 1999 (1992). *Vaccines: Are They Really Safe and Effective?* Santa Fe: New Atlantean Press.

Morris, Errol (director). 2004. *Fog of War*. DVD lecture. Studio: Sony Pictures.

Moravec, Hans, 1999, *Robot*, Oxford University Press: New York

Moss, Ralph. 2002 (1980). *The Cancer Industry*. Brooklyn: Equinox Press.

Mueller, Denis, and Ellis, Deb (directors). 2005. *Howard Zinn: You Can't Be Neutral on a Moving Train*. DVD lecture. Studio: First Run Features. ASIN: B0007TKOSC.

Murphy, Timothy. 2004. *Case Studies in Biomedical Ethics*. Cambridge; MIT Press.

N

Nace, Ted. 2003. *Gangs of America: The Rise of Corporate Power and the Disabling of Democracy*. San Francisco: Berret-Koehler Publishing, Inc.

Napoleoni, Loretta. 2005. *Terror Incorporated: Tracing the Dollars Behind the Terror Networks*. New York: Seven Stories press

Nelson, Jane. 1996 (1981). *Positive Discipline*. New York: Ballantine Books

O

Olds, Ian, and Scott, Garrett (directors). 2005. *Occupation Dreamland.* DVD lecture. Studio: Rumur Releasing, ASIN: B000DZ7XYI.

Olmsted, Dan. 2005. "No Autism for the Unvaccinated Amish? The Age of Autism: 'A Pretty Big Secret." United Press International. December 7, 2005.

Orwell, George. 1977 (1949) *1984.* New York: Signet Classic, Centennial Edition.

Owen, Stephen. 2003. "Absolute Power, Absolute Corruption." In Herival, Tara, and Wright, Paul. *Prison Nation.* New York: Routledge. Pages 23-29.

P

Paglen, Trevor, and Thompson, A.C. 2006. *Torture Taxi: On the Trial of the CIA's Rendition Flights.* Hoboken, NJ: Melville House Publishing.

Paine, Chris (director). 2006. *Who Killed the Electric Car?* DVD lecture. Studio: Sony Pictures. ASIN: B000I5Y8FU

Palast, Greg. 2004. *The Best Democracy Money Can Buy.* New York: Plume.

Pappas, Robert Kane (director). 2003. *Orwell Rolls in His Grave.* DVD lecture. Studio: Go-Kart Records.

Pawlick, Thomas. 2006. *The End of Food: How the Food Industry is Destroying our Food Supply, and What You Can Do About It.* Fort Lee, NJ: Barricade Books.

Perloff, James. 1988. *Shadows of Power: The Council on Foreign Relations and the American Decline.* Boston, Los Angeles: Western Islands.

Pinto, Christian J. (director). 2006. *The Secret Mysteries of America's Beginnings. Volume One: The New Atlantis.* DVD lecture. Studio: Antiquities Research Films. ASN: B000FIGJ84. This documentary consists of two hours of interviews with the premier experts on freemasonry, and the secret societies at the origin of America.

PNAC (Project for a New American Century). 2000. *Rebuilding America's Defenses: Strategy, Forces, and Resources for a New Century.* A report from the Project for a New American Century. 1150 Seventeenth Street, N.W. Suite 510. Washington, D. C. 20036.

Proctor, Robert N. 1999. *The Nazi War on Cancer.* Princeton: Princeton University Press.

Q

Quigley, Carroll. 1966. *Tragedy and Hope: A History of the World In Our Time.* MacMillan Company: New York.

R

Rampton, Sheldon, and Stauber, John. 2002. *Trust Us, We're Experts: How Industry Manipulates Science and Gambles with Your Future.* New York: Tarcher/Putnam.

Rich, Andrew. 2004. *Think Tanks, Public Policy, and the Politics of Expertise.* New York: Cambridge University Press.

Richards, Byron. 2006. *Fight for Your Health: Exposing the FDA's Betrayal of America.* Tuscon: Truth in Wellness, LLC.

Rosemann, Nils. 2005. "The Privatization of Human Rights Violations—Business Impunity or Corporate Responsibility? The Case of Human Rights Abuses and Torture in Iraq." *Non-State Actors and International Law.* 5: 77-100.

Rubin, Jordan S. 2003. Patient Heal Thyself: A Remarkable Program Combining Ancient Wisdom with Groundbreaking Clinical Research. Freedom Press.

Ruppert, Michael. 2004a. *Crossing the Rubicon: The Decline of the American Empire at the End of the Age of Oil*. New Society Publishers.

Ruppert, Michael. 2004b. *The Truth and Lies of 9-11*. DVD recording of Portland State University lecture that occurred on November 28, 2001. From the Wilderness Publications, at www. fromthewilderness.com.

Russon, John. 2003. *Human Experience: Philosophy Neurosis, and the Elements of Everyday Life*. Albany: State University of New York Press.

S

Schechter, Danny (director). 2004. *Weapons of Mass Deception*. DVD lecture. Studio: Cinema Libre. ASIN: B00074DXFS.

Schechter, Danny. 2002. *Media Wars: News at a Time of Terror*. New York: Rowman and Littlefield.

Scheibner, Viera. 1993. *Vaccination: 100 Years of Orthodox Research Shows that Vaccines Represent a Medical Assault on the Immune System*. Victoria Australia: Australian Print Group.

Schor, Juliet B. 2004. *Born To Buy*. New York: Schribner.

Scott, Peter Dale. 2003. *Drugs, Oil, and War*. New York: Rowman and Littlefield.

Silverstein, Ken. 1998. *Washington on $10 Million A Day*. Monroe Maine: Common Courage Press.

Simmons, Matthew. 2005. *Twilight in the Desert*. Hoboken: Wiley.

Simontacchi, Carol. 2000. *The Crazy Makers: How the Food Industry is Destroying Our Brains and Harming our Children*. New York: Tarcher/Putnam.

Simpson, Christopher. 1994. *Science of Coercion*. New York: Oxford University Press.

Singer, P. W. 2003. *Corporate Warriors: The Rise of the Privatized Military Industry*. Ithaca: Cornell University Press.

Slaughter, Anne-Marie. 2005. *A New World Order*. Princeton: Princeton University Press.

Smith, Craig R. 2001. *Rediscovering Gold in the 21ˢᵗ Century*. Phoenix: My Idea Factory.

Smith, Jeffrey. 2003. *Seeds of Deception: Exposing Industry and Government Lies About the Safety of the Genetically Engineered Foods You're Eating*. Fairfield Iowa: Yes Books.

Smith, James. 1991. *The Idea Brokers*. New York: The Free Press.

Standing, Brian (director). 2004. *War is Sell*. DVD lecture. Studio: Prolefeed Studios. ASIN: B000BWFSNQ.

Stein, David B. 2001. *Unraveling the ADD/ADHD Fiasco: Successful Parenting Without Drugs*. Kansas City: Andrews McMeel Publishing.

Stinnet, Robert, 2000, *Day of Deceit: The Truth About FDR and Pearl Harbor*. New York: Touchstone.

Stone, Robert (director). 1986. *Radio Bikini*. DVD lecture. Studio: New Video Group. ASIN: B0000TPAMO.

Sutton, Anthony. 2002. *Wall Street and the Rise of Hitler*. San Pedro, CA: GSG and Associates Publishers.

Sutton, Antony C. 1995. *The Federal Reserve Conspiracy*. Boring Oregon: CPA Book Publishers.

Swinburne, Richard. 2001. *Epistemic Justification*. Oxford: Oxford University Press.

Szasz, Thomas S. 1974. *The Myth of Mental Illness*. New York: Harper and Row.

T

Tabor, Nathan. 2006. *The Beast on the East River: The UN Threat to America's Sovereignty and Security*. Nashville: Nelson Current.

Taicher, Robert (director). 2005. *Rush to War*. DVD lecture. Studio: RTW Productions, LLC. ASIN: B0007NA3ZC.

Tarpley, Webster Griffin. 2006. *9/11 Synthetic Terror: Made in the USA*. 2nd Edition. Joshua Tree: Progressive Press.

Tarpley, Webster G., and Chaitkin, Anton. 2004 (1992). *George Bush: The Unauthorized* Bibliography. Joshua Tree: Progressive Press.

Taylor, Kathleen. 2004. *Brainwashing: The Science of Thought Control*. Oxford: Oxford University Press.

Taylor, Richard, 1992, *Metaphysics*, 4th Ed., Prentice-Hall, Englewood Cliffs.

Tenpenny, Sherri. 2005. *Vaccines: The Risks, the Benefits, the Choices*. DVD lecture. Studio: NMA Media Press. ISBN: 0-9743448-1-8.

Thomas, William. 2004. *Chemtrails Confirmed*. Carson City: Bridger House Publishers.

Thorn, Victor. 2003. *The New World Order Exposed*. Happy Valley, PA: Sisyphus Press.

W

Walsh, Roger N. 1990. *The Spirit of Shamanism*. New York: Tarcher/Putnam.

Williams, Lindsey. 1980. *The Energy Non-Crisis* (2nd Ed.). Master Books.

Winslow, George. 2003. "Capital Crimes: The Corporate Economy of Violence." In Herival, Tara, and Wright, Paul. *Prison Nation*. New York: Routledge. Pages 41-56.

Z

Zepezauer, Mark. 2004. *Take the Rick off Welfare*. Cambridge: South End.

Zepezauer, Mark. 2003. *Boomerang!* Monroe Maine: Common Courage.

Zinn, Howard. 2003 (1980). *A People's History of the United States*. New York: Harper Perennial.

Zinn, Howard. 2004. *The People Speak: American Voices, Some Famous, Some Little Known*. Audio Book. New York: Harper Audio (Harper Collins Publishers).

INDEX

More Books by Prof. Jeffrey Grupp

The Telescreen is the pervasive media screen put in front of, and injected into, the eyes and ears of humans in the American electronic techno-culture. From birth it moulds consciousness into a less-than-human, despiritualized semi-consciousness. This pseudosphere destroys humans, who give their attention, consciousness, and vital spirit to the telescreen. As in Plato's Cave or *1984,* shadow images substitute fiction lives for the empty ones of a brainwashed population. Grupp demonstrates that this is the dream-world we live in. One of materialism, robotic, shallow stooges, degrading images, down-dumbing education, of war propaganda fed on pure fakery and repetition by the media. History is twisted on "educational" TV shows. Journalists who stray from the party lines into real issues are eliminated. The herd instinct is exploited to impose a tyranny more effective than brute force. Feb. 2010, 199 pp., $14.95.

The Invisible Government. America is going into revolution. But even before it's fully underway, there is tremendous evidence that the New World Order is hijacking and steering the revolution — taking it away from the people, and turning it into a divide-and-conquer operation: where the highest echelon of the New World Order works for the annihilation and sacrifice of the lower echelon ("the puppets") by the people of the world. Such operations are routine in history (Hitler, Bolshevik revolution, etc.); another one is already underway. Release in 2010.

Telementation: *Cosmic Feeling and the Law of Attraction.* Deep feeling rather than thought or faith is our secret nature and key to self-realization. Prof. Grupp, a long-time Buddhist, shows the way in this simple guide-book. May 2009. 124 pp., $12.95.

Light, Ufology and Ecstasy. There is a divine dimension everywhere in the universe. It is freedom, compassion, and an ineffable joy. All things seek to flow with it, mimic it. Awareness of this God-ecstasy is the highest task in life. Grupp explains spirituality and religion as its vehicles, and the ultra-advanced ancient civilizations who brought it to us. He tells how to carry out the meditation and prayer exercises simply but in detail, so that any reader can open up their inner God-communion. Release in 2010.

More Top Sellers from Progressive Press

Seeds of Destruction: The Hidden Agenda of Genetic Manipulation. F. Wm. Engdahl, author of *A Century of War,* reveals a diabolical world of greed, intrigue, corruption and coercion. A tiny corporate elite is out for complete control over the world by patenting the basis of survival: food. Inside the corridors of power, corporate boardrooms and backrooms of science labs, it reads as a crime story, because it is. A hugely important and unique work. Published by GlobalResearch.ca. 340 pages, $24.95

Illuminati: The Cult that Hijacked the World. Contemporary Canadian political philosopher Henry Makow PhD tackles taboos like Zionism, the British Empire, and Holocaust revisionism, as he relates how international bankers stole a monopoly on government credit, and took over the world. They run it all: the wars, schools, media, the works. 249 pages, $19.95. In ***Cruel Hoax: Feminism and the New World Order. The Attack on Your Human Identity***. Makow shares unusual insights on social aspects of the conspiracy to enslave humanity. 232 pages, $19.95.

Webster Griffin Tarpley

Surviving the Cataclysm, Your Guide through the Greatest Financial Crisis in Human History, updated edition, by Webster Griffin Tarpley. The unwinding of the hedge funds and derivatives bubble, and with them, life as we knew it in the USA. Richly detailed history of the financier oligarchy, how they plunder this nation. Provides solutions for the crisis for individuals and the nation. May 2009, 668 pages, $29.95.

Obama – The Postmodern Coup: Making of a Manchurian Candidate. Remember Bush's compassionate conservatism and humble foreign policy – and what happened next? Webster G. Tarpley reveals that the Obama puppet's advisors are even more radical reactionaries than the neo-cons. A crash course in political science, it distills decades of political insight and astute analysis, from a unique perspective. 320 pages, $15.95.

Barack H. Obama: the Unauthorized Biography Tarpley at his best: erudite, witty, insightful, activist, iconoclastic. Complete profile of a puppet's progress, cavorting in the trough of corruption of the Chicago Combine, and the oligarchy that backs him. Obama's regime will be one of brutal economic sacrifice and austerity to finance Wall Street bailouts, and imperialist confrontation with Russia and China. 595 pages, $19.95.

George Bush: The Unauthorized Biography. This 700-page classic blockbuster of research is a vivid X-ray of the Anglo-American oligarchy dominating U.S. politics. The Bushes and their Skull and Bones brethren, Brown Bros. Harriman, made a fortune building up Hitler and his Nazi war machine. Bush Sr. is linked to Iran-Contra, Watergate, the attempt to shoot Reagan when Bush was VP, and war crimes in Iraq. 700 pp., $19.95.

9/11 Synthetic Terror: Made in USA. The Bible of 9/11 Truth, with its working model of the state-sponsored false-flag terrorism: a rogue network of moles, patsies, and killers, in privatized paramilitary settings, and covered by corrupt politicians and corporate media. The simplistic Big Lie – that "it's paranoid to think 'our own government' could do it" – is exploded. Only state actors have the resources for spectacular terrorism. 512 pages, $17.95

More on 9/11

Truth Jihad: My Epic Struggle against the 9/11 Big Lie. 9/11 Truther Prof. Kevin Barrett's rollicking autobiography sends critics like Sean Hannity, the Secret Service and neocon politicians packing. Insights on academic freedom, bigotry, and media blindness. 224 pages, $12.95.

9/11 on Trial: The W T C Collapse. Presents 20 mathematical and scientific proofs by the rules of evidence to show that WTC buildings 1, 2 and 7 were downed by controlled demolition. 192 pages, $12.95

America's "War on Terrorism" Concise, wide-reaching, hard-hitting study on 9/11 in geopolitical context. The "war on terrorism" is a complete fabrication, an illusion that one man, Osama bin Laden, outwitted the $40 billion-a-year American intelligence apparatus. Chossudovsky peels back layers of rhetoric to reveal a complex web of deceit, aimed at luring the American people and the rest of the world into accepting a military solution which threatens the future of humanity. With a chapter on the London 7/7 false-flag bombings 387 pages, $22.95

Terror on the Tube: Behind the Veil of 7/7, an Investigation, by Nick Kollerstrom. First book to compile all the evidence that the four Muslim scapegoats were completely innocent. 7/7 is Bliar's Big Lie and Reichstag Fire, False Flag Terror as pretext for war and an Orwellian, neo-fascist British police state. July 2009. 232 pages, $17.77.

More Modern History

Enemies by Design: Inventing the War on Terrorism. A century of Anglo-American skullduggery grabbing Gulf oil, in 4 parts: biography of Osama bin Ladeen; Zionization of America; Afghanistan, Palestine, Iraq; One Nation under PNAC. 416 pages, $17.95.

The Nazi Hydra in America: Suppressed History of a Century exposes how US plutocrats launched Hitler, then recouped Nazi assets to lay the postwar foundations of a modern police state. Fascists won WWII because they ran both sides. Includes a blow-by-blow account of the fascist takeover of US media. 700 pages, $19.95.

The Complete Patriot's Guide to Oligarchical Collectivism: its Theory and Practice by Ethan. A nonfictional exploration of Orwell's *1984* for our times, and a guide to taking ownership of our lives and our world. August 2009, 484 pages, $19.95.

Witness in Palestine: *A Jewish American Woman in the Occupied Territories*, by young Fulbright scholar Anna Baltzer. A beautiful achievement, a journey of discovery of the nuts and bolts of everyday oppression, on her five-month sojourn in Palestine. Color photos adorn almost every one of 400 pages. $26.95.

Classics now available from ProgressivePress

How the World Really Works by Alan B. Jones. A crash course in the conspiracy field, with digests of 11 works like *A Century of War, Tragedy and Hope, The Creature from Jekyll Island*, and *Dope Inc*. 336 pp., $15.

Propaganda for War: How the US was Conditioned to Fight the Great War by Stewart Halsey Ross. How propaganda by Britain and her agents like Teddy Roosevelt suckered the USA into the war to smash the old world order. June 2009, 356 pages, $18.95.

Inside the Gestapo: Hitler's Shadow over the World (1940). Intimate, fascinating defector's tale of ruthlessness, spy intrigue, geopolitics and bizarre personalities of the 3rd Reich. 287 pp, $24.95.

Descent into Slavery? covers the Founding Fathers, Rothschilds, the Crown and the City, the two world wars, and globalization. 320 pp., $16.

1,000 Americans Who Rule the USA (1947, 324 pp, $18.95) and *Facts and Fascism* (1943, 292 pp., $15.95). By the great muckraking journalist George Seldes – whistleblower on the American plutocrats who keep the media in lockstep, and finance fascism. Key source books for *The Nazi Hydra*. How little has changed in 65 years: must reading for activists.

The Rape of the Mind: The Psychology of Thought Control, Menticide and Brainwashing (1956) by Joost Meerloo, M.D. The good Dutch doctor escaped from a Nazi death camp, only to discover the subtler mass mind control of McCarthy's America. Wide-ranging study of conditioning in open and closed societies. Ideas to help resist all forms of it, from torture to everyday social and media brainwashing. Reprint, 320 pages, $16.95.

Coming in 2010

Final Warning: A History of the New World Order by David Allen Rivera, updated, Part One. In-depth research nails down the Great Conspiracy in its various aspects as the Fed, the CFR, Trilateral Commission, Illuminati.

Dope Inc.: Britain's Opium War against the United States. "The Book that Drove Kissinger Crazy." New edition of the Underground Classic.

Global Predator: US Wars for Empire by Stewart Halsey Ross. A damning account of the atrocities committed by US armed forces, in Mexico, the Philippines, Europe, Korea, Vietnam, Iraq.

Triumph of Consciousness Over Fake Environmentalism, Lapdog Media, and Global Government. The environmental movement hijacked to facilitate globalization. Is Earth really overheated and overpopulated?

Terrorism and the Illuminati, A 3000-Year History. "Islamic" terrorists are tentacles of the satanist Illuminati cult. The Luciferian bloodline since the Crusades and back to ancient times. By David Livingstone, 2nd edition.